The Politics of Resentment

Chicago Studies in American Politics

A SERIES EDITED BY BENJAMIN I. PAGE, SUSAN HERBST,
LAWRENCE R. JACOBS, AND ADAM J. BERINSKY

Also in the series:

The Politics of Resentment

Rural Consciousness in Wisconsin and the Rise of Scott Walker

KATHERINE J. CRAMER

THE UNIVERSITY OF CHICAGO PRESS   CHICAGO AND LONDON

KATHERINE J. CRAMER is professor of political science at the University of Wisconsin—Madison, where she is also director of the Morgridge Center for Public Service and an affiliate faculty member in the School of Journalism and Mass Communication, the LaFollette School of Public Affairs, the Department of Forest and Wildlife Ecology, the Wisconsin Center for the Advancement of Postsecondary Education, and the Center for Community and Nonprofit Studies. She is the author of *Talking about Race* and *Talking about Politics*, both also published by the University of Chicago Press.

The University of Chicago Press, Chicago 60637
The University of Chicago Press, Ltd., London
© 2016 by The University of Chicago
All rights reserved. Published 2016.
Printed in the United States of America
25 24 23 22 21 20 19 18 17 16   1 2 3 4 5

ISBN-13: 978-0-226-34908-4 (cloth)
ISBN-13: 978-0-226-34911-4 (paper)
ISBN-13: 978-0-226-34925-1 (e-book)
DOI: 10.7208/chicago/9780226349251.001.0001

Library of Congress Cataloging-in-Publication Data

Cramer, Katherine J. (Katherine Jean), author.
    The politics of resentment : rural consciousness in Wisconsin and the rise of Scott Walker / Katherine J. Cramer.
        pages cm— (Chicago studies in American politics)
    ISBN 978-0-226-34908-4 (cloth : alkaline paper) — ISBN 978-0-226-34911-4 (paperback : alkaline paper) — ISBN (978-0-226-34925-1 (e-book)   1. Wisconsin—Politics and government—21st century.   2. Walker, Scott (Scott Kevin), 1967–   3. Rural-urban divide—Wisconsin.   I. Title.   II. Series: Chicago studies in American politics.
    F586.2.C73 2016
    977.5'044—dc23

                                                              2015025701

TO ROSEMARY

Contents

Acknowledgments

Knowledge is something we often create with other people, and that is the case with this book. My gratitude extends far beyond these pages and into the future. But it's my pleasure to spell it out as best as I am able here.

First and foremost, I am deeply grateful to the people who allowed me access to their conversations for this study. I do not take it lightly that you allowed a stranger to sit with you in spaces you have carved out for yourselves as havens. Your hospitality, good humor, and honesty are sticking with me.

Secondly, I am grateful to the many University of Wisconsin–Madison (UW–Madison) students who helped me with this project. Tim Bagshaw, Emily Erwin-Frank, David Lassen, Ryan Miller, Tricia Olsen, Helen Osborn, Kerry Ratigan, and Paula Uniacke helped with transcription, translation, and gathering census and other background data. Special thanks to Dave Lassen for his excellent work on the news media content-analysis project in chapter 4. Also, Sarah Niebler spent many months on crucial analyses that helped me understand the lay of the land in terms of partisan leanings and distribution of resources in Wisconsin and across the country. Ben Toff, thank you for your assistance with so many aspects of this book, including the many long and valuable conversations. Thank you also to the participants in the American Politics Workshop and the Political Behavior Research Group at UW–Madison.

I had the pleasure of presenting various aspects of this work to many groups, and I am grateful to you all for the invitations to do so. Thank you to the members of the Center for the Study of Democratic Politics colloquium at Princeton University, the Center for American Political Studies at Harvard University, the Department of Political Science at the University of Illinois at Urbana-Champaign, the Center for Political Studies at the University of Michigan, the Chicago Area Political and Social Behavior Workshop at Northwestern University, the Center for the Study of Democratic Institutions at Vanderbilt University, the Center on American Politics at Indiana University, the American Politics Workshop at the University of Chicago, the Cornell Conference "Homogeneity and Heterogeneity in Public Opinion," and also the Oxford conference "Popular Reactions to the Economic Crisis."

Also, many groups on the UW–Madison campus as well as groups off campus in Madison and around the state asked me to share what I head learned about attitudes toward UW–Madison and about divides in our state. From those fifty-plus presentations, I learned a tremendous amount from the participants' questions, comments, and follow-up conversations. Thanks to all of them for inviting me to share this work. We are all in this together, and our interactions have gone a long way toward reminding me of that.

Thank you also to the many people who discussed various aspects of this work at conferences, reviewed my submissions to journals, or offered feedback on works in progress. In particular, thank you to Chris Achen, Adam Berinsky, Nancy Bermeo, Nancy Burns, Nick Carnes, Dan Carpenter, Dennis Chong, Jamie Druckman, Jack Edelson, Chris Ellis, Peter Enns, Luke Fuszard, Jim Gimpel, Dan Hopkins, Kent Jennings, Don Kinder, Allan Linton, Leslie McCall, Tali Mendelberg, Spencer Piston, Sam Popkin, Ethan Porter, Markus Prior, Elizabeth Rigby, Meredith Sadin, Byron Shafer, Theda Skocpol, Tim Smeeding, Jim Stimson, Kent Tedin, John Transue, Christopher Wlezien, and several anonymous reviewers. Thank you to Charles Franklin for access to Marquette Poll data. Thank you also to Lew Friedland, Dhavan Shah, Chris Wells, and Mike Wagner in the Contentious Politics Research Group at UW–Madison. Our collaborations and conversations are such a joy.

In the course of this project I have been privileged to develop friendships with two scholars whom I have admired from afar for decades, John Zaller and Larry Bartels. They are both legends in their own time, and it is a happy circumstance for us all that they are also thoroughly decent people and encouraging colleagues as well. I am grateful to John for his enthusiastic encouragement at an early stage of this project, for insisting that I publish in highly visible venues, and for his incisive and invaluable review of the manuscript. Larry, thank you for your unconditional support, your long conversations, and your incredible thirty-two pages of feedback on a draft manuscript.

Thank you also to Alexander Shashko, Jacquie Boggess, and Noam Lupu, three dear friends who went out of their way to read an entire draft manuscript and offer their sage advice. Joe Soss, thank you for teaching me so much of what I know and always being willing to share your wisdom and encouragement. I couldn't have done this without you. Thank you, also, to Kent Jennings and Nancy Burns for your ongoing support and inspiration.

I am so grateful to the people at the University of Chicago Press for treating my work with such care and respect. John Tryneski has my deepest gratitude and admiration for his encouragement, insight, and all-around mastery of publishing a social science book, as well as of life. Thank you to Rodney Powell for your good humor while dealing with me and my work for the third time around. Thanks also to Yvonne Zipter for her copyediting and interest in my work. Thank you also to series editor Larry Jacobs for detailed feedback, tough love, and enthusiasm.

Thank you, also, to Kristin Harley for creating the index for this book.

Some material in this book also appeared in Cramer Walsh (2012, 2014). I am grateful to the *American Political Science Review* and Oxford University Press for use of that work.

I am grateful to the Ira and Ineva Reilly Baldwin Wisconsin Idea Endowment Grant that funded the first year of this research, to Peyton Smith for making that possible, and to Gina Sapiro for suggesting that I apply. I may not have pursued this research otherwise. I am also grateful to the UW–Madison Department of Political Science, a Vilas Associates Award that enabled this work, and a Leon Epstein Fellowship that helped me to finish it. In addition, I am grateful to the staff of the Morgridge Center for Public Service at the UW–Madison for their camaraderie and inspiration. Thank you to John and Tashia Morgridge for their generosity, which makes that work possible, and to Julie Underwood, the dean of the School of Education, who encouraged me to do the job.

When I finished my previous book (on community racial dialogue programs) and earned tenure at UW–Madison, I promised myself I would get involved in racial justice work in the Madison area. Through that work, I became friends with a group of women who have challenged me, loved me, and nourished my civic soul. Thank you for everything you have taught me and continue to teach me. During the years I worked on this book, the roller coaster that is life took some particularly sharp twists and turns, and I could not have made it through without my friends and without my family. From the bottom of my heart, thank you. I am grateful to be the daughter of two devoted, loving, and generous parents. Thank you to my mom and dad, Pat and Kip Cramer; to my brother and sister-in-law and their kids, Scott, Joan, Ben, and Matt Cramer; and to my whole extended family for your support and understanding. Thank you to my former husband, Bailey, for your constant kindness.

Finally, I dedicate this book to Rosemary, my daughter, who had no choice but to come along on much of the fieldwork necessary for this book. Your intense sense of justice inspires me.

CHAPTER ONE

Making Sense of Politics through Resentment

I have a story I would like to share with you. It is a story that my friend Tom recently shared with me. We both live in Madison, Wisconsin, which is the state capital and home to the state's flagship public university, the University of Wisconsin–Madison. Tom tells me that not too long ago he was filling up his car at a gas station here in town. He drives a Prius, and has two bumper stickers on his car that say, "OBAMA 2012" and "RECALL WALKER."

Walker, for anyone who may not know, is our current governor, Scott Walker. He is a Republican and was first elected in November 2010. He took office on January 3, 2011, and soon after, on February 11, 2011, introduced a budget repair bill (Act 10) that called for an end to collective bargaining rights, except with respect to wages, for all public employees except police and fire employees. It also required all public employees to increase their payroll contributions for health and pension benefits (to the tune of a 10 percent cut to many of their paychecks).[1] Over the following weekend, union leaders organized protests at the Capitol. By Tuesday, February 15, over ten thousand protestors gathered on the Capitol Square, and thousands more packed the inside. Two days later, fourteen Democrats in the state senate fled to Illinois, in an effort to block the bill. The protests continued for weeks, peaking on Saturday, March 12, when approximately a hundred thousand protestors packed the Capitol Square. Earlier that week, the legislature passed the collective bargaining provisions by removing some parts dealing with fiscal matters, which allowed them to reach quorum in the senate despite the fourteen missing Democrats. By mid-March, efforts to recall sixteen state senators (of both parties) and the governor were underway. In the summer of 2012, recall elections for nine state senators were held.[2] On June 5, 2012, Walker himself survived a recall vote in a campaign against the same Democrat he had competed against in 2010, Tom Barrett, the mayor of Milwaukee—becoming the first American governor ever to survive a recall. Then in November 2014, he was reelected, with 52 percent of the vote.

The partisan divisiveness in Wisconsin reflects broader political trends in the United States. The country as a whole has seen increasing partisan polarization since the mid-1970s (Layman, Carsey, and Horowitz 2006; McCarty, Poole, and Rosenthal 2008; Barber and McCarty 2013). Democrats and Republicans in both the U.S. House and Senate are increasingly further apart on many issues. Also, state legislatures have become more and more polarized. Wisconsin stands out in this respect—its state legislators are further apart than most—but the trend is universal (Shor 2014). Our political leaders are increasingly taking stands that are ideologically distinctive and far apart (McCarty, Poole, and Rosenthal 2008; Barber and McCarty 2013). And members of the public are increasingly polarized as well (Layman et al. 2006; Jacobson 2010; Abramowitz 2013; Haidt and Hetherington 2012).

Some argue that the public is not actually polarized, that people are just better sorted ideologically into partisan camps than in the past (Hetherington 2009; Fiorina, Abrams, and Pope 2010). But others observe that there is more at stake here than ideology. Divides between identifiers with the two parties in terms of religious preferences, attitudes toward race, and racial demographics themselves are deeper than ever (Abramowitz 2013, 2014). The divides are not just about politics but about who we are as people.

These divides are also reflective of the central debate in American politics today: What is the proper role of government in society and who should pay for it (Stonecash 2014)? There are those who believe government ought to be expanded in order to deal with the challenges we face, and there are those who feel that government itself is a major obstacle that should be shrunk. The emergence of the Tea Party is one manifestation of this fundamental divide.

So back to my story. It is in this contentious context that Tom is pumping gas into his clearly liberal/Democratic car. A cool vintage convertible pulls in to the station. Tom starts chatting up the driver when he gets out of his car. The man looks at Tom, looks at Tom's car, and says, "I don't talk to people like you."

This is a little shocking. Unfortunately, it is not unusual in Wisconsin anymore. It has gotten downright nasty around here. People, in casual conversation, are treating each other as enemies. And this is in a place in which people are notoriously nice. Seriously nice. But times change.

I am a life-long Wisconsinite, and proudly so. I am also a political scientist. So I know from my daily work that besides partisan divisiveness, another key feature of the times we live in is economic inequality (Piketty and Saez 2003). Yes, families at all parts of the income distribution have experienced growth in income since World War II, even when adjusting for inflation. But the growth among the wealthiest folks has skyrocketed, while it seems to have stagnated since the 1970s among the 40 percent lowest in income (Bartels 2008, 7–8).

When you consider how much the very top income earners make compared to the bulk of the population, economic inequality in the United States looks even worse. According to 2005 tax returns, the average income for the top 1 percent was $1,111,560. For the bottom 90 percent, it was just $29,143 (Winters and Page 2009, 735).[3] Of course, since those figures were calculated, the Great Recession hit us all. And this meant a hit to household wealth—the savings, investments, and ownership of things like homes that people can tap into during rough times. Here, too, we see inequality: Those in the ninety-fifth percentile of wealth lost a great deal of wealth in the Great Recession but then recovered quickly. However, those in the bottom twenty-fifth percentile have lost a great deal—approximately 85 percent of their net worth—and not regained it.[4]

This economic imbalance has apparently produced a widening gap in political access between the rich and everyone else. The policies our elected officials put into law reflect the preferences of the affluent, but not so much the opinions of other folks. For example, when you compare the votes of U.S. senators to the preferences their constituents express in public opinion polls, the preferences of the lowest third by income are hardly reflected at all in the senators' votes. The preferences of the middle third are reflected somewhat, but just by the Democratic Party. It is only the opinions of the wealthiest that correspond in any substantial way with senators' votes (Bartels 2008).[5]

I offer another piece of evidence that national politicians seem to listen only to the affluent from political scientist Martin Gilens, who compared the opinions of the nation as a whole with policy outcomes. He used responses to 1,935 questions concerning a variety of policy areas from surveys conducted between 1981 and 2002 (Gilens 2005, 2012). When wealthy and low-income people had similar preferences, their opinions corresponded with policy outcomes. But when their preferences diverged, policies did not reflect the wishes of the low- or middle-income people. They reflected the wishes of the wealthy.

Similar results have been found at the state level. State-level economic policy more closely corresponds to the desires of the rich and hardly matches the desires of the poor (Rigby and Wright 2011). On specific policies, including the death penalty, abortion, gun control, level of education spending, gambling, and scope of AFDC eligibility, state policy again is unresponsive to the ideological leanings of the lowest-income residents (Flavin 2012). If our legislators are listening to anyone (Jacobs and Shapiro 2000), it looks like they are listening mainly to the people with a great deal of money.

There are some who disagree with this interpretation. Ura and Ellis (2008) and Soroka and Wlezien (2008) argue that the evidence of unequal representation is not so strong, since on many policies, preferences do not vary greatly by income level and tend to move similarly over time. But even if that take on public opinion is correct, we are left with another puzzle: as income inequality has risen in the United States, low-income voters' preference for redistribution of income has moved in a conservative fashion. Their preference for redistribution has moved in the same direction as that of high-income voters, even though presumably low-income voters would benefit, directly in their pocketbooks, from more redistributive policy (Kelly and Enns 2010).

This puzzling trend is not just among low-income voters, at least internationally. Among affluent member countries of the Organisation for Economic Co-operation and Development, when the distance in income between low- and middle-income voters is small compared to the distance between the rich and the middle-income, there is greater support among middle-income voters for redistribution (Lupu and Pontusson 2011). But that does not hold in the United States. There seems to be less support for redistribution here than in other countries with similar levels of economic inequality (Kenworthy and Pontusson 2005).

Why? Why is it that most voters continue to elect officials who apparently do not represent the vast majority of us?[6] Or if one does not believe that interpretation, why is it that many low-income voters who might benefit from more government redistribution continue to vote against it? Why, in times of increasing economic inequality, have the preferences of the lowest-income voters moved in a conservative, rather than liberal, direction? And why is it that, here in the United States, we have less support for redistribution among middle-income voters than in comparable countries?

This book provides at least part of the answer to these questions. Back in May of 2007, I started inviting myself into conversations in over two dozen communities chosen throughout Wisconsin.[7] My aim was to listen. I wanted to hear how people made sense of politics and their place in it. I kept going back to those groups of people for over five years, through November 2012.

Their conversations enabled me to examine what it looks like when people who might benefit from more government instead prefer far less of it. Listening closely to people revealed two things to me: a significant rural-versus-urban divide and the powerful role of resentment. This book shows that what can look like disagreements about basic political principles can be rooted in something even more fundamental: ideas about who gets what, who has power, what people are like, and who is to blame. What might seem to be a central debate about the appropriate role of government might at base be something else: resentment toward our fellow citizens.

This book shows people making sense of politics in a way that places resentment toward other citizens at the center. It illuminates this politics of resentment by looking closely at the manner in which many rural residents exhibit an intense resentment against their urban counterparts. I explain how people make sense of politics when the boundaries they draw between "us" and "them" coincide with real, geographic boundaries. I show that, although this form of thinking about politics is often criticized as ignorance, these understandings are complex, many layered, and grounded in fundamental identities.

I learned, as a city girl, that many rural residents have a perspective I am going to call "rural consciousness." To folks who grew up in rural areas, a fancy social science name like that probably seems unnecessary. But it is my shorthand for referring to this: an identity as a rural person that includes much more than an attachment to place. It includes a sense that decision makers routinely ignore rural places and fail to give rural communities their fair share of resources, as well as a sense that rural folks are fundamentally different from urbanites in terms of lifestyles, values, and work ethic. Rural consciousness signals an identification with rural people and rural places and denotes a multifaceted resentment against cities.

When I heard people using this lens to interpret their world, I heard them claiming that government and public employees are the product of anti-rural forces and should obviously be scaled back as much as possible. Viewing politics through the perspective of rural consciousness makes wanting less government a commonsense desire.

We political scientists often claim that whether a person feels closer to the Democratic or Republican Party is the most important predisposition for predicting what people think about politics, including how much government and redistribution people want. But in this book, I show how partisanship can be part of a broader understanding of who one is in the world and a less meaningful identity than we often assume.

Instead of partisan identities, many of the people I spent time with in rural areas used identities rooted in place and class, this perspective I am calling rural consciousness, to structure the causal stories they told to each other—and to me—about the state of the economy before, during, and after the Great Recession.[8] It informed their frequently negative perceptions of public employees. Even though there were public employees in their towns, and sometimes even in their groups, many rural folks did not view public employees as truly rural. They did not see them as hard working and deserving as rural folks in general, for example. This perspective provided an environment ripe for the Tea Party, Scott Walker's success, and support for small government generally.

I call this book *The Politics of Resentment* because there are other ways to make sense of politics than by relying primarily on ideas about which of one's fellow citizens are getting more than their fair share and who among them is undeserving. I draw attention to a kind of politics in which people do not focus their blame on elite decision makers as they try to comprehend an economic recession. Instead, they give their attention to fellow residents who they think are eating their share of the pie. These interpretations are encouraged, perhaps fomented, by political leaders who exploit these divisions for political gain.

This is a different argument than is commonly made about U.S. public opinion and its manipulation by political elites. Contrary to the arguments of political observer Thomas Frank (2004), the interpretations that I am describing are not devoid of economic considerations. The conversations I observed suggest that politicians are not distracting people from economic considerations by convincing them to focus on social and cultural issues. People *are* taking economics into account. But these considerations are not raw objective facts. Instead, they are perceptions of who is getting what and who deserves it, and these notions are affected by perceptions of cultural and lifestyle differences. That is, in a politics of resentment, people intertwine economic considerations with social and cultural considerations in the interpretations of the world they make with one another.

The possibility I am raising here is that we may be missing something if we think of votes in terms of issue stances, as political scientists normally do. Perhaps issues are secondary to identities. Perhaps when people vote for a candidate their overarching calculation is not how closely does this person's stances match my own, but instead, is this person like me? Does this person understand people like me? The answers to those questions *include* a consideration of issue stances, but issue stances are not necessarily the main ingredient.

This is a study of public opinion, but it is atypical in that my goal is not to tell you *what* people think, whether Wisconsinites or any other general population. My goal is not to predict voters' candidate choices or policy preferences. Instead, my goal is to better understand *how* people think about politics. Some public opinion scholars have argued that opinions about redistribution are not just a function of economic considerations but are, instead, the products of people embedded in particular social locations and social environments (Brooks and Manza 2007). In this book, I do the listening required to study how people combine their sense of themselves in the world with their perceptions of economic conditions to arrive at policy preferences. My goal is to uncover the understandings that make a politics of resentment possible. I want to know what it looks like when people use social categories to understand the political world, and how they connect resentment toward particular groups to the broader stance of wanting less, not more, government redistribution.

Let me also say that this is not a study of how *well* people interpret the political world. American citizens already get a great deal of criticism from public opinion scholars and political pundits for being inept (as Lupia [2006] has noted). The pages that follow do contain a good bit of dismay about the way people make sense of politics, but my point is not to echo that argument. The purpose of the book is not to blame the average citizen. Instead, its purpose is to illuminate how we blame each other.

Why the Focus on "Us" versus "Them" and Social Identities?

The politics of resentment is fueled by political strategy but it is made possible by basic human cognition. When people try to make sense of politics, what do they rely on? Psychologists tell us that when people try to understand the world in general, not just the political world, they categorize (Chi, Feltovich, and Glaser 1981; Medin and Cooley 1998). A particularly powerful set of categories in the realm of politics are social identities, more casually called notions of "us" and "them" (Tajfel 1981; Turner et al. 1987). My definition of social identities is simply this: Identities with social groups. These may be small or large—from friendship groups to society-wide categories like "women"—but they serve as reference points by which people compare themselves to others. These identities help us figure out which people are on our side. They help us figure out how we ought to behave and what stances we should take. They even influence what we pay attention to. Because of all that, they affect what and who influences us (e.g., Tajfel et al. 1971; Brewer and Miller 1984; Sears and Kinder 1985; Tajfel and Turner 1986).

These social identities are important politically. They play a central role in political attitudes and behaviors (Campbell et al. 1960, chaps. 12, 13; Conover 1984, 1988; Huddy 2003). Identifying with the broad category Republican or Democrat alone captures enough of individuals' sense of themselves that those identities predict a whole host of political behaviors, particularly voting (Green et al. 2002).

Not all social categories are relevant to politics, but it does not take much for a social category to have an impact on the formation of preferences regarding the distribution of resources—an issue at the heart of politics. When people are simply told to identify with an arbitrary social group, such as Klee or Kandinsky fans, they become more likely to allocate more resources to members of that in-group as opposed to people in the out-group (i.e., the "minimal group result" [Tajfel et al. 1971]). Identifying with a group does not necessarily entail vilifying members of out-groups (Brewer 1999). However, in the realm of public affairs, the distribution of resources is often portrayed as a zero-sum game. There is only so much money to go around. If I allocate it to my group, yours will not get it. Therefore, how people conceptualize the outlines of us and them likely influences what types of policies they are willing to support.

When people feel unsure and insecure about the amount of money available to go around, the situation is ripe for a politics of resentment. People are especially likely to rely on their group identities in situations of uncertainty (Grieve and Hogg 1999; Mullin and Hogg 1999). When people perceive that they are not getting their fair share and that others are but do not deserve to, the emotion of resentment is a likely result (Feather and Sherman 2002; Feather and Nairn 2005). The combination of a reliance on social identities and the emotion of resentment can create a situation in which people regularly view politics in terms of opposition to other social groups.

Resentment is both public and stubborn. It is more socially acceptable to express than envy (Feather and Sherman 2002), making it a potential tool for political arguments. And it is stubborn because even when members of better-off groups are suddenly on the short end of the stick as well—as when public workers must suddenly devote more of their paychecks to benefit contributions—those who resent them are not likely to feel sympathetic toward them (Feather and Nairn 2005). Also, victories over people perceived as underserving tend to produce schadenfreude, or a feeling of pleasure over their failure (Feather and Sherman 2002).

A politics of resentment arises from the way social identities, the emotion of resentment, and economic insecurity interact. In a politics of resentment, resentment toward fellow citizens is front and center. People understand their circumstances as the fault of guilty and less deserving social groups, not as the product of broad social, economic, and political forces.

Some people are more prone to interpret the world in terms of us and them than others (Kinder and Kam 2009). My intent here is not to figure out who uses us/them divisions more than others—I am not claiming that rural residents do this more than urban residents. Instead, my goal is to show what it looks like in practice when people interpret politics by focusing on whom they are against and whom they resent.

My Window Is Wisconsin

My window to the way the politics of resentment works is Wisconsin. This is a state in which the debate over the appropriate role of government has played out prominently and over a sustained period. It has been central to the conservative response to the disarray of the Republican Party after the George W. Bush presidency and Barack Obama's 2008 presidential victory. Wisconsin was a predominantly Republican state until the 1950s, but Democratic presidential candidates have repeatedly carried the state since 1988. Since 2000, however, it has been a partisan battleground, or swing state.

You can see the push-and-pull of partisan fights here in multiple ways. Wisconsin scored highest on the number of "Bush-Obama counties"; no other state had as many counties that went for George W. Bush in the 2004 presidential election and then for Barack Obama in 2008 (Achenbach 2012). Wisconsin went from having a Democratically controlled state legislature with a Democratic governor and two Democratic senators in 2009–10 to having a narrowly Republican-controlled state legislature, Republican governor, and a split U.S. senate delegation in 2012. The state senate has been narrowly balanced, and has alternated between the parties, for decades.[9] The 2010 elections saw a sharp shift toward the Republican Party. Those elections involved a defeat of three-term Democratic U.S. senate incumbent Russ Feingold to Tea Party–backed Republican Ron Johnson, and Walker's ascent to governor (a position previously held by Democrat Jim Doyle, only the second Democrat to ever win reelection to the Wisconsin governorship). But the state continues to be closely divided. Although Walker won his gubernatorial recall election in June 2012, exit polls showed that approximately 9 percent of the electorate had voted for Walker and intended to vote for Obama that coming November (Gilbert 2012b). In the 2012 presidential election, Obama won Wisconsin, and in a race for an open U.S. senate seat, Democrat Tammy Baldwin defeated Republican Tommy Thompson, one of the most popular politicians to ever serve in the state (a former Republican governor and secretary of Health and Human Services under George W. Bush). In the same election, however, Wisconsinites elected a majority Republican state assembly and senate.

These recent elections show that Wisconsin does not lean clearly toward one party or the other. The state's political leaders have real and visible debates about the appropriate reach of government and the merits of market- versus government-based approaches. This makes Wisconsin a fascinating place to study the politics of resentment because it is a laboratory for some of the most fundamental political issues of our time.

To be honest, I did not initially choose to study Wisconsin for these reasons. I was not looking for a laboratory for arguments about the right size of government or even a way to examine the Tea Party. I set out, in

May of 2007, to learn more about the way social-class identities matter for the way people make sense of politics. I chose Wisconsin because average household income and local economies vary widely across the state, and I knew the people here were likely to hold a variety of perceptions with respect to social class. I also wanted to better understand attitudes among state residents toward my alma mater and the university I work for, the University of Wisconsin–Madison. I was also the faculty investigator of a state-wide public opinion poll and wanted to use conversations with people across the state to help set the agenda for our surveys instead of relying solely on conversations with politicos in Madison, the state capitol.

I had a lot of reasons for studying Wisconsin. But the three most important ones were these: I grew up here, I love this state, and I care deeply about it.

I did not foresee the rise of the Tea Party. I did not foresee the Great Recession, Barack Obama, or Scott Walker. But as this intense political context took shape, I was already in the field, listening and gathering data on what residents in the state were thinking. I had sampled my research sites in an attempt to take myself to a wide range of places in the state. My hope was to listen to people of varying socioeconomic backgrounds, across different types of communities. This meant that I spent a lot of time in smaller communities, and more time outside metro areas than ever before in my life.[10]

Listening to conversations in a broad assortment of places alerted me to a rift that surprised me. As I listened closer and longer, I learned that it is a rift through which our economic tensions and our ambivalence about the proper role of government gets played out. This rift is, on its most basic level, a rural-versus-urban divide.

Rural Consciousness

As a female social scientist driving my Volkswagen Jetta out from Madison, the state capitol and the second largest city in the state, I heard a lot of criticism of cities from people in small-town Wisconsin. I heard that urbanites ignore people in rural areas, take in all of their hard-earned money, and fundamentally disrespect and misunderstand the rural way of life.

What I heard while inviting myself into conversations around Wisconsin taught me that the rural-versus-urban divide is an important—if quite overlooked—divide in American politics today. We tend to talk about red versus blue when we look at electoral maps, but perhaps a more important divide is urban versus rural (Meckler and Chinni 2014). We have known for a long time that that this divide matters, but not in the way I am suggesting.

History shows us that the rural-versus-urban divide has long been a factor in American politics. But what I am describing in this book is not just the correlation between place and votes. Instead, I am arguing that place matters because it functions as a lens through which people interpret politics, and I am showing *how* it matters. When previous studies have examined how or why location matters, they have not, in fact, examined how place-based consciousness matters for the way people make sense of politics. In this book, I show how consciousness as a rural resident itself can make the stands that people take in these conflicts seem appropriate and natural.

I am calling this lens rural consciousness to describe a perspective that is at its core an identity rooted in place and class. But it is infused with a sense of distributive injustice—a sense that rural folks don't get their fair share.

I heard this perspective in just about every rural community in which I spent time.[11] In general, it had three elements: (1) a belief that rural areas are ignored by decision makers, including policy makers, (2) a perception that rural areas do not get their fair share of resources, and (3) a sense that rural folks have fundamentally distinct values and lifestyles, which are misunderstood and disrespected by city folks.

I label this perspective rural consciousness in order to build on a line of research in political science regarding "group consciousness." That work focuses on social identities that are infused with a sense of distributive injustice. Such scholarship argues that a group consciousness is a social identity that has particular importance politically. People with a group consciousness prefer their in-group, are dissatisfied with that group's status, believe that members of the group are not getting their fair share, and perceive that this state of affairs is the product of systematic decisions, not just chance or individual-level behavior (Miller et al. 1981). When such attitudes are attached to a social group identity, that identity tends to matter for politics. It affects political preferences and whether people become politically engaged.

The Importance of Place in Contemporary American Politics

In this book, I focus on the urban-versus-rural divide and the perspective of rural consciousness as a window into understanding the politics of resentment.[12] I regard this divide as one of many through which the politics of resentment can operate. However, this particular axis of resentment is hugely consequential for American politics today. Yes, the population of rural residents in the United States is quite small—about 15 percent of the total population. However, contemporary Republican Party power depends on rural residents. According to a recent *Wall Street Journal* analysis, "Over the past 15 years the percentage of rural Americans represented by Republicans in the House has grown sharply, while urban Americans have shifted slightly to House Democrats. . . . As Democrats have come to dominate U.S. cities, it is Republican strength in rural areas that allows the party to hold control of the House and remain competitive in presidential elections" (Meckler and Chinni 2014).

Take Wisconsin, for example. Milwaukee's suburbs lean increasingly Republican, and yet Madison leans increasingly Democratic. There is a lot of attention to the culture war between these two urban areas and, also, to the tensions between the overwhelmingly Republican and white Milwaukee suburbs versus the Democratic and racially diverse city of Milwaukee.[13]

But the rural-versus-urban divide matters. Almost half of the population in Wisconsin lives outside the fourteen counties that make up the greater Milwaukee and Madison metropolitan areas (48 percent according to the 2010 Census).[14] And these nonmetro areas are a political battleground. Of these fifty-eight nonmetro counties, only six voted for the Democratic gubernatorial candidate in 2010. But just two years earlier, only eight of them went for Republican John McCain in the 2008 presidential race. And in 2012, the counties outside the major metro areas basically split: twenty-seven of them went for Obama, and thirty-one went for Republican challenger Mitt Romney. There is an independent streak in the rural areas, and it has mattered in recent elections.[15]

Also, at the same time that the United States is becoming increasingly urban, and increasingly racially and ethnically heterogeneous, there are places that are experiencing something different. Wisconsin is one of them. The changes in Wisconsin represent a change common to the Midwest, but one that is often overlooked by journalists living on the coasts. Here in "flyover" land, the population in Wisconsin is indeed becoming more racially and ethnically diverse. But the largest overall growth in Wisconsin is in the Milwaukee suburbs, which tend to be predominantly white and predominantly Republican.[16]

You can look at demographic change and conclude that urban areas represent the future, and rural areas the past. You could say that conservatism is woven into the fabric of rural life. Maybe. But the alliance of Republican and rural is not inevitable. Nor is the correlation between small towns and support for less government. My interest is in the interpretations of the world that make these correlations happen.

What I argue in this book is that paying attention to identities rooted in place is key to understanding these interpretations. We should pay attention to place because rural areas are political battlegrounds, our system of representation is based on geography, and conflicts between rural and urban areas over who should get what are intensifying (Gimpel and Schuknecht 2003, esp. 385). But we should also pay attention to place because it is central to the way many people understand the political world.

Americans' perceptions of who gets what and our notions of fairness about these distinctions are often linked to place (Hochschild 1981). These perceptions of place and justice also correlate with perceptions of who has power and how it is exercised (Hayward 2000). Our identification with particular communities is also associated with our willingness to pay taxes (Wong 2010, chap. 3).

The links we make between place and justice, fairness and inequality are powerful because they involve race and social class. By social class, I mean our perceived social standing relative to each other, which is rooted in economic characteristics such as income, occupation, and education. It is inescapable that there are haves and have-nots in the United States in terms of objective wealth, and on that basis I argue class matters in American politics. Place is intertwined with the objective indicators of class (Burrows and Gane 2006),[17] defined by a long pedigree of scholarship as income, wealth, occupation, and relationship to authority in the workplace.[18]

When it comes to figuring out how the politics of resentment works, people's perceptions of their social class make a difference—and that is also intertwined with place. Objective measures of class do not necessarily predict how people will perceive their own social class (Walsh, Jennings, and Stoker 2004). A person we type as "upper class" according to income may instead think of herself as "middle class." Social-class identities are a function of income, occupation, and education, but they also incorporate a sense of what people value and the lifestyles they prefer (Jackman and Jackman 1983).

Class is not something that people just have—it is something that they *do*. They give meaning to their social-class status through the food they eat, the clothes they wear, the sports they play, and so on (Bourdieu [1979] 1984, chap. 3; see also Lareau 2008). People give meaning to their identities through their everyday life and interactions with others, and those meanings in turn structure how they make sense of the world.[19]

The connection between social-class identity and geographic place may be particularly important for politics. Because identities are perceptions, not necessarily consistent with objective circumstances, other people, including politicians, can influence and manipulate them. And because dividing lines may be most easily exploited when they have physical markers, identities rooted in geographic spaces are ripe for the politics of resentment. Geographic boundaries allow us to actually draw lines between types of people, particularly between the haves and the have-nots.

I am focusing on place as a dimension of the politics of resentment because it is intertwined with another social category that is highly relevant to redistributive policy in the United States: race. Race has been central to debates over what role the government should play in redistribution since at least the Civil War. In their book, *Fighting Poverty in the US and Europe*, Alesina and Glaeser (2004) explain that, until the Civil War, the federal government did not have the capacity to redistribute wealth. After the war, three things came together: a stagnant economy among farmers, enormous increases in wealth for some people (this was what we call the Gilded Age, after all), and a government with increased power, not only real but demonstrably so—it had just successfully freed the slaves.

At that point in time, the rural-versus-urban divide, race, and redistribution collided. Rural economies were particularly hard hit and various rural-based movements arose, in which people argued for redistribution. Their focus was on increasing inflation so that farmers could pay their debts. But in essence they were asking for the federal government to take from the very rich and redistribute to the rural poor.

These movements became what we now call populism. As populists tried to make their arguments, they tried to appeal to African Americans—an overwhelmingly poor population at the time. And pretty quickly, enemies of populism invoked racism to combat these calls for redistribution.

President Franklin Delano Roosevelt's New Deal legislation to combat the Great Depression changed the debate about redistribution, and the United States practiced significant redistribution until the 1960s. The Republican Party found itself out of power—until a change that began with Barry Goldwater's successful candidacy for his party's nomination in 1964 provided a blueprint that the party built on in later years. He gained support in that race by appealing to a coalition of McCarthyites (anticommunists), anti–New Dealers, and Southerners committed to segregation. That coalition has underpinned Republican success ever since. As Alesina and Glaeser (2004) argue, whether or not Republican politicians were intentionally using race, when they ran on an anti–New Deal platform, they were appealing to those opposed to integration.

Arguments against redistribution still benefit from the unfortunate fact that racist sentiments persist. As Alesina and Glaeser show, across the globe opponents of the welfare state have succeeded by tapping into cultural heterogeneity, whether racial, religious, or otherwise. In the United States, it is in the interests of the Republican Party for attention to class to be diverted to attention to race.

In fact, race is quite likely the reason that public opinion in the United States has not shifted in a redistributive direction as much as it has in other countries, despite rising economic inequality. In most affluent member countries of the Organisation for Economic Co-operation and Development, governments have responded to rising inequality with greater redistribution—but not in the United States (Kenworthy and Pontusson 2005). Some say that the relative weakness of labor unions and socialist movements (Korpi 1983) and the low voting rates among low-income voters (Kenworthy and Pontusson 2005) in the United States have resulted in less pressure for redistribution than in other countries.

Another part of the story, though, is the composition of the poor in the United States. As I noted at the start of this book, support for redistribution among middle-income voters in the United States is much lower than it is in other countries of the Organisation for Economic Co-operation and Development with comparable levels of affluence and structures of inequality (Lupu and Pontusson 2011). Scholars argue this is because a greater proportion of the poor in the United States are racial minorities (Alesina and Glaeser 2004). They argue that racial difference reduces the connection that middle-income voters feel toward the poor. Without a psychological connection to the poor, middle-income voters are less likely to support redistributing resources toward them (Lupu and Pontusson 2011; see also Lane 2001).

The history of the intertwined nature of race, place, and class underscores that the alliance of rural voters with a party pressing for less government has roots in human action—it has not popped out of thin air. In fact, in the populist era, the relationship was reversed: farmers were allied with populists calling for more redistribution. Looking closely at the way rural residents understand politics today helps uncover the many layers of the publics' interpretations of who is on their side and where they place the role of government in these battles.

Listening closely to rural voters also helps reveal how the meaning of "populism" has changed in the contemporary United States. Political actors often claim to be populist as a shorthand for conveying that they are especially close to the people and are railing against politics as usual. Present-day U.S. candidates who call themselves "populist" are not necessarily so.[20] Because we live in a time when distrust in government is the norm, there is often a political benefit in running against government and in making the claim that government is out of step with the concerns of the public.

But the white-collar composition of our national, state, and local governments calls into question the extent to which those seeking office are on the side of "the people" in a populist division of people versus the powerful elite (Carnes 2013). Also, how often are so-called populists these days operating outside the party structure? For example, are Tea Party candidates really separate from the Republican Party and the organizations that support it? That does not appear to be the case, as Republican Party elites and the Fox News network have been key players in Tea Party activism (Williamson, Skocpol, and Coggin 2011).

When populist appeals are made, do we really have genuine "discontent stem[ming] from the disparity between those who hold no power versus those who do" (Barr 2009, 31)? For example, in the rural consciousness I observed, many people living in rural places thought that their communities were not receiving their fair share of resources. And yet, empirically the evidence on this is unclear, as I explain in greater detail in chapter 3. Also, on many issues their stances were similar to the policy priorities of the party in power: Act 10, gun control, and reducing taxes, for example. In this way, many appeals that are labeled populist rarely cut against the grain of society or against the grain of elite values.[21] The claim we will encounter that public employees are lazy and undeserving is not exactly against the interests of the established elite, for example.

The approach I take in this book enables us to better understand the operation of what contemporary political pundits call populism. I show what some of these us-versus-them divides look like from the public's point of view. I also show why people find these categories appealing and useful, even if focusing on such categories ultimately benefits not themselves but, instead, the powerful elite.

Public Opinion among Ordinary People

My attention in this book is focused on "ordinary" people who find themselves in a caustic political environment and who, unfortunately, through their own sense making, contribute to that environment. By ordinary people, I mean people who are not themselves political elites—not elected officials, staffers for elected officials, public employees involved in the policy process, or journalists and others who live and breathe politics. (As much as I would like to think of myself as an ordinary person, this leaves out political scientists, too).[22]

Because I listen intensively to particular people in particular places in this study, you can say this is a bottom-up study of public opinion. But I am not assuming that the opinions I hear in these communities exist in a vacuum, independent of mass media or political leaders. I am also not assuming that ordinary people simply parrot the views of Fox News, Barack Obama, or anyone else. The reality I will try to convey to you is of a much more complex process of sense making and understanding.

Here are my assumptions about the way public opinion operates. First, we can predict the aggregate shape of public opinion quite accurately from the content of mainstream news media (Zaller 1992). Second, differences within the population can be accurately predicted by politically important predispositions like partisanship, attitudes toward war (Zaller 1992), and attitudes toward racial groups (Kinder and Sanders 1996). People pay attention to and hear things that resonate with their preexisting beliefs. Third, when we judge whether the ordinary citizen is capable of making "good" judgments with respect to politics according to how much they "know" (Delli Carpini and Keeter 1996) and to what extent they base these judgments on an overarching ideology (Converse 1964), they do not in general perform very well. Fourth, when you listen to the way people make sense of politics, they have justifications for what they think, and these justifications make sense to them and are steeped in their personal sense of who they are in the world (Cramer Walsh 2004). Fifth, the identities people use to make sense of politics are constantly evolving and change salience in response to the context (Turner et al. 1994; Green, Palmquist, and Schickler 2002).

Sixth, public opinion is not just what polls measure. Before we had survey research, people did not define public opinion as poll results. Instead, scholars thought of it as the product of groups of people competing with one another (Blumer 1948) and the back and forth between citizens and journalists (Bryce 1913). When the technology of mass sample surveys was emerging, it seemed crazy to some people to think of public opinion as the mechanical aggregation of the expressions of isolated individuals. Even today, for many decisions, especially at lower levels of government, it is not practical to capture public opinion through polling. Politicians with small constituencies or limited budgets figure out what their constituents think and feel—public opinion—based on things other than polls (Fenno 1978). They talk to people. They do "polling by walking around" (Cramer Walsh 2009). I am trying to revive this definition of public opinion as more than just what polls measure. It is also the understandings that emerge from communication among people.

In this view of public opinion, bottom-up and top-down processes are occurring at the same time and influence one another. Elites mobilize public opinion. That does not mean that they create public opinion from scratch. Instead, they tap into preexisting sentiments and values they find it advantageous to activate. Market research and campaign consultants try to figure out what messages will work—what will resonate and what will successfully ignite opinions that are lying dormant (Key 1961). In addition, political strategy does contribute to the opinions and sentiments that are out there. The seeds of resentment are sown over long periods of time. In other words, political elites reap the benefits of the divisiveness they help create.

In the conversations of this book, we see how the weeds grow as people sow them in the minds of each other. We also see how certain contexts create a bounty harvest as politicians fertilize certain resentments for particular political purposes. My focus here is on processes among ordinary people, but my aim is to explain how they fit into an overall political ecology.

Why Study Group Conversation?

You might have gathered that this is not your typical public opinion study, meaning a study conducted via scientific opinion surveys. This book is based on data gathered by inviting myself into the conversations of ordinary people. I find mass-sample public opinion surveys enormously helpful for capturing what a large population of people think at a given point in time. But for the task of figuring out *why* people think what they do I have found no better substitute than listening to them in depth—sitting down with them in groups in the places they normally hang out and hearing how they piece the world together for themselves. This is sometimes called an "ethnographic approach" (Schatz 2009). It is ethnographic in the sense of observing life in a place in order to understand the meaning people construct of their own lives and the world around them.

I said at the outset that my main motivation was not to get at *how well* people make sense of politics, but to get at *how* they do so. I am trying to discern what people have rather than what they lack, in terms of the tools they have for making sense of politics. I take this approach because, as I said above, I tend to think of public opinion as the understandings that people create together. That is, if a person was to talk about an issue one way in her morning coffee klatch and yet another way in response to a telephone interviewer later in the day, which one is her real opinion? Both are real and both have importance.

My hope is to better explain how the perspectives people use to interpret the world lead them to see certain stances as natural and right for someone like themselves (Soss 2006, 316). This is in line with an approach to social science called "interpretivism" (Schwartz-Shea and Yanow 2012). This kind of work generally shares the goal of trying to provide a coherent account of interpretations or understandings in order to explain why people express the opinions they do. My assumption is that providing such an account is necessary for a true explanation.

Even before I noticed that place identities were a prominent way in which people in the rural communities I sampled were making sense of politics, I wanted to take into account the way the socioeconomic context of their communities mattered in their conversations. An ethnographic approach enabled me to do this. I also wanted to spend time with people having conversations in their own environments because doing so allows me to see the work of social identity. Social identity is hard to measure with surveys. Our best attempts involve asking people how close they feel to certain social groups, but when we do so we have to anticipate what groups matter to people. I find that we learn a lot when we allow people to tell us what their identity reference points are (Walsh 2004). In addition, when you watch people interacting with people they normally spend time with, you can hear and see them using these reference points in a way that does not necessarily occur in a one-on-one interview with a researcher.

Another thing I should point out about this study is that it is not about causation. I am not trying to predict how X causes Y. For example, my question is not whether living in a rural place causes rural consciousness, or whether politicians activate rural consciousness. Instead, this study is a "constitutive" analysis. That is, it is an examination of what this thing, rural consciousness, consists of, how it works, and how it is part of a broader politics of resentment (Taylor 1971; McCann 1996; Wendt 1998). The point is not to argue that we see consciousness in rural areas but not in other places, or to estimate how often it appears among rural residents, or to describe what a population of people thinks. Instead, my purpose here is to examine what this particular rural consciousness is and what it does: how it helps to organize and integrate thoughts about the distribution of resources, decision-making authority, and values into a coherent narrative that people use to make sense of the world. In addition, the goal is to illuminate how this perspective fits in with a broader politics in which tapping into resentment is an effective political strategy. This is not a study of Wisconsin; it is a study of political understanding that is conducted in Wisconsin (Geertz 1973, 22).

To clarify what this study needs to show in order to contribute to our understanding of politics, and what exactly it does contribute, allow me to contrast it with positivist approaches. By a positivist approach, I mean one that tests data to demonstrate causality and discover scientific laws that explain human behavior and society. One of the things that I do in this book is to examine how people weave together place and class identities and their orientations to government and how they use the resulting perspectives to think about politics. A positivist study of this topic

might measure identities and orientations to government, and then include them as elements in a statistical analysis that is attempting to figure out which things predict policy or candidate preferences.

Such an approach is problematic for my purposes. The positivist
model set-up assumes that values on one explanatory (or "independent")
variable move independently of the other variables. Or, if claiming an
interaction between two explanatory variables, it assumes that people
with particular combinations of these characteristics exhibit a significantly different level of the variable we are trying to explain (the "dependent" variable). However, the object of my study, or my dependent variable, to put it in positivist terms, is not a position on an attitude scale but,
instead, the perspectives that people use to arrive at that position. My
object is to understand neither the independent effects of identities and
attitudes (such as trust) on a given political opinion nor how people having different combinations of characteristics and attitudes compare to
others in terms of their issue positions. Rather, my goal is to distinguish
how people themselves combine attitudes and identities—how they create or constitute perceptions of themselves and use these to make sense
of politics.

What does this study need to demonstrate, if not that X causes Y?
I have to show, convincingly, that a particular perspective is influential
for the way some people think about politics.[23] The burden is on me to
show that rural consciousness structures how the people I spent time
with think about politics—that is, that their use of rural consciousness
screens out certain considerations and makes others obvious and com-
monplace. I have to show that the work of this perspective contributes to
a broader context in which politics is understood as a matter of resentment toward other members of the public.

Plan of the Book

My plan for the remainder of this book is to first explain the approach
that I took in doing this research, what rural consciousness is, and then
how it functions to structure political understanding and contributes to
a politics of resentment. After I specify what rural consciousness is and
what it does, I will develop in detail how this lens structures interpretations of politics.

In short, here is what I will do in each chapter. In the next chapter,

I explain my methods in full and introduce the reader to the groups who allowed me to join in on their gatherings. It is conventional to put this information in an appendix at the back of the book. I am asking you to read it as part of the story because knowing how I went about collecting these data is important for understanding what I learned from them. Also, since most people—scholars and ordinary citizens alike—are used to thinking about public opinion as the results of public opinion polls, I need to provide some extra clarification concerning how to evaluate the kind of data I present in this book.

In chapter 3, I lay out the nature of rural consciousness, the geography of Wisconsin, and its historical relationship to politics in the state. With the use of survey and conversational data, I argue that there are three major components of the rural consciousness perspective: a perception that rural areas do not receive their fair share of decision-making power, that they are distinct from urban (and suburban) areas in their culture and lifestyle (and that these differences are not respected), and that rural areas do not receive their fair share of public resources. I examine the importance of understandings about who works hard in the population and the manner in which rural consciousness has provided an extra grounding for even this basic part of U.S. culture. I also carefully consider racism in these conversations and ask the reader to take a nuanced understanding of its role in the resentment we hear.

In chapter 4, I analyze whether there is empirical support for the idea that rural areas are the victims of distributive injustice. I argue that even though per capita allocations do not consistently support this view, the nature of the challenges facing rural areas in the United States means that there is a reasonable basis for these perceptions. Finally, the chapter presents results of an investigation into evidence of rural consciousness in local news coverage in Wisconsin. I use our null results from that analysis to argue that rural consciousness is one aspect of public opinion that is likely communicated primarily through interpersonal interaction, again suggesting the importance of public opinion methods that place listening front and center.

In chapter 5, I move from explaining what rural consciousness is into what it does—how it works for helping people make sense of politics. I look closely at conversations about education, particularly higher education, to analyze how rural consciousness has structured conversations about public institutions and public employees. As I contrast conversations among groups of people meeting in rural areas with groups meeting in urban and suburban places, I show how rural consciousness provides extra grounding for interpretations that center on resentment.

In chapter 6, I show how rural consciousness provides fertile ground for arguments in favor of less redistribution and smaller government. I examine the way people connect resentment toward government in general and toward public employees in particular with the conclusion that government ought to be cut back. I argue that, in a politics of resentment, attitudes toward social groups do the work of ideology. In this kind of politics, we see people arguing in favor of small government based on resentment toward other citizens, not libertarian principles. I show how rural consciousness provides an extra footing for these understandings. Ambivalence in the public about the proper size of government means these interpretations are not inevitable, but the narratives that resentment offers make them seem that way.

In chapter 7, I show how the lens of rural consciousness has structured understandings of the Great Recession, Barack Obama, and the ruckus around Scott Walker in Wisconsin. I dissect conversations about public employees to examine how rural consciousness served to reinforce the politics of resentment before, during, and after the Great Recession. I also examine conversations about Barack Obama, Scott Walker, and the legislation by Walker that effectively ended collective bargaining for public employees and required them to contribute much larger amounts from their paychecks toward their health insurance and pensions. Finally, I analyze Walker's public comments to suggest how politicians tap into resentment to win elections and further their policy goals.

These analyses help develop the argument that the politics of resentment is about more than making sense of politics with the tools of social identity. It is about using perspectives that make resentment toward social groups inevitable and reasonable. In this style of interpretation, people blame other residents rather than broader structural forces.

In the conclusion of the book, I reflect back on the nature of rural consciousness, how people use it to structure their understanding of politics, and how it is part of a broader politics of resentment. I underscore that perspectives that are often denigrated as ignorant seem quite complex in these conversations. I consider what the results tell us about the importance of place identity in public opinion, as well as the importance of place in practical understandings of social class. I use the results from the various analyses throughout the book to argue that understanding contemporary public opinion requires considering both bottom-up and top-down forces. I describe some of the insights this interpretivist study offers for positivist approaches. Finally, I conclude that this study gives us some serious warning signals about the tendency of modern democracy toward resentment. When arguments about how we ought to allocate resources to each other are made on the backs of our resentment toward each other, what does the future hold?

CHAPTER TWO

A Method of Listening

In Wisconsin, the months of May and June are something to behold. Driving around the state at that time of year, the green of the fields and the blue of the sky are brighter than the best postcard. I have lived here most of my life, but when I started my fieldwork for this project in May of 2007, the landscape nevertheless took my breath away. I love the geography of this state and the character of the people within it. Those facts matter, because they meant that it took me years to characterize what I observed in these conversations as resentment. I went into this project with a love of Wisconsin; I came out of it with a deep concern for the nature of democracy in this state and in the United States in general.

My job as a political ethnographer is to describe what I observed in enough detail that you, the reader, can judge my observations for yourself. I want to show you how I arrived at my conclusions, not just tell you what they are.

On one particularly bright and beautiful June morning in Wisconsin in 2012, I was in a dairy barn, just outside a town in the central part of the state. The owner's brother had invited me out for a visit. I had first met both men at a local diner about five years prior (Group 11b).[1]

I had been at the diner that morning. Most of the regulars were there, playing dice like they usually do, but not Henry, the dairy farmer whose farm I was now visiting. At the diner, Henry's brother had explained to me that Henry no longer came to the diner in the mornings. Political discussions had gotten too intense since Walker became governor. No one seemed to want to clarify whether Henry had been kicked out or he had decided of his own volition to quit being a part of the group.

So on this particular glorious morning, I am in Henry's dairy barn while the cows are getting milked. I am in what I call my "nondescript fieldwork clothes," an outfit that is intentionally professional but not too fancy—nice pants and a button-down short-sleeved shirt, with decent sandals, all in darkish but not black colors (navy blue, basically). Like I said, it is not too fancy, and yet I am mindful that cow poop is splattering up from the cement onto my toes. The farmers and the others in the barn chuckle a little as they notice me grimace.

Henry introduces me to several family members working in the barn. I have told Henry and his brother I am a faculty member at the University of Wisconsin–Madison (UW–Madison) and given them my business card each of the four other times I have visited with their dice group over the past five years. But they have a different interpretation. "Here's a politician, up from Madison," Henry says as he introduces me. "Oh I am NOT a politician," I say as I laugh. "I'm here to get the wisdom of people around here on recent events in the state."

A man working with the milking machines looks around the back of the cow at me and says, "I'm glad Walker did what he did. It's about time someone takes something away from those bastards."

The bastards, in this case, are public employees. I am one of them. Walker's budget repair bill, or Act 10, introduced shortly after he took office in early 2011, eliminated most collective bargaining for most public employees, and also required them to contribute more of their paychecks to their pensions and health care benefits. The resulting protests at the capitol were the largest in the state's history and as visually striking as a June day in Wisconsin. The sheer volume and duration of the protests were historic but so, too, were the recall efforts that followed.

Of course, the most famous of the recall attempts was a recall of Walker himself. Walker opponents gathered over 900,000 signatures to force that recall vote (over 360,000 more than necessary). The recall campaign was vicious. The ads (MacGillis 2012) and road signs were nasty but so were the interactions among ordinary folks.[2] People stole yard signs from each other. They stopped talking to one another. They spit on each other. They even tried to run each other over, even if they were married to one another. I am not kidding.[3] Suddenly, national reporters were calling Wisconsin "The Most Politically Divisive Place in America" (Kaufman 2012).

Even with these divisive politics going on, Wisconsin looks gorgeous on this June morning. But it is not any June day here in Wisconsin. It is

Recall Election Day, June 5, 2012. Walker and his lieutenant governor, Rebecca Kleefisch, are both up for recall, as are four Republican state senators.

When Henry's son-in-law refers to us public employees as bastards, nobody laughs. But it is not exactly an uncomfortable moment either. They have welcomed me into their barn, after all. And then Henry offers to give me a tour and shows me the various animals he is raising to amuse his grandkids. There are chickens, pigs, a cat, and a dog. The farm in general is pristine, especially so because Henry is about to host the county's annual farm breakfast. As I start back to my car to head back to Madison, he urges me to return in a few days for the big event. I promise to try, but it's a three-and-a-half-hour drive one way, and I have a four-year-old at home. As it turns out, I will not make it back.

After leaving the farm, I go back to my room at the local Super 8 Hotel, then meet up with a group of women for lunch at a family-style restaurant. This is a group of older women (some working, some retired) who get together once a week at various restaurants (Group 11c). One of the men that gathers at the diner told me about this lunch bunch. It was my first time meeting with them. They welcomed me in warmly. I was glad to have on my nondescript fieldwork outfit. Most of them were dressed for lunch: bright T-shirts, careful hair, and tasteful earrings.

On my way back to Madison, I stop at an exclusive spa where two of my dearest friends are spending the night to celebrate one's fortieth birthday. As I visit with them at the resort, I am mindful that I look a little out of place in my fieldwork uniform. I worry I am not fancy enough. Later that night, we check in on the recall results via Twitter. It appears Walker has won, and so have three of the four Republican state senators up for recall. It comes as a bit of a shock. Living in Madison, support for Walker was invisible, and pretty much taboo. I had expected a close race based on what I had seen and heard in other parts of the state, but the strong Walker win surprised me nonetheless. We all learned later from exit polls that many people voted for Walker as a way of voting against the recall process itself. Call it Midwestern good manners, I suppose: we are neither supposed to throw people out midstream nor "waste" taxpayer dollars to do so.

This was just one day in my fieldwork. I share it with you because it illuminates the upsides and downsides of this research. First and foremost, this research was personal. I got to know people. I spent time in their barns, at their favorite hang-outs, in their chairs. They asked to

see pictures of my daughter, and I asked to see pictures of their families in return. I got manure on my toes. I got insulted, and I got and gave
hugs. Also, I had to pay attention to my own identities and make sense of
how they affected what I observed. I had to pay attention to how I presented myself and how people were altering their own presentations in
response. I had to find a way to be authentic—be myself—without turning people off in this hyperpolitically charged atmosphere.

Choosing the Communities, Finding the Groups

When I started this study, I was not focused on rural-urban divides. My
interest was in social-class identity. I had been curious about social-class
identity throughout my career and I wanted to know more about how
it mattered for the way people made sense of politics. I knew I wanted
to observe group conversations among people who got together on their
own, not among people whom I had recruited.

I knew I wanted the groups I studied to vary in terms of socioeconomic status, not only in terms of their own incomes, educations, and
occupations but also in terms of the socioeconomic status of the communities that I visited. For this reason, I chose the places to include in
my study so that they varied by community wealth, expecting that this
would give me some variation in individuals' social-class identity as well
as in their communities' class statuses.

I wanted the communities to vary with respect to other community
characteristics that I thought might be related to social-class identity. To
do so, I sampled communities using what is known as a stratified pur-
poseful approach (Miles and Huberman 1994, 28). That is, I divided the
counties in Wisconsin into eight regions and then purposefully chose
communities within each of those regions. To divide the state into regions, I analyzed a variety of information about each of the seventy-two
counties: their partisan leanings in recent elections, median household
income, population density, total population, racial and ethnic heterogeneity according to the 2000 Census, type of industry, and agricultural
background. Within each region I chose the municipality with the largest
population and randomly chose a smaller municipality. To provide additional variation, I added eleven municipalities. The result was a sample
of twenty-seven communities.

Once I had chosen these communities, I sought out groups within them that met regularly and in a place in which I could easily introduce myself. Two sources of information were invaluable: University of Wisconsin Cooperative Extension educators and local newspaper editors. These folks know the counties they work in well. I would call them up and ask for suggestions of groups of regulars whom I could get access to—where and when they met and any tips for introducing myself. Sometimes the informant said, "Don't tell them I sent you." Sometimes he or she offered to come with me to help me get a foot in the door.

The places they usually sent me to were early morning coffee klatches that met in diners, cafés, McDonald's, or, oftentimes, in gas stations. In many small towns, the main morning meeting place is the gas station, where people gather around the coffee urns to get the latest news and some social interaction. In appendix B, I give a brief description of each of these groups, the communities in which they met, and the dates of my visits with them. As I mention these various groups throughout the book, I provide the numbers I use to label groups in that table so that you can use it to look up more detailed information about the groups and the communities in which they met.

The first group I spent time with met in Madison (Group 22b). In a way they were my "practice" group, but that label does not do justice to how much I learned from them over the years. This was a group of retirees, men and women, who met every morning, including weekends for many of them, in a coffee shop near downtown. Most of them had lived in Madison their entire lives. They, like nearly all of the groups, welcomed me warmly and seemed to enjoy telling me their stories and sharing their views with me. They were somewhat notorious in town. Over the years the daily newspapers have done several feature stories on them. Most of the groups I spent with were like this—an obvious group of regulars in the community.

Other groups were harder to find. For example, Henry's former group met in a diner in a town in the west-central part of the state (Group 11b) but not in the main dining room or even at the double U-shaped counter. Thankfully, a prominent attorney in town accompanied me on my first visit and led me through a curtain at the back of a restaurant to the room full of men playing dice. Over the years I realized that everyone in town knew about this dice game except outsiders like me.

In another town a bit farther west, I had been told by a local news editor that a group of retired and current businessmen met every day, mid-morning, in a certain diner on the main street (Group 13). On my first visit, I walked into the restaurant and did not see a group of people meeting, just a few pairs of people at the booths and tables. So I ordered some eggs and coffee and lamented the fact that I had driven across the state for nothing. But then I heard voices beyond a partition near the back of the restaurant. And there they were: the "Ding-a-Lings." This was what they called themselves. It described the way they would clink their water glasses when they needed the server to pour more coffee.

With the groups that met in gas stations, all I had to do was find the coffee urns. The regulars would be right there. In some places, they would be sitting in chairs or stools given as hand-me-downs from a local tavern. I learned in time that meeting up with these groups required some sensitivity to the seasons. Visiting during deer hunting season was a little silly. Most of the folks were in their deer stands, not on the beat-up bar stools in the gas station. Also, loggers met up in gas stations at slightly different times of the morning depending on the season. In the slow months like late March and April—when the ground was too soggy for their trucks to get to the trees—they slept in a bit and lingered longer around the coffee urns. But in the later spring, when the ground was passable and the weather good, I learned I had to get there by 5 A.M. in order to hear their conversations. The way the rhythm of daily life varied with nature was something I had to learn. I am a city girl who works behind a desk, not outdoors.

Presenting Myself

My identity as an urbanite matters for how I perceive things. But it also matters for the way I presented myself. My training, like that of political scientists in general, was predominantly positivist. In other words, much of what I learned in school was how to analyze causation. I learned that the goal of a good social scientist is to approximate the scientific method as closely as possible. In such an approach, one aims to have little or no effect on the research setting. Ideally, a different person could replicate the same study to a T.

That way of thinking still enters my thoughts, but I no longer think it is appropriate for my ethnographic work. When I first started my fieldwork for this study, I tried to wear the same outfit to every research site in a given round, or set of visits. My purpose was to try to interact with each group in precisely the same way, to act as a scientific instrument as much as possible. But as my work went on, it seemed that it did not matter that I dressed the same across groups. Blue-collar groups in low-income communities knew I was wealthier by virtue of my job. They knew I was different because I rolled up to their diner or gas station in a Volkswagen Jetta wagon, and parked it next to a bunch of Made-in-USA pickup trucks. I learned that, rather than obscure who I am, I had to be a human being in order to be welcomed into their conversations.

I learned more by being attentive to their reactions to me than from trying to convince them and myself that my own identities did not matter (Schwartz-Shea and Yanow 2012). In my everyday life I tend to dress with a little flair—lots of color and bold patterns—and it probably helped to tone that down in order to make the conversation less about me. But psychology tells us that people make sense of each other by categorizing. People categorized me—and how they did so was an important source of information. It helped me to notice what they noticed—what they thought was important. Was it my presence as a woman that mattered? The fact that I was a white person? A younger person? A state employee? Academic? Urbanite? Wisconsinite? I tried to take advantage of the way my presence altered the conversations, rather than fool myself into thinking I could somehow present myself as somebody who appeared neutral on every dimension (Schwartz-Shea and Yanow 2012).

It is one thing to say that my presence made some topics more salient, but didn't it also bring rural consciousness itself into the conversation? My obvious status as an urbanite very likely made the out-group of urbanites more salient (Turner et al. 1994). But rural consciousness was not an artifact of my presence. I say this for a variety of reasons. Rural consciousness was not just about rural versus city folks. It contained perceptions of the distribution of power, values, and resources that could not have been constructed suddenly in my presence. Second, the people I listened to revealed the perspective of rural consciousness quickly, suggesting that they used this perspective quite a bit, not suddenly when meeting me. Third, for the people who used this perspective, it was so fundamental to the way they talked about politics that when I asked about it directly they were often downright astonished that I found it necessary to do so.[4]

For example, in a small hamlet on the Wisconsin River about an hour's drive from Madison (Group 8), a male and female group of retirees and people on their way to work met every morning in a gas station. Over the course of several visits I asked them to tell me about the major concerns in their community. They spoke about injustices in the way property taxes are implemented, the inefficiency of state government, and state workers' exorbitant salaries and health benefits. Eventually, on my third visit (April 2008), I asked them directly about this obvious antigovernment attitude.

> KJC: So sounds like the state government, boy, doesn't have a very good reputation out here.
> THEODORE: It doesn't in most rural areas
> MICHAEL: No.

Their blunt response suggested that a central aspect of their antigovernment attitude was geography. Even given my question wording ("out here") and my presence as an urbanite, the quickness of their response and the astonishment in their voices suggested that the rural-versus urban divide was salient before I arrived.

My presence likely altered the conversations in one other way. I am pretty sure that when I visited groups of men, they cleaned up their language. When I visited a group in a very small town in central Wisconsin in 2011, three years after my first visit, one man joked, "Hey Ronny, I just said to Brad, I said 'I believe it's been five or ten minutes and I haven't heard a cuss word.' I said, 'that's the longest it's been since the last time she was here'" (Group 1, April 2011).

On my first visit to a group meeting in the back of an all-purpose store in northwest Wisconsin (Group 6) in June 2007, the female cashier called back to us toward the end of my visit:

> CASSIE: You guys behaving back here? This is a naughty bunch!
> KJC: This has been great. Oh they are great. Thank you so much.
> JOHNNY: We barely even swore this morning.
> CASSIE: You did what Johnny?
> JOHNNY: I said we barely even swore this morning.
> [Laughter]
> KJC: Oh you go right ahead—you don't have to—
> JOHNNY: Usually a lot of potty mouthing back here.
> KJC: Yeah I knew that would happen.
> SAM: Well Cassie doesn't work every morning so she didn't know any better— she let you come in. The other regulars woulda never let you come back here!

Because I was using myself as a scientific tool, these were human interactions, and they were hard at times. Pulling up to a gas station at 5 A.M., parking my foreign yuppie car among a bunch of Fords, and walking in to cold-call announce that I was there to invite myself into a conversation took some gumption. I am somewhat of an introvert, so I often resorted to a chunk of dark chocolate and a deep breath for courage. Most of the time people welcomed me warmly. Sometimes, I had to have a tough skin. For example, in the gas station group on the Wisconsin River (Group 8), on my fourth visit (April 2011), most of the regulars got up from their table and stood on the other side of the room until I left. In one diner in a suburb north of Milwaukee (Group 14), I could hear and see one regular mutter, "here comes trouble," as I approached the door.

In some groups people saw me as a representative of UW–Madison, the city of Madison, or the state government. They took me directly to task for policies they disliked, as if I was one of the people who made the decisions. Sometimes they held me personally responsible for things that had happened in Madison, regardless of my connection to the events. In one case, a man's daughter had been badly injured by falling snow while walking on a Madison street, and he took his anger out on me. Those incidents revealed the symbolic place that Madison holds in many Wisconsinites' perceptions of power, their sense of distance from it, and their desire to criticize it.[5]

Probably the most difficult interactions were not those that emphasized I came from power, but those that positioned me as less powerful—as a woman. In my daily life, I do not experience a lot of overt ogling. But I got ogled on these visits. People asked me out on dates, despite the wedding ring on my hand at the time. On my first round, when I traveled with a visibly pregnant belly, several groups of men joked with each other about which member was the father of my child-to-be. Walking in the door to a men's group with one of the men resulted in a pretty embarrassing barrage of comments assuming we had just had sex. When I would move over to make room for a late-arriving regular, some folks saw my moving closer to someone as license to make a wisecrack like, "Be careful of that guy you're scooching up to—watch his hands!" I tried to take all that in stride and take it as data. Honestly, remarks about my appearance or gender were so common that sometimes I noticed them more in the transcripts than I did in real time.[6]

The Evolution of the Project

My aim in doing this research was to illuminate understandings, rather than establish causality. I wanted to figure out the kinds of tools people used to understand politics, explain what constitutes these tools, and explain how people use them. Such a study is often called "interpretivist." In this kind of work, we are seeking information about how people understand their world. We start with a guiding research question, identify a strategy to begin to answer it, and then sort through data to develop answers. We then gather more data to make sure we are drawing valid conclusions. In this way, our questions evolve as we gather data. This means that fieldwork has an initial research design, but by necessity it has to be adapted, updated, and extended.

In this particular case, my initial questions about social-class identity led me to plan three rounds of visits to the initial twenty-seven sites. I wanted multiple visits because past experience in research and life (as well as an extensive scholarly literature on the dynamics of human interaction) had taught me that cooperative relationships are more likely with people who believe you are coming back (e.g., Axelrod [1984] 2006). Most of the groups I visited appreciated my first visit, were surprised by my second, and were downright impressed by a third or more. I learned more about them and their community by spending multiple visits with them, and I conveyed my sincerity in wanting to learn from them by showing up again when I said I would. In the end, I visited most of the groups two or more times and conducted these visits between May 2007 and November 2012.[7] I had been awarded a sabbatical during the 2007–8 academic year to conduct the first three rounds of fieldwork (spring/summer 2007, January/February 2008, and spring/summer 2008). In subsequent years, it was a bit more difficult to get out and around the state while teaching full time, but I was able to do so during the summers and in between teaching days.

My fieldwork lasted longer than I expected for two main reasons. First, my observations from the first two rounds alerted me to the importance of a rural-urban divide, and I had to alter my questions and revisit the groups in order to learn more about it. Second, Wisconsin politics went from quirky to incredibly fascinating during this time and I wanted to listen to the way people were making sense of the ruckus.

I added some groups as my research progressed. In several places, I added another group to get some leverage on the way conversations varied not by geographic place but by type of participant (Groups 4b, 10b, 11c, 12b, 16b, 18b, 18c). I also added four 4-H groups when it became clear that my strategy for identifying groups was leading me to groups of predominantly older men (Groups 24, 25, 26, and 27).

My intent in the way I chose communities and groups was not to have a sample that was representative of all of the people in Wisconsin. Instead, I wanted to listen to a wide variety of people. Wisconsin is a very white state (83.3 percent non-Hispanic white according to the 2010 Census), but it was important to me to listen to people from a variety of racial and ethnic backgrounds.[8] My own background is European/Caucasian, and I had to take some extra steps to get access to groups of people of color. In Milwaukee, I gained access to a group of African Americans through a friend. He referred me to a man who was part of group of African American activists that met every Sunday after their church service (Group 23a). To get access to Latino immigrants, I spent time at a pro bono health clinic in Milwaukee. Through the help of an interpreter at the clinic, we invited people waiting in line for appointments to talk with us in an adjoining room (Group 23b). To listen to Native Americans in the state, a friend who is a prominent Native American leader introduced me to a member of the Oneida Nation, who invited me to join him and his family for a fish fry at a diner on their reservation (Group 7).

In several other municipalities, I could not find a group of regulars meeting in a place I could easily invite myself into, so I asked a community member to assemble a small group for me. In one case, a librarian posted an invitation in the public library for residents to come and talk with me on two different visits (Groups 4a_1 and 4a_2). Other cases included the member of the Oneida Nation (Group 7), a female friend who invited a group of women to talk with me at a café (Group 16b), and a high school teacher who assembled groups of coworkers to meet with me at the end of the school day (Group 18a). Most of the thirty-nine groups I spent time with were informal, but there were several that had a formal purpose and welcomed me as a special guest at a scheduled meeting. These include the activist church group in Milwaukee (Group 23a), a Kiwanis club meeting in a central Wisconsin town (12a), and a group of parishioners who met occasionally after their Saturday evening service in the "thumb" of Wisconsin, or Door County (Group 5).

The groups I spent time with varied in size from two people to approximately thirty. Between four and ten people was typical. The membership for the groups varied on any given visit, although most had a core of regulars present each time I was with them. The people I spent time with were predominantly male, non-Hispanic white, and of retirement age. Of the thirty-nine groups I studied, twelve were composed of only men, six were exclusively female, and the rest were of mixed gender but predominantly male. Most groups (twenty-one) were composed of a mix of retirees and currently employed people, though retirees were in the majority in these groups. Of the other groups, five were composed solely of retirees, nine of people currently employed or unemployed, and four of high school students (4-H groups). Although the groups taken as a whole were fairly homogenous with respect to occupational and educational background, individual groups varied. Some groups were composed of people "one step from homelessness," and others were mainly wealthy business owners.

What Were These Visits Like?

I noted earlier that inviting myself into these groups required audacity, but it might help to know what these visits actually looked like. The first time I visited a group to which I was showing up unannounced, I would walk in, say, "Hi! I'm Kathy Walsh from the University of Wisconsin–Madison. Do you mind if I join you this morning?"[9] The people would look at me a little baffled, chuckle, and then say something like, "Sure. We got nothing better to do." And chuckle some more.

I quickly learned that depending on their reactions, I would have to acknowledge my affiliation with UW–Madison and the city of Madison with something like: "I know that might raise your hackles, but I'm sincerely here to listen to what you think." As I learned, and as you will see, I had to contend with the common perception that visitors from Madison usually parachute in and pronounce what is right and good and then leave without respecting local wisdom, wants, or needs.

Once they gave me an initial OK, I passed out my business cards while explaining, "I'm a public opinion researcher at UW–Madison, and I'm traveling around the state trying to better understand how people think about various things going on in the state and to understand how the university can better serve the people of the state." Then I passed out "tokens of my appreciation": University of Wisconsin (UW) Badger three-year football schedules, UW–Madison pens and pencils, UW–Madison sticky notes or, if I had run out of all of those, temporary tattoos of UW Bucky Badger (the university's mascot). Here is another lesson that is both substantive and methodological: I found out fast that I had to explain that these tchotchkes were donated by the UW–Madison Alumni Association, "not paid for by your taxpayer dollars." If I didn't, usually someone would ask.[10]

Once I had given them a token of my appreciation, I asked if I could record our conversation. I said something like, "Do you all mind if I record this? It's just for transcription purposes—I'm not going to play this for anyone. I just don't want to have to write notes while I'm listening to you all—I'd rather look at you than look down at my notes. But if anybody is uncomfortable with this, I can take notes." Only two of the thirty-nine groups refused to let me record them. Once I got their permission, I placed my digital recorder and a big microphone on the table in front of us, so that it was clear for everyone to see, including latecomers to whom I would point out that I was recording while giving them my card and a tchotchke.[11] I learned to use an additional cassette recorder, just as backup. On several occasions, I had driven across the state to meet up with a group, enjoyed a fantastic conversation, and then got into my car to discover that the recorder had not worked. I must have looked kind of funny in some of those small towns—a city girl, sitting in my Jetta, swearing to myself.

Even when my recorder worked, the results were not always ideal. In larger groups, the conversation at one end of the table would drown out other remarks, and the recordings did not offer much confirmation of direct quotes. It was in those cases that I was especially glad that after each visit, I would record a summary and as many verbatim statements as I could as I drove away.

To start out the conversations, I asked something like, "What are the big concerns here these days?" People interpreted this in a variety of ways. One man said, simply, "Who is sleeping with whom." He was probably right, but I asked them to focus on more boring things like taxes, immigration, health care, and their perceptions of UW–Madison. The first three were topics that my previous work had suggested were likely to spark talk about economic issues and social class (Cramer Walsh 2007). The latter was a topic my university had asked me to investigate. Asking about perceptions of the university and higher education proved very fruitful, since attitudes about education are intertwined with social class and convey a good deal about people's perceptions of where public resources go, who deserves them, and who has the power to make such decisions.

Over the course of my visits, I added, deleted, and changed the questions I asked. Appendix C provides the list of questions I carried with me on these visits. The changes were based on what questions generated useful responses and my need to probe differently due to my evolving research questions. I did not ask all of these questions of every group. These visits were less like interviews and more like conversations. I tried my hardest to let the conversation flow. I wanted to know what people thought was important and the connections they perceived between topics, which required that I steer the conversation as little as possible. I went in with a sense of what questions I *had* to ask, and what questions I *could* ask if I had extra time. Since my time with each group was limited, I had to raise some topics and ask some questions, not just wait for people to raise them on their own. I adjusted the order of questions during each visit to try to make the conversation as natural as possible.

Most people talked with me readily. Often, the conversations felt like no one had ever before asked these people for their thoughts on public affairs. It was if I had turned on a spigot. In general, I find that if you sincerely convey to people that you are interested in what they think and are there to listen, not to preach or lecture, they have a lot to say.

On the other hand, some people did not want to talk with me. They would get up and leave or sit across the room (like the men in Group 8 on one visit) or just not contribute anything to the conversation. On several occasions, though, groups that were initially skeptical were pleading with me forty-five minutes later to stick around a little longer.

Some of the people I learned the most from were consistently grumpy, and there were times I was reluctant to go back because they were so unpleasant. But I learned things from their grumpiness, and from the way they grumpily described me, within my earshot, to other regulars in their group.

If you could hear me talking about this, you would notice that there is something about me that probably made the first few minutes of getting access to these folks easier—I have a substantial Wisconsin accent. I grew up in Wisconsin, went to college at UW–Madison, and moved back here with gusto on finishing my PhD. My grad school friends tell me my accent is thicker since I moved back. That is not necessarily intentional, but I do think it helped with this project.

I am not sure my ability to signal my identity via language is an advantage in general, though. If I had more clearly been an outsider, people might have explained themselves to me a bit more. I often had to pretend not to understand common Wisconsin wisdom, such as what people mean by "up north" (i.e., the tourist/vacation areas in the northern part of the state), so that I could listen to the way they explained such terms. I might have seemed a little less obtuse if I had really not known those things.

What I learned from this study is all the more striking since I did grow up in this state. Until 2007, I explained myself to others as someone who had grown up in small-town Wisconsin. My home town, Grafton, was about seven thousand people in size and just north of the Milwaukee suburbs during the years I was growing up. I now understand that is *not* small-town Wisconsin. Small-town Wisconsin is a place where your entire high school class could fit on one floor of a dorm at UW–Madison. I get that now.

I also understand now the pervasiveness of the rural-urban divide in Wisconsin. The rural-urban split is deep and complex and obvious to many people in small-town Wisconsin but invisible to us city folks who have had little experience in such places, except as tourists. Even if we do get up north in the summer, we might not notice the lack of wealth the locals complain about. There is expensive food in the grocery stores, Starbucks on some main streets, and OK cell phone reception most places. What we do not necessarily notice is that these "necessities" are not for the locals—they are amenities marketed to us urbanites.

One of the lessons of this book is that animosity toward government is partly about feeling overlooked, ignored, and disrespected. It is a political science lesson in particular because winning elections depends in part on candidates conveying to people that they *do* understand the hardships of ordinary people and are doing something concrete to remedy them. But it is also a professional lesson because it underscores the importance of listening as a researcher, in two respects. First, listening conveys respect. It is in my interest as an ethnographer to make it clear that I'm listening—to put the recorder on the table, to have eye contact with people as they are talking, and to convey with my body language that I am trying to digest every word they say. I try not to cross my arms—I do not want to signal that I am at all closed to what they are saying. I try not to jump into the conversation. I try not to smile too much or nod my head too much when people are talking to avoid disclosing my own biases, but I do tend to nod along in a slow way to try to convey, "I am with you. Please say more."

The second respect in which this work drove home the importance of listening is related to my role as an ambassador of my university. Chapter 5 details a perception I encountered frequently about university faculty: the view that we are arrogant and elitist. Listening is good for establishing and perhaps improving the ties citizens have to their institutions of higher education. I do not mean that in a shallow sense—I did not pretend to listen so that people were fooled into thinking my university cares about them. I made a point to make it clear that I *am* listening, because thankfully I work at a place in which many people, including the people in charge, care deeply about public service. The future of higher education, especially public higher education, depends on demonstrating that such institutions are relevant to the public. Visibly listening is one small way I can advance that.

From the start, I told people I would protect their confidentiality. I did not ask for their names. Over time, I did learn some of their first names, or at least what they called each other in my presence, but I seldom learned last names. In the pages to follow, I use pseudonyms and do not identify the communities by name except for the largest municipalities of Madison and Milwaukee.

When I refer to a group or individual members as lower income or upper income, I am inferring this from the work they reported doing currently or before retirement. I wanted to know their household incomes, but income is personal information to many people and in my attempt to gather it, I learned it was "none of my business." (The high rates of refusal to answer income questions on mass sample surveys is one way to see the widespread sensitivity of these questions.)

The people I studied were spending time in these groups voluntarily. Because they are folks who make a point to get out of the house or workplace and socialize with others, they are unusual from the population at large (e.g., Putnam 2000). They are likely more aware of current events, more talkative, and have larger social networks than the average person. They do not necessarily pay more attention to the news than others, but their groups of regulars usually contained one or two people who gave them ready access to such news.

Many of these people were leaders in their community. Some of them held local office, were prominent in the local business community, or were active in civic organizations. Their relative prestige varied across the places I sampled. In some places they were executives of multinational corporations; in others, they owned businesses on Main Street. In other words, these folks were often opinion leaders (Lazarsfeld, Berelson, and Gaudet 1944). Their perceptions may not be representative, but they are likely consequential for the way others in their community think about many public issues.

There is one other aspect of these conversations that I would like to acknowledge again: the opinions that I heard are not necessarily reflective of the opinions that each individual would offer up in a one-on-one conversation with me. There were loudmouths who dominated the conversations. There were shy people who hardly said anything at all. What I observed are the things that people say when they interact with one another. This is the opinion of a group as people create it together, not the opinion of a group measured as an aggregation of their privately expressed beliefs.

Analyzing the Data

One question I often get from researchers who are trying interpretive work for the first time is, "How do you analyze your data?" Here is how I go about it. Since I am interested in how people make sense of politics, I look to these conversations for evidence of what tools people use to do so. What are people using to make sense of health care? Of the economy? Of Barack Obama? I carefully look through the transcriptions of the conversations for evidence of tools—usually categories and frames, or the perspectives through which they are perceiving the topic at hand. I look for patterns across groups and create what is called a "data display" as I do so (Miles and Huberman 1994). My version of a data display is a spreadsheet in which the rows are particular visits to particular groups and the columns are different characteristics—either of the group or of the conversation.

As I read through the transcripts and fill in the cells of this spreadsheet, I write memos to myself about the patterns I am observing (Feldman 1995). I use the data display to see how common the patterns are across my groups and visits and whether they vary across group type (Miles and Huberman 1994, chap. 10). I think about the evidence I would need to see in order to validate my conclusions and convince myself and others how I know what I say I know (Manna 2000), and then I make plans to go and get this evidence. This, at times, means altering my interview protocol and, at other times, means adding additional groups to my sample.

I do other things to make sure the conclusions I am reaching are valid. I think about how my presence affected the conversations. I look back over transcripts of conversations that do not seem to fit the patterns, think about alternative explanations for what I am seeing, and ask the people I am studying if they agree with my conclusions (Miles and Huberman 1994, 262–77). At times this meant sending a report via e-mail to a group member who had given me an e-mail address. Other times this meant sending the report via surface mail to a gas station addressed to "The Group That Meets at 6 A.M. by the Coffee."

I have not received a letter, phone call, or e-mail in response to these mailings, but I have had conversations about them with some groups on return visits. No one has disagreed with my conclusions. That does not mean that everyone I listened to agrees with my conclusions. It might simply mean my conclusions are more interesting to me than to anyone else, and these folks have better things to do than argue with me. Would disagreement mean I am wrong? Not necessarily. I would have to think carefully about what their disagreement conveys about their perception of the world, while being open to the idea that I am misunderstanding the points they were making.

There are some things I would do differently if I could start this study from scratch. In particular, I would have asked more of the group members about their own length of residence in the community, and their time in rural areas in general. Knowing more about which rural residents had spent time in urban areas and vice versa would have enabled me to better understand variations in the rural consciousness I heard.

In addition, I would have observed more groups that contained public employees, particularly women, prior to Walker proposing Act 10. It would have been useful to have an overtime comparison of their conversations. But I did not foresee the centrality of attitudes toward public employees during this time period.

I also wish that I had had the courage to go into taverns on my own and listen to groups spending time there. This would have enabled me to listen to more people in their twenties and thirties.

But aside from wishing that I had the capacity to listen to a wider range of people, I mainly regret having to dip in and out of these twenty-seven places. It would have been revealing to spend extended time in each of these communities, to listen to more conversations and a wider range of people in each location to more thoroughly observe the manner in which the sense of place and the sense of politics interact. I would have been able to watch people live their lives in a manner infused with their rural consciousness, not just convey that perspective through their words. I also would have been able to provide much more detail about the nature of these places. But I balanced the desire to listen to a wide range of conversations with a desire to learn a great deal about each community and opted for many occasional visits to many places rather than extended visits to just a few communities.

Conclusion

The methods I used to do the research for this book are unusual for a scholar of public opinion. I hope this chapter has provided a clear picture of what this approach looked like in practice. And I hope the chapters to come that follow will demonstrate that the time required to take part in these conversations was fruitful for advancing our understanding of how people think about politics, and why we see a strong relationship between rural areas and support for small government and limited redistribution.

CHAPTER THREE

The Contours of Rural Consciousness

In May of 2008, I visited a group of men who gathered in a service station in the morning in a small town in central Wisconsin (Group 1). It had been difficult identifying a group of regulars in this town. After two months of phone tag with the university extension office and the local paper, I started calling members of the county board. Eventually one board member said, "Oh you need to go and talk to the guys at the service station—the 7–8 A.M. group."

And so I did. On a cold May morning, I pulled up to a vintage service station, parked my Jetta in the gravel lot in the row of pickup trucks, and walked inside.

There was a group of four middle-aged and retired men sitting in molded plastic lawn chairs in the front room of the station. The huge plate glass window provided a view of vintage gas pumps no longer in operation and a quaint but mostly boarded-up main street. The men were in jeans, sweatshirts, and baseball caps. On the walls and ledges were potted plants and lots of Milwaukee Brewers baseball memorabilia. A coffeemaker on a shelf on one side of the room seemed to be the lone source of heat.

I could hear the laughter even before I opened the door. When I went inside and quickly explained who I was, they welcomed me in and invited me to use the one empty chair. I was reluctant—it seemed like the kind of place where somebody owns each chair. But I sat down, and I am glad that I did. This group—"The Downtown Athletic Club" as they called themselves—opened my eyes to rural consciousness.

That first morning with them, I passed out my football schedules and other tokens of gratitude and asked if it was OK to turn on my recorder. They said sure, I pushed the record button, and I bumbled out, "I'm interested—what are the big concerns for people living up here?"

I quickly learned that all four of those men were former public school teachers. One had been a principal. Right away, they voiced concerns about state legislators raiding tax dollars out of the highway fund (they wanted that to stop), the liquor tax (they wanted that higher), the price of gas (they wanted that lower), and the cost of health care (they wanted someone to do something about it). I asked them to dwell on that last one a bit.

> KJC: Well that's a good question, what do you do about health care reform, you know? I visited a lot of places last summer and based on what we heard, we asked a question on the telephone poll [of voting-age Wisconsinites that I had been conducting with the University of Wisconsin Survey Center] that basically said, you know, "What should we do about health care?" and gave four options. Let me know if any of these are viable, or some combination of them—we ought to pursue. So one would be to expand the existing programs like Badger Care and Medicare, Medicaid. Another would be to mandate that everyone have health care, and those who can't pay it, then the government pitches in at that point. A third way would be to encourage people to have their own health savings accounts, and the final one would be to have a state-sponsored program, where the state government runs the health care and everybody has coverage that way. What do you think? Any of those options sound—
>
> JOE: Explain the last option. Is that for everyone?
>
> KJC: Yeah, I mean—
>
> JOE: So they'd be in competition with an insurance company?
>
> KJC: That's a great question. I mean, I think initially that's what would happen . . . it's partly what you all think ought to happen . . .
>
> [. . .]¹
>
> GARY: This doesn't really answer your question, but we were just talking about this issue today is that probably one of the biggest values of your insurance plan now is not necessarily the bill they pay, but the way they're able to negotiate the bill down. . . . But the person without that insurance now, they're billed the full amount. . . . I just got new glasses. I went in, and I have had eyeglass coverage in my life, but when I was teaching, WEA Insurance [the teacher's union insurance] always had a discount, so you

might get 30 percent off or something like that, and we always kind of appreciated that. . . .

LOU: Your fourth choice makes sense in some ways, but there's—if the state
of Wisconsin was to insure everybody, you'd have a large, large pool. However, when I retired and I looked at insurances, the state of Wisconsin
medical plan was three to four hundred dollars more than WEA. Now
the reason for that is they don't have the expertise in that, so if they were
to do the whole state they would bid it out to the insurance companies,
the lowest bidder, which maybe would drive it down. The insurance company would have to administer it because they wouldn't have the bureaucracy. . . . But if you put everyone in it, maybe it would cheapen because
you'd have an entire state. . . .

KJC: Yeah, OK.

JOE: I think the last option with the state-sponsored would be the best option out of all of them. And the one where you would put into a fund
wouldn't fly very good because everybody's income is different, umm . . . I
don't know what kind of an insurance plan someone could buy for, that's
working on an eight- or nine-dollar-an-hour job, you know . . . basically
nothing.

To this point, this conversation was not particular to any type of place.
But then I heard a theme common in rural communities.

STU: Well, that's where it's affecting a lot of the little guys is with gas and food
competing against insurance, and gas and food is going to have to win out
because you gotta eat, and you gotta get to work.

JOE [*Joking, mimicking someone critical of driving a long way to work.*]:
"You gotta quit driving! Don't drive as much." [*Rolls his eyes.*] You gotta
drive twenty miles to work? How you gonna . . . you can't cut it in half!

[. . .]

STU: But [the cost of gas] was a rapid increase, it wasn't a gradual buildup, I
mean, it was all of the sudden . . .

GARY: I mean, yeah, in the last ten years, what has it gone up? Eight hundred
percent?

LOU: Four years ago it was under two dollars a gallon for gasoline, and look
at it now. It's double that price. . . . The government jumped in and subsi-
dized ethanol. It takes five hundred bushels of corn to make thirteen gal-
lons of gas, uh, ethanol gas, so what does that tell you? We're not producing

as much gas, the price goes up. Look what the corn does now to everything else. It's just: one thing drives another.

Few people like rising gas prices, but to people in rural communities—
who typically drive long distances to everything—they are a major
source of concern. By the time I met this group, I had come to realize
that there was something important about the way many people in small
communities thought about their towns in relation to more urban places.
So I nudged the conversation in that direction:

GARY: The other big issue I think for our whole nation is the discrepancy
  between . . . oh, the common economics and the CEOs of corporations,
  where the top of the corporations are taking off profits greater than ever
  before in history, when the companies may be challenged, or the product line may be challenged. There's still that huge amount of money for
  the people at the very top. And that's really driving a bigger separation
  between the richest in America . . . and the common belief is that we're
  losing the middle class.
KJC: Right. How do you see that in . . . Do you feel like the middle class in
  [this town] is disappearing?
GARY: Well the business element is—the town is dying. All the small towns in
  the area are having a hard time keeping grocery stores and gas stations,
  and everything, because of competition from people buying from the bigger chains, like the Walmart.
[. . .]
KJC: Do you feel like most people around here struggle to makes ends meet?
  Or do people live comfortably?
GARY: The big thing that affects the rural areas in the last fifteen years is the
  change in the agriculture where you don't have the mom-and-pop farms
  anymore. They're all corporation farms. Where people used to make their
  livings on 8–140 acres of land, I mean it's . . . now, eighty acres of land is
  hobby land, it's not a living. I retired with my farm, and I have seventy-five
  to eighty cattle. Thirty cows, when I was a kid, could feed a family. Now
  thirty cows is a big hobby. I mean, the amount of income off of that versus expenses is not very great, so it just changes. Another confusion is if
  you look at the corn in some years were a $1.90, now last I bought $5.50 a
  bushel. And, uh, during this time of rising corn prices, hogs, sows are now
  ten cents a pound. And chickens have crashed, and it's kind of confusing
  for some of those ag products, and raw materials going in are four to five

times more expensive than the actual money available for the end product, which is reduced. And part of the problem with agriculture is we have perishable goods. It's not like a barrel of oil you can let sit there for ten years. The milk has to go, that cheese has to go, pretty much. The livestock has to be slaughtered, has a short lifespan. There's so many things where people can set the process, whether it be gasoline or whatever it is, but farmers are typically—somebody else is setting the price for the farmer.

As the conversation continued, their concerns about their local economy extended past farming to schools and property tax issues.

STU: I think two other major issues: one is schools, and the funding, and the funding coming from the state has dropped off dramatically, and that property taxes have specifically, I would say, the taxes on "rec" land, that would be one issue, as opposed to the taxes on ag land. And ag land, I'm guessing, is about 40 percent of what taxes are on "rec" land. There's too big a discrepancy. It's good for the farmers because they're getting by a lot cheaper, but, you know, the money's got to come from someplace . . . And in an area like this where you have nothing but ag land, basically, you know, they're not paying their fair share, you're short on money. Everybody's short on money, the state cuts back, and that compounds the issue with school. Every area would be different, but that tax issue I think is a big deal.

LOU: The schools, because the state's not living up to the law, what the law says, special education should be funded at 63 percent. When I retired ten years ago, it was down to 38 [percent]. It's probably less than 20 percent today, and that's a high cost. When you take two kids today in special ed, it can cost twenty thousand dollars a year, and you're only getting 20 percent?

GARY: And mandate how you manage that: individual teacher, separate transportation in some cases—all those things they have mandated. The style of education—right now, what are they saying is our shortfall with the budget?

LOU: Six hundred million.

[. . .]

GARY: As far as schools, the whole transition from [former Governor] Tommy Thompson forward was to take a . . . schools weren't handled uniformly, so tech schools versus private schools versus colleges and universities were all handled in different ways, and I know the political motivation of

> Thompson when he did that, but it's really created a problem with fund-
> ing formulas for schools, and we know that many areas in northern Wis-
> consin and central Wisconsin, there are schools that are going to be forced
> out of their communities, and the problem with that really in a small town
> like this is that the only identity this town has any more is the school. The
> school is the most important business in town, and if the school wasn't
> here, especially with the higher fuel costs, there's really no reason that
> all the people who live here would choose to live in a small place because
> many of them work in Stevens Point or [Wisconsin] Rapids or whatever it
> is, and . . . it's not the first time in history that small towns have been dried
> up and blown away, you know, in the boom days of the west, they did that
> all the time, but it's really going to change the fabric of rural America.[2]

As they talked, a lightbulb went on for me. People in groups in a variety of places—rural, suburban, urban—had expressed concerns about
health care and education. But in this place, their concerns about those
issues were rooted in their sense of themselves as members of a rural
community. Health care is hard to afford. That's the case for many people in many places. But these folks were telling me that, in rural places,
the escalating price of gas was crippling their ability to buy insurance.
Why? Because in rural places people drive to work. Far. They drive far to
many things, including to the store that provides their daily necessities.

Funding for education was an issue, too. Why? Because rural communities get the short end of the stick, they were saying. The Wisconsin
"funding formula" meant that revenues are shared across school districts,
but wealthier communities can spend more than the state allocation by
using revenues gathered through local property taxes. As the population
in rural places dwindles, the possibility of school consolidation increases,
and the identity of a town—its schools—dry up and blow away.

In other words, health care and education mattered to folks in a lot
of places. But in this community, as in many of the rural communities I
visited, people viewed these issues through a rural lens. As I tried to understand why these men felt the way they did about health care and education, it helped to hear these things while looking out that big service
station window onto the main street buildings that were now just brit-
tle husks of their once lively past. It helped to know where these people
were coming from.

When I turned my recorder off that morning, the conversation continued. As soon as I got back to my car, I left myself a note on my recorder describing as much as possible of those last comments. This is what I said: "Lou said that 'You know another thing is that they make all the rules in Madison with respect to schools and they don't really apply to us, because you know—because the governor's office and such—if first graders are not learning to read and the parents show up at the school board meeting and you know we fix it, it just doesn't work the same as in Milwaukee. Those rules don't apply here.' And I said in response, 'That's really interesting because you hear a lot of talk about the difference between Milwaukee and Madison and the rest of the state and usually it's in terms of resources, where all the resources get sucked down to that part of the state, but that's not—that's not what you're talking about. You're talking about the rules not necessarily applying in the right way.' And he said, 'Yeah, yeah that's what I mean.'"

"Lou also mentioned: 'Yeah well Madison is the most liberal area of the state.' And then he talked about how in that way things don't apply to other parts of the state as well. 'You know people in that environment make the laws and they don't necessarily—not necessarily what people need or want in other parts of the state.'"

When I got back to Madison and transcribed those notes, I added this: "Just very interesting getting the perspective of people in rural areas—something very important going on there." I wondered whether this rural perspective was unique to this group. They were former educators, and as they had told me, community identity and the schools are closely intertwined. Maybe as teachers they were especially likely to talk about public issues by referring to the place in which they lived.

So I looked back over my transcripts and notes from my other fieldwork sites. I kept doing more fieldwork. I presented my work to groups on my campus and elsewhere in the state and country and found increasing support for this conclusion: For many people in rural communities in Wisconsin, people understand public issues through a lens of rural consciousness. This is a perspective that encompasses a strong identity as a rural resident, resentment toward the cities, and a belief that rural communities are not given their fair share of resources or respect.

The next time I went back to this group, three years later in May of 2011, I brought this perspective up directly in our conversation. One man asked me, "What are the issues in other communities [that you've been visiting]? You know, we sit here jabbering, what do *they* jabber about?"

KJC: You know, kind of the same things. It's been really eye-opening to me.
I mean, growing up in Grafton I always thought of myself as a small-town
Wisconsin kid, but then you really spend time in the rest of Wisconsin you
realize Grafton is kind of, I mean *this* is small town you know?

[*Several voices*]: Yeah, the smallest.

[*Laughter*]

KJC: I mean, the issues are the same, I mean, people wonder where the heck
the money is going. They're struggling to make ends meet all over the
state. Um, there's a sense that nobody's listening.

LOU: Yeah, I think that, um, I think that is an issue. That seems, bothers a lot
of people in this neighborhood, is that people in Madison are just simply
not listening to what the people have to say. You can tell your representative and they go down there and vote whatever the party tells 'em to vote,
not what you said.

FRED: The state is considered Madison-Milwaukee.

LOU: Right.

FRED: It really is.

I returned one year later, in May of 2012. I spent the night before at a
Super 8 Hotel twenty miles away. I drove to the station as the sun came
up, and I was looking forward to the conversation, feeling a little bad
that I could not bring them donuts because the grocery store near the
Super 8 was not open yet.

But when I got there, the gravel lot around the service station was
empty. There was no one there. I was stunned. The station was closed,
and the owner had taped the following sign to the window:

FIRST I WANT TO SAY I'M SORRY TO ALL
MY CUSTOMERS FOR ABRUPTLY CLOSING
THE SHOP. AN OPPORTUNITY CAME
ALONG FOR ME TO WORK LESS HOURS
DOING WHAT I ENJOY WHILE ACTUALLY
GETTING A REAL PAYCHECK AGAIN. NOT
THAT I DIDN'T ENJOY WORKING, FOR THE
MOST PART, WITH ALL OF YOU. IT HAS
BEEN A STRUGGLE FOR THE PAST FEW
YEARS KEEPING THIS SHOP OPEN WITH
THE POOR ECONOMY AND A SMALL TOWN
WHERE EVERYONE DRIVES 25 MILES TO

WORK, SHOP AND ULTIMATELY GET WORK
DONE ON THEIR VEHICLES. I DID NOT
REGRET MY DECISION BACK IN 1993 TO
COME TO WORK HERE BUT AS TIME WENT
ON, OUR LITTLE VILLAGE KEPT GETTING
SMALLER AND SO DID THE PROFIT MARGIN
IN THE SHOP.
TO ALL THE MEMBERS OF THE
"DOWNTOWN ATHLETIC CLUB," I HOPE WE
CAN FIND A NEW HOME TO CONTINUE TO
MEET. MAYBE WE CAN MOVE TO [ONE OF THE MEMBERS'
BUSINESSES]. I WILL DONATE EVERYTHING I HAVE LEFT TO
KEEP THE COFFEE GOING IF A NEW
MEETING PLACE IS FOUND.
THANK YOU EVERYONE FOR THE 19 YEARS
I WAS ABLE TO PROVIDE YOU SERVICE.

The service station had closed and the Downtown Athletic Club was without a home. Ironically, by ceasing to exist, the Downtown Athletic Club convinced me that something important *was* going on in rural communities.

Republican and Rural: Not Just a Correlation

Scholars and political pundits have known for decades, over a century even, that there is a correlation between votes and rural-urban location in the United States. But as I puzzled through my field notes and the relevant literature, I realized that scholars knew very little about the way rural-versus-urban divides function *as a perspective* through which some people think about politics.

Since the mid-twentieth century, Wisconsin has looked pretty much like national electoral maps: blue cities and red rural places. In Wisconsin, the Democratic Party's success in the larger cities is due in part to stronger union organizing (Fowler 2008, 184) and the concentration of African Americans in those places. Also, some of the Republicanism in the rural areas may be a holdover from anti–Democratic Party attitudes that rose up during World War I and II. Many Wisconsinites have German relatives somewhere in their family—43 percent of residents claimed German heritage in 2000 (Fowler 2008, 205). German American voters were strongly isolationist during World War I and II and, therefore, likely to vote against the Democrats, especially in rural areas, where unions had little influence (Fowler 2008).

Rural-urban divides have been an important part of Wisconsin's politics for at least a century. One of our famous quirks is that we were home to both Joe McCarthy and Bob La Follette, two decidedly different characters. McCarthy was the U.S. Senator who is responsible for "McCarthyism"—the post–World War II anticommunist scare that led to the interrogations of many Americans, particularly government employees, people in the entertainment industry, and those involved in labor unions. La Follette, in contrast, is the father of Progressivism. He served in the U.S. House, the U.S. Senate, and was governor of the state in the first few decades of the twentieth century.

Some say that rural-urban tensions help explain how both of these folks were successful in the same state. Granted, the fact that La Follette and McCarthy were both from Wisconsin is a little less mysterious when you consider that they both started out as Republicans. Wisconsin was overwhelmingly Republican for much of the first half of the twentieth century (Epstein 1958). But the rural-urban divide helps solve part of the La Follette–McCarthy mystery, too. Both of them tapped into rural consciousness to win votes. When La Follette's Progressivism took hold, Wisconsin was mainly a nonmetropolitan state—as it is now. In that context, skepticism of party organizations among rural residents was a stronger force than was support of political machines among urban residents (Epstein 1958). Some scholars argue that McCarthy won his senate seat by exploiting the skepticism that small-town residents had of globalization and distant institutions.[3] Even the breakthrough of the modern Democratic Party—the election of Democrat William Proxmire to the Senate in a special election after McCarthy's death—is commonly understood as the result of Proxmire's successful appeal to "rural discontent" (Fowler 2008, 173). Also, he is the senator who devised the monthly Golden Fleece Award, an award he bestowed on a public official who had made an excessive government expenditure. Although a member of the Democratic Party, the party typically associated with "big government," he was a champion of government frugality.

For some time, then, there has been a correlation in Wisconsin, as in most of the United States, between rural and Republican. But that correlation is not inevitable and is not simply the result of people voting the same way their parents did. People have perspectives and understandings that make support for Republican candidates seem appropriate and natural.

The conversations among the people in the service station awoke me to one such perspective, the perspective I am calling rural consciousness. Its broad contours had three main elements. First, rural consciousness was about perceptions of power, or who makes decisions and who decides what to even discuss. Second, it showed up with respect to perceptions of values and lifestyles. Third and finally, it involved perceptions of resources or who gets what.

These are the outlines of the rural consciousness I encountered. Every expression of this perspective did not sound exactly the same. As with all identities, people in particular places put their own twist on who they are. In this chapter, I am going to show you in detail what this perspective looked like.

Where Is "Rural" in Wisconsin?

The Downtown Athletic Club met in central Wisconsin, north of the two main metropolitan areas of the state. (You can see what I mean by looking at the map in appendix A.) There is Madison, the state capitol and home to the flagship public university, and there is Milwaukee, the main industrial area of the state. They are both located in the southern part of Wisconsin. The places outside these metro areas are sometimes referred to as "Outstate" or "out-state Wisconsin" (though this name annoys some people who live in those areas of the state) and the northern tier of the state, largely a tourist area, is typically called "up north."

This division of the state into Madison and Milwaukee versus the rest of the state was common knowledge to the people I encountered outside of Madison and Milwaukee. When talking about the big issues of the day, many of the people I visited in small towns automatically referred to this geography. Sometime they did so with reference to highways that split the state into north and south. For example, a group of middle-aged and retired people meeting in a church basement for coffee, in one small, far northwestern community (Group 3) described it to me this way:

MARTHA: We were told many, many years ago that anything north of Highway 8 is all recreational land.

[*Groups says "yep" and "yes" in agreement.*]
MARK: No! People that are retired and on welfare!
[*Laughter*]

And in a northern logging community (Group 6), which was not far from
that town:

JIM: You get north of Highway 29 and there's, we're in the end of the world.
KJC: That's what a lot of people say, I mean . . .
JIM: Wha—that's the way it is, that's the way it's always been.
CINDY [*cashier, chiming in*]: And then if you ever live south of there, they're
    glad it's like this up here.
JIM: Well yeah.
KJC: Yeah.
CINDY: I lived down there for (all my life . . .) [*She had explained that her
    husband was from this northern community, and they had returned to live
    there together six years ago.*]
KJC: Yeah.
JIM: We like our poverty. We enjoy it. Right?

On these mental maps, the places that get attention and resources are in
the southcentral and southeast parts of the state.

There are cities in Wisconsin besides Madison and Milwaukee. Those
places aren't exactly "rural" communities.[4] They are residential and
commercial centers in their own right. But they are distinctively less urban than the metropolitan centers in the southern part of the state.

The rural consciousness perspective I heard was most common in
communities one would readily identify as rural—lots of green space,
few stoplights, and far from an urban center. But it also emerged in areas
best described as nonmetro: more populous areas but beyond the major metro centers of Madison and Milwaukee. Rural consciousness was a
matter of degree. Sometimes, for convenience, I use the term "rural" to
refer broadly to all areas outside the two major metro areas in the state.

Power

The Downtown Athletic Club made me sit up and take notice of the
place-based sense of injustice among rural residents, but they were not

the only ones to voice it. I heard it in many of the groups I spent time with outside the Madison and Milwaukee areas. Of the thirty-nine groups I spent time with, twenty-five met in places outside the major metro areas.[5] Of these twenty-five nonmetro groups, nineteen called themselves "rural people," or people "out here," or "up here."[6]

The rural consciousness perspective I want to show you was more than just identity as a rural person. Besides place identity, it encompassed perceptions of power, values and lifestyles, and resources. So to show you what it looked like, I want to invite you into some of these conversations and explain what these three elements looked like as we go along. When I heard people talking about rural consciousness in these conversations, they were often talking about several of these central elements.

To show you what I mean, a good place to start is the issue that meant so much to the Downtown Athletic Group: education. Their complaint that Wisconsin's funding formula for education unfairly hurt rural communities was a common concern across groups meeting in rural places. For example, on my first visit to the dice game group in central west Wisconsin (Group 11b, May 2007), I started out with my "what are your big concerns here" question:

KJC: Anything—it can be any kind of concerns—I'll ask you more directly about the UW later on. What kind of issues? Partly the reason I want to know is that we do a phone survey at the UW and usually when we decide which topics to—

MARK: One thing we were bitching about yesterday is that you—is the state's penchant for unfunded mandates—what three times, two times they got a referenda in the community that was not wanted. And so now—they keep jamming the cost down to the county so they can avoid spending it on the state's nickel, that has to stop.

ERNIE: Things that are mandated should be paid for.

MARK: Yeah, the tax structure in this state is weird. I think that is a fundamental problem with the state is that they have to reorganize their tax structure. Local schools, local municipalities, and of course the state— what they're doing is they're just redirecting tax burden on the local taxes which ends up being more evident to the locals, so they more complain and then what ends up happening is they say it isn't their fault.

RICHARD: We don't have the economic base here to pay the kind of taxes that comes out of Madison. You know I mean down there if things go up 1 percent it doesn't—but 1 percent means a hell of a lot more here than it does in Madison or what Henry calls south of the Mason Dixon Line, the line east and west going through Wausau.

DALE: Or Portage [a city about an hour's drive north of Madison].

RICHARD: Well—

MARK: But I mean you know, right down to the tax form or the support form for the schools—why is a kid worth fourteen thousand dollars in Mequon [a suburban Milwaukee city] and what is he up here, Henry? Seven?

HENRY: Oh yeah—the consistency in schools that we're spending money—ridiculous. . . . Why don't they give each school X number of dollars per kid? If they want to spend eleven thousand dollars on a kid, tax the school district for the difference.

ERNIE: Have it averaged.

HENRY: Yeah, have it averaged. Everybody gets eight thousand dollars and if you want to spend eleven, tax the local district for it. Comprehensive plan.

MARK: This goes with the schools, in terms of facilities—facilities are gorgeous because they have the money to spend on it.

HENRY: If you take the state of Wisconsin and take a ruler and start at Green Bay and diagonally and just go fifty miles north of Madison, right over to the corner of the state, all your money lies in the south end of the state, your votes weight there. You're never going to get nothing changed to the north.

DAVE: That is absolutely correct.

HENRY: That's it.

MARK: That's not just the schools.

HENRY: We listen to the—being on the school board, we went several times to testify to the legislature to tell you that the formula was wrong, but they don't change it, because we haven't—if anybody on the south end would say change the formula for the schools, they never would get elected another two years and that's why all they are is looking for their own job.

Somebody makes a comment about the University of Wisconsin–Madison, and then Henry offers up his thoughts.

HENRY: And another thing, every time the state has a program, where do they, where do they implement it? Madison, Lake Geneva, in Milwaukee. They give everything to Milwaukee. You know all the programs in education—they want to try a new program, where do they put it? Milwaukee. Dead at the start. Why don't they put it out here where we can do something with it? Dead at the start.

RICHARD: Far as I can—like with—kept their schools up, Milwaukee let theirs

fall down, and then they take our tax money to deal with the schools after
we kept ours up. And they let theirs fall down.

HENRY: First of all, they oughta take that formula they give Milwaukee—they
give Milwaukee a whole wad of money right off the top first and whatever
is left, we divide by the other 425 schools in the state, which is wrong. Let
Milwaukee do their own—get their fair—same share as we get, don't give
a whole wad of it to them and then turn around and divide the rest among
the rest of us.

In this conversation, the men complain about taxes and unfunded
mandates—complaints that could come from someone in any type of
municipality—but then they talk about this unfairness in terms of geography, namely, that a 1 percent tax increase "means a hell of a lot more
here" than it does in the metro areas. They perceive that the decision
making or the exercise of power in the major cities victimizes people
in small towns by giving them less than their fair share of resources. In
their eyes, decisions about funding for schools mean that small communities are the victims of distributive injustice.

Across the state, in a north-central tourist town, I asked a group of
people at a diner counter early in the morning (Group 9, June 2007) if
they "feel like you're paying your fair share up here? Or heck no?"

NELSON: Well we'd like to keep more of our money for our school districts up
here instead of sending it down below.

HELLEN [*The only other woman at the counter at that moment who is somewhat a little apologetic that she is about to leave me alone with them*]: I'm
going to leave you with them.

KJC: Nice to meet you.

HELLEN: Good luck with these guys.

KJC: Oh thank you. So I'm sorry [to interrupt]—the schools. . . .

NELSON: They're taking so much of our money away from us. Want to close
our schools and that sort of stuff, and the schools in Milwaukee and Madison and everyplace south of us, they've got all the foreign languages and
everything else, and they got their curriculum is so much better than what
we can give—because the fact that the state is not allowing us to have our
money to educate our kids the way we should.

TREVOR: Talking about state schools? I thought that money came from here.

NELSON: Yeah—all of our money goes to Madison gets distributed back
down to us.

KJC: A chunk of it—I don't know what percent but a good chunk of it.

NELSON: Yeah—the bureaucracy gets bigger and bigger. Their secretaries have to have secretaries . . .

PETE: Gotta figure with all the out-of-staters here, pay a lot of taxes.

NELSON: Oh sure—exactly true. People come up here to retire, the taxes eat 'em up. They have to move off [the lakes], but that's been their dream to get up here.

KJC: Oh no kidding.

NELSON: You know, as far as I'm concerned, I pay it, I don't protest, but I would like it if the city, the state would get fairer with the money. Why can't we have a foreign languages and that sort of stuff? Prepare for life after high school. They [kids from our community] get down to the colleges [which are almost all located south of this town], they are behind. . . .

Conversations about school funding often echoed the view that the rural areas were not getting their fair share. In such comments, people conveyed their identity as rural folks as well as their sense of injustice over the distribution of power and resources. I heard the claim that people in rural communities are helpless to change these funding formulas because no one downstate is listening to their concerns. They perceived that politicians and government in general are tone deaf to people outside the major cities.

Resentment about a lack of power compared to city people came through on many topics besides education. A group of people meeting in a gas station in a gorgeous hamlet on the Wisconsin River in southwest Wisconsin were very critical of what they saw as the state government's concern for tourists from the major cities and the Chicago area rather than themselves (Group 8). On my first visit, in June 2007:

GLENN: Just like everything else in Wisconsin, the most important thing to politicians in Wisconsin and in the state government is getting the tourists in here and the people out of Illinois. . . . You go to a boat landing around here and hell you can't unload your boat because there will be a dozen Illinois people there and they are top priority to the state and anybody with a supposed tourist label on 'em.

LARRY: Be there with their canoes, bring their food with 'em, their water, all they leave on the sand bars is shit.

[*Laughter*]

Four years later, their animosity toward the state government's neglect of their community's concerns came out as a complaint against unfunded mandates (Group 8, April 2011).

> GEORGE: And where I see a lot of wasted money is garbage that I receive in the mail that doesn't have . . . I've been on the town board for about thirty-five years already . . .
>
> KJC: Oh bless your heart.
>
> GEORGE: And all the garbage I get, mail that doesn't even have anything to do with this area here whatsoever.
>
> KJC: Huh. What kind of stuff?
>
> GEORGE: Oh, from the state. Mandating everything, you know, do this, do that and our township doesn't have any curbs and gutters, there's so much stuff that the rural area doesn't even have that, you know, people in Milwaukee and Madison think, you know, that it's a big deal, but out here it's nothing.

As far as this group was concerned, city folks sent little to their community but junk mail and poop.

Even in a left-leaning group of retired women in an artsy community in northern Wisconsin (Group 2, April 09), many of the members thought government paid no attention to their concerns.

> KJC: OK, "How much attention do you feel the government pays to what the people think when it decides what to do? A good deal, some, or not much?"
>
> [*Long pause*]
>
> SUE: I think they're starting to get, that they're starting to listen with all this mess [the Great Recession].
>
> KJC: Some. Yeah?
>
> SUE: Before this I don't think. . . . I think it's changing.
>
> DOROTHY: I think it's in the Beltway and out the Beltway. I mean Madison might listen to Madison people. Washington, DC, is a country unto itself. I know it; I spent time there. They haven't got a clue what the rest of the nation is up to, they're so absorbed studying their own belly button.

It is not a stretch to say that people in many places—not just rural areas—feel ignored by the government. But the complaints I heard in rural areas were not simply distrust of government—people in rural areas often perceived that government was *particularly* dismissive of the concerns of people in rural communities. Half of the groups outside the major metro areas expressed that belief.[7] These attitudes were antigovernment thoughts, but they were rooted in residents' place identities.

Let me show it yet another way. In a logging town in northwestern Wisconsin, during the run-up to the 2008 presidential election, I had this conversation with the two men remaining that morning out of a group that gathers in the back of the grocery store/gas station/liquor store/gift shop/hardware store (Group 6, April 2008):

> KJC: Do you . . . what are your hopes for this presidential election? How would you like it to turn out in November?

Both of them laughed in response to the question before answering as follows:

> SCOTT: Doesn't make any difference to me . . . Never has. I'm not a big political . . . I can't stand it because I've been around it for thirty-four years. County boards and stuff. I have no use for any of it. I'm sorry, I just—I'm sorry. That may be kind of a horseshit attitude, but I just, I'm sorry, I just don't.
>
> KJC: A lot of people feel that way. The presidential candidates, you know, sometimes Wisconsin—
>
> SCOTT: I can't see the difference it's gonna make up here anyway. We've been in a recession up here for thirty years, forty years. We don't know any different. People talk about recession, you oughta come up here.
>
> KJC: Yeah?
>
> SCOTT: Doesn't get any different.

Scott thought candidates did not care about his community and that his community, his place, had been ignored for decades. This was part of a widespread perception that small towns like his were generally overlooked. A group of women meeting for lunch in a central-west village on the day of the gubernatorial recall election in 2012 felt small communities like theirs had been "hung out to dry" (Group 11c, June 2011). I fumbled around with the question, but they ran with it.

KJC: Who do you think represents your concerns? I mean . . . do you . . . are there . . . does . . . do you feel like your state senator or state assembly person? Do you feel like anybody—

GLADYS: I think we are just hung out there to dry.

DOLORES: Great. I would agree with you. [*chuckles*]

KJC: That was the answer I feared, I mean—

DOLORES: There isn't anyone, I don't think, that really addresses the concerns of the smaller communities.

BEVERLY: No. I don't think so.

GLADYS: And being an agricultural dairy state, I understand that some of these farmers haven't got a lot more or maybe right in the same ballpark that they get for their milk that we got when we were farming twenty-three years ago and look at what else has gone up. The money it costs for the crops to go up . . . Nobody . . . We got the news. OK. "This big building burned in some area." It's all over the news. [But if] some farmer loses his barn, which is probably the same amount of money and the same catastrophe, it barely gets three seconds. It's not good.

Ignored by government and by the news media, these folks felt neglected by the powers that be. One way I noticed this was in the way they reacted to me. Several groups could not quite believe that I had made the effort to come "all the way from Madison" to talk with them. For example, in the town with the dice game in the central-west city, I spent time with a group that met up in the *early*, early morning at a gas station. At the end of my first visit, in May 2007, I had this exchange (Group 11a):

KJC: Nice to meet you. Here's a football schedule for you—would you like one? Football schedule? Good for three years. Convenient, yeah? You're welcome. I would love to come back like January or February to talk to you guys again, could I?

[*"Sure!"*]

MARK: I think we need more input out of Madison in your small areas. Even like your senators, and everything. I mean they've gotta get around to do things like this.

Even higher income people in places outside the Madison and Milwaukee metro areas expressed this kind of surprise. They saw themselves as less important than people in the metro areas in the eyes of politicians and other decision makers. For example, one group of professionals meeting for coffee every morning in a diner in a central Wisconsin city (Group 16a) said they were surprised that I, a university employee from Madison, was taking the time to drive around the state to listen to people like them: "I think that we are impressed [that you come up here to visit with us]. Because most of us, particularly in a state like Wisconsin where politicians—none of the national ones come and see us—you know we only have ten electoral votes. I mean none of the politicians come to see us at all." The Downtown Athletic Club perceived that the focus of politicians on cities rather than rural areas was a fact of politics nationwide (Group 1, November 2012):

> KJC: Well, what's your take on the presidential election?
>
> JOHN: You don't even want to know.
>
> [*Fred laughs*]
>
> KJC: Yes, I do! Sure I do. I don't want to start any fights. I want to know what you think.
>
> JOHN: I don't know. How's that?
>
> KJC: Oh you, yes you do. Why don't you . . .
>
> JOHN: You had the state of Ohio, what was it? No. Pennsylvania. Where four precincts voted nineteen thousand some odd to nothing. For Obama.[8] That just doesn't make a lot of sense, does it?
>
> FRED: I didn't hear that story.
>
> KJC: A little fishy. I didn't either.
>
> JOHN: There was like four or so precincts where Romney never got a vote. Not one. You would think that any precinct that there'd be one person contrary to the norm. And at least I would.
>
> MATT: Yeah, makes you wonder there, don't it.
>
> JOHN: But uh no, I don't know. The election? The president knew where to campaign. He campaigned in all the metropolitan areas. The cities and stuff. That's where all the vote was. If you looked at, I go back to Ohio cause that was the swing state they all talked about all the time, and if you look at it on the map, I'm going to say there's sixty-five counties and Romney—so characteristic throughout the whole nation won—the vast majority of territory, he did not win the cities. I mean that's . . . somebody was attacking—
>
> FRED: By square miles he'd have won.
>
> KJC: Here in Wisconsin, too, right?

JOHN: Easily. What the . . . what did they say? All you have to do is win eleven
cities and you can win the election?

KJC: Really?

JOHN: Someone was just saying that. The populist . . . the vote is that manner
[set up in a way] that if you win eleven cities, you can win the election. I
don't know if that's true but. . . .

To me, much of what is getting talked about here is power, and that
power comes in several layers. The most obvious example of this power
is the ability of governments to force rural places to abide by laws they
dislike. This is the classic definition of power—the ability of A to get B to
do something B otherwise would not do (Dahl 1961). "Unfunded mandates" is one example. But there is another dimension of power getting
talked about here, too: control over which concerns even get recognized
and discussed (Bachrach and Baratz 1962). I heard people in rural areas
say many times that all of the major decisions are made in the urban areas, by urban people, and dictated outward. They complained that authority flowed out from Madison and Milwaukee but never in reverse.
They felt that they did not have the power to get people to listen to their
concerns.[9]

While the inability to get their concerns heard is a subtle instance of
feeling powerless, it is nonetheless important. Power is partly about respect, recognition, and listening. People whose voices are never heard
by decision makers have no power. When those in power listen to some
group, they convey that they are worthy of attention and, implicitly, that
they share their power.

Many of the people I spent time with in rural areas felt like their
towns were drying up and blowing away because the spigot of resources
had been turned off. In addition, though, there was also a sense that
these more subtle forms of power had been denied them as well.

One member of a group of retired and working women meeting for
breakfast in a rural, far northern resort community (Group 2) explained:

THERESA: As a former educator, I resented, highly, comments such as, "There
is no education north of Highway 8 [a U.S. highway that runs East-West
across the middle of the state.] These kids aren't—" and we send them
such absolutely excellent and well-prepared students there that they—the
attitude that the hick area of the state—was painful.

KJC: So who did you get that from? Recruiters?

THERESA: Professors.

KJC: Really? When they would visit?

THERESA: Yeah, or publish in newspaper articles or other, you know—and that was a little distressful because I think northern Wisconsin feels a little far away from Madison anyway. And we keep waving our hands and saying, "Yoo-hoo, there's another half of a state up here! Up north is not Wausau [the main city in the central part of the state]!"

This is not just alienation, or a lack of trust, or low efficacy with respect to powerful institutions. These sentiments are tightly bound to a sense of place identity. Simply put, many folks I met in small places identified as rural people and equated membership in that category with being a person who is systematically ignored and left out of the exercise of power.

Values and Lifestyles

When people talked about public affairs from a rural consciousness perspective they were telling me that city people have a lack of listening skills, exhibit a chronic lack of respect for the rural way of life, and regularly ignore rural communities. Many people talked about this as part and parcel of a fundamental aspect of the rural-versus-urban divide: city people just don't seem to get it. They don't understand rural life or pay attention to it.

Part of the reason people in rural areas felt misjudged by urbanites were the widely known stereotypes of rural folks. Many rural residents believed that city dwellers thought they were just "a bunch of rednecks," for example. A third of groups ($N = 18$) in places with populations under ten thousand assumed that public decision makers in the major metro areas held common negative stereotypes of rural residents, such as "hicks," "country bumpkins," "rednecks," and uneducated folks (Creed and Ching 1997; Jarosz and Lawson 2002).[10] One group that I interviewed even went so far as to call themselves the "Mediocre Redneck Coffee Klatch" (Group 11a).

They were defensive, but they were also proud. And they had their own stereotypes of city folk. Slightly more than a third of these groups ridiculed urbanites' lack of common sense. Many of them made a point of emphasizing that in contrast to city folk, they understood how to really hunt and fish and knew what it was like to really interact with nature. Also, many people took enormous pride in using their hands rather than what they saw as what most city folks did for work: sitting behind a desk all day.

This combination of pride in one's group and sense that their group is deprived relative to other groups is characteristic of group consciousness in general. So notice that although many rural residents resented cities, they did not necessarily want to live in one. Conversations in eleven of the twenty-one groups located in places with populations of less than ten thousand included comments to the effect that, despite the hardships of rural life, they preferred their lifestyles to rootless, fast-paced city living. "Down in the cities, they don't even know their neighbors most of 'em!" one man exclaimed to me (Group 6). People took pride in the face-to-face nature of their interactions, as opposed to the bureaucracy and technology they perceived to be typical of urban life. For example, one woman in a small town (Group 3) explained to me that, in her community, people do not do inspections when selling a house. "It's seen as insulting," she said. "If I give you my word that the house is in good shape, why would you need to inspect it?"

This perception of differing lifestyles for rural and urban residents fed the belief that city dwellers could not make decent decisions on behalf of rural communities. Such concerns were more focused on differences in ways of life and values than on differences in partisanship—that, say, city folks were Democrats and rural folks were Republican. In particular, many rural residents perceived a different pace of life in cities and were downright mad about attempts to appeal to tourists by urbanizing their own towns. For example, in the group of loggers in the northwestern village (Group 6), during my first visit, I asked a general anything-else-I-should-know question, and here's what the group offered up (June 2007):

KJC: But is there something else I oughta know about—I don't know—your lives in [this town] or what is going on up here? I know you can learn a whole lot in half an hour, but this is really helpful, actually.

[*Long pause*]

SAM: Well it's a lot less rat race than Madison.

KJC: Yeah, really peaceful.

JOHNNY: Yeah it's nice. I wouldn't live anywhere else.

KJC: Yeah you want to stay here—I can see that.

SAM: Drives to work, his house within a mile you're in the country—I mean not that [far] even.

KJC: Aw, it's beautiful.

SAM: Yeah, it's a lot less hectic. When you grow up this way. I guess if you grow up in the city, people say they can't stand it here. But if you grow up here—

KJC: Well, I think even city people, when they come up here, it's just like, "Wow it's so relaxing!" or they'll say things like—

SAM: Then they want to change everything. Have you been to Minocqua [a popular northern tourist town]?

KJC: Yeah.

SAM: Or Hayward [another popular northern tourist town]?

KJC: Not in a long time.

SAM: Hayward was like [this town] twenty years ago, and now it's got Walmart.

KJC: Hayward has a Walmart?

SAM: McDonald's, Menards, Subway—you turn around, you make a little Madison. Just strip malls. Downtown turns into antique stores because everything is out at Walmart. Lost all your businesses. Like this was all stores [as he waves his arm at the boarded-up Main Street outside].

A few hours west of that group of loggers, I met up two times in the town hall with a handful of leaders from the local government and the public schools who would turn on the lights and the Mr. Coffee machine and huddle together there every morning (Group 4b). The men resented outsiders' desire to urbanize northern Wisconsin (January 2008).

DEAN: What generally happens is that one or the other likes it here, either the husband likes it here or the wife, and the other just hates it because they want to go downtown every day, and shop. But if they wanna go shopping they have to drive twenty miles. So eventually, we've got like two- or three-million-dollar homes built, and they were there like five years, and one or the other of 'em didn't like it, and they sold out and went back to Florida.

KJC: Wow, did somebody buy that home? I mean, who's gonna? . . .

JACK: Oh yeah.

KJC: Really.

JACK: They had, you know, snowmobiles, all kinds of equipment, fishing rods and boats and all that, but she hated it here. Well, just to be in that party system in the city, and you come up here in the wintertime, there's nothing. I think that more spread between the very, very wealthy who move up here, and, it seems like to me, what we might call the middle class is shrinking, and the ones on the bottom. I don't have any facts, but that's the way I look at it.

Although most of the commentary about the contrast in urban and rural lifestyles was not overtly political, sometimes people did bring in politics directly. The men who gathered around the Mr. Coffee shared this (Group 4b, June 2008):

FRANK: Well, we're very conservative in the Northwoods and they're very, very, very, very, very, very, very left in those cities. Just think if Madison and Milwaukee and La Crosse did not vote in an election. What would've happened? I mean our votes mean nothing because of the population and the votes [the large number of votes coming from cities, as opposed to small towns]. That's how I look at it. Same reason [upper] Michigan years ago wanted to leave lower Michigan. Form their own state.

KJC: So you feel like the show is pretty much run by the people—

FRANK: Oh yes, oh yeah. Yeah. We don't have any say.

KJC: So how about with the DNR [state Department of Natural Resources]? When you were working with the DNR?

FRANK [sarcastically]: Fine group of men. [laughs]

KJC: No, because the reason I ask is because connected with the state government did you feel like in your job you still didn't have much of a say—it was pretty much the folks in Madison telling you what you—

DEAN: You work long enough you have something political—we had decent working conditions—

AL: And that was the end of it. Now the governor appoints all the big shots and they don't know, before a guy had to work from the bottom all the way up and then become the head of the DNR. Now they just pick some guy off the street.

JACK: Oh yeah.

AL: A buddy of the governor and . . . That's the way I think about it. The DNR's changed.

Most of the people in this group were themselves elected officials or vocal commentators on public affairs. Their resentment toward the decisions people made in the cities had a clear partisan tone.

But when people talked about the inability of city dwellers to adequately represent rural concerns, partisanship was not front and center.
Even for the group around the Mr. Coffee, they referenced "conservatism" not "Republicanism." There was a sense that urban residents lived
differently. They were carving up the world into "us" and "them," but
partisanship was not the key divider.

In addition, when they talked as if city people lived by different values, they were not emphasizing abortion, or gay marriage, or the things
that are typically pointed to as the cultural issues that divide lower-
income whites from the Democratic Party. Instead, the values they
talked about were intertwined with economic concerns. When they
talked about city folks being unable to understand rural life, those conversations were typically about how they had no understanding of the
economic realities of rural life and how hard people had to work to make
ends meet in small towns.

Here is one example of rural residents talking about how they struggled harder to get by than did people in cities. This exchange took place
among a group of women meeting for lunch in the central-west town
where the dice game takes place. They brought up the topic of health
care and complained about politicians making choices out of step with
ordinary people like themselves (Group 11c, June 2012).

> DOLORES: I have this feeling that—I don't know who mentioned this it might
> have been Bill Cosby—that if all of these senators and congressman and
> all of these people took a cut in their wages, you know, and their bene-
> fits . . . and took the benefits that we have to take—
> GLADYS: Yeah!
> DOLORES: Live on the kind of salary that we have to live on, you know. They
> have no idea what small, rural America is like . . . small towns, you know!
> They couldn't begin to fathom what's it like to live on the incomes that we
> live on.
> KJC: Do you feel that way about the state politicians too?
> DOLORES: Up to a point. Yeah. You know, their thing is to win . . .

In a tiny town in the northwestern part of the state I met with a group
of people that gathers in the basement of the local church every Tuesday
morning: stay-at-home moms and some kids, retirees, and people taking
a break from work (Group 3). For a good chunk of time, the first time I

met them, they complained about how disrespectful one of their state legislative representatives was and about how clueless state inspectors are. One example they gave me was the time an inspector checked the temperature of food in a salad bar in a restaurant a few towns over by sticking her thermometer in the ice.

When I asked them what the University of Wisconsin–Madison does not do well, they stated bluntly that people in Madison and Milwaukee have qualitatively different lifestyles than do people in the rural parts of the state.

> KJC: What do you think the University of Wisconsin–Madison does not do well? When you think about [it] . . .
>
> MARTHA: Represents our area. I mean we are like, we're strange to Madison. They want us to do everything for Madison's laws and the way they do things, but we totally live differently than the city people live. So they need to think more rural instead of all this city area.
>
> DONNA: We can't afford to educate our children like they can in the cities. Simple as that. Don't have the advantages.
>
> ETHEL: All the things they do, based on Madison and Milwaukee, never us.
>
> MARTHA: Yeah, we don't have the advantages that they give their local people there, I think a lot of times. And it is probably because they don't understand how rural people live and what we deal with and our problems.
>
> KJC: I think that's right. I think there is a whole lot of distance between— especially this corner of the state.
>
> MARTHA: Oh we're, like, we're lost up here!
>
> ROSEMARY: They don't even understand how we live in [our community]!
>
> [*Laughter*]
>
> MARTHA: Yeah that's right! It's very true. They won't even come and help us with our roads until you demand it.

In that conversation, in response to my question about the main concerns in their community, they had talked about their representative in Madison as someone unlike themselves, and about the state workers that regulated their livelihoods as oblivious to the basics of their businesses. The sense of being "strange to Madison" and living "differently than the city people live" was about fundamental difference in lived experience. And much of that difference was tied to economics: "We don't have the advantages that they give their local people there," Martha had said.

Conceptions of Hard Work

One key value that rural residents emphasized as they contrasted their communities with city life was the value of hard work. Many Americans value hard work (McClosky and Zaller 1984, chap. 4), and working-class Americans seem especially likely to emphasize hard work, compared to their upper-income counterparts (Lamont 2000). But when I talked with people in small-town Wisconsin, many of them told me that hard work was especially necessary in rural places. They said that, because their economic realities were perpetually tough, the people trying to make a living in those communities had to be tough as well.

Ideas about who works hard are important for the way people talk about public policy because they are closely tied to notions of who deserves taxpayer support. People we perceive as not working hard—as lazy—are undeserving. We tend to perceive hard workers, in contrast, as deserving our respect and our support (Feather 1999; Soss and Schram 2007).

I want to demonstrate how this worked in the conversations to emphasize again the way these perceptions went beyond partisanship. Republicans and Democrats talked about hard work differently.[11] But people viewing the world through the lens of rural consciousness had an understanding of hard work that was rooted in place identity as much as in partisanship.

Many Republicans I met, regardless of the type of place they lived in, linked ideas of hard work with opposition to social welfare programs. They would say that people do not work hard like they used to or that certain people worked less than others and thus were less deserving of taxpayer money. For example, at a breakfast meeting in a diner in a central Wisconsin city (Group 18c), when I asked whether the group favored one of the presidential primary candidates, one man said:

> No, I don't like any of them. I'll take—I'll take somebody that will let me keep some of my money rather than have to, have to pay for everybody's free lunch. And what happened to this world where we all started out in a world where we had to work our ass off to, uh, to get where we are. Nowadays nobody wants to work their ass off and they just want to have [the money] handed to them. And I mean, that's—that's the scary part.

Likewise, a suburban Milwaukee breakfast group of retired men and women, all Republicans, argued that they were not supportive of Democrats because they believed that "Democrats take hard-working Americans' money away."

Rural Republicans, in contrast, would talk about the value of hard work by referring to rural life in general. They would claim that the demands of rural life simply required hard work. At times, they would use this sentiment to explain why young people in their communities often chose to move to a city after high school. When I asked the group of conservative men around the Mr. Coffee in the northern tourist town (Group 4b) about poverty in their area, they explained:

> DEAN: There's lots of jobs, but everybody, the younger generation, they want twenty dollars an hour to rake leaves, you know? These retired people can't afford to pay some guy twenty dollars to come in. But everybody wants big money, and . . . the greed, everybody wants big money to come in and work. . . . Instead of like us guys; we had to work hard all our lives.
> [laughter]
> JACK: I was cutting pulp with an ax and a sweep-saw when I was thirteen, fourteen years old.
> KJC: No kidding?
> JACK: Put myself through college.

Democrats tended to have a different take on hard work. At the same time that they valued hard work, they would remark that working hard could only do so much—that sometimes people needed additional help to get ahead. For rural Democrats, living in a rural place meant that it was especially tough to make ends meet, even if you worked hard. For example, Democrats among the group of loggers in the northwest town (Group 6) talked about how much people in their community work and said that people in general should work for the benefits they receive. In that way they sounded just like the Republicans in other groups. But when I asked them a standard survey question to probe their ideas about income inequality, something else emerged:

> KJC: "In America today, some people have better jobs and higher incomes than others do." Why do you think that is, that some Americans have better jobs and higher income than others do? There is a bunch of different

reasons people typically give—and you all tell me whether you think it is a bunch of bunk, or whether you think that is a good reason. One is, "because some people have more inborn ability to learn." How important do you think that reason is for why some people have better jobs?

CHARLIE: Basically what it amounts to is who has more ambition than the next person.

KJC: More ambition? Yeah?

CHARLIE: Some people don't have any ambition and they don't wanna work.

SAM: That doesn't mean you're going to make more money. Mexicans got more ambition than anybody. They keep the wages low.

KJC: Yeah? So one of the standard reasons they give is because some people just don't work as hard. Is that—is that kind of what you are talking about?

JIM: Yeah Sam kind of hit the nail on the head.

SAM: He goes to work every day, does the same thing, if they cut the price [of timber], you ain't gonna make no money. Cut the price, work longer.

STU: Yeah—I worked all weekend.

KJC: So even working hard, that's not what counts for earning a higher income?

JIM: Well no—what are you going to do? We're in that industry—

SAM: You're really not rewarded a lot as far as—

JIM: No you're not.

SAM: And we'll all fault unions but there is a lot of reasons why—because you keep bringing all the Mexicans in, it keeps the wages down.

KJC: So does that hurt you all in the end? The fact that Mexicans take the lower-paying jobs?

SAM: Well nobody's going—

JIM: Well I'm not going to—

SAM: To do that work for eight dollars an hour. Especially—

JIM: I'm not going to go pick tomatoes, or go milk cows.

SAM: But if they gave you twenty dollars an hour you might.

JIM: Well yah! But I still don't think I would go milk cows. [*laughter*] The paper mill has been shitting on us, I don't want no cow shitting on us! I gotta go to work. [*Gets up and leaves.*]

Like the Republican rural groups, the Democrats in this group talked about the value of hard work by bringing in the fact that they lived in a rural area. They talked about their discomfort with the notion that hard work leads to success by referencing their distinctively rural industry, logging. They saw themselves as rural people: people who worked hard and who are by definition of a place that is economically disadvantaged. To them, one could work extremely hard and still not earn enough to make ends meet. Their perception was that the deck was so stacked against communities like theirs that even hard work could not allow them to get ahead. In other words, people in many types of places brought in notions of hard work to talk about social welfare policy, but when rural residents did so, they often talked about hard work in terms of place.

A few years later, in this same group, the only people who had shown up the morning I visited called themselves conservatives, Republicans, and Scott Walker supporters (Group 6, May 2011). They also talked about themselves as rural folks but gave a very different picture of social welfare than had the Democratic-leaning loggers on my previous visit.

RON: I have no compassion for people that are lazy. We live in America, we've all got the way to make a good living. I've made a good living because I've worked hard all my life. I got, I mean I got a lot of stuff, I'm not. . . . But I worked for it, nobody gave it to me. I've been working since I was ten years old; I've never taken a sick day.

KJC: Oh my God.

RON: I've never missed a day of work because of being sick. And I've been sick, you know?

KJC: Sure.

RON: But I go to work. I got hurt a couple times where I missed some time, but to take a sick day, that's what, all these people get all these sick days. Come on! What is, this whole country that, I mean that you gotta have twelve sick days a year?

KJC: Yeah?

RON: Then, I mean like the state employees, it ain't all the, it's not all of the deals in the state, but certain ones, if you've got one sick day when you retire at fifty-five, you're gonna retire at fifty-five and you can use one sick day a month to pay for your health insurance. Now one sick day, is that worth that fifteen hundred dollars a month of health care coverage? One sick day is worth what you should make in a day. . . . I worked in the woods most of my life, I've never had an easy job. They want to raise, they want to raise the social security age, you know. I mean, can I work, doing my job till I'm seventy? Somebody sitting at a desk could probably do it, but that's not manual labor. But, by the time, I'll be sixty-two in October, I mean I'm gonna keep working till I'm sixty-five, but after sixty-five, you're burned out, you know? If, like working construction, or, you know?

KJC: Sure. You've gotta give your body a break.

RON: Manual labor job. Yeah, yeah.

This man interpreted the hard life that he had had to live in his rural community as evidence that anyone can do it, and that those who can't are lazy. Was this sentiment what led him to support the Republican Party and Scott Walker's attempts to undercut public employee unions and make public employees contribute more to their pensions and health care insurance? Or was his support for the Republican Party what made him interpret the difficulty of his life as evidence that other folks ought to pull themselves up by their bootstraps rather than advocate for an increased safety net? I do not know, but from where I sat in these conversations, they seemed all of a piece.

When pundits look at low-income residents in Republican areas and exclaim that they are voting against their interests, they are often assuming that somehow the Republican Party has fooled people into not noticing that they are opposing the very kind of government programs that might help them out. But those kinds of claims neglect that a "safety net" may not translate as "help" to everyone. In rural areas, there is a great deal of pride in the idea that "help" is about letting people work hard enough so that they can make it on their own. The sense I got from these conversations is that help, for many, is about providing jobs, not welfare. When Ron told me he had never missed a day of work, and he did it "working in the woods," he said it with pride. To him, rural life is tough, but he drew a good deal of esteem from claiming that he was a person who was living that life.

Resources

When people in small towns claimed that they lived differently and had different values than city folks, they were often simultaneously claiming that they were people facing unique economic challenges. I want to hone in on their perceptions of economic injustice to show you the depth of these understandings. When people perceived that rural life was economically tough, this carried with it many complaints: about the injustice in the distribution of public dollars, unfair taxation, and more. Those complaints were intertwined with other aspects of rural consciousness, in particular, with their sense of being ignored and disrespected and of having fundamentally different values and lifestyles than city dwellers.

Here is a common narrative for how people wove these perceptions together: Rural life was a source of pride for many because it was different from urban living—it involved different lifestyles and values, including a special emphasis on hard work. That rural hard work ethic was a point of pride, but for many, it was a problem because in order to work hard, you needed a job, and rural communities were on the short end of the stick in terms of jobs. Why? Because rural communities had no power. Politicians and others with the ability to make the decisions to bring good-paying jobs to their communities paid no attention to their places.

In the rural communities I visited, I often heard people stating, as though a matter of fact, that jobs, wealth, and taxpayer dollars are in the "the M&Ms," as people sometimes referred to Madison and Milwaukee. They complained that rural areas are being left on their own to fight a losing battle. Conversations in seventeen of the twenty-five groups outside the Madison and Milwaukee areas included statements conveying that their communities did not receive their fair share of resources and that metro residents did not understand this. Their comments conveyed that the rural-versus-urban distinction was *the* main way to characterize the distribution of taxation, wealth, and the cost of goods and services in the state. In short, many people in small towns perceived that their tax dollars are "sucked in" by Madison and spent on that city or Milwaukee, never to be seen again.

On this mapping, wealthy people live in the cities (cf. Bell 1992, 78). "Everybody in [the] northern [part of the state] makes money off of tourists . . . [the tourists] bring some of that fresh money up," one man in the diner group in the north-central tourist town told me (Group 9). On a different visit to the same group, another man said simply, "When you get down in the city, people are making more money."

Many people equated the cities with wealth because they perceived that the cities are where the good jobs are. One man in the group meeting in the small town on the Wisconsin River explained to me during my first visit (Group 8, June 2007), "Our salaries are less than what they are in Madison, by far, our hourly wages. And I would think salaried jobs as well. People here don't make as much, but there again, it's—that's why we don't have . . . that's why a lot of our young people have gone someplace else." About four years later, I heard a similar conversation in that group (April 2011):

RANDY: I'd like to see, you know, I'd like to see a lot of new young families move into town. . . . That's one thing you do see is too many older, retired persons in your communities—to be real active it makes a difference . . .

GLENN: A lack of good-paying jobs for the younger people to live on. You know it takes money to live or play or anything else and you get into a town like this and the people who are on the boards and stuff are people who usually own their homes and have a job and their interests are more in the parks and the fire departments and different things like that where it takes jobs for these young people to keep 'em around. And, you got jobs, you get young people, you get homes being built, and you get things being done.

RANDY: That's the problem with rural America.

GLENN: Right.

RANDY: You start here, go down along the river or whatever, you pick any of these communities, we're fortunate in [this town]. . . . we're fortunate here that we got two or three good industries in town which we're very fortunate to have.

[. . .]

GLENN: In any of these towns. You go around Madison, thirty-, forty-mile radius, the majority of 'em are driving to Madison you know and it's, you know, they want to live in a small town but they gotta have a job, a decent paying job. With four-dollar gas, that's gonna make it tough.

Along with complaints about gas prices, I often heard concerns about utility bills in rural areas. For example, in the breakfast group of women in a rural tourist town (Group 2):

SALLY: The cost of the water and sewer here is outrageous compared to what they pay in Madison. So here is big rich Madison, with all the good high-paying jobs, getting the cheapest water, and we have people up here who have three months of employment [because of the short tourist season], what are they paying? And I feel like there should be more sharing—less taxes going to Madison to help offset—

DOROTHY: I just moved from [a city in the central part of the state]. A quarter of water in [that city] is seventy bucks . . . seventy dollars every *three* months for [that] water. Up here, which we constantly have been paying, every second month, the bill—and sometimes we're not here—is seventy dollars every *second* month.

A bit later in the conversation, they continued on this theme.

SALLY: You've also got to look at Madison and the growth of Madison. There's new sewers going in in every single day, the result of the businesses. You go down there and you don't know where Madison starts and Mount Horeb—I mean it is just one big sewer. . . . Like Walmart, buy it in volume, get it cheaper. But I think we don't look at places here—I mean I was coming up here eighteen years ago with a business, and I was shocked at how little the people got for services here. You pay for your garbage collection here on top of paying high taxes. I mean Madison, I throw out sofas [and don't have to pay.] There should be more sharing with these communities that are really struggling with stuff like that.

SHIRLEY: But in Madison there are all these big businesses that are paying taxes that we don't have here.

SUE: Exactly, but it should be a shared thing. I mean, why can't we look at that? Or at least put a state office building up here, with all the communication.

[*Agreement all around: "That would help."/ "That's a thought."/ "Great idea."/ "Absolutely."*]

SALLY: We could. I've worked for the state of Wisconsin, in a lot of offices, and a lot of offices could be—

DOROTHY: Outsource it to northern Wisconsin!

LAURA [*to me*]: You could be here all the time!

[*Laughter*]

KJC: That would be delightful—I would love it.

In the rural consciousness perspective, not only were the cities wealthier but they were also advantaged in terms of gas prices, utility bills, and infrastructure like sewers. These perceptions of injustice burned so brightly because they carried perceptions of blame. It was not just that cities were advantaged, but also that decision makers in them were intentionally overlooking the smaller communities in the state.

A man in the northwest logging group (Group 6) lamented, "I mean, rightfully so, you know, population centers, that's where the majority of the stuff has eventually got to go. It just makes sense. But you can't ignore everything up here either, you know." Likewise, a group of men at a diner in a rural northern-central tourist town (Group 9) almost laughed at the notion that the Obama administration stimulus proposal would help their community. They assumed none of the funds would focus on rural areas. One man said, "But the trickle down won't get to here because we don't have any business. So the trickle down will stop at Green Bay, Wausau [cities south of where they live] . . ."

Taxation was a seriously raw issue for many people in small communities. In general, the perception was that taxation hurt rural areas. At least one person in ten of the twenty-five groups outside the Milwaukee and Madison metro areas assumed that people in those cities are taxed at much lower rates than rural residents are.

Property taxes in particular were treated like an invasive species killing off native life forms. And people were sure it had come from the cities. Many rural folks blamed urbanites for driving up property values in their communities by purchasing expensive vacation homes. Some claimed this had driven locals out of their own communities or, at least, away from their lifetime dreams of finally buying a house on a local lake. They described these rising property values, driven by urbanites, as a threat to their personal and community identities (cf. Bell 1992, 76). For example, on the first morning that I met with the group of women in the rural northwest tourist town (Group 2), one member showed me a list she had written in a small notebook of sixty people who had been forced out of their homes by urbanites buying expensive vacation homes. "The old-time families have left or are leaving," she said. "The character of the town is changing, and it is just too bad."

In Door County, the "thumb" of Wisconsin, I heard a similar thing from a woman taking part in a conversation after a church service:

Having been raised and grown up here, it has gotten to the point that I think Door County is becoming very elitist. Thank God I have a home. I was lucky enough that my husband and I had worked for it and paid for it before he died. On my wages, I could not have bought a home by myself. The cost of all of the surrounding land has become so expensive because of all the people who don't live here more than six weeks out of the year, and build three-quarter-million-dollar homes, million-dollar homes, and basically visit, and so they've driven the property values so high that those people who have lived in a home their whole lives and were able to afford, can no longer afford because the tax rate has gone up so high. The wage scale is not that great in Door County. People say, "Well, you know, you make a good living." No. And they somehow get the impression that we go to the gas station and we pay less for our gas, and pay less for our food because we live here. Ah, wrong! We pay the same price [*laughter*], but we don't make the wages, and we're paying for what has been driven up, and it's—I see it as a real hardship. I'm fortunate, but I look at my children and my grandchildren and I wonder will they be able to live here and own a home? Maybe they'll be able to rent, but to live here and own a home and take pride in that? That's scary. Really is scary.

The sentiment that city people were oblivious to the economic hardships that rural residents face was simmering on the back burner in many of these conversations. People living in tourist communities acknowledged the income that tourism generated but resented the perception that people living "up north" led leisurely lives. A woman in a northwest rural town (Group 2) said to me, "Just remember that up here many people have two and three part-time jobs to survive." Across the state, one man explained to me that, yes, he lived in a beautiful wilderness area, but when the weather got nice enough to be outside, he hardly had time to enjoy it. It was during those summer months that he and most of the people he knew had to work multiple jobs to get by throughout the rest of the year (Group 9, June 2011): "I live on a lake— lived there twenty-three years. I've fished it three times. Just not enough time. When we want to fish, we go to Canada or Minnesota to get away from it all."

Four years earlier, some people in his breakfast group expressed exasperation at how clueless city people were about the economic realities of tourist towns (Group 9, June 2007).

NELSON: Yeah—people in town here, they sell their home in Milwaukee or Madison or Illinois and they come up here and buy one of these small businesses. Christ!

PETE: Yeah—wake up!

NELSON: You won't make any money for twenty years, if you can stay in business for that long, pay your taxes and everything else.

KJC: Wow.

NELSON: It's a different world up here than it is in the southern part of the state.

PETE: Looks great in the summer time!

NELSON: Yeah looks great.

PETE: Nine months are winter, and three months are tough sledding.

In Door County, the "tough sledding" sounded like this (Group 5, June 2007):

PAM: What you make in six months has to stretch all year.

BECKY: And many of 'em are working two and three jobs during this period of time.

PAM: Exactly.

BECKY: Yeah, they're not doing just one job,

PAM: You don't really have a summer—it consists of working. When my kids were home, I worked two jobs, so you know—it goes by quickly.

SHELLY: People always say, "You are so lucky to live [here] in the summertime!" Well, any of us who live here, live here and work here and never enjoy it. First of all we're irritated [*half-jokingly*] because we can't get to our job because of these tourists driving so slow.

KJC: I'm sorry! [*Apologizing for being a slow-driving tourist.*]

SHELLY: And then when we get there we work, leave that and go to another job and come home and then we are following another tourist to come home [*laughter*], and so we really don't get to enjoy what everybody else does, although I am so appreciative that I can live here, I really can't imagine—I just thank God every day that I am able to live here in [this town] where I was born.

DON [*sarcastically*]: You don't want to go to Milwaukee and live there?

SHELLY: No and I'm willing to give up a lot to do that, and I think a lot of us have done that.

The way they described it, making a living in a tourist community was a challenge, characterized by constant hardship and uncertainty. And they believed that urbanites just did not understand this.

People resented the economic hardships they faced, the fact that city people and those who held the reins of power did not seem to recognize these hardships, and, also, the unfulfilled promise of tourism. They did not necessarily like city people coming in to their communities but were willing to put up with it in order to make a living. In some places, however, people talked about city people infiltrating their communities, yet not helping the local economy in any way. Local residents would complain that tourists passed right through without spending any money. One example was the "all they leave on the sandbars is shit" comment noted earlier. Randall, from the group of loggers in the northwest corner of the state (Group 6, April 2008), also expressed this objection: "A lot of people tell me, well, if it wasn't for tourists, your taxes would be higher. Well, they don't spend much money here. They bring their own gas, they bring their own food, they might stay in a motel, you know. We're not really gaining anything from tourism."

In these conversations, the distinctiveness of rural economies was obvious to people living in them. In one case, a woman gave this a label—"the rural class" (Group 2): "If you look at the *rural class* [emphasis added] . . . we've never had jobs here, it's not like this is part of the economy that there are no jobs, but I think one of our big concerns is the coming tourist season and the decrease in funding from the state for tourist-related activities, cause so many people here rely entirely on tourists coming so it's just a real uneasy feeling about what's gonna happen this year."

Talk concerning rural economies ranged from this "uneasy feeling" to downright anger. Sometimes the resentment about the economic inequality between the major cities and small communities was so strong I wondered if I should end the conversation and get out. Other times it was downright comical. One group in west-central Wisconsin (Group 11b) actually imagined a geographic line that represented this unfairness. This was State Highway 29, which cuts east-west across the state through the central city of Wausau. This is what Henry and Richard referred to as "the Mason/Dixon Line" in a conversation I quoted earlier. In their eyes, communities to the south of this line got all of the resources, while those to the north were ignored. One man said simply, "I think you've forgotten rural America."

This is the gang of men who played dice every morning before work. The first time I visited this group, when a local attorney led me through the curtain at the back of the diner to the group sitting at their L-shaped table, they stopped playing dice for a while and talked with me. At the end of our conversation, they asked me if I knew how to play Ship, Captain, and Crew. I said, proudly, "Why, yes I do." My Wisconsinness came in handy here, as I had played this dice game many times with my family growing up.[12] They asked me to "turn off that machine [my recorder] and we'll shake for a buck" in their dollar round (before most of them left and went to work or their other tasks for the day), and I promptly lost. They asked me to "come back and shake dice" and "bring your quarters." It was clear that I was welcome to come back, but I had better plan on playing dice when I did.

On my third visit (in April 2008), there was a horse auction going on in town, and the group members joked with me about buying a horse. This led to some colorful comments about Madison. When several of them asked me if I was going to check out the auction, I answered:

> KJC: I think I will go up once, yeah, I went up—I looked through the fence yesterday evening.
> HENRY: Why don't you buy one of them horses? I got a trailer.
> KJC: Not sure where I'd keep him. [They knew by this point that I lived right in Madison, a mile from the football stadium at the time, where there was room for them to park next time they come down for a game. But there is certainly no room to keep a horse.]
> HENRY: Huh?
> KJC: I'm not sure where I'd keep him!
> HENRY: Keep him in Madison. That's where they keep all the bullshit.

After everyone got a good laugh out of that one, Henry continued on:

> HENRY: Well, basically all you gotta do is buy the front end of the horse, they got the back end in Madison!

The group laughed, and I almost snorted my coffee, but then I started to get uncomfortable—not because of the anti-Madison comments, but because I had been winning round after round in the dice game. Most of the members of the group thought this was funny, but at least one was visibly irritated. To try to soften the situation, I joked,

> KJC: I come and ask for your thoughts and I take your money!
> RICHARD: I'll tell you what, that's good though. Because we have so little of it.
> KJC: And it all goes to Madison anyway [*joking along with them*].
> HOWARD: We expect nothing less from Madison!
> RICHARD: It won't cost any postage to get it down there now!

This resentment was good-natured, but it was ubiquitous across the rural communities I visited. It didn't seem temporary, either, and wasn't just a product of the Great Recession. People talked about economic injustice as a fact of rural life.

Isn't This Really Just about Race?

Many people in these small towns perceived that someone or something was responsible for the decline of their communities. Someone or something was siphoning off their money, they told me. They believed that wherever their tax dollars were going they sure were not going to their own towns.

Who or what was doing this? Who was getting their hard-earned money? "They" often had something to do with cities: decision makers, wealthy people, liberals, and the undeserving.

Cities represent a lot in American life. One thing they conjure up is race. In short, cities are often shorthand for people who are not white. When the dice game group in central Wisconsin (Group 11b) referred to the line dividing rural Wisconsin from the metropolitan centers in the southern part of the state as the Mason-Dixon line, the racial implications of that term were probably not accidental.

The urban-versus-rural divide is undoubtedly in part about race. Cities have perhaps always "been the places where we have first and most fully confronted the task of living alongside people who do not necessarily belong to our own tribe" (Conn 2014, 4). There is a widening policy conflict between urban and rural areas, and it is no secret that it is driven in part by racial mobilization (Gimpel and Schuknecht 2003). Research on implicit racial priming tells us that the term "inner city" is racialized—that this term activates racial attitudes (Hurwitz and Peffley 2005). It is likely the term "urban" does so as well. This may be especially the case in Wisconsin, which is extremely racially segregated. Only 29 percent of the state's African American population lives outside the cities of Milwaukee and Madison, and most of the state has little experience to date with Latino immigration.[13] Also, the Milwaukee metro area is extremely segregated with respect to African Americans and Latinos. According to a Brookings Institute analysis of 2005–9 data from the Census Bureau's American Community Survey, the Milwaukee metro area is one of the most racially segregated in the country (Frey 2010).

So yes, it is highly likely that when people refer to "those people in Milwaukee" they are often referring to racial minorities. But notice how complex this is. The urbanites that rural folks were referring to were not predominantly racial minorities. When white outstaters (i.e., those living outside the major metropolitan areas) complained of the laziness in the cities in these conversations, their comments were almost always directed at white people: government bureaucrats and faculty members at the flagship public university.

In that way, antiurban resentment is not simply resentment against people of color. At the same time, given the way arguments against government redistribution in the United States have historically been made by equating deservingness with whiteness, these conversations are about race even when race is not mentioned. Also, animosity toward public workers and wealthy folks in the city may be driven by conservative views on race. Since the cities, particularly Madison, are perceived as liberal and vote Democratic in elections, people who harbor racial resentment may indeed be equating city people with racial liberalism. Now, as in the past, racial animosity is directed toward groups of whites that help minorities, such as government employees and academics.

When rural folks did make openly racist comments, they did so about Native Americans, an overwhelmingly rural population in Wisconsin. There are eleven reservations in Wisconsin, located primarily in the northern third of the state. Hostility toward Native Americans did not arise often in these conversations, but it is no secret that relations between Native Americans and whites in Wisconsin have been tense historically and in recent history.[14] Violent protests erupted in response to a series of federal court decisions in the 1980s, beginning in 1983. Those decisions affirmed spearfishing treaty rights to the Chippewa tribe and imposed no limits on how many fish tribal members could harvest (Bobo and Tuan 2006, chap. 2). White residents protested at boat landings, held demonstrations and rallies, and called for the end to treaty rights as well as the reservation system. Much of this opposition was rooted in racism, as social science research has documented (Bobo and Tuan 2006).

In recent years, these tensions have become salient to the broader population again, as the Walker administration has passed legislation that is facilitating the start of an iron ore mine in northwestern Wisconsin. To some, the mine signifies hundreds of jobs for people in the area who are sorely lacking them, but to others it means extensive disturbance to the way of life and natural environment and health of Native Americans on the adjacent Bad River Reservation (Seely 2011).

It is very possible that the lack of references to urban racial minorities in the conversations I observed is a manifestation of the threat hypothesis, or the idea that racial prejudice is heightened when people of different racial backgrounds are in proximity to one another (Key 1949; Blalock 1967). Given the extreme racial segregation in Wisconsin, there is little interaction here between whites and people of color. Thus the immediate racial tensions in most rural areas are not between whites and African Americans and Latinos but, instead, with Native Americans and, in a few communities, with Hmong refugees, who were relocated to Wisconsin in the decades since the Vietnam War.

The point I want to make is this: race is a part of rural consciousness. However, I ask the reader to notice the complexity of these perspectives and not think of them as simply about race. If we boil rural consciousness down to race, we ignore the ways in which these perspectives comprise many things: identities with place, a sense of oneself as a person of a particular place in the class hierarchy, identities as people with particular values, and sometimes ideology. Resentment is operating because people perceive they are not getting their fair share. They are making sense of this injustice by resenting those whom they think are getting more than they deserve, and perceptions of who works hard and who is deserving are infected with racism (Winter 2006, 2008). But those notions of distributive justice are *intertwined* with race—neither separate from nor synonymous with a simple distinction of white versus other.

Finally, if we conclude that rural consciousness is just racism dressed up in social science jargon, it allows us to overlook the role of antigovernment attitudes and preferences for small government here. Tea Party messaging appeals to racism (Burghart and Zeskind 2010; Parker and Barreto 2013), but it also resonates with many of the perceptions of inequality and alienation from government observed in the conversations presented in this book. As I have argued, attitudes about redistribution rest on a long history of racial discrimination in the United States. But that long history has enabled an accretion of meaning around attitudes of injustice.

This is how the politics of resentment operates—it works through seemingly simple divisions of us versus them, but it has power because in these divisions are a multitude of fundamental understandings: who has power, who has what values and which of those values are right, who gets what, and perceptions of the basic fairness of all of this. It is opposition to other people, and the overlap of urban and racially "other" is a powerful combination.

This is part of the reason racism is so persistent. Because it is in-tertwined with other fundamental attitudes, it can be invoked and ex-pressed in seemingly socially acceptable ways (Mendelberg 2001). In the conversations I observed, when people expressed racist sentiments, they did so while weaving them with values and allegiances of which they were sufficiently certain and proud that they were willing to express them in front of me, a relative stranger. Take for example these com-ments to me, by a man in the group of loggers in northwest Wisconsin, in May 2011:

> RON: Yeah. You know. Well like him that just left, that was here before to get coffee?
>
> KJC: Yeah.
>
> RON: He's an American Indian. [One sentence deleted for confidentiality.]
>
> KJC: Oh really?
>
> RON: He's a good guy.
>
> KJC: Yeah.
>
> RON: Works hard. Yeah.
>
> KJC: Well sure.
>
> RON: But he won't live on the reservation where they get all the free housing and stuff, he's self-supporting, you know?
>
> KJC: Yeah.
>
> RON: And, there, there's too many programs down there for a bunch of peo-ple, you know to have it for them to want to go to work. You know? They got the casino down there shoving our money through 'em, they got the federal government shoving our money through 'em, and they wonder where they got drunken alcohol problems, they got nothing to do all day besides sitting around and do what they want to do. And they keep giv-ing 'em money to do it, well how do you expect to get anything out of any-body? There's an old saying: A hungry dog hunts harder. Hey, you keep feeding a dog or a cat, they're not gonna hunt, they're not gonna look for food, they're gonna lay around and get fat.

If I said these comments in a classroom, I would expect to get accused of racism. But for Ron, this was about hard work and deservingness. To call this just plain racism misses the complexity of the sentiments involved here.

In chapters 6 and 7, I will dive further into the role of race in the work of rural consciousness.

Conclusion

"Rural consciousness" is the term I am using to describe a strong sense of identity as a rural person combined with a strong sense that rural areas are the victims of injustice: the sense that rural areas do not get their fair share of power, respect, or resources and that rural folks prefer lifestyles that differ fundamentally from those of city people. I have claimed at various moments in this chapter that this perspective is important for the way people make sense of public affairs. In chapters 5–7, I will show more specifically what I mean.

When I argue that rural consciousness structures the way people understand politics, I am suggesting that something other than partisanship is driving their political preferences. Support for the Republican Party is not what causes people to have these complex, intertwined understandings of economic injustice, place identity, class identity, race, and values. And the complexities of this understanding do not inevitably lead to support for the Republican Party. You may have noticed that some of these rural groups contain a good number of Democrats. In fact, the northwestern and southwestern corners of Wisconsin, although predominantly rural, lean Democratic. Booth Fowler, one of the wisest scholars of politics in Wisconsin, reasons that this is due in part to high levels of poverty in those areas, the influence of the city of Superior and of Great Lake shipping unions in the northwest corner, and the effect of commuters or out-migrants from Madison in the southwest (Fowler 2008). Whatever the reason, it is clear that the correlation between where people live and how they vote are not set in stone. They are the product of people actively trying to make sense of their lives.

In the following chapter, I take a pause from these conversations to consider whether the claims I heard in rural areas about their towns being the victims of injustice were legitimate. When people tried to make sense of their lives, were their understandings of where tax dollars go, tax rates, and relative wealth accurate? And, if not, where do these perceptions come from?

CHAPTER FOUR

The Context of Rural Consciousness

In the rest of this book, I want to demonstrate how rural consciousness plays out in terms of interpreting politics, how it helps structure support for small government, and how it influences interpretations of specific political actors and events. But before I go there, I know many readers will be wondering whether this thing I am calling rural consciousness is justified—that is, whether it reflects real or simply perceived disparities in government resources, concern, and attention.

I know this because when I describe complaints of injustice among small-town residents to urban audiences, I am almost always asked whether it is *actually* the case, for example, that rural areas get fewer public dollars than urban areas do. In the conversations I observed in rural Wisconsin, many people thought they were getting the short end of the stick with respect to taxpayer dollars. But was that really the case?

Taxes and Spending by the Numbers

The evidence is mixed. In Wisconsin, rural counties do receive fewer public dollars than urban counties. In the aggregate, measures of both state and federal government expenditures at the county level in fiscal year 2010 show that more than 75 percent of this money went to counties with urban metropolitan communities (fig. 4.1).

However, there are far fewer people living in rural counties than urban ones, so a more apt comparison might be one that uses a per capita basis for comparison. Figures 4.2 and 4.3 show two correlation plots, with each dot representing a single county in Wisconsin. This pair of figures shows almost no relationship between how rural a county is and the

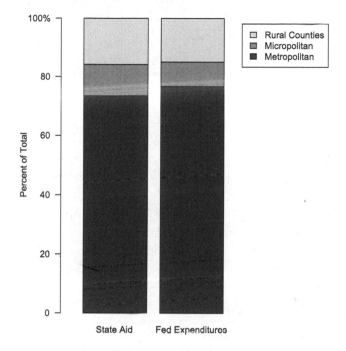

FIGURE 4.1. Aggregate distribution of state and federal government spending by type of county in Wisconsin. Sources: U.S. Census Bureau, "Principal Cities of Metropolitan and Micropolitan Statistical Areas," February 2013, (http://www.census.gov/population/ metro/data/def.html); Wisconsin Department of Revenue, "State Taxes and Aids by Municipality and County for Calendar Year 2010," November 2011 (http://www.revenue.wi .gov/ra/10StateTaxesAndAidsByMuniCo.pdf), U.S. Census Bureau, "Consolidated Federal Funds Report for Fiscal Year 2010," September 2011 (http://www.census.gov/prod/ 2011pubs/cffr-10.pdf).

dollars it receives in expenditures per capita from the state and federal government.[1] Excluding outliers, a slight upward trend is evident, with more rural counties receiving slightly more dollars per person; however, the relationship is weak.[2] But the evidence certainly does not support the notion that urban counties receive far more than their share of tax dollars per resident.

Do rural counties pay more on average into the system? Here the evidence is fairly conclusively the reverse. When we plot the average amount of tax revenue paid per capita in each county by how rural the county is, a steep inverse relationship is evident, with rural residents paying, on average, less per person into both the state (fig. 4.4) and federal (fig. 4.5) government coffers than their urban counterparts.[3]

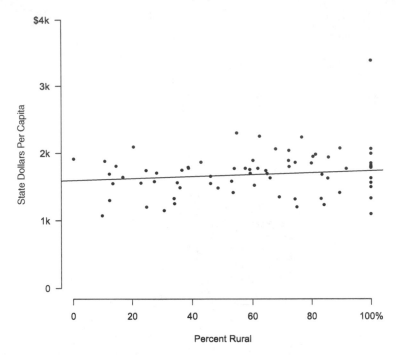

FIGURE 4.2. Wisconsin counties by percentage rural plotted against state aid per capita. Sources: U.S. Census Bureau, "Percent urban and rural in 2010 by state and county" (see under "Lists of Population, Land Area, and Percent Urban and Rural in 2010 and Changes from 2000 to 2010" at http://www.census.gov/geo/reference/ua/urban-rural -2010.html); Wisconsin Department of Revenue, "State Taxes and Aids by Municipality and County for Calendar Year 2010," November 2011 (http://www.revenue.wi.gov/ra/ 10StateTaxesAndAidsByMuniCo.pdf).

Indeed, combining these two sets of data, it is possible to calculate what might be called an average "return on taxes paid" by residents of each county in order to evaluate whether rural residents get more or less than their "fair share" back from what they put in. Figures 4.6 and 4.7 are another pair of scatter plots showing the relationship between how rural a district is and what kind of "return" the residents receive, on average, from the state and federal government.

Evaluating the fairness of tax policy with respect to rural counties is ultimately an artificial comparison. Residents in different counties, after all, have different needs and different capacities to pay for government services. Rural residents who feel the government is less responsive to the needs of their communities may be accounting for these differences

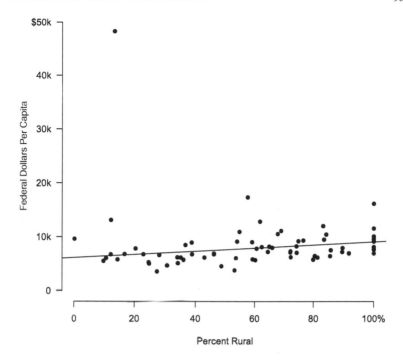

FIGURE 4.3. Wisconsin counties by percentage rural plotted against federal expenditures per capita. Sources: U.S. Census Bureau, "Percent urban and rural in 2010 by state and county" (see under "Lists of Population, Land Area, and Percent Urban and Rural in 2010 and Changes from 2000 to 2010" at http://www.census.gov/geo/reference/ua/urban-rural -2010.html); U.S. Census Bureau, "Consolidated Federal Funds Report for Fiscal Year 2010," September 2011 (http://www.census.gov/prod/2011pubs/cffr-10.pdf).

in need and ability. And sure enough, although rural counties in the ag-gregate may pay somewhat less in taxes per person and receive approxi-mately similar amounts of money in return, they also tend to experience greater levels of poverty, lower wages, and modestly higher rates of un-employment. These three measures are plotted in figures 4.8–4.10.

What the Numbers May Not Reveal

While this evidence does not back up the perceptions I heard among many rural residents that there is vastly disproporationate spending in urban counties and higher tax burdens falling on rural communities, many would also be quick to point out that what these numbers do not

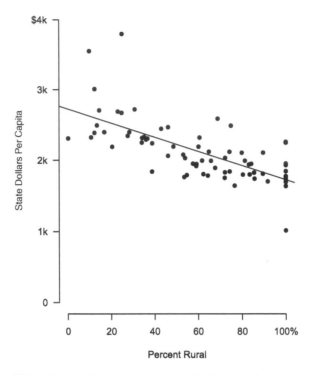

FIGURE 4.4. Wisconsin counties by percentage rural plotted against state tax revenue per capita. Source: U.S. Census Bureau, "Percent urban and rural in 2010 by state and county" (see under "Lists of Population, Land Area, and Percent Urban and Rural in 2010 and Changes from 2000 to 2010" at http://www.census.gov/geo/reference/ua/urban-rural-2010.html); Wisconsin Department of Revenue, "State Taxes and Aids by Municipality and County for Calendar Year 2010," November 2011 (http://www.revenue.wi.gov/ra/10StateTaxesAndAidsByMuniCo.pdf).

reveal is how effectively the money was spent. Even if the spending were proportionate across type of place, if the spending failed to meet the needs of people living there, it really would not matter. Some services simply cost less per capita in cities because of economies of scale.[4]

But even though these figures do not clearly support the idea that rural areas are receiving a lesser share of public resources, there are many ways in which people living outside major metro centers might perceive that they are on the short end of the stick these days. Rural places have been experiencing a long, slow death for decades (Davidson 1996) and perhaps have always been struggling (Macgregor 2010). More specifically, rural economies are fighting a losing battle. Driving through most small towns reveals main streets pocked with abandoned storefronts.

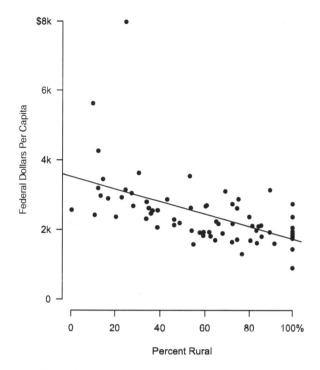

FIGURE 4.5. Wisconsin counties by percentage rural plotted against federal tax revenue per capita. Sources: U.S. Census Bureau, "Percent urban and rural in 2010 by state and county" (see under "Lists of Population, Land Area, and Percent Urban and Rural in 2010 and Changes from 2000 to 2010" at http://www.census.gov/geo/reference/ua/urban-rural-2010.html); "Total Tax Liability" for Wisconsin at Internal Revenue Service, "SOI Tax Stats—County Data—2011" (http://www.irs.gov/uac/SOI-Tax-Stats-County-Data-2011).

Local ownership is a thing of the past, and that loss strikes at the heart of small-town life (Macgregor 2010; but see Varghese et al. [2006] on the complex nature between local ownership and community prosperity).

Also contributing to this decline of local business is what some have called the farm crisis. Osha Gray Davidson, in a 1996 book called *Broken Heartland: The Rise of America's Rural Ghetto*, argues that agricultural policy in the United States has created an uphill battle for farm owners since the beginning of the nation. In his view, farm debt has always been a problem. Although the Homestead Act of 1862 was designed to give land to settlers, by 1900, only one in six of the acres intended for allocation had been given to individual farm owners.

In more recent history, the post–World War II boom and then subsequent bust were perhaps magnified in rural America. In the 1970s, farms

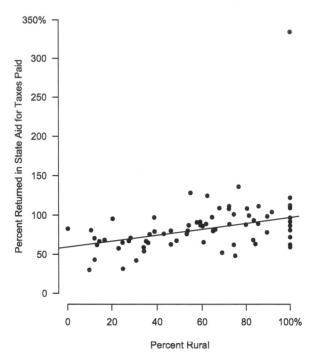

FIGURE 4.6. Wisconsin counties by percentage rural plotted against percentage returned for taxes paid (state). Sources: U.S. Census Bureau, "Percent urban and rural in 2010 by state and county" (see under "Lists of Population, Land Area, and Percent Urban and Rural in 2010 and Changes from 2000 to 2010" at http://www.census.gov/geo/reference/ua/urban-rural-2010.html); Wisconsin Department of Revenue, "State Taxes and Aids by Municipality and County for Calendar Year 2010," November 2011 (http://www.revenue.wi.gov/ra/10StateTaxesAndAidsByMuniCo.pdf).

were prosperous and seemingly invincible. As inflation rose, so did farmland values, which farmers borrowed against in spades. But other countries started producing and exporting, and soon the markets were overflowing with grain, Davidson explains. Farmers started producing more to try to make up for lost profits. The result was an even greater glut in product, pushing prices even lower. In 1979, farms felt a double whammy: the Federal Reserve raised interest rates in 1979, and land values started to fall. The farm crisis was underway. One astounding figure that Davidson presents is that between 1981 and 1983, the average net farm income in Iowa fell from $17,680 to –$1,891 (1996, 17). Those of us old enough to remember the Farm Aid Concert of 1986 are reminded that things have been tough for rural economies for at least several de-

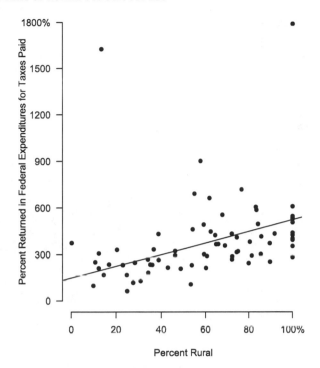

FIGURE 4.7. Wisconsin counties by percentage rural plotted against percentage returned for taxes paid (federal). Sources: U.S. Census Bureau, "Percent urban and rural in 2010 by state and county" (see under "Lists of Population, Land Area, and Percent Urban and Rural in 2010 and Changes from 2000 to 2010" at http://www.census.gov/geo/reference/ua/urban rural 2010.html); "Total Tax Liability" for Wisconsin at Internal Revenue Service, "SOI Tax Stats—County Data—2011" (http://www.irs.gov/uac/SOI-Tax-Stats-County -Data-2011), U.S. Census Bureau, "Consolidated Federal Funds Report for Fiscal Year 2010," September 2011 (http://www.census.gov/prod/2011pubs/cffr-10.pdf).

cades, particularly for those places in which many people are employed in agriculture (Johnson et al. 1995).

Some of the loss that rural places are feeling is due to the new global economy, but some of it can be blamed on the structure of government, too. Relationships between local, state, and federal governments have changed a great deal since the late 1970s, and these changes have exacerbated the economic challenges rural areas face. Devolution since the late 1970s means that local governments have been increasingly left to their own sources of revenue to provide services. Many of these services are unfunded but mandated by higher-level governments (Johnson et al.

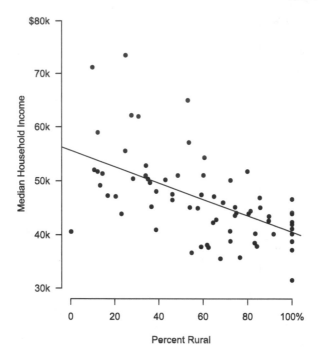

FIGURE 4.8. Wisconsin counties by percentage rural plotted against median household income. Sources: U.S. Census Bureau, "Percent urban and rural in 2010 by state and county" (see under "Lists of Population, Land Area, and Percent Urban and Rural in 2010 and Changes from 2000 to 2010" at http://www.census.gov/geo/reference/ua/urban-rural-2010 .html); U.S. Census Bureau, "Small Area Income and Poverty Estimates," last revised April 29, 2013 (http://www.census.gov/did/www/saipe/data/statecounty/data/2010.html).

1995). Also, local governments now have a greater reliance on state aid (Dewees Lobao, and Swanson 2003, 184).

Rural places are facing all of these demands as they attempt to protect themselves from the changing macro environment. Their tools for doing so are limited. Some scholars call the difficult economic position rural counties find themselves in "rural disadvantage" (Lobao and Kraybill 2005). Specifically, rural communities have smaller tax bases to dip into and are therefore less able than more populous places to raise funds. At the same time, they face higher costs when attempting to provide services due to economies of scale (Reeder and Jansen 1995, cited in Johnson et al. 1995, 386; Dewees et al. 2003, 184). For example, providing broadband service is a more daunting task in a sparsely populated community than it is in a dense urban one (Gillett, Lehr, and Osorio 2004).

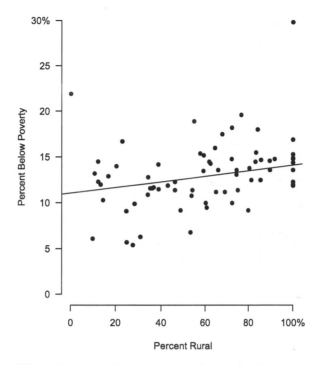

FIGURE 4.9. Wisconsin counties by percentage rural plotted against percentage below poverty line. Sources: U.S. Census Bureau, "Percent urban and rural in 2010 by state and county" (see under "Lists of Population, Land Area, and Percent Urban and Rural in 2010 and Changes from 2000 to 2010" at http://www.census.gov/geo/reference/ua/urban-rural -2010.html); U.S. Census Bureau, "Small Area Income and Poverty Estimates," last re-vised April 29, 2013 (http://www.census.gov/did/www/saipc/data/statecounty/data/2010 .html).

Providing K–12 public education is also difficult for rural municipalities. In 2003–4, one-third of public schools in the United States were in ru-ral places, but these schools served only one-fifth of the public school students that year (Provasnik et al. 2007). Also, local officials as well as staff members in rural governments tend to be less experienced and professional than their urban counterparts, making it harder for them to take advantage of economic opportunities such as grants and tax abate-ments (Dewees et al. 2003, 185–86). In addition, poverty rates tend to be higher in rural areas (Milbourne 2004, 75–78; Weber et al. 2005; USDA Economic Research Service 2015), particularly in the southern states (Milbourne 2004, 79).[5] Education levels tend to be lower as well (Provas-nik et al. 2007; Byun, Meece, and Irvin 2012).

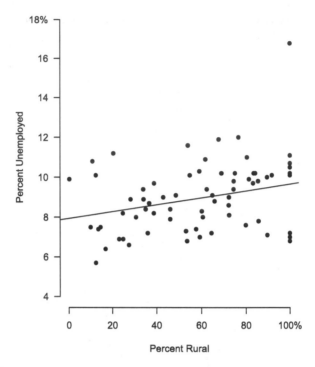

FIGURE 4.10. Wisconsin counties by percentage rural plotted against unemployment rate. Sources: U.S. Census Bureau, "Percent urban and rural in 2010 by state and county" (see under "Lists of Population, Land Area, and Percent Urban and Rural in 2010 and Changes from 2000 to 2010" at http://www.census.gov/geo/reference/ua/urban-rural-2010.html); U.S. Bureau of Labor Statistics, "Local Area Unemployment Statistics" (http://www.bls .gov/lau/#cntyaa).

In this context, rural communities can pursue one of several less-than-ideal development strategies, if they muster the resources to pursue development at all (Dewees et al. 2003; Lobao and Kraybill 2005). Lawson, Jarosz, and Bonds (2010), looking particularly at the American Northwest, note that changes in the nature of relationships and responsibilities across levels of government are taking place as the economy in that part of the country shifts from "extractive resource and agrarian economies toward tourism, services, and retailing" (663). The result is that rural counties have been treated either as "playgrounds" (tourism havens), dumping grounds (places with relaxed environmental and other regulations in order to attract investment, even undesirable development), or unseen grounds (areas that receive little attention from politicians or economic investment). Although the Lawson et al. study was specific to the Northwest, Lobao and Kraybill's analysis of a 2001 national survey of county governments found that "remote" counties, or nonmetro counties not adjacent to metro counties, were more likely to pursue "fiscally less sustainable business attraction activities" (2005, 252).

Many rural Wisconsin communities have focused on tourism to try to keep their local economies afloat. But the concerns that I heard about tourist economies were not imagined. Counties that have a large tourism or recreation industry are often seen as wealthier because of the revenue they bring in. However, Johnson et al. (1995) note that tourist counties have higher infrastructure costs for things like more highways and larger sewage and water systems, and more police officers, firefighters, and paramedics than would a nonrecreational county of the same size. At the same time, their revenue stream is precarious because of the reliance of tourism on weather (390).

Rural life is sometimes romanticized as less expensive than urban living and therefore less susceptible to a bad economy. But some argue that it is not actually cheaper to live in rural areas (Zimmerman, Ham, and Frank 2008). As the conversations presented in this study illustrate, one big expense rural residents face is gas. And this is not merely a perception: members of rural households drive 38 percent more miles on a daily basis. Rural poor drive 59 percent more than urban poor (Zimmerman et al. 2008, 465–66, citing Pucher and Renne 2004). Food prices also tend to be higher, and there is evidence that mortgage rates, electricity prices, and health care premiums are higher as well (Zimmerman et al. 2008, 467–68). These are just some of the differences in the costs of living. There are other costs as well: maintaining a septic system, for example (468).

One might argue that there is a pervasive work ethic in rural areas or a fighting American spirit that is preventing the death of these communities and helping them evolve into something new (Wuthnow 2013). That may be the case in some places, but it is not the broader trend that I have seen. First of all, when communities change their local economy and community identity, even if to attract development attention from urban areas, that is a kind of loss for many long-time residents. Also, there is a troubling brain drain, in which the best and brightest youth in rural communities tend to emigrate to urban areas after high school (Domina 2006; Carr and Kefalas 2009).

This brain drain impinges on community vitality in a variety of ways, not least of which is the effect on the local schools. As the average age of rural residents becomes older, the need for local public schools dwindles, and schools consolidate. This means the loss of a very important source of community identity.

As communities lose members, they must continue to provide many services with revenue from an even smaller tax base (Johnson et al. 1995, 382–83, citing Reeder 1985). School aid from higher levels of government to the local level has changed since the 1970s toward more population- or pupil-based allocations, further disadvantaging nonmetro areas (Johnson et al. 1995, 384).

Politically, rural areas have also experienced a loss in terms of representation. In 1962 the U.S. Supreme Court decided a case called *Baker v. Carr*, which mandated that representation to state legislatures as well as to Congress would be apportioned according to population, not geographic surface area ("one person, one vote"). The result was fewer representatives from rural areas, and more from urban, which has led to less attention to rural areas in resource allocation than before this reapportionment (Ansolabehere and Snyder 2008).[6] In Wisconsin, state legislative seats have been apportioned by population since 1954 (Epstein 1958, 27).

The perception that all the wealth in Wisconsin is in the cities, and that this is at least in part the fault of government, can be traced back decades, if not centuries. The northern third of the state that is often referred to as "up north" (at least by those in the southern part of the state) is also known to some as "the cutover." In the early twentieth century, the intrusion of European settlers made it increasingly difficult for Native Americans to continue living off the land.[7] The tribal leaders agreed to a series of treaties in the late nineteenth century that essentially removed Native Americans from the region and forced them to live in several discrete areas. This made it possible for commercial lumber barons to clear much of northern Wisconsin of its forests—hence, "the cutover," that is, timberland cleared of trees. White settlers moved into this environment and attempted to farm it and were encouraged to do so by business and political interests eager to find a new economic basis for these former logging communities.

It was clear several decades later, though, that the soil, short growing season, and lack of planning were not going to make it possible to have an agricultural economy in northern Wisconsin. In response, the government tried to reshape northern Wisconsin's economy into one dependent on forestry and tourism.

In my fieldwork, I did not hear comments about the failed policies of that era, but its history helps explain the pervasive sentiment that the economy in northern Wisconsin is a fragile one. It also illuminates the perception that "the government," for a long time, has at best failed to solve and at worst exacerbated the dire economy in Wisconsin's North-woods. People commonly interpret even the government programs of the New Deal as a mixed blessing. They helped many people in the cutover region stay out of poverty, but they also brought in some aspects of "the outside world and its more strictly commercial economy" that made it hard to maintain family farms (Gough 1997, 191).

Based on this history, it seems to me that the sense of loss that of-ten hangs in the air—which is also present in the way people in northern Wisconsin describe their communities—has been there for generations. When farming dwindled in the cutover region in the first few decades of the twentieth century, many young people left their hometowns. Robert Gough estimates that "by the 1930s in the cutover perhaps only about one child in four remained as an adult near where he or she had grown up" (1997, 212).

The promotion of tourism has been a blessing to many communities in that region because it has provided jobs, but it has also been a curse. The rise of tourism brought the relative wealth of vacationing urban-ites into the plain view of rural residents. Some historians recount the resentment rural residents felt toward "'messy' tourists who seemed to chain them to businesses—motels, fishing boats, roadside attractions—with high rates of failure."[8] It has also meant increased property values as more and more urban residents have bought vacation or retirement homes in Wisconsin's picturesque Northwoods. While rising property values can be a plus for many homeowners, the rise in property taxes that goes along with that has made it increasingly difficult for many to stay in their homes.

Another important change in the rural Midwest is the influx of La-tino immigrants. At the same time that many rural communities are ex-periencing a loss of young white adults, the Hispanic population is grow-ing, and as a 2004 U.S. Department of Agriculture (USDA) report put it, it is "now the most rapidly growing demographic group in rural and small-town America," especially in the South and Midwest (Kandel and Cromartie 2004). Since Native Americas were forced from their geo-graphic homes, rural communities in the Midwest have been almost completely white, except for a small population of African American farmers (e.g., Cooper 1994; Vincent 1999), and Native American reservations. Because of this, the arrival of Latino immigrants has meant a challenge to many communities' long-term racial identity and is a local reminder that that demographics of the country are changing.

Most of the rural people I listened to while doing the research for this book were older folks, and it may be that espousing a view that your community is "falling apart" is something that older people just tend to do. Maybe Midwestern rural communities have had this view for a long time (see Varenne 1977, 92). Possibly. But it seems to me that something important and distressing is happening in rural America in recent years, and this something is not just one aspect of life changing but is instead a confluence of many things that is contributing to rural residents' perception that their way of life is under attack.

This is not to say that urban and even suburban areas are free of challenges. Obviously, they are facing serious economic challenges. The Great Recession and the rising economic inequality I referred to at the beginning of this book have affected most places in the United States. In fact, economic inequality is not as great and has not increased as much in rural areas as it has in urban areas.[9] However, the many difficulties rural places and rural residents face in the contemporary economy make perceptions of injustice understandable. In addition, when wealthy urban tourists visit economically challenged rural areas, the contrast in standard of living is often rather blatant to the local residents. For example, the locals know that it is not their year-round neighbors who are buying the $200 bottles of champagne in the grocery store. Whether rural areas are objectively worse off than other places is not, at root, the issue. Instead, for the politics of resentment, what matters is that many rural residents perceive that rural communities are the victims of economic injustice.

Measuring Perceptions of Unfairness

Regardless of the empirical evidence, the rural residents I spent time with were sure that rural areas were worse off. And survey evidence suggests that these perceptions are widespread among rural residents in Wisconsin. In late June and early July of 2011, the University of Wisconsin Survey Center and I fielded a statewide opinion poll of voting-age adults in which we asked a variety of questions that measured different aspects of rural consciousness. We asked respondents: "How much attention do you feel the state government in Wisconsin pays to what the people in your community think when it decides what to do: none at all, only a small amount of attention, a moderate amount of attention, a large amount of attention, or a very large amount of attention?" A majority—56 percent of all respondents (including those who said they "don't know" and those who refused)—said they thought that the amount of attention the government pays to their community was "none at all" or "only a small amount." In other words, many people felt government ignores their community. However, this was especially true of rural folks: 70 percent of them said government represents their community only a small amount or not at all (by way of comparison, 52 percent of urban and 47 percent of suburban respondents said this).[10]

In that poll, we also asked Wisconsinites whether the state government represents their community's values.[11] Rural as well as urban respondents were less likely than suburban respondents to think state government represented their community in this way.[12] This perception among urbanites may have been due in part to partisanship. The urban centers are strongly Democratic, but at the time of the survey, the governor and both state legislative chambers were majority Republican. But urban centers in Wisconsin have been demonized by politicians in the state for decades.[13] Notice, though, how remarkable it is that rural respondents, despite being predominantly Republican, also felt government did not represent their community's values.

We asked about rural consciousness in one other respect as well—resources. Once again, rural residents expressed a sense of disconnect. We asked: "How well does the state of Wisconsin do in distributing government resources equally across rural, urban and suburban areas of the state: not at all, only a little, somewhat, very well, or extremely well?" We then asked: "Are rural areas of Wisconsin given much more than their fair share, somewhat more, somewhat less, much less than their fair share, or about their fair share?" The same question was repeated about urban and suburban areas.

The answers show that rural folks have particularly strong perceptions of not getting their fair share. A startling percentage of them felt that their type of place was not getting its fair share. Just 16 percent of suburban and 25 percent of urban respondents felt rural areas received "much less" or "somewhat less" than their fair share. But 69 percent of rural respondents felt rural areas received much less or somewhat less than their fair share.

Where Does Rural Consciousness Come From?

Where does rural consciousness come from? Where do people get these identities that encapsulate so many fundamental sentiments, particularly if the sense of injustice that people express is not clearly supported by hard data on the distribution of tax dollars and by income and poverty figures? A logical source is mass media. Maybe the messages people in rural places receive about urban places and about the allocation of goods in their state suggest that they are the victims of distributive injustice.

To investigate, a graduate student researcher, David Lassen, a team of undergraduate coders, and I engaged in an extensive search for such perceptions in local newspapers. But we found little evidence that news media are the source of rural consciousness. We focused on local newspapers because that was the source of local news for which we could gather content data. Many of the people I talked with reported that a main source of news is radio, especially Wisconsin Public Radio, but transcripts of such broadcasts were unavailable. We were confident, though, that the content of newspapers was a reliable indicator of the local news environment since previous research has shown that other news sources tend to follow the general contours of newspaper coverage (McChesney and Nichols 2010).

We sampled thirteen daily newspapers in addition to the printed dailies in Madison and Milwaukee (the *Wisconsin State Journal* and the *Milwaukee Journal Sentinel*, respectively). We also analyzed content in a popular weekly in northern Wisconsin, the *Lakeland Times*.[14] We collected articles from each source that specifically referenced a state-level political actor (people holding or running for statewide elective office as well as those holding an appointed/hired position with a state government organization or agency). We focused on state government since in the conversations I observed, people used rural consciousness most clearly when talking about state politics. We coded all articles related to state politics published in the *Milwaukee Journal Sentinel* and the *La Crosse Tribune* from 2007 to 2011, in the *Wisconsin State Journal* between 2008 and 2011, and in the other papers in 2008 and 2009, as well as in 2010 and 2011 for several of them. These years coincide with my fieldwork period. In all, we analyzed 1,218 articles, which included over 3,551 mentions of different government actors (which included local, county, and federal actors as well as state actors and state public officials from other states).[15]

We looked for whether papers outside the Madison and Milwaukee metro areas talked about the distribution of resources more than the Madison and Milwaukee papers did. We found no evidence of this. If anything, the Madison and Milwaukee papers talked about these issues more, including the possibility that rural areas do not get their fair share.

We also looked for differences in the values these news articles emphasized. For example, we wanted to know if there was a regional difference in how much the papers emphasized hard work. (We analyzed what the journalists said as well as the people they quoted.) But we found very few articles that mentioned values like hard work and frugality, as well as values with a more direct relevance to politics like a desire to give citizens more power in policy decisions. Just 152 of the 1,218 articles we coded clearly mentioned any value at all. There were no discernible regional differences in whether articles mentioned values or in what types of values they mentioned.

We did, however, find some slight differences in the tone that articles expressed toward state government actors. We coded whether the article discussed a state government actor using a negative, positive, mixed, or neutral or unclear tone. We considered coverage negative if the majority of the article's discussion of a given actor was negative or critical, no matter the criticism's origin.[16] We expected papers outside the major metro areas to be more critical of state actors. But we found that papers outside census-designated metro counties were actually slightly more positive toward state actors.[17]

Another small difference was that Madison and Milwaukee papers were slightly less likely than the outstate papers to cover economic issues (e.g., taxes, government budgets, government spending, and the recession).[18]

In general, we did not find large differences across daily papers in the state in the way they discussed state politics or rural-versus-urban tensions. There are a variety of likely explanations for this. First, many of these "local" newspapers are not all that local. For example, the *Green Bay Gazette* is the local daily paper for many small towns in northeastern Wisconsin, and yet it is generated in what people in those places see as a relatively large city—Green Bay. There are very few daily papers in the state that are published in Census "noncore" counties, or even in micropolitan (i.e., an urban area with a population of at least ten thousand but less than fifty thousand) as opposed to metropolitan counties. Also, many of these papers are published by the same company, Gannett, and use the same pool of reporters, not reporters located in a specific community.

Taking into account other aspects of the way the news is made also suggests that it should not be surprising that the values, tone, and topics covered in the less populous places in the state are not all that different from those expressed in the news in the major metropolitan areas. The content of news media is a function of the need for media to make a profit and thus create content in the most efficient way possible. The result is that journalists and government officials exist in a kind of symbiosis (Cook 1998) or at least collaboration (Schudson 2002, 2003). This means that journalists get most of their information from official sources (Fishman 1980, cited in Schudson 2002, 255), and most of the sources quoted in stories are government officials (Sigal 1973; Tuchman 1978; Bennett 1989; Corbett 1995). In this view, the content of the news is not a function of local perspectives but of sophisticated government public relations apparatuses.

Also, even though news media outwardly claim to serve as a check on power (e.g., the critical coverage detailed in Patterson 1993), in practice they rely on the official line (Herman and Chomsky 1988). Because representation in the state government is allocated according to population (Ansolabehere and Snyder 2008), the balance of power in Wisconsin is arguably located in the major metropolitan areas. If journalists and news organizations rely heavily on public officials, then we should not expect them to call this balance of power into question in any strident way, regardless of where in the state the news is being produced.

There are different ways to view how news gets produced, of course, but even sociological perspectives of news making (rather than economic ones) point toward more homogeneity across newspapers than toward difference. Most journalists are motivated by a desire for professional prestige. Obtaining that requires covering the news in an objective and efficient manner (Weaver and Wilhoit 1996). Relying on official sources is a way to achieve what is widely regarded as objectivity (Bennett 2011). That reliance is likely to result in similarity in coverage across the state.

A sociological perspective might suggest some slight difference by region. It is possible that journalists' attempt to cover news in a way that is both accessible and meaningful for their audiences would lead to differences between the major cities dailies and the others. Also, there is some evidence that journalists at less prominent organizations are more conservative (Weaver and Wilhoit 1996), again suggesting some differences across regions. It is also possible that regardless of reporters' backgrounds, coverage might differ depending on the cultural milieu in which it is created (Corbett 1995, 401). But our analysis suggested that none of these are a strong counterforce to the processes producing homogeneity in coverage of state issues.[19]

What does the lack of rural consciousness in daily papers circulated to rural communities say about rural consciousness and where it comes from? It may simply be the case that our coding process was not sophisticated enough to pick up differences across newspapers. Also, we did not analyze the content of agricultural newspapers and magazines. Or maybe rural consciousness is just less prominent than the conversations I observed suggests. However, the survey data earlier in this chapter make that conclusion unlikely.

Another explanation for the null results is that the lack of a rural consciousness perspective in the daily news actually reinforces what many people in rural areas told me: that their communities are overlooked, ignored, and misunderstood by urbanites. In the conversations that exhibited rural consciousness, people talked about "the news media" as yet another institution that is out of touch with ordinary rural Wisconsinites. Perhaps most journalists are trained to report from an urban perspective and write in a way that resonates with a broader journalism community, rather than with the rural communities to which the papers are circulated. With that in mind, we should not expect to see a reflection of rural consciousness in newspapers, except perhaps in the most irreverent rural publication, the *Lakeland Times*.[20] However, among the few significant differences we found was evidence that the *Lakeland Times* and the two other nonmetro papers were more positive toward state actors than the other papers.

Maybe the important lesson here is the possibility that some aspects of public opinion are not directly absorbed from mass media but, rather, are cultivated through good old-fashioned face-to-face socialization. Scholarship on media effects has evolved to teach us that media audiences are not passive receptors but are instead active processors who interpret media messages through their own lenses and biases.[21] If local newspapers are not covering issues relevant to rural residents, the effect of that content on rural residents may not be to cause their views to become more similar to that of urban residents overtime. Instead, it could reinforce rural folks' perception that rural communities like their own are ignored.

In other words, it is likely that rural consciousness exists not because it is communicated via news media but because we teach these things to each other. News media content did not reflect rural consciousness, but my fieldwork and the survey data certainly did. That is cause for concern for public opinion scholars. We often use news content as an indicator of public opinion, especially historically, when survey data from the past are not available (Herbst 1998). We would do well to acknowledge that sometimes there is no substitute for sitting down with people and listening to their perspectives in order to measure what those perspectives are.[22]

Conclusion

Suburbanites or urbanites might be surprised to have read here that rural citizens believe they face tougher lives than people living in cities. Those holding such beliefs might be perceived as being wrong, misinformed, or both. What I have tried to convey in this chapter is that there are solid and understandable empirical reasons that rural folks might think that they are the victims of distributive injustice. Furthermore, it appears that they are not sold these perceptions through local media but, instead, make these interpretations with each other in the course of their daily rural lives.

I do not mean, however, to privilege these interpretations over those of urban and suburban folks. Though I am drawing attention to the views of rural residents in this book, it is not my intention to claim that they are any more right or righteous than are people who live in more urban areas. My intention is to listen to and draw attention to these perceptions in order to better understand the political choices that they bring about.

CHAPTER FIVE

Attitudes toward Public Institutions and Public Employees

I want to spend some time demonstrating what attitudes toward public institutions and public employees looked like through the lens of rural consciousness. Often, when I was in rural areas, conversations about public institutions and employees would be rooted in a sense that rural areas are on the short end of the stick with respect to power, resources, and respect. One public institution and set of public employees I heard a lot about was the University of Wisconsin–Madison and the people who work there because I was specifically asking about UW–Madison. But I heard a lot about public institutions and employees generally. In this chapter I highlight conversations about the university and other public institutions. The conversations show how the lens of rural consciousness has structured the way many people think about government and government employees.

"Hi! I'm from the UW–Madison. . . ."

Doing research for this book was possible, in part, because administrators at the UW–Madison wanted me to probe attitudes about the university while I was visiting different communities across Wisconsin.[1] They gave me a research grant and approved my sabbatical time during the first year of this project on the condition that while I was out and about in the state, I ask about attitudes toward the university. So at some point in most of these conversations, I worked in three questions about UW–

Madison: What do we do well? What do we do not so well? And what should we be doing in your community?

My presence alone, though, brought the university into the conversations. The first thing I usually said to these groups, especially during my first visits in 2007 and 2008, was, "Hi! I'm Kathy. I'm from the UW–Madison." So I want to acknowledge up front that it is likely that these groups would not have talked about the university and higher education as much if I hadn't inserted myself into their conversations. But my focus was not how much they talked about the university or other aspects of government, but how they made sense of it when they did so. Their conversations about UW–Madison provide a window to their attitudes about government and public employees more generally.

The University of Wisconsin–Madison is the flagship school of the University of Wisconsin System. This is a *big* public university system. There are thirteen four-year institutions and thirteen two-year colleges in it, scattered throughout the state. In addition, the system includes a vast and historic extension system. Each of the seventy-two counties have a University of Wisconsin Cooperative Extension office, and the educators that work in them provide a variety of popular services, from agricultural outreach to 4-H clubs to master gardening classes. These educators (formerly "extension agents") are often pretty immersed in the communities they serve. Many residents know them by name if not also by appearance.

The people I encountered during these visits around Wisconsin had a lot to say about UW–Madison, and many of those comments were quite positive. Residents of Wisconsin are very proud of UW–Madison and of the UW System in general.[2] Over 260,000 state residents enroll in these colleges and universities in a given year.[3] And Bucky Badger is everywhere. If you are not from Wisconsin, I am guessing you nevertheless know whom I am talking about. Bucky is the UW–Madison's mascot, one of the most beloved members of the weasel family on earth. It wasn't unusual for me to show up at a gas station or diner to do fieldwork and find at least one person wearing some kind of Wisconsin Badger gear. This was not for my benefit—those folks did not even know I would be showing up that day.

Many Wisconsinites are rabid Badger fans. In fact, when I asked my "what-do-we-do-well" question, the most popular response was Badger sports of some sort, particularly men's football, basketball, or hockey. People also love our marching band, a highlight of UW Badger sporting events. That was the second most common thing they mentioned when I asked, "What do we do well." I know that some readers will roll your eyes at the thought that sports is what people value the most about UW–Madison. But this enthusiasm is a powerful connection for many people—and for many people I spoke with, it was their only connection. About 141,000 residents of Wisconsin are UW–Madison alumni.[4] But there are over 5.6 million people in Wisconsin, and the vast majority have never set foot on the campus. One man, Tim, in the small community on the Wisconsin River said, "Really with the University of Wisconsin, our affiliation here is, all kidding aside, athletics. That's all we get" (Group 8, June 2007). There is a deep sense of ownership of the UW–Madison and the university system in Wisconsin, and it is cultivated in large part by Badger sports.

The people I spoke with loved other things about the university—the hospital, the extension system, research that had appeared in the news, and the university's overall reputation for providing a great education. But when I asked, "What do we do not so well?" there was no shortage of answers. I realized over time that what I was hearing was not just resentment toward the university but also resentment toward cities, government institutions, and public employees in general.

Distance from the University

Many rural residents perceived that their community was distant from the university, just as it was distant from a variety of powerful institutions and the government in general. The distance they talked about was not exclusively geographic but symbolic as well. They felt that UW–Madison did not really want rural students to attend. They also talked about its admissions and tuitions policies as completely out of touch with the financial reality of rural people. I found a wide variety of people expressing an attitude of ownership toward UW–Madison. They talked about it as their university, an institution that belonged to the people of their state. But they also wished it were more attentive to people like themselves—people who saw rural communities and rural kids as disadvantaged compared to suburban and urban kids in the state.

During my first visit to the tourist community in Door County (Group 5, June 2007), several people in the group were proud alumni and talked fondly of their time on the UW–Madison campus. But then I asked:

KJC: So here's the most important question about the UW. What do you think the UW should be doing here in [this town] or in Door County? And I leave that very broad, so in terms of doing for students, doing for residents, doing in general.

BECKY: They could probably do a better job of trying to recruit kids to the campus. I don't see—when you go through a list of graduates from say [a local high school], and you hear where they're going to school, you don't hear very many that are going to UW–Madison. There's a few that go to [UW–]Milwaukee and go to Marquette [University]. I think the private schools do a much better job of recruiting and getting students to their campuses. Then what—

KJC: OK so actually coming out here and saying—

BECKY: Yeah.

STEPHANIE: Recruiting to the rural areas—I don't think they do a big job of that.

PAUL: No they don't.

DON: They don't have to.

These folks, like many folks in rural places, perceived that the UW–Madison did not find it necessary to physically send someone out to their community to convey that "we want your kids in Madison." The "they don't have to" comment at the end of this conversation referred to the fact that UW–Madison has no shortage of applications every year, and this group realized that perhaps recruitment was not a necessity. But the perception that UW–Madison does not actively recruit in rural areas fed a perception that UW–Madison does not care about rural areas and does not really care if rural students attend.

Many of the parents I encountered in small towns hoped to send their kids to UW–Madison, but they had two main worries about that prospect. They worried about (1) their kids falling flat on their faces in such a big campus in the big city of Madison and (2) their kids not getting admitted or not being able to afford tuition, given the economic disadvantages they perceived themselves to have as rural folks.

With respect to the first worry, that young people from small towns in the state would fall on their faces in big Madison, here are some examples of that topic coming up in my conversations. The group of women meeting once a week for breakfast in the northwest tourist town put it this way (Group 2, June 2007):

KAREN: And when you are as far as we are living up here, one of the problems of the kids going to Madison is that they haven't had the experience of going away and getting this—they can't go to Madison. It's too far away. [*"Yes" from several others.*] Emotional adjustment. Far better that we send them to Superior or even Eau Claire [cities with other UW System schools] but Madison—we lose kids when we send them down there. They self-destruct because the change is too traumatic.

DIANA: They don't have the home support.

When I went back to this group in April 2008, I heard the same concern from Sally:

I worked for [a retail supplier] when I was in Madison, and I had a store on the [State Capitol] Square, and I heard a lot students, and one thing I noticed were young kids coming in from small towns seem to come to . . . they came in from small towns in Wisconsin and fell flat on their faces. They were either out of school in the semester or they had gone from planning on being premed or engineering to art, I mean, it was strikingly sad to see it, and I wondered what they really do for these freshmen coming in from—because they're coming in and meeting up with these foreign students who are *so* dedicated to learning, I think the freshmen get lost in that big a school. And I know that you can go to a smaller school, you can go to Superior and maybe work your way down [to Madison], but I think a lot of kids, the freshmen, are still . . . I had at least four young women that were valedictorians that actually were just *gone* before the end of the semester, and I wonder what the ratio is. . . .

An hour or so south of this community, in the northwestern logging town, the loggers also worried about students from their town having a hard time fitting in (Group 6, April 2008).

RON: Well, it's not [UW–Madison's] fault, but they're so big, so a student goes to a school . . . [Our town has] probably got three hundred kids, K–12, and they go to Madison, they could be pretty well lost, and most of them go to the other state, the small state schools . . .

It isn't actually the case that the students from rural communities who do attend UW–Madison fall on their faces. They have similar levels of success in their first years compared to students from more urban areas of the state (Huhn 2005). Nevertheless, the belief that small-town kids would not succeed there was common in the conversations I heard. It is possible that those attitudes may, in turn, have prevented many kids from rural areas from even applying to UW–Madison.[5]

People in small towns worried about their students making it once they got to Madison, but they also looked at UW–Madison as "distant" in terms of admissions and tuition. And those perceptions were rooted in their sense that rural folks were at a disadvantage.

The men in the dice game in the small town in central Wisconsin also talked about local kids being at a disadvantage (Group 11b). During my first visit, Mark told me that their district couldn't afford the college prep that the suburban schools could (May 2007).

> In fact the UW, your program will only take the top-end students, straight As, 3.8s maybe, I don't know. I don't know what the average ACT is—30, 28? Well, it's obviously having an impact here where they are cutting and cutting and cutting where we can't afford programs, so instead of having two or three foreign languages we're lucky if we have one. That in itself is a negative incentive to students to really excel and thrive. I mean, if you want to go to the UW in Madison, you gotta have AP [advanced placement] everything, gotta have three or four years minimum of a language, you're going to have four years of all the curricular or academic subjects, well if that's all that's offered, it certainly is an indication to the students that it can't be that important. And I think that's gotta—you're losing bright kids who aren't filling or meeting the academic criteria—a portion or a reason of it is that we don't have the money to do that, and that impacts negatively on what they think is important because the state is telling them that you aren't important.

People saw the lack of resources in their communities as an indicator of neglect. Many believed kids in their communities were at a disadvantage because their communities were not given the resources they deserved. They also perceived that people from their kind of community did not make enough money to afford an education at UW–Madison. Here is an example from one father in the group of loggers in northwest Wisconsin (Group 6, June 2007):

> SAM: I think one thing I think the UW can do is be a little less restrictive on in-state kids.

KJC: Yeah? Let more of them in you mean?

SAM: Like my oldest son Ben that is the helicopter pilot. Back then he coulda never got in to Madison and he's—those two kids [his two sons] are what the future of this country is. If they are not going to get in to a big university, then we are really losing out. Madison was so damn restrictive when Ben graduated, early nineties, he coulda never got in and he was towards the top of his class, top five anyhow, not a big class. Only twenty-two kids in his class. Pilot. He scored ninety-nine on his ASVAB or whatever you call it, that military test, but he couldn't have got into Madison. Makes sense that we are bringing kids in from India, but then telling Chris now you can't go to Madison. And he ended up going to Gogebic [Community College] in Michigan cause it was a two-year school and he could live at home and you know he didn't go in debt to go to school. [Gogebic is less than an hour from this town]. Matt's paying his way through the GI bill, and then Wisconsin had a—if you were in Iraq you had two years of free college. Iraq or Afghanistan. So I mean he's doing actually pretty darn good in college financially. Plus he has a full-time job, too.

KJC: And he's in the reserves?

SAM: And he's in the reserves.

KJC: Holy cow.

SAM: But he won't have much debt you know that's the other thing. Bankrupting the kids to go to college. Did you go to Madison?

KJC: I did yeah, I did as a kid.

SAM: Did you have to borrow tons and tons of money?

KJC: Yeah tuition was a lot cheaper then.[6] And still you know, Wisconsin compared to Minnesota is even cheaper, but still.

SAM: I listen to Minnesota public radio a lot and the ex-governor was on, big hockey star in the sixties, but he mentioned his first year at the University of Minnesota was twenty-seven dollars.

KJC: No way!

SAM: Now can you imagine what it costs to go to school?

KJC: It's like six thousand dollars a semester or something, right? I mean I should know exactly what it is,[7] but—

SAM: When I went to school it was cheap and they had all kinds of loans, and half the time [now] you can't get any kind of loans.

KJC: Lot of kids work while they go to school

SAM: Well they have to. Some of that's all right. But we're pricing college out of . . . How are you going to pay for that when you're working—[turns to Johnny] Piling lumber down there, what are they paying now?

JOHNNY: Like eight or nine if you've been there a few years.

SAM: Yeah if you've been there fifty years, you get nine dollars an hour.

KJC: Wow that's tough.

SAM: You're not going to be able to send your kids to school.

JOHNNY: Nope.

SAM: How many people work there that got kids?! I don't know how they can, how they do it.

KJC: So most people just don't go on to school, huh?

JOHNNY: There's lots that don't, then like I said most that do just go to local technical school. Like outta my class there's probably maybe two kids that went to university, I think one of them went to Madison and—

KJC: How many in your class?

JOHNNY: Mine was a little bit bigger—closer to thirty—compared to most. Not huge by any means.

KJC: OK, OK. Wow.

SAM: Let's see when I went to school, almost half started college, I think maybe a quarter, but we had a superintendent that pushed college. Nothing wrong with vocational school, either.

JOHNNY: No.

KJC: No, you said it.

JOHNNY: I think most everybody in my class did go to some sort of college, but—

KJC: Yeah? Just depends what type? Yeah, OK.

SAM: Well it's so much cheaper.

KJC: And if you can live at home

SAM: When Ben went to Gogebic—[*talking to Johnny*] you went to Gogebic too, huh? It wasn't much more than eight hundred dollars tuition, was it?

JOHNNY: Yeah I think mine was just a little over a thousand.

SAM: Yeah, probably. When Ben went it was eight hundred dollars.

JOHNNY: I only went one semester.

In their tourist town in northern Wisconsin, the folks at the diner counter put it this way (Group 9, June 2007):

KJC: So let me ask you if I can a few questions about UW–Madison. You won't hurt my feelings. I have thick enough skin I think. So I want to know what you think the UW–Madison could be doing better, in terms of . . . in terms of anything. Whether it is sports teams, or you know, we don't have a whole lot of contact up here.

NELSON: I know they do a good job—one of the top schools in the country, it's one of those things where the programs are very good. Costs are getting up there. Live in northern Wisconsin? Not going to go to the University of Madison. You're going to take one of the smaller colleges they're going to. Can't afford it.

PETE: James [local student] going there?

NELSON: Yeah—Rhinelander.

KJC: So most kids if they're thinking about going to college they go to, like, another UW system school?

NELSON: Or going to tech schools and . . . not the tough courses, going through the easier ones to get out and get back to work as quick as they can because they can't afford it. I'd say the average income in this town is probably less than 20K a year. So trying to live on $20K a year, go to the University of Madison? You ain't going to do it. There's no way. Borrow the money, then you get out of college, don't get the job you were trying to get, now you got fifteen years, can't even afford to pay for the God dang thing.

Notice how social class and attitudes toward education are intertwined in these comments. People in all kinds of places, from rural communities to wealthy suburbs, conveyed attitudes toward education and higher education that were related to social class. It tended to be the case that higher-income folks talked about education as a means toward self-actualization, networking, and professionalization and as an important element of a healthy democracy. But lower-income folks talked about it as a means toward a job. They wondered aloud why anyone would spend all that money on a degree from UW–Madison when a two-year degree would get the person into a job more quickly or when attending another decent UW system school would get the person a much cheaper degree.

So you might say then that the resentment I heard in rural places toward the university was not really about place but was, instead, about class. But rural consciousness is, as any identity rooted in class, not just about income, wealth, or occupation. Many people understood their disadvantage as a more general distance from power and lifestyles that were more closely connected to access to things like the flagship university. They believed that those in the cities had it better than they did. The believed that people in Madison and Milwaukee had more money and better-paying jobs and were privy to the game and how to play it.

For example, in the dice game, during my first visit, Mark explained to me:

> The kids who end up—most of the kids—the ones who end up going to the UW, going to the top-tier schools outside the state, usually have parents [who] are educated and know what the game is to be played. We have a lot of kids— can't even talk to 'em, don't understand that getting into college is a game. You've gotta punch your tickets, you gotta do certain things if you want to get into a really good school. So if your parents aren't beating on you like they are down in Waukesha [a Milwaukee suburb] because all their parents are probably graduates and have probably really nice jobs, these are poor people up here. We have a great brain drain. Most of our kids leave. [Looking to a friend next to him.] Your kids all left. Mine left. There is nothing for them to do up here. So what we're left with is, people who are good folks but they are unsophisticated in the ways of what goes on in education.

This perception that there are people systematically left out of the game was tied to a sense of economic injustice. People interpreted the distance from powerful institutions such as UW–Madison as having concrete, palpable effects on their lives.

"UW and San Francisco Got about the Same Initials"

Intertwined with this sense of distance from the university was a degree of resentment: many expressed that they did not necessarily want to be closer to the university. At the same time that some people wanted access to the resources of UW–Madison and the metro areas, many lived where they did because they wanted the lifestyles and values of their rural communities. In some of these places, people told me they wanted to keep themselves and their kids as far away from Madison as possible.

In the group meeting at a gas station in small town on the Wisconsin River about an hour west of Madison, I asked about the UW–Madison on my first visit in 2007 (Group 8):

> KJC: Why don't [students from here] go to Madison? I mean I have all kinds of guesses why, but why do you think?
> TIM: Cost is the biggest thing.

DAN: Tuition is higher in Madison than it is in La Crosse or Platteville [cities with other UW System schools] for one thing.

TIM: And we have a lot who commute back and forth.

KJC: Do they?

TIM: Sure.

KJC: So when you think of the UW–Madison, what comes to mind about what they don't do well? Besides high tuition? [*long pause*] And don't—you're not going to hurt my feelings.

GLENN: Oh I think probably the whole Madison scene, including the UW is over-liberal. That's—

TIM: That's from a conservative speaking. [*chuckles*]

KJC: Yeah, sure.

DAN: How do they say that? "It's an island of—"

GLENN: You want the truth, or do you want to hear what you want to hear?

KJC: The truth!

GLENN: One of the two. Yeah?

KJC: Yeah!

GLENN: Well . . .

KJC: Absolutely.

RANDY: Professors are underpaid yet they pay the coaches a fabulous salary. Take some of that coach's salary and give it to the professors. After all, they go to school to get an education, not to play football or to play basketball. The education is more important to them, as far as I'm concerned.

I'm not sure whether Randy was joking with me or not, but Glenn had a different point to make:

GLENN: UW is the only place where you can be a hippie for forty years and not be out of place. [*chuckles*]

DAN: Sometimes you can't tell them from the professors, either. [*laughs*]

TIM: Well that's true, too.

KJC: Right, right.

GLENN: UW and San Francisco got about the same initials. [*chuckles*]

KJC: So what do you think the UW–Madison should be doing here in [this town]? And I mean that very broadly, like from students to ordinary folks who live here, you know beyond student age, are there things they should be doing?

TIM: I don't know what they could do—I guess I'm like Glenn and the rest of

'em as far as the liberal—I'm not a Madison person. There's a reason that I
don't live in Madison, I like [this town]. I don't like Madison at all. It's big,
it's . . . to me, I don't like to drive in the city—

GLENN: Best part about Madison is the fifty-five miles that it is away.

TIM: Yeah. You know it is the political hub, which every state has to have one,
but I'm—I personally I think Madison is doing everything for me that I
would like to have—

KJC: Just keep their distance?

TIM: Stay where they're at.

KJC: Alright.

Three hours north of there, a group of folks at a gas station in the
town where the dice game met also worried about getting exposed to, or
exposing their kids to, the overly liberal nature of Madison (Group 11a,
May 2007).

DOUG: Very liberal—they've brainwashed all the kids that go down there.

KJC: Do you really think so?

HANK: He's a got a daughter down there!

[*Laughter*]

KJC: So tell me what happened with her?

[*Laughter*]

HANK: Lost common sense, right? [*Makes sounds like she went loopy.*]

[*Laughter*]

WARREN: Peace Corps! I mean, good God!!

KJC: She wants to go into the Peace Corps?

WARREN: She *didn't*. She *was* there.

KJC: Where did she go?

WARREN: Africa. It didn't go very well.

DOUG: Didn't it?

WARREN: No. She got robbed at knife point and back she came. But she was
going to save the world.

But then again, in this group, as was the case at other times, someone with personal experience in Madison piped up that the place isn't all
that bad.

ALEX: They say there are a lot of kooks down there, you know. But the first
time I went to UW–Madison, driving on University Avenue, and I saw a

[mechanical] barn cleaner sticking out of a truck. They have a veterinarian hospital and all and I figured, "Oh, these people are OK!"

"Got That Book Learning"

I share these conversations to convey that people felt a sense of disadvantage with respect to the university compared to people in the urban centers in the state, but economic disadvantage was just one element in a broader sense of distance from this public institution. These perceptions of distance are very much about resources and economics, but they are about so much more: respect, acknowledgment, and understanding. All of these things together—not just resources—constitute peoples' perceptions of their relationship to power.

Let me try to convey this in one more way. Through the conversations, I heard about interactions with the rare UW–Madison employees who traveled out to do work in rural parts of the state. The issue people raised with me in these conversations was not that UW–Madison ignored their communities but that it ignored the knowledge and the norms of the people living in their communities.

The group of men meeting in the town hall early in the morning in north-central Wisconsin had a variety of stories along these lines. Toward the end of my first visit, we had this conversation (Group 4b, January 2008):

> KJC: Wow, before I run out of time, I want to ask you: are there . . . well, first of all, when you think of the UW–Madison, are there things that come to mind about what it should be doing differently, or could be doing differently, if you think about UW–Madison at all. You know, it's probably not—
>
> JACK: Winning the Big Ten!
>
> [*Laughter*]
>
> KJC: Yeah, really, what's with this Ohio State business?[8]
>
> DEAN: What does the university do over here at Bass Lake?[9] What is their big thing?
>
> KJC: You know, I don't know for sure.
>
> JACK: Well it's an experimental—
>
> KJC: Is it a UW–Madison thing?
>
> JACK: Yeah.

KJC: I'm not sure.

DEAN: They're in all our lakes.

JACK: Zoology, biology, zoology . . .

KJC: Are they taking samples of stuff?

DEAN: No, but what is it Field Lake or whatever it is, they filled out a whole bunch of trees in the water and tied them down with cement blocks and put tags on them, and they go around every year and check them. But now the water's low, so all those trees are on high ground!

[*Laughter*]

KJC: Oh I see, they were trying to watch how quick they deteriorate or something?

DEAN: That's what it is. You go to all the lakes around here, you'll see tags on the logs down there in the water. I don't know what the idea is, what—

JACK: They were taking core samples out of the deepest part of Bay Lake two years ago. They were dropping one of those weighted things down to see, you know, I don't know what they're looking for, whether it's acid rain, or, you know, I don't know.

DEAN: They do some of the funniest things. I go over there to Leaf Lake, and they put up, it must have a been a mile of little plastic traps for some kind of mouse that's supposed to be in there so they could watch him all winter.

KJC: A mouse?

DEAN: Yeah, they had it all piped in . . . I don't know if it was for a deer mouse or one of those little, long-eared, what do you call it?

JACK: Kangaroo mouse.

DEAN: Kangaroo mouse.

KJC: How curious.

DEAN: They had these pipes and they had boxes like that where the mouse could go in there and they could somehow monitor what they were . . . I mean they spent days and days . . .

KJC: How funny!

DEAN: And then they take clothes baskets, and I don't know what they do, and they put them all the way around the lake . . .

JACK: Cut the bottom out of them.

KJC: You mean the plastic . . . ?

[*Laughter*]

JACK: Stake them in the shallow water.

DEAN: Another thing is that none of them seem to tell anybody what they're doing, you know?

JACK: That would be a good idea. They could do a little more publicity in the local papers, so people . . . like Night Lake years ago they had like garden hoses all the way around the lake with holes in it, and with weights and floats, so once you got in there, you had a tough time fishing because . . . then at the end of the year, I went back duck season and hunted there, and they must have just grabbed onto it with a long cable from the boat landing and dragged it up onto that bog and left it. And that irritated me. I wrote a letter to them.

KJC: Did you? Good for you.

JACK: They left it there, you know, just trash. I don't know whether anybody came and got it later or not, but I was—

DEAN: They have little birdhouses I see every thirty feet . . .

JACK [*sarcastically*]: Oh, that's, that's good.

[*Laughter*]

DEAN: Wiley Lake there has about a hundred and fifty of them. You know, why would you put one every hundred feet?

KJC: And there's no sign on it?

DEAN: It's a post in the ground, a metal post in the ground with a little birdhouse on it. They must be trying to find what kinds of birds are there, or—

JACK: Now is it the DNR or the university that's putting up the little things to trap the gypsy moths?

DEAN: That's a private outfit. It's the DNR, but they hire people.

JACK: I didn't know who was in charge of that.

DEAN: Guys making big money doing that.

JACK: But again, it should get a little more publicity to tell people what that is and to leave them alone.

KJC: Yeah, it would be nice to have just a little sign up there even, if they're not going to do more publicity than that, just a little tag to tell you what it's . . . I would love to know what's with the laundry baskets . . . how funny!

JACK: Well they had the metal garbage cans in Albatross Lake years and years ago, too like that, staked in with holes drilled in the side. And I remember we looked in there and couldn't see anything, and so he said let's give them something, and he put a little northern and threw it in there, and wondered when they came by, you know, "How did *that* get in here?"

[*Laughter*]

On my next visit, I heard yet another story from this group, from a man named Al who had not been there on that previous January morning. He told me about his encounter with researchers on a remote lake where he frequently goes to fish. He said that they had constructed a set of elaborate and expensive cribs for fish to spawn around.

> I went looking along and they had, there were bass spawning and there was a little peg in the ground with a little red flag with a number on it. I seen these all over the lake. Well, they were there one day when I was fishing and I said, "What's with the red flags?" and [they] said, "Oh we're trying to determine if bass spawn in the same place every year." And I said, "Well if you'd have asked anybody who lives up here they could've tell ya 'yes' and just save yourself a whole bunch of trouble." [*Laughter*] They don't want anything to do with ya. They think they're smarter than ya. Got that book learning. People go to college they come out dumber than they went in. They got the books there, those books, it's not like the experience.

These comments conveyed a sense of lack of recognition but also a lack of respect. Just earlier in this conversation, Al had complained about UW researchers flagrantly ignoring laws that the locals abided by.

> AL: Their image is tarnished because there are many lakes up here that are electric motors only and posted—prominently posted at the landing. Two years ago I was up here at my lake, a little lake, it was daylight, all state land. Absolutely gorgeous lake, electric motors only. . . . And here comes the University of Wisconsin one day with four young people in a boat with an outboard motor and they're going down the lake wide open and I hollered at them, waved and they shut the motor off and I said, "What're you doing?" "Well, I work for the University of Wisconsin. We're out here doing research on"—they're going to take core samples out in the deep part of the lake. And I said, "Well, did you see the sign at the landing? There's no electric, no gas motors." "Well yeah, but we're from . . ." I said, "I don't care if you're from Washington, DC!" Started the motor and away they went. And came back by me again and kind of waved at me like you know, "Hahaha!! We can run our motor, you can't!" I got home that night and I was fuming.
>
> KJC: I don't blame you.
>
> AL: And I mean it's a lake that loons are there, people kayak just to see the, you know, I called the local game warden. And he says, "I can't do a thing about it. We have word from the town, hands off, we cannot do anything, whatever they do, we can't do anything about." I says, "Well that's great."

This man was clearly resentful of what he perceived as a lack of respect for local knowledge and the standard ways of behaving in his town. In his view, even though university employees had traveled off of the campus into outstate Wisconsin, they did not care about behaving themselves, even with respect to the simplest things like no outboard motors on certain lakes. The experience of the men in this group was that there was plenty of UW–Madison activity going on in their neck of the woods, but it was for the benefit of the researchers, not the residents.

I want to remind my readers, especially those of you who work at an institution of higher education that puts considerable effort into serving the broader public, that these are perceptions. They are not necessarily accurate. Maybe the stories I just relayed were examples of miscommunication. I certainly encountered claims about UW–Madison activity that were false, such as claims that UW–Madison no longer runs "short courses" for farmers (Group 11b, May 2007).[10] The important thing, however, is that these perceptions exist, and they structure the way people think about the university.

Rural Resentment toward Public Employees and Institutions in General

We could just chalk up the above conversations to a general perception that academics are elitist and aloof. But the comments of the folks in these rural groups about other public employees suggest that this is not simply about resentment toward academics as much as it is about government employees generally.

Notice, for example, the way Department of Natural Resources employees were lumped in with comments about UW–Madison employees above. The DNR was a frequent target of rural resentment. It, too, was widely perceived to be an urban entity that was out of touch with rural life.

When I visited with the group of loggers in northwest Wisconsin in April 2009, I asked them some standard survey questions about trust in government and the group lashed out at the DNR (Group 6).

> KJC: Alright. [Question] three. Agree/disagree. People like me don't have any say about what the government does. Do you agree or disagree?

FRED: A hundred percent. They don't care what we think.

SAM: No.

FRED: You can go right with your DNR. They just have meetings around about, you know, the deer herd and everything else. You tell them, "There ain't no deer around." But they keep telling ya, "Well there's twelve thousand deer in Unit 6." Well we hunt in Unit 6. You know?

KJC: You don't see them?

FRED: There aren't that many deer there. We tell them that. Oh, no. "Well we're just gonna do what we wanna do."

The men in the town hall in northern Wisconsin said similar things (Group 4b, January 2008).

JACK: Now there's that fish virus loose in the state.

KJC: Yeah, has it gotten up around here?

JACK: Yeah, it's affecting us up here because . . . are you familiar with the new regulations from the DNR on this?

KJC: No.

JACK: I go to Joe's Minnow Stand, and I buy four dozen minnows, and I go to Lake A, and I fish there for two hours and nothing is biting, and I decide I'm gonna go from Lake A to Lake B, I gotta dump all those minnows and buy more. And now, where do I dump them because it's illegal for me to dump them on the shore, so . . .

KJC: What are you supposed to do with them?

JACK: Well we asked the warden the other day. "What . . . are you supposed to dump the water out of your bucket and then leave the minnows somewhere where it's legal to dispose of them, like on your own property?"

[*Laughter*]

KJC: Wow, who's gonna be doing that?

JACK: And the wardens are upset about it. The local warden, he says, "Nobody asked *us* about the rule, the legislatures went ahead and made it." He said, "It's unworkable, it's gonna be a nightmare." So he said, "I give it about a year, and they're probably gonna make some changes in it." So . . .

DEAN: The ice fishermen are furious about it, too. You have to dump your minnows out on the bank when you leave or do something with them.

JACK: You can't dump them in the ice. That's against the law, too.

DEAN: I think what a lot of them are doing is throwing them on the ice, and the eagles are eating them.

JACK: Yeah, but if you do it and you get caught, you're gonna get a citation, and so . . .

Many people perceived that the DNR—or the legislators making the decisions behind the DNR's action—had little actual understanding of the practicalities of everyday life in the Northwoods. Many people perceived that their own wisdom was not book learning, but it was far more valuable and realistic. And they felt like folks from Madison ignored that kind of knowledge, even when the locals made a point to communicate their concerns.

The DNR and UW–Madison employees were targets of these types of concerns, but they weren't the only ones. I heard similar complaints with respect to Department of Transportation employees, for example. On my first visit to the group at the diner in the northern tourist town, I asked those gathered to tell me what their concerns were in their town. The group was all male that day except for one woman, and she helped me get the conversation going (Group 9, June 2007).

KJC: Anything at all—the things that you normally shoot the breeze about.

HELLEN [laughs]: Race cars. [long pause] You had better start talking because she's running out of tape.

KJC: Don't worry. I won't run out—whatever is on your mind these days.

HELLEN: What's on your mind? He's a retired fireman.

KJC: My first response yesterday was, "Who's sleeping with whom."

[Laughter, followed by a long pause]

HELLEN: Better talk to her, she's going to get up and leave.

KJC: No, I won't leave. Take your time.

NELSON: Biggest issue around here right now is Armory Road.

KJC: What's going on with that?

NELSON: We want to improve the road and make it a little bit wider so that the trucks and cars don't run into each other and the school buses don't get in the way of the big trucks and stuff. And we have a group that don't want to have it fixed up. Cause they don't understand it. Business people that have equipment don't want to see it fixed either because of taxes, but also you want to get it wide enough so you don't kill somebody.

KJC: Have there been a lot of accidents?

NELSON: A lot of 'em.

KJC: Really.

NELSON: Then they say, there hasn't been a lot of deaths out there in the last few years. Well, there hasn't been. But some people that have been paralyzed and stuff like that.

KJC: Oh gosh.

NELSON: Hit by other vehicles—trees and posts and slippery roads—it's dangerous. So the local people want it but the southern part of the state don't want it.

KJC: They don't?

NELSON: A hundred feet of it is national forests and all the roads are in the national forests right around there, slow paced where there isn't anybody, and the trees are right up against the road.

KJC: Yeah I do—I know Armory Road real well.

NELSON: So it is kind of an important thing to the people around here because we're here in the winter, you know we stay here. It is very dangerous.

KJC: Wow.

When I returned in January 2008, I asked the folks at the counter if there were any updates on that road.

DAVE: The thing that upset a lot of us was that article [op-ed] that was in the *Milwaukee Journal Sentinel* [against the widening of the road]. Well I thought, well, you know, OK, if you don't live there, it's a road to nowhere, but there's a lot of people who live there, and he was not there in the middle of winter when it's not nice and smooth [*sarcastically, referring to the very icy conditions on this road*]. It's nice and smooth today, right?

KJC: Sure.

DAVE: Sure, OK.

[*Laughter*]

KJC: I didn't know he [the Milwaukee Journal Sentinel columnist] wrote an article about it.

DAVE: Sure. Yeah, I wasn't happy with him at all. I quit reading him.

KJC: Did you tell him? You should write him a letter.

DAVE: Well, I guess all of the other articles I read were bullshit, too.

KJC: Well, it makes you wonder.

DAVE: You know, you know. I thought, well, he's really lopsided on a lot of these articles obviously, because this one he sure was.

In that conversation, Dave directed his anger at a journalist. But the broader issue was about the decisions of public officials on a part of this man's everyday life that mattered a great deal to him and the people in his community: the safety of a road that he and others regularly used to meet their daily needs. I have driven that road many times, including the winter. And I have never noticed my city girl naïveté more so than on the icy April morning I spun out on a road near it, into a ditch.

To this point, I have been talking about public employees as urbanites, and that has been my intention. Because even when public employees were referenced who were actually residents of a rural community, people talked about them as if they were controlled by urban concerns and values. For example, people talked about the public school teachers in their town as outsiders, even if they had grown up just a few towns away.[11] People often assumed that public employees in their community were driven by urban regulations and incentives and had the same flaws as people from Madison and Milwaukee: a laziness and tendency to waste tax dollars. In other words, people did not claim that all public employees were themselves urbanites, but they treated them as if they exuded the values and priorities of people from urban places.[12]

People perceived that public employees were urban, but their resentment toward those people was more than a perception of difference and lack of respect. It was intertwined with a strong sense that public employees did not deserve the salaries and benefits they received. And many people in rural places perceived that public employees did not work nearly as hard as rural residents do.

Take, for example, university employees, especially professors. When people expressed animosity toward "university types," part of that was an aversion to elitism. Many rural individuals saw professors as urban and "them" and believed they looked down on local, rural folks. But part of it was an aversion to laziness and a sense that university types did not work hard for a living. Those talking through a rural consciousness lens saw professors as part of that broad class of urbanites who sit behind a desk all day. And they hardly appear in the classroom. ("They have teaching assistants, after all.") They "have the summer off." In one of the best summary statements I heard, "they shower before work, not afterwards."

To be honest, I felt sheepish explaining to people during my first year of fieldwork that I wasn't teaching any classes. In the midst of conversations about the wear and tear of common rural occupations on one's body, I had a difficult time thinking of my job driving around the state, inviting myself into coffee klatches as hard work. For example, here's a conversation from the group meeting up early in the morning in a gas station on the Wisconsin River, about an hour west of Madison (Group 8, April 2011):

> DAN: Who teaches your classes then when you're out on the road like this?
> KJC: Nobody, I just zip in and out in between. I just stayed in [a nearby town] last night, just drove [there from Madison late last night] after dinner so I could come out here this morning.
> DAN: Give 'em an automatic passing grade since you aren't there?

It wasn't as if they thought public employees did not do anything. But whatever it was they were doing, people said, it did not seem to be making much of a difference. When I first visited the group of loggers in northwest Wisconsin in June 2007 (Group 6), I asked whether they thought they paid their fair share in taxes. That sure opened a can of worms. They launched into a conversation about state government expenditures on road projects.

> JIM: Too many studies.
> FRED: Not enough work.
> JIM: Too much bureaucracy in the system.
> FRED: They do waste a lot of money on surveying roads.
> SAM: All those state employees we look at 'em, and we don't think they do much.

Later in the conversation, I asked the group about hard work:

> KJC: Sometimes people say . . . survey researchers ask about different occupations and they ask people which one they think works the hardest. Tell me what you think—if you compare a professor, a public school teacher, a waitress, a farmer, and a construction worker, which ones do you think work the hardest?
> SAM: The last three.
> STEVE: Yeah.
> SAM: And for no benefits.
> KJC: Yeah? How about those first two—like—
> SAM: I think a school teacher—I know it can be hard. But they got great benefits. Tremendous benefits. And if you've been there for fifteen, twenty years, you're making fifty grand a year. There's nobody in town other than

them making fifty grand a year. The guys in the [local] mill make twenty thousand.

In a metropolitan area, it might seem crazy to claim that people working in the public sector make more money than those in the private sector. But in low-income areas, at least in Wisconsin, that appears to be the case. Data from the U.S. Census Bureau's American Community Survey suggest that, in areas with lower average total income in Wisconsin, public employees make more than private employees.[13] That is especially the case in the city of Milwaukee and in the northwest corner of the state, two of the most impoverished areas of Wisconsin. In wealthier areas, private worker incomes far outpace public worker incomes. There is more variability in private-sector salaries across the state, so in high-income areas, public workers are making relatively less, but in low-income areas, they are making relatively more.

Figure 5.1 displays the distributions of incomes for public and private workers in low-income areas (where the average total income was under $30,000) and then also in higher-income areas (where the average exceeded $33,500).[14] What we see here is that in both low- and high-income areas, for low and middle ranges of incomes, public workers are making more than private workers. In low-income areas, only among the very highest income percentiles are private workers earning more than public employees. But in high-income areas, the top 15 percent of private workers are making a great deal more than the top 15 percent of public workers.

What accounts for the visibility of these differences would be a fascinating research project on its own (and one I did not undertake here), but several things are likely responsible. First, the salaries of public employees are a matter of public record and their jobs are often visible. That is not necessarily the case with private workers. Because public employees are by definition public servants, many people come into contact with them on a daily basis. Postal workers, public school teachers, and maintenance workers are just a few examples. Second, politicians, such as Walker, have found it advantageous to feed the perception that public workers are overpaid. For example, during the second 2010 gubernatorial general election debate, he said, "We can no longer have a society where the public-sector employees are the 'haves' and the people who foot the bill, the taxpayers, are the 'have-nots.'"[15]

To get why that kind of argument has an appeal, one has to remember

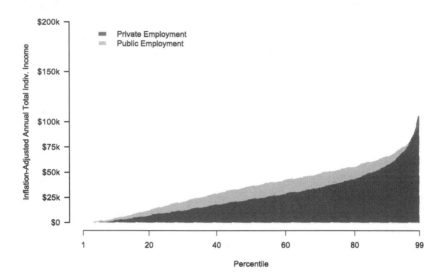

Distribution of Income, Low-Income Areas

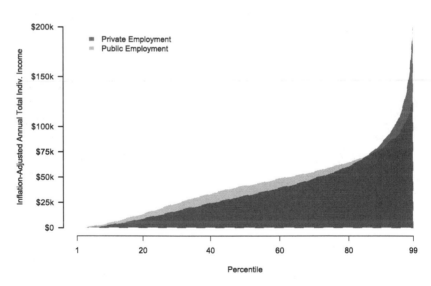

Distribution of Income, High-Income Areas

FIGURE 5.1. Comparison of public and private worker incomes across low- and high-income areas of Wisconsin. Sources: U.S. Census Bureau, "2006–2010 ACS 5-year PUMS," American Community Survey: PUMS Data, http://www.census.gov/acs/www/data_documentation/pums_data/.

that, in many of these small towns, people perceived that their type of community—a small, rural community—faced especially difficult economic circumstances. Even before and during the Great Recession, many people perceived that rural areas had it especially bad. In the northwest logging town (Group 6), the men felt that, unlike the metro areas, their community's economy was not in a temporary downturn or recession but, rather, was in a permanent recession and enduring a long, slow death. During my first visit to their group in June 2007, they explained:

> LOUIS: [It's a great place to live] if you like poverty.
> FRANK: Yeah, it *is* poverty [describing their town]. [*The group chuckles*] There ain't no businesses going in up here.
> KJC: Yeah, a lot of folks leaving?
> LOUIS: No, most of us can't afford to leave.
> FRANK: Yeah.
> CHARLIE: Well I stayed here all my life; I never made enough money to leave.
> KJC: Gosh.
> FRANK: No industry up here.
> JIM: Only thing we have up here is lumbering, trees, or logs or what have you. Every one of us here—
> FRED: We're all a bunch of sawdust heads.

In April 2008, when I asked them what they thought about the presidential race, they said the outcome did not matter to people so far removed from the urban centers, as I noted in chapter 3 when I quoted Steve's claim that they had been in a recession already for decades. One woman who met for lunch once a week with her pals in the dice game town (Group 11c) explained to me (as the other women nodded and said, "Yes") in June 2012 that "we don't have the highs and lows here that so many places do. We may go along and dip down, but we don't reach those real high peaks that some of those places [do]. I think you all agree with that, right?"

This mattered for perceptions of public employees because many people in rural places perceived that the good life that public employees were enjoying was at their expense. They believed that public employees were enjoying extravagant salaries, health care benefits, and pensions paid for by ordinary taxpayers. And rural people were enduring a special burden in this respect because many of them were physically working very hard to earn relatively low salaries. They perceived that a large chunk of what they were able to earn went to pay for the benefits enjoyed by public employees—who they believed did not work as hard.

The group of loggers in northwest Wisconsin made it clear to me that government pensions were a luxury they resented (Group 6, April 2009):

> SAM: If somebody can retire at fifty years old but then the government wants the rest of us to work till we're sixty-five or sixty-seven, I mean—
>
> RANDALL: Yeah.
>
> SAM: I'd have a better chance working till sixty-seven being a teacher and not doing any physical work than being out in the woods working. You know or somebody working at the mill or the lumber yard.
>
> KJC: Right, right.
>
> SAM: At sixty-five years old you're worn out. You should be able to retire.

Adding fire to their resentment was a perception that public employees did not realize how good they had it. One logger in the group I just quoted remarked, "The people that do have health insurance don't realize [how lucky they are]." A farmer in the central part of the state pointed out that public employees did not have to pay income tax on the benefits they receive and that they didn't realize how unfair it was that other folks were paying taxes on the income that they had to funnel into health insurance. And they looked at people in Madison as especially oblivious to these concerns. The men in the gas station across town from the dice game explained it this way during my first visit in May 2007 (Group 11a).

> KJC: OK. So here's a question about financial security. Thinking about your overall situation here, do you . . . would you say that you kind of struggle to [make] ends meet, or that most people live pretty comfortably in [this town]? You've already given me a good sense of this—
>
> KJC [reading their nods]: Struggle? OK.
>
> HANK: Nowadays it's at least—it's a two-person—
>
> WARREN: Gotta pay your health care!
>
> HANK: Both parties in the family gotta work.
>
> WARREN: Gotta work.
>
> HANK: One job, at least one, and a lot of times two, so you are actually working three jobs for two people.
>
> KJC: Do most people pay their own health care you think? Most jobs—

HANK: Well, I would say, just as many pay as don't.

KJC: Really?

HANK: I pay my own, you pay your own, you pay your own [*looking around at the guys in the room*], you pay your own, you pay your own, you pay your own, you pay your own . . .

KENT: One without.

HANK: Rest of 'em here, you got one, two, three, four, one doesn't have it, and one gets it paid. I get half of mine, a third of mine.

DAVE: Public—there's not a—unlike Madison, there's not a large public employee base, or a large union base. So a lot of people here, they don't have health insurance as a matter of their job description. That fringe benefit isn't there. That is because of the huge rise of the cost of health care, is one that drains the economy here more so than it would in a place like Madison.

HANK: Big issue here as far as insurance. As far as the care: we got good care—

KJC: I'll bet that's something that folks in Madison don't quite get. I don't know about the state legislature, but because so many people are employed by the state—the university or the state government, you know.

HANK: [They] forget benefits are 30 percent of your wages.

WARREN: Yeah—pay big for that.

KENT: By the time you're done—you know, now you got your health, you got your vacation, your 401(k).

ALEX: Boy, state employees, too, they get to keep their sick leave, and when they retire, they get to use that to pay their health care.

HANK: All that adds up.

DOUG: Big thing around here now, teachers that have retired, in a lot of your smaller school districts, you got teachers that are retired that get their health care paid after ten years up to sixty-five. That's something your school district—

ROLAND: Some they bought out too, for as long as they live, too, they have got their insurance.

People in small towns resented university employees and public employees in general because they received great benefits. And who paid for these benefits? Taxpayers, like themselves. They perceived that they worked harder than other people to make ends meet because they had to survive in a rural economy. Even though they were working hard, many of them could still not afford health care. But their hard-earned money was going to pay for wages and benefits for people who they did not think were working very hard and whom they therefore perceived as undeserving.

Comparing to Conversations in Other Places

Rural consciousness is something best understood as a matter of a continuum. People did not either have it or not. What I am describing is a constellation of sentiments that taken together can be characterized as rural identity combined with a sense of distributive injustice. But identity varies across people. Particular people give it meaning in particular places.

There are many people who live in areas outside the Milwaukee and Madison metro areas that are not really living in rural communities. They live in small or medium-sized cities or even suburbs of those cities. And yet many of those folks exhibited something like a rural consciousness—they identified as residents of communities that were outside the orbit of power, resources, and respect of the main cities in the state.

I mention these folks to make the point that rural consciousness is not a fixed identity and also to argue that those farther along the continuum—with the strongest identity as rural people and the most intense sense of distributive injustice—seemed most likely to resent public employees. Strong rural consciousness provided an extra foothold for resentment toward public employees.

To show you what I mean, take, for example, the group of professionals in a central Wisconsin city (Group 16a). They, like many people in rural, urban, and suburban places also had many economic concerns and criticism of public employees. But unlike the conversations in the rural communities, they did not view tough economic conditions as inevitable for people living in their type of town.

The members of this group did not consider themselves rural. The city they lived in has almost forty thousand people in it. And yet this city was located several driving hours north of the Madison and Milwaukee metro areas. Many of them had personal relationships with state politicians, as well as close ties to local officials. Some of them spent a great deal of time in Madison doing business and engaged in long conversations with me about their favorite restaurants and shops there. When they complained about the government, they did not convey that their geographic and socioeconomic location meant it was inevitable that government ignores people like them (Cramer Walsh 2011). Instead, their complaints about economic policy were complaints about the people they considered the dolts in there right now. They talked as if *they* could hold state office themselves if only they would be crazy enough to run.

And yet they felt ignored and looked down on by people in the cities. In addition, although their comments, occupations, and neighborhoods suggested they did not struggle to make ends meet, they nevertheless talked about their community as a victim of distributive injustice and as being overlooked by decision makers. Part of this injustice was attributed to place. In short, this group exhibited some aspects of rural consciousness that we see in smaller communities—they identified as people geographically outside the Madison-Milwaukee orbit of power—but they neither identified as rural folks nor conceived of public employees as others because of geography. These professionals felt ignored by power holders in the state, but their social class as lawyers and wealthy business owners put them within the social networks of political and business leaders. They expected to be listened to.

A closer look at the professionals' comments will help illustrate their attitudes. During my first visit (June 2007), the members worried about a variety of economic concerns: the loss of manufacturing jobs in the community and the country, the low state bond ratings in Wisconsin compared to other states, an unbalanced state budget, and the fact that Wisconsin's economy seemed to be lagging behind neighboring Minnesota's.

They also complained about public employees' benefits. They teased me that as a state university employee, I would enjoy a luxurious retirement:

> ED [*nodding at another man in the group*]: You and I would love to retire at
> 70 percent of our income.
> KJC: I am very fortunate.
> ED: You are one of the few that appreciate it. I'm just saying that the majority
> of 'em sit there and say it is an expectation, it's a right.
> STANLEY: God given right.
> ED: But I am saying, ask most people here if they are going to retire anywhere
> close to that. They won't be anywhere close to that.

Their sense of distributive injustice associated with their geographic location outside the major cities came up in two ways in other parts of this conversation. First, they complained about the high price of gas and high property taxes in their city compared to other parts of the state. Also, as they criticized public employees, they talked about how oblivious decision makers in Madison were to real economic concerns, exhibiting the same kind of people-in-power-are-out-of-touch-with-ordinary-Wisconsinites attitude that I had heard in many rural areas. One lawyer talked about the inability of UW–Madison to educate journalists properly, and others chimed in about professors at the university being ignorant of real economic concerns. And they talked about state employees in general as being out of touch. One summarized simply, "There is no reality in Madison."

What this group did not share with many of the people I spent time with in rural areas was socioeconomic status. They were professionals who were not manual laborers and therefore did not get into arguments about how they were breaking their backs to pay for health care and pensions of lazy public employees who never got their hands dirty. So their perspectives as outstaters did play into their comments about public employees, but they were not as intense as people who identified as people from communities who were so clearly less well off than the metro areas of the state.

Conclusion

I started out this chapter by explaining resentment toward UW–Madison and then showed how those sentiments were related to resentment toward public employees in general. Let me end this chapter by acknowledging that people of many walks of life feel distant from institutions of higher education and also public employees.

First, consider that public opinion surveys suggest that many people feel a sense of disconnection from institutions of higher education. For example, a December 9–13, 2009, Public Agenda poll of 1,031 U.S. adults found that 60 percent of the public perceives that "colleges today are like most businesses and mainly care about the bottom line," as opposed to "colleges today mainly care about education and making sure students have a good educational experience."[16] Also, that same poll found that 33 percent "agree strongly" and 27 percent "agree somewhat" that "colleges could take a lot more students without lowering quality or raising prices." And with respect to public higher education institutions in particular, that same poll found that 49 percent believed that "your state's public college and university system needs to be fundamentally overhauled" came closer to their own view than "your state's public college system should be basically left alone" (39 percent).

Second, resentment toward public employees is not new and is certainly not exclusive to rural areas.[17] As early as 1936, public employees were referred to as "tax eaters."[18] Until recently, Wisconsin was often looked to as one of the leaders in labor rights for public employees, but collective bargaining started in Wisconsin in 1959 only after a long struggle. There was a fear, or at least an argument, that collective bargaining for government workers would inhibit the provision of public services to citizens. The Taft-Hartley Act, passed in 1947, made the existence of public unions seem less threatening by allowing employers to resist union activity. After Wisconsin allowed public-sector collective bargaining, President John Kennedy and the federal government followed suit, along with other levels of government.

When the postwar economy slowed and inflation and unemployment rose in the 1970s, the relatively warm attitudes toward unions changed, and it seems there has been an increasing resentment toward public employees ever since. Government budgets became tight, leading to more confrontations with public unions. As private workers felt the economic downturns in their own pocketbooks, resentment toward public workers grew. People revolted against taxes and political entrepreneurs parlayed such attitudes into antigovernment sentiment (as I explain in more detail in the next chapter). Arguments that public-sector unionization was a step toward socialism gained prominence (Petro 1974–75). When President Ronald Reagan broke the Professional Air Traffic Controllers Organization strike in 1981, it emboldened public union opponents and suggested that conservative politicians had much to gain by attempting to weaken public unions (McCartin 2011).

In other words, the contemporary resentment toward public employees is not just a fleeting sentiment. It has been brewing for some time.

And it is not exclusive to rural places. In my own fieldwork, I heard resentment toward public employees from people across a range of political leanings and in a range of places. The ordinariness of this resentment was striking to me. Opinion polls suggest it is indeed a common sentiment in the state. In a June–July 2011 Badger Poll, 27 percent of respondents said that public employees had "too much influence." This is only roughly a quarter of the population—nowhere near a majority of the public—expressing anti–public employee attitudes, according to this measure. But it is a little striking that even at this time, a few months after Walker successfully passed Act 10, which undercut public employee unions, more than a quarter of the public still said they had too much influence.[19] Also, this level of negative attitudes toward public employees is substantial compared to other leanings that we treat as politically important in the contemporary context. It is larger than the level of support for the Tea Party expressed in the same poll—18 percent—in a state in which a Tea Party–backed candidate for U.S. Senate had defeated a longtime and popular incumbent in 2010.

Even though this sentiment that public employees have too much influence is fairly widespread, it is worth noticing that almost two out of three Wisconsinites did not feel that way in 2011.[20] The people I listened to from this study came disproportionately from the other third. The manner in which I sampled communities and people for this study exposed me to the perspective of people who were resentful of public employees. A different study could have presented different attitudes toward people who are paid out of public funds.

You might also be wondering what I would have heard had more of the people I listened to been women. In the early stages of my fieldwork, most of the people I encountered were men. As my fieldwork progressed and I became increasingly aware of this, I made extra attempts to invite myself into groups of women because I expected they might sound quite different than those among men. I was especially concerned about this after I realized the pervasive resentment against public employees. Since most public union members are women, I thought groups of women might be more supportive of public employees (see Vargas-Cooper 2011). Also, in the course of my fieldwork after Walker came to power, several men told me about female relatives who had stopped talking to them because of their pro-Walker stances. Available poll data do not suggest that women were more supportive of public employees.[21] But exit polls for the recall and the 2014 gubernatorial election show a clear gender gap in support for Walker. In the recall, Walker lost among women (52 percent of them voted for his opponent), although he won among men with 59 percent of their vote.[22] In the 2014 gubernatorial election, Walker's Democratic opponent was a woman, Mary Burke, a business executive and Madison school board member. Again, Walker lost among women (54 percent voted for Burke), but won among men (60 percent of men voted for Walker).[23]

So after the 2011 protests, in several of my twenty-seven communities I sought out groups of women to try to broaden my understanding of resentment toward public employees and the way rural consciousness structured this resentment. These included the group of women (Group 11c) in the central-west village where the dice group met and a group in a central Wisconsin city (Group 16b). The sentiments toward public employees in these groups were not noticeably different from those among the predominantly male groups. This does not mean that women on average do not have different views toward public employees than do men. As I have noted before, the data I have collected do not tell us what views of the population as a whole look like. Instead, what it tells us is that, among the universe of people I encountered in small-town Wisconsin, gender was not a key component of the way they made sense of public employees.

Instead, what I have demonstrated in this chapter is that viewing the world through an identity as a rural person who lives in a place perceived to be the victim of distributive injustice provides an extra foothold for resentment against the university and against public employees generally. Looking across the conversations from all of the thirty-nine groups I observed across all of the twenty-seven communities I sampled in Wisconsin, there were several common elements about the resentment toward public employees that I heard. Public employees were perceived as (1) lazy and undeserving, (2) inefficient bureaucrats, (3) recipients of exorbitant benefits and salaries paid with hard-earned taxpayer money, (4) guilty by association with the government, and (5) often represented by greedy unions. But in rural areas, oftentimes the resentment of public workers had an additional layer: public employees were perceived as members of another out-group, urbanites. For many folks in rural areas, a rural-versus-urban distinction represented the distribution of political power, the distribution of wealth and resources, and the location of people who worked hard. They described urbanites as lazy bureaucrats who did not know how to work with their hands. Attitudes toward university employees provided examples of this general perspective.

I have focused in this chapter on resentment toward public employees, but the rural consciousness perspective is not reducible to attitudes toward just one social group. The category urban contained many groups—public employees but also liberals, academics, people of color, wealthy people, and people with a different work ethic. The fact that the social divide of rural versus urban is so rich with meaning is perhaps the reason that it is an appealing perspective for politicians to tap into. Activating one component of this perspective can mobilize resentment against other aspects of it. For example, notice the things that "Madison" invoked for many people: state government, which ignores people like them; public employees, who are living high off the hog at their expense; liberal academics who are arrogant, overpaid, and challenging their way of life; city people, whose lifestyles and values just breed the mess we are in; and more.

These divisions, indicative of the politics of resentment, are not simple. They have roots in many things: place, power, and distributive justice. It is kind of ironic. Often when people try to explain why members of the white working class vote for Republicans, they explain it as a product of ignorance or, perhaps, a lack of sophistication. But there is another way to read these conversations. These understandings, whether or not one agrees with them, have roots and reasons behind them.

CHAPTER SIX

Support for Small Government

When I was traveling around Wisconsin, inviting myself into conversations in gas stations, diners, and other local hangouts, many times I got into conversations about health care reform with people who said they could not afford health insurance. They wished they could afford health care and dental care, too, for that matter. They talked about how people in general in their community could not afford health insurance. As the years went on, Barack Obama became president, and went about pursuing substantial health care reform.

But people in those groups, even the folks missing teeth, rarely supported government-sponsored health care reform. Why?

A common way to answer this question is to say that people are simply ignorant; they vote against their interests. But I would like to suggest the possibility that the issue is not about what facts they know. Instead, the issue has to do with the perspectives through which they encounter facts and conceive of possible solutions.

When we stop to notice the way rural consciousness undergirds resentment toward public employees, support for small-government policies and the conservatism of candidates in rural areas is not so surprising. In this chapter, I am going to make the bold claim that support for small government is more about identity than principle.

Why is this a bold claim? We can look back on "Obamacare" or the "Affordable Care Act" and note that which side people took is related to partisanship. And we can say that whether people side with Republicans or Democrats in general is related to their attitudes about the appropriate role of government (e.g., Green, Palmquist, and Schickler 2002; Goren 2005; Carsey and Layman 2006). But those correlations do not help us understand why someone without teeth would not support government-funded dental care. Is it really the case that such a person is thinking to himself, "In principle I believe the less government the better; therefore, I am going to vote for the Republican Party and against single-payer health care, even though I need health care myself"? I don't think so.

Instead, what I heard over and over again is some version of the following: "I wish I could afford better health care, but I can hardly make ends meet as it is. And the harder I work, the more my taxes go up. I don't want my taxes to go up anymore. I can't afford it. And wherever it is those tax dollars are going, they sure aren't going to people like me, in communities like mine. Because look at this place! This community is dying! It seems to me that I'm paying for health care for people who aren't working half as hard as I am, and even though I am working myself to death, I can't afford to pay for my own health care."

A fundamental aspect of rural consciousness is the perception that "people in my rural community are not getting their fair share of resources—in particular, we are not getting our share of taxpayer dollars." We can imagine that people holding that belief would want *more* government resources, as they sometimes did when talking about wanting more state aid for the tourism industry or for their local schools. But that is not the conclusion I heard people reaching. Instead, I much more commonly heard them concluding something like "the government must be mishandling my hard-earned dollars, because my taxes keep going up and clearly they are not coming back to benefit people like me. So why would I want an expansion of government?"

These are summaries of what I heard—but let me give you examples of actual conversations. In the group of women meeting once a week in the northwest tourist town, I heard this in January 2008 (Group 2):

> ELAINE: A lot of people here have less money than other parts of the state so how can they buy their insurance?
>
> KJC: Yeah, OK [*quietly, overlapping other people talking*] . . . important to remember.
>
> KATIE: A lot of times people up here have health insurance but they have a huge deductible 'cause that's the kind of health insurance they can afford, so you can still get stuck with a big, big bill.

In the northwest logging town, several hours south, earlier that morning (Group 6, January 2008):

JIM: Well *you tell me.* Somebody that's working in these industries around
here that are making eight, nine dollars an hour. With a family of two,
how are you going to afford eight hundred dollars a month for health
insurance?

KJC: You can't.

JIM: On eight dollars an hour?

KJC [*quietly*]: You can't.

JIM [*really mad now*]: Eight, ten dollars an hour? At fifteen, fifteen dollars an
hour how can you afford it?

Several hours west of there, among the group of people meeting at the
diner counter in the north-central tourist town, I heard this in June 2007
(Group 9):

KJC: How about health care? Is that a big issue?

NELSON: Health care has always been an issue because the average person up
here can't afford health care.

KJC: Do you think most people up here just kind of take a risk, don't buy it?

NELSON: Well they get . . . they don't go to the doctor when they should,
checkups, no. I've always been lucky.

KJC: So what do you think should be done about health care? There is a lot of
talk these days about universal health care and such . . .

NELSON: Well, see what's happening right now is that we're getting more and
more hospitals opening up, making enough money where they are building 'em. They are crying about not making any money, but they sure as
heck are—should see the doctor's houses out here. They are beautiful!

[*Agreement all around: "Yeah."*]

A half a year later, in January 2008, I asked that same group what
they thought should be done about health care, and Nelson was skeptical that a government mandate for people to buy insurance would work
in their type of town (Group 9, January 2008): "Well, when you get down
in the city, people are making more money, so you can afford to do it, but
when you're in northern Wisconsin making ten dollars an hour, and you
try to stretch that over for a family, you're not gonna get health care. As
a matter of fact, you're lucky if you can pay your bills. You're going to be
running an old car and hopefully that will get you back toward working,
but you're not going to be able to pay for health care."

If people perceived that they could not afford health care themselves, then why didn't they support government-subsidized health care? In many conversations, people perceived that even government-subsidized care would still cost them a great deal. In the dice game, in west-central Wisconsin, during my first visit in May 2007, I asked this (Group 11b):

> KJC: Do you think a lot of people who are retired in this community decide not to do health care at all? Just decide to take the risk?
>
> HENRY: Some of 'em can't afford to do health care.
>
> RICHARD: Not a matter of choosing—it's a matter of what you have to do. You pay some insurance company, or do you buy groceries? Whatever.
>
> ERNIE: Well if they would let us buy the insurance out of the state, that would be a hell of a lot cheaper—but they say well you can't buy insurance out of the state. Gotta be in state. That's stupid.
>
> RICHARD: You look at the average income in the southern part of the state, look at the average income here and you could tell me who is more prepared to buy their health insurance?
>
> MARK: We're about the second poorest county in the state.
>
> ERNIE: Yeah.
>
> MARK: After Menominee, Dave, is that right?
>
> DAVE: Uh, I think so. One of the poorest counties right now.
>
> MARK: So we're what? Number 2? And the state-run health program is—I'd like to say well that's going to take care of this, but that ain't gonna work. There ain't a damn thing the state ever does that's cheap.

The sense of identity as people from a place that was disadvantaged economically coexisted with the perception that wherever their hard-earned money was going, it was not coming to them. It seemed instead to be going, in part, to bloated government programs and overpaid and underworked public employees. That resentment toward government and toward public employees fueled support for small government. In this chapter, my intent is to show, in greater detail, what this looked like.[1]

The sentiments above about health care seem to include a bit of parroting of conservative media or Republican arguments. (Take, for example, the complaint about prohibitions against buying health insurance across state lines. That was a plank in Mitt Romney's platform when running against Obama in 2012.) But again, understanding these sentiments should entail more than looking just at the facts mentioned. While the facts that people pick up and repeat are a product of what they consider valid and credible ways to view the world, it is important to dig deeper. In the sections that follow, I will examine more closely the way the people I listened to understood the appropriate size of government.

Ambivalence about the Size of Government

Often, when scholars have reflected on why Americans have not supported universal health care, they have noted the strong tendency to avoid such large-scale government intervention in this aspect of their lives (e.g., Popkin 2007). But in order to understand what underlies support for small-government policies and candidates, it is important to acknowledge that the American public is far more ambivalent about the size of government than many contemporary political arguments allege (Sears and Citrin 1982; Cook and Barrett 1992; Quadagno and Street 2005; Martin 2008).

There have been significant expansions of government in U.S. history, particularly around the time of the Industrial Revolution and the New Deal, and the three decades following World War II (Cook and Barrett 1992; Martin 2008). Public education, Social Security, and Medicare are three notable examples (Quadagno and Street 2005).

When the economic downturn of the 1970s occurred, criticism about government social programs intensified (Cook and Barrett 1992, 5). The economic crises of the 1970s were a stark contrast to the prosperity of the two preceding decades, and people felt it. Government programs felt costlier as public revenues increased primarily from inflation rather than actual expansion of the economy (Sears and Citrin 1982, 225).

One result was protest against property tax hikes at the local and state levels, as Sears and Citrin argue in *Tax Revolt* (1982). In 1978, voters in California passed Proposition 13 (Prop 13) via referendum on a two-to-one margin. That proposition changed the state's constitution such that property taxes dropped and instantly were limited in how much they could escalate in the future.

Prop 13 is an example of an issue or event that some tout as a clear showing of widespread support for small government, but it is understood by others as something else. The passage of Prop 13 was spun by national political elites as support for downsizing government. But Martin (2008) argues that Prop 13 was not a show of support for limited government more generally. Instead, he argues, Prop 13 was a reaction to a specific, noticeable change in policy. It won the public's support because the property tax had been modernized in the 1960s and members of the public were steaming about the relatively sudden hike in their taxes.

Sears and Citrin write that the conservative wing of the campaign for Prop 13 "portrayed itself as a movement of 'the people' against a punitive government" (1982, 15). When Prop 13 passed, officials of many leanings interpreted it "as a symbol of public hostility to government in general, rather than the property tax in particular" (Martin 2008, 15). Even Jimmy Carter said publicly in 1978, "I do believe that Proposition 13 is an accurate expression of, first of all, the distrust of government" (quoted in Martin 2008, 126).

Notice, though, that Carter said "distrust of government." But distrust of government or antigovernment sentiment is not the same as a preference for limited or smaller government. By antigovernment sentiment, I mean criticism of the government, lack of trust in government, or perceptions of corruption or incompetence in government. By support for limited government, I mean a belief in the adage the less government, the better. A person can be highly critical of the people currently in government or current government procedures while at the same time believing in principle that society ought to invest heavily in government, even beyond defense (e.g., public education, public assistance, or health care). At the same time, a person might believe strongly in limited government (e.g., most government programs ought to be privatized), while believing that current policy makers are doing a competent job. Walker supporters in Wisconsin are one example.

Even though antigovernment sentiment is not the same as support for limited government, the conservatives of the Reagan revolution succeeded in melding the two. Conservatives used the hostility to government they claimed Prop 13 revealed to justify cutting taxes in general (Martin 2008, 15). In the midst of the shifting party coalitions in the postwar era, the parties were looking for ways to distinguish themselves. Republicans found such a strategy in antitax and anti-big-government stances (127). Martin (2008) argues that Prop 13 changed American politics because it changed how much attention the parties paid to taxes.

It was in that context that Reagan became president. One of the main targets of his efforts to scale back government was the welfare state. But some argue that, despite these attempts, there were actually few cutbacks to the welfare state in the 1980s because the public, and their congressional representatives, actually expressed widespread support for social welfare programs (Cook and Barrett 1992). Cook and Barrett's analyses of public opinion data show that public opinion in favor of social welfare did not drop in the 1970s and early 1980s, despite conservative arguments to the contrary (25).[2]

The health care debate during the first part of the Clinton administration is another example in which a political outcome that was interpreted as evidence of a widespread preference for less government may have been something else entirely. Theda Skocpol argued in *Boomerang* (1997) that the failure of the Clinton health reform did not result from the public bluntly rejecting an expansion of the government. Instead, she argues, the public may have been reacting to the nature of that specific policy. Clinton proposed increasing regulations, rather than increasing taxes, to achieve reform. Skocpol argues that the public does not take kindly to regulation without observable payouts, such as the payouts people receive from social security. In that way, political elites who mobilized against the bill, motivated by a desire to make large Republican gains in the 1994 midterm elections, were able to take advantage of that vulnerability and defeat it.

These battles over the expansion of government suggest that U.S. public opinion has rarely if ever been overwhelmingly in favor of limited government. Although a strong distrust of government is a familiar theme in American history as it is commonly told, that is just one strain of our political culture that politicians at times successfully mobilize (Quadagno and Street 2005, esp. 67) and parlay into support for cutting government back, including reducing redistributive efforts.

We can see from figure 6.1 how support for small government has wavered even in the past several decades. This figure plots responses from a nationally representative sample of eligible voters collected by the American National Election Studies conducted at the University of Michigan. Since 1990, the American National Election Studies has asked three questions that tap into attitudes about limited government.[3] Several things are notable here. First, support for limited government has not been the same over time, from a relative high in 1996, then a low in 2008, then a rebound in 2012 to the highest point since the questions were included. Second, the responses seem to correspond to the partisanship of the president at the time. The chart indicates that, since 1990, support for small government tends to rise after a Democrat becomes president. The rebound in small-government views after the 2008 election of Barack Obama suggests that his election provided fertile ground for the Tea Party movement to nurture support for limited government.

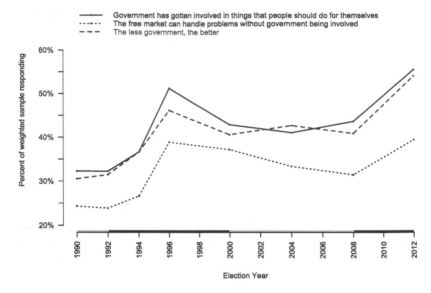

FIGURE 6.1. Small government views over time. Source: American National Election Studies, "Time Series Cumulative Data File [dataset]," Stanford University and the University of Michigan [producers and distributors], 2010, http://www.electionstudies.org/studypages/anes_timeseries_cdf/anes_timeseries_cdf.htm. Darkened portions of the x axis correspond to time periods with a Democratic president.

Indeed, people tend to be less trusting of the government when their party is not in control of the White House (Haidt and Hetherington 2012). Trust in government has declined significantly among Republicans since Obama has been president. Republican ideology has developed into arguments in favor of less redistributive policy. So here we are, in a time in which one party is advocating for smaller government and supporters of that party in the public are also the least likely to trust government right now. The time is ripe for Republican leaders to say, "Look, government stinks. So let's cut it back."

What Support for Small Government Sounds Like

We may be in a historical moment when politicians have successfully melded distrust in government with support for cutting back. But again, it is not inevitable that people will respond to disenchantment with government and their own quality of life with a call to scale back government. Distrust and disenchantment with government is not the same as support for limited government.

Let me demonstrate this using the words of the people who invited me into their conversations. Some people were highly critical of government, but they did not necessarily want to cut it back. One case in point was a group of middle-class African Americans in Milwaukee (Group 23a). In the first ten seconds of talking with them, one man argued that the city needed to spend more on policing in his neighborhood and explained to me thus: "We live in a war zone, OK? I'm gonna be honest with you. We are at the mercy of urban terrorists, you know, in some cases, and it seems like that message is not getting through like it should. People don't really have an idea of what really is going on in Milwaukee. They brush over it, politicians brush over it, there are times—to receive votes—and once they get into office, it's like that's going on the back burner, and it's never going to be anything done about it." This man wanted more government, even though he felt ignored by it. I encountered other instances of people complaining about government yet favoring *more* services, rather than less. For example, many people complained about the lack of regulation of the health care system and wanted to see government play a stronger role in it, especially before the debate over the Affordable Care Act (or "Obamacare") heated up and people adopted partisan stances (Groups 18a, 18b, 22b, 17, 21b).

I also encountered clear support for limited government. The members of a group of retirees in the Milwaukee suburban area that met every morning at a diner for breakfast and coffee (Group 18c) provide the clearest example of this. They introduced themselves to me as "conservatives" and time and again asserted that government programs should be scaled back. They believed in people pulling themselves up by the bootstraps and lamented the inability of many people to do so. There were a few exceptions to their general belief in the less government the better: defense spending, and "programs like the WPA [Works Progress Administration] and the CCC [Civilian Conservation Corps] that rewarded hard work."

Those attitudes are attitudes in favor of limited government. And notice how even this seemingly principled group does not hold principles that are immune to the political context. They supported WPA and the CCC because those programs presumably rewarded hard work, but they were not supportive of such government programs in the context of the Great Recession.

When I talk about "antigovernment attitudes," I am including complaints that government only cares about wealthy people and big business, not ordinary people, or that people in government are not to be trusted because they ignore and avoid important issues.

I am dwelling on this distinction between support for small government and distrust in government to emphasize that political attitudes are not inevitable. Despite the evidence that there is a biological basis for some political leanings and beliefs (e.g., Hibbing and Smith 2007; Hatemi and McDermott 2011), people still have to do the work of interpreting the political world around them. People have to make a connection between disenchantment with government and wanting less of it.

Political scientists look around for the basis for political beliefs—political ideology, value systems, and partisan guidance. What is it that guides these choices? Why do people think what they do? The way rural consciousness structures understanding teaches us that a big part of the answer is identity, including questions such as: What kind of a person am I? What is appropriate for someone like me to think and do? Where am I and where are people like me in relation to others in terms of power, resources, and respect?

The conversations I observed suggest that rural consciousness is one of the identities that makes support for limited government the logical choice. Resentment toward cities often served as the glue between antigovernment and small-government attitudes.[4]

This worked in three main ways. First, when people talked about specific issues and whether government spending was a solution or an obstacle, people in these rural places would often contrast their community's wealth against that of Madison and Milwaukee. They said that, sure, their community needed government services, but people in their type of town simply could not afford to pay higher taxes in order to afford these services. "There ain't shit here" one logger in northwest Wisconsin told me (Group 6). When I sat with his group in April 2008, we got around to talking about sewer pipes. It sounded to me like the men in the group knew their town needed new sewer pipes, but they thought people in town simply did not earn enough money to be able to afford them.

> SAM: If only we had more money to fix our sewers. Twenty percent of the water is unaccounted for. We got no money to fix them, you know?
> KJC: Wow.

RANDALL: Well all these were put in back in the forties.

KJC: In the forties . . .

SAM: They just can't even patch them anymore.

RANDALL: So you just put in close to three million dollars in sewer pipes three years ago. They did an income survey, a private income survey, away from the town . . . saw the results of the engineering permit. The average income in the town I live in is eleven thousand dollars.

KJC: Eleven?

RANDALL: And the sewer bills are fifty-three dollars a month.

KJC: A *month*?

RANDALL: A majority of people—

TOM: Wow, now my sixty-five and a quarter ain't too bad at all.

RANDALL: And a majority of the people, it was over half if I remember, are elderly, single people on a fixed income.

KJC: Awful.

RANDALL: We were promised 90 percent grant money. We got under seventy. So the federal government won't work with us at all . . .

KJC: Oh my, yeah. What are you gonna do in a case like that? I mean, you need a sewer, right? I mean—

SAM: Yeah, you gotta have something done . . .

RANDALL: I'll say. In order to fix anything, you can't keep raising the rates on it, you know, those people can't afford it.

The second way that rural consciousness fueled limited-government stances was by providing a set of arguments against government regulation. Many people openly resented having decision makers in the cities impose regulations on rural life that they felt displayed an obvious lack of understanding of what life in their community was like. In the previous chapter, I mentioned some of these complaints with respect to the state's Department of Natural Resources, or DNR—or in some of these circles, "Damn Near Russia." The DNR came up in many conversations as a government entity that imposed what were perceived as ridiculous regulations.

People in rural areas mentioned the DNR more than any other government agency. It was a prominent force in their lives. Many of them made a living working with natural resources, and many people spent a good bit of their leisure time outdoors hunting and fishing. When I first met the loggers in northwest Wisconsin, I asked them, "So what do you do, when you have leisure time, if you do, what do you like to do around [this town]?" (Group 6, June 2007).

SAM [*laughs*]: They go to taverns . . .

KJC: Hang out and visit?

CHARLIE: Go to work!

SAM: Sure yeah, go back to work.

JOHNNY: Hunt and fish. That's what lots of people do.

KJC: That's great, that's great.

JIM: Four-wheel it.

Later in our conversation, they brought up the cost of hunting and fishing licenses.

CHARLIE: No, they keep raising the prices of everything, hunting license, fishing license, and your wardens and stuff—you're on this side of the river then the trout has gotta be twelve inches long, and you go down here, a hundred yards underneath the bridge, and it's gotta be fourteen inches long, and then you get picked up and the warden don't even know what kind of fish they are.

KJC: Oh gosh!

CHARLIE: You know, it's—I haven't bought a fishing license in—

KJC: Do they keep close track of you, keep track of what you fish?

CHARLIE: I used to love to fish but I quit buying a license.

JIM: Yeah, I quit buying a license

CHARLIE: I won't even fish anymore because they don't know what they're doing, and I'm not going to go out there and get caught. As far as I'm concerned, the DNR thinks they are God. You know? We drop a half quart of oil out there or break a little hose or whatever and you gotta spend six months out there cleaning it up. It's good, but their good can go overboard. I can't walk out into a federal forest and go behind a tree and take a leak.

KJC: You can't?

CHARLIE: No! It's that bad. Really.

KJC [*laughing*]: Good grief! Do DNR folks live around here?

JIM: Oh yeah—

CHARLIE: We run into 'em all the time.

KJC: Be friendly with your neighbors, you know.

FRED: Well some of the guys—like in the forestry department, [of] course you got your forestry department, then you got your law enforcement then all your environmental stuff you got—

SAM: So guys turn them in, then they gotta go investigate.

KJC: Is deer hunting a big thing up here?

CHARLIE: Oh yeah.

KJC: I'm sure. And do they overregulate?

JOHNNY: What's that?

KJC: Deer hunting?

JOHNNY: Yeah, getting out of control.

SAM: If you ask five guys you'll have five different answers.

KJC: That's all right.

CHARLIE: It's just like the bear season, you know? You apply for a bear tag, you apply for a bear tag, takes you seven years to get a bear tag. But there are so many bear up here.

SAM: Yeah, got way too many.

CHARLIE: Every year you pay in to get that tag, and bear problems all over the place.

JIM: My mother lives down by Glidden, and they are ripping her bird feeder down every night, they are taking the humming bird feeders down, and you call the DNR and: "We ain't got time. We ain't got time to come up and check and see," you know. So what you do is you shoot the sucker. Got to. Got to protect your own property.

I heard criticism of the DNR as an agency getting in their way, even though its employees, according to the locals, knew less about the environment than they did, in many small towns. On the other side of the state, in Door County, I heard this (Group 5, June 2007):

DORIS: Talking about the environment up here, we've gotta do something about this algae that's running around [in the Great Lakes]. [*People in the group groan in agreement.*] Now you can get a fifty-dollar permit from the DNR to clean up your beach, but supposedly the people next to you don't do anything. And it comes back, I don't know how many times are you supposed to do this, and how are you going to get down [to the beach from the cliff above], like where I live, to get something down there to scrape it all up, and then what are they going to do with it?

PAM: And why do you have to pay?

DORIS: Yeah? Supposedly giving you a break because it was supposed to be five hundred dollars.

KJC: So—

BECKY: Why are they going to charge you to clean?

[*Several people*]: Have to have a permit.

KJC: Yeah—so for the $50 you just get a permit, it's not like the tools, or sup-
plies you need?

DORIS: No, just to clean it up

SHELLY: And get rid of it.

PASTOR CORRIE: Yeah, that doesn't make any sense at all!

KJC: That doesn't make any sense.

PAM: Right now—

DON: The DNR is very difficult to understand.

Many DNR employees live in rural areas, and are even from rural areas. But people in small-town Wisconsin would often talk about the DNR as one of these arms of government that is driven by decision makers in Madison. The perspective was that even if a given DNR employee was him- or herself a rural person, the regulations they had to enforce were made by people who were oblivious to rural life. In this way, resentment toward cities and toward the way urbanites ignored and disrespected rural folks fed opposition to government regulation.

A third way in which rural consciousness provided grounding for limited-government stances was by providing a story about where their tax dollars go. The basic narrative was that taxes are high and they must be going somewhere besides rural communities because rural communities are dying.

In that view, even if a person was willing, in theory, to give up some of their own income to support something like education, in practice they resented the idea because they believed that those dollars would go to the big cities, not to their town. Their disgust with the cost of public education was not aimed at spending on education in general. Instead, it was a resentment that public education spending systematically disadvantaged rural areas.

Take, for example, the conversations about education that took place in a rural group that leaned liberal but contained vocal conservatives as well. In a far northwest tourist and artistic community, a group of older and retired women met every Tuesday morning for coffee in the back of a restaurant, on the edge of town beyond the tourist-prone places (Group 2). Some of the women were big Obama supporters. Their leftiness was clearly signaled when one woman bellowed, "Rush Limbaugh should be hung." Another member stated outright that she moved to Wisconsin because of its reputation for great public education. She knew that quality education required higher taxes, and she was more than willing to pay them.

> You know, on the other hand, though, this maybe seems strange, I've always felt that if I'm living in Wisconsin I'm going to be paying taxes. I've already accepted that. And I don't want to live in Florida, and I don't want to live where education is poor. If my paying taxes supports kids, that's what I need to do. We feel that—I mean my husband and I both feel that way. So even though taxes are creeping up and they do and they do and they do, I think—if I want services, I'm going to pay taxes, they have to go to schools.

However, some of the women in this group were not as liberal. Many of them complained about high local property taxes. Their view was that urbanites bought or built expensive vacation homes, pushed up property taxes, made it hard for the locals to keep their homes, and changed the character of their town. Even the more vocally liberal members of the group nodded in agreement with these sentiments. Like many of the other rural groups, these women were willing to pay for public services but perceived that the money they put into the public pot would not come back to their small town. They lamented the way income tax took money out of their community, but were not at all positive about the way property taxes kept it there.

As noted in chapter 3, one woman, Carol, kept a notebook of all of the names of locals who had to leave town because of what they saw as skyrocketing property taxes driven by the price of urbanites' summer homes. When others expressed surprise at the length of the list she had accumulated in just nine years (sixty names), she said in June 2007:

> CAROL: This *is* a phenomenal thing. My notebook with all the pages of people that have left or are thinking about leaving. The majority for tax reasons.
> LAURA: And did they move, like, to . . . nearby areas? But just out of [this town]?
> CAROL: Out of [this town].
> LAURA: But still in the same county.
> CAROL: Mostly.
> ROSE: And one of the things, too, almost everybody has got a view of the lake. Almost everybody. And you pay for having a view, and that just doesn't seem right.
> LAURA: Conversely, because of the high cost of living, people, especially fam-

ilies, aren't moving in because there is not a job to support them to be able
to live here. So the school enrollment doesn't increase and we still have to
pay the burden of the school as part of the taxes.

SUE: And I think with shared revenues in the state of Wisconsin it is always
going to be that way. The money is collected here, it is sent to Madison,
and it is dispersed to Milwaukee and Madison primarily, and so our return on what we spend is very little, you know? And we struggle with our
school system here for the same reasons.

This was a general pattern for ambivalent rural groups. They were not
necessarily opposed to government spending in principle but, instead,
perceived that the government spending that did take place was unfair to
people like them—rural folks. Again, these perceptions were not always
accurate. The school-funding formula in Wisconsin is designed to ensure
that every district has a minimum level of spending per pupil. Districts
that have lower wealth in property values obtain proportionately more
in state aid.[5] But it is the perceptions that matter for how people interpreted small government.

Some of the people in these groups were clearly not opposed to government involvement in their lives. For example, although the group at
the diner in the northern tourist town (Group 9) passionately resented
regulations on hunting and fishing, they also supported stricter drunk
driving laws. The opposition to "big government" was more commonly
rooted in a perception that government was not functioning on behalf of
people like themselves than in a belief that government in general should
do less (Williamson, Skocpol, and Coggin 2011, 34).

Some of the ambivalence may also be related to the way the people I
listened to tended to meld different levels of government—local, county,
state, national—together when they talked about the government. Complaints about one level seemed to flow right into complaints about another. An issue with DNR regulation (a state agency) was often cause to
complain about "the government" in general.

The conversations in the Downtown Athletic Club, the group that had
been meeting in the old service station in the small town in central Wisconsin, can help illustrate the way groups were willing to pay for public
services if they could be convinced that their tax dollars would actually
come back to the people of their rural community. After I showed up
one morning to find the station shut down, I wrote a letter to the owner,
and we eventually got in touch. They had moved to a new location, and

I joined up with them one November morning in 2012. It was a small crowd because of deer hunting season (Group 1, June 2012). There were just two men there that morning when I arrived: the former service station owner, and the owner of the business that had become the new location for their morning meet-ups. For a few minutes, the wife of the latter business owner joined us, as did another man after about an hour. None of the retired public school teachers were there that morning.

During my earlier visits, the members of the Downtown Athletic Club expressed a lot of pride in their local schools and worried about their town blowing away if the state decided to consolidate the school district with the schools from a nearby town. Even without the retired school teachers in attendance, these small business owners said they were willing to pay tax dollars for the public schools, but they were not willing to pay higher taxes to support benefits for school teachers.

> FRED: Exactly, that's why Obama won cause he got the black vote, he got the Hispanic vote, and he got the women vote. He preyed upon the people who want to sit back and do nothing and keep receiving the handouts. And—
>
> SHARON: That's what irritates me.
>
> FRED: Nobody is ever going to get in there and win an election if they go in and tell the truth. Nobody will ever win any election if you go in and say we have to raise this tax 2 percent for this reason. We have to do this. We have to cut this for this reason. You'll never get in. It's like I told Lou and all them guys at the schools with these referendums. I says, If you can tell me the school needs a million-dollar referendum to buy computers for the junior high, new labs for the senior high, and a science class or whatever, I'd be more than happy to pay extra taxes and do my share. If it's truly for what the kids need. Now but that referendum just means the school can use it for whatever they want. And if they need this million dollars to pay the teachers' health insurance when we're paying thirteen hundred dollars a month with a twenty-five-hundred-dollar deductible.
>
> SHARON: Yeah, no, forty-five hundred dollars for the family deductible.
>
> FRED: I'm sorry, now you're starting to hit, where I won't 'cause it's not for the kids anymore. It's not about kids.
>
> SHARON: No dental, no vision.
>
> MATT: You know, but—
>
> SHARON: And that's, I told Fred, I said I would just as soon pay my kids a tuition to go to school. And I realize there are people out there that can't do

that. But I really feel like there's too much free shit in the world that people are abusing. Way too much.

KJC: That's frustrating. When times are tight.

Fred's wife, Sharon, who had joined us for a little while, says goodbye
and leaves, and I continue.

KJC: Yeah, that's so hard when you're busting your butt to make ends meet
and it feels like, you know, the government isn't paying any attention to
people like you.

MATT: No, it's like we've always said, small business, we're not a small
business—him and I aren't. I don't know what the hell we are.

FRED: We're just . . . We gotta carry umbrellas so the ants . . . we've got to
carry umbrellas so the ants don't pee on us.

[*KJC laughs*]

MATT: Yeah, small business is fifty employees. That's not us.

KJC: Micro? Micro-business.

MATT: Micro-business I guess you'd call it. There is no category for us. They
just kind of skim over the top of us.

People in other small towns were similarly willing to devote their tax
dollars to education, but reluctant to give it away to people who seemingly ignored or were unconcerned about them and their town (including the local public school teachers, who were often treated as outsiders). When I went back to the dice game in west-central Wisconsin on
recall election day (Group 11b, June 2012), I sat down at the table, apologetic for winning so much money during a previous visit. Amid shouting
about the score on the previous roll, Dale said to me:

DALE: You should get your money out.

KJC: You know the one time I did that, I won and won and won and never
lived it down. I won't play again and take all your money. Partly because
I come up here and hear that Madison sucks away all your money, so
that wouldn't be very appropriate for me to just sit here and take all your
quarters.

DALE: That was a lesson to remember. Madison sucks it all away.

KJC: I know. [*laughs*]

RICHARD: Well they do suck a lot of property tax[6] away north of the Mason-

Dixon line[7] for school aid. I wonder what—look at what they get per student down there for school aid versus north of Highway 21.

ERNIE: They shouldn't get any.

DALE: You're getting to the problem now if they would bring us their school district money back, we wouldn't have to raise taxes.

RICHARD: We're supposed to pay the teachers at the union scale and keep up all this stuff the same that they pay down there and we're expected to do it with less dollars than they do it south of [Highway] 21.

DALE: We keep our schools up and they let theirs fall apart and we pay them more.

RICHARD: The problem is with Milwaukee, of course. For years, the policy was the worst we're doing down here, let's just throw some more money at it. You think afterwards you would say, "It ain't working. There has to be fundamentally something else wrong."

DALE: We have to tax them enough to get it.

RICHARD: Who you gonna get them from though? Who you going to tax from?

DALE: The [same type of] people that they're taxing.

RICHARD: Why do you think they come up here and identify—and come up with a new term, "recreational land." You know what all that is about. It's about collecting more property taxes here to go south of the Mason-Dixon line. That's all it is. That's the only reason to do something.

DALE: We can halfway agree on something.

ERNIE: What's that?

RICHARD: The politics down there . . . they saw all this wooded land and of course that's God's country and why are all these people able to own that and they're paying nothing for property tax on it, you know. Well there's a reason property taxes are different up here than down there.

Hours south, well south of Highway 21, but nevertheless in a very rural area, I heard similar complaints. In the hamlet on the Wisconsin River, the people in the gas station resented the manner in which Madison sucked their tax dollars away for what they saw as unnecessary problems, but they also resented that the state government mandated that their local schools provide city-like programs (Group 8, January 2008).

DAN: It's like, have you ever seen a politician ever cut out a program? No, because the more programs you have the more politicians and government employees it takes to run them. So they want as many programs as possible, whether they're any good or not.

[*KJC laughs*]

RANDY: So are you, you go right there. [You're doing the same thing.] Right there. You know the legislature used to be part time in Wisconsin.

KJC: I know. Very different isn't it?

DAN: It's no different than all the programs that are mandated in the schools. They're never gonna back off in those programs because it takes that many more state employees to administer them. So they want as many programs as possible. And the health care is no different. The more programs they have, the more government-controlled programs, the more government employees it takes to run them. So they never talk themselves out of a job.

LARRY: I remember when the schools were paid for by our local taxes. The state of Wisconsin said, Well, you know, your small schools here, you're not giving the number of different classes that these kids could take. We want the kids in [this town] to receive the same classes as the kids in Madison. So the state of Wisconsin took it over. And we still are not getting the same classes that they do in Madison and they're not paying to run our schools.

DAN: But we're helping pay for the Milwaukee programs.

LARRY: That's right. Our schools are going into debt every year.

That kind of a conversation suggested to me that opposition to government spending was rooted in part in a perception that school policies were unfair to small towns. Part of the opposition here is due to a belief in government waste. But part of it stems from rural consciousness. Why support education spending when you believe that the money collected will not be used to benefit your own district? In these conversations, no one considers the possibility that any of these policies—school aid policy, recreational land designations—were created with rural interests in mind. Instead, the lens is of unfairness to rural places and rural people.

Political Principle? Or Identity and Resentment?

When people in rural areas claimed that government did not represent their interests, they were often rooting these claims in their identities as rural people. When they tried to make sense of the proper role of government, the concept of deservingness mattered just as it did in more urban areas. However, their understanding of *who* is deserving was often rooted in contrasts between themselves as rural people and nonrural people who did not face the same challenges and did not share the same work ethic or values.

Hard work was a key consideration for the consistently conservative groups but also, arguably, for the vast majority of the groups, including the groups who were ambivalent about small government. This is important. It suggests that support for limited government is not driven mainly by a belief in small government as a principle itself but, instead, by attitudes about a particular program's recipients (Schneider and Ingram 1993; Nelson and Kinder 1996).

It is important to pause a moment and consider once again the work of race here. When people were complaining that their hard-earned dollars were being taxed away and unfairly spent on the cities, wasn't that just racism? As I argued in chapter 3, I would like to suggest that the answer is not a simple yes. There is ample evidence to suggest that racism underlies much of the opposition to government spending, particularly on welfare (Kinder and Sanders 1996; Gilens 1999), although some scholars argue that such opposition is based on the principle of individualism, not rooted in racist beliefs (see the outlines of the debate in Huddy and Feldman 2009). Particularly since the Progressive Era (the late 1800s through the 1920s), cities in the United States have represented the expansion of government and cultural diversity (Conn 2014). That is, what we think of when we think of city is often about both of these things, together. We know that drawing attention to race, subtly or overtly (Huber and Lapinski 2006, 2008), influences support for policy. When race is sa-licnt, racial stereotypes play a role in whether people support a given candidate or policy choice (see also White 2007). Race can be made salient in a variety of ways, including images of people of color (Valentino 1999; Mendelberg 2001; Valentino, Hutchings and White 2002), the race of the president proposing the policy (Tesler 2012), the demographics of a policy context (Soss, Fording, and Schram 2011), or the use of words like "inner city" (Hurwitz and Peffley 2005) or "welfare" that have become near-synonymous with people of color (Gilens 1999).

Because support for policy is often driven by notions of deservingness and hard work (Soss and Schram 2007), and perceptions of who works hard are tinged by racism (Winter 2006, 2008; DeSante 2013), racism is unfortunately an inescapable part of public opinion in the contemporary United States.

However, I am reluctant to explain the work of rural consciousness as simply the work of racism because in contemporary parlance "racism" is often understood as blatant discrimination against people of color. That is not what is going on here. As I mentioned before, I observed little overt racism in rural Wisconsin.[8] But I heard ample amounts of it in urban and suburban areas.[9] I searched my field notes for a conversation in a rural community in which at least one person made a comment that directly linked urban residents with being lazy welfare recipients, for example. I found exactly zero such exchanges in rural communities, but several in urban and suburban locations.

When the rural residents I observed complained about urban people sucking tax dollars away, they were talking about their perception that urban residents paid fewer tax dollars than rural residents and received more government services such as better schools and better roads and infrastructure (e.g., Group 8). When I heard rural residents talk about "those people on welfare," they were talking about their white neighbors, not people of color in the cities (e.g., Group 8). Also, when they talked about lazy urbanites, they were talking about government employees or wealthier people who did not have to work as hard as themselves. The lazy and undeserving were also often young people (see Skocpol and Williamson 2012, chap. 4; e.g., Group 3). In this way, the perception that government programs benefited urbanites and not rural residents was not racism as it is commonly understood.

But racism today is not simple. Race is not something that we can siphon off from place and class in the contemporary United States. Patterns of discrimination over centuries mean that race colors our impressions of what kind of people are where and our willingness to share resources with them.

Unfortunately, particularly in a time of economic recession, the seeds of racism in U.S. political culture make it possible for public officials to use racism to mobilize support for small government. If one wishes to mobilize opposition to a government program, a powerful way of doing so is to suggest that the recipients of that program are predominantly people of color, precisely because support for policy hinges so strongly on notions of deservingness, which are rooted in notions of who in the population works hard. The persistence of racial stereotypes that contain beliefs that some racial groups are lazier than others makes it likely that those arguments activate racial resentment among many people and, therefore, even stronger opposition to government spending, as we have seen in the mobilization of support for Tea Party candidates (e.g., Burghart and Zeskind 2010; Parker and Barreto 2013).[10]

In the contemporary era, many people in the population feel that the government is not responsive to their concerns, as we have already seen. If people perceived that it is the affluent whose preferences are most closely reflected in policy decisions, then reducing the size of government is not necessarily what they would prefer. Instead, their response might be to favor increases in taxation of the rich and big business or, perhaps, reforms to campaign-spending laws. But if the focus is placed on the "undeserving" poor instead, the logical solution is to eliminate or reduce programs that provide a safety net for the undeserving, thereby shrinking government spending. To be blunt: conservative politicians encourage people to focus on the undeserving as a way to achieve their goal of limiting government without harming the interests of the wealthy.

In the following chapter, I look in closely at conversations that directly involved race, as I analyze reactions to Barack Obama.

Conclusion

It may not take much for you to agree with me that the people I observed are not reasoning about politics on the basis of political principle. We do not expect people to reason on the basis of coherent ideologies, and we often denigrate the average American voter as ignorant and incompetent in the realm of politics. But what is support for small government, if not a function of principle? To suggest that people are being hoodwinked does not mesh with what I have just presented to you. People have reasons for not wanting more government programs, even if an outside observer might conclude that stance is not consistent with their interests.

Why might the rural folks introduced here vote for a candidate whose policies support the idea of less government? Is it likely because they support an array of that candidate's specific policies? Are they voting on the basis of issues?

I suggest that whom people support in the election booth has to do with something rather different than issue voting—namely, identity. I heard people making sense of health care, education, and property taxes as a function of the kinds of people they believed themselves to be. Their sense of themselves as a part of a local community with a particular kind of challenging economy and relationship to government meant that they wanted less interaction with government, not more.

In the following chapter, I show how those perceptions and an identity-driven assessment of government programs played a role in the way they interpreted the Great Recession, Barack Obama, and Scott Walker.

CHAPTER SEVEN

Reactions to the Ruckus

W hen I started this project, I did not know the Great Recession was coming, that Barack Obama would soon be elected leader of the free world, or that Scott Walker would soon become my governor and propose Act 10. And I certainly did not foresee how interesting Wisconsin politics were about to become. I tried to take advantage of the fact that I was already in the field as these events happened. Because I had by that time established relationships with people taking part in regular coffee klatches across the state, I was able to ask for their permission to listen to how they were making sense of all this ruckus.

Noticing the Great Recession

The remarkable thing to me about the way people in small towns made sense of the Great Recession was just how unremarkable the recession seemed to many of them. For people who viewed the world through the lens of being victims of economic injustice because of where they live, the recession was just not that big of a deal. The recession *did* affect their towns. But they treated the effects as unremarkable. They said economic struggle was nothing new where they lived.

Because my fieldwork started before the Great Recession began and lasted well past its technical end, I was able to get some sense of when people noticed it. When I first visited twenty-three of the thirty-nine groups in this study in May and June of 2007, the financial crisis had not yet occurred. At that time, the Dow Jones was still rising (it hit its pre-recession peak on October 9, 2007). By most official accounts, the recession did not begin until August 2007, when problems with subprime

mortgage-backed securities came to light and the credit markets began to freeze up. Attention to the crisis intensified over the course of
my fieldwork, but many of the groups—especially those meeting in rural
communities—had serious concerns about the economy even before the
recession began.

During my first visits in the summer of 2007, no group anywhere
talked about "the recession." But economic concerns were nevertheless
prominent. To the question of what the big concerns were in their communities, the top three responses across all types of locations were the
cost of health care, lack of jobs, and high taxes. Another big concern was
the cost of gas, the price of which soared to over three dollars per gallon
in the Midwest in May 2007.

I did my second round of fieldwork in January and February of 2008.
By that time, the recession was here. The U.S. Federal Reserve had in-
jected over $80 billion for banks to borrow at a low rate in November
and December, and it had lowered the interest rate several times to 3.50
by mid-January. Nevertheless, "the recession" was again not a top concern, in any of the different places I visited. Instead, people talked about
health care and jobs. Occasionally, someone would mention "recession,"
but even then, others would argue a recession was not occurring.

At this time, of course, the 2008 presidential election was ramping up.
It was far from clear who was going to be the Democratic nominee. Before
the Iowa caucuses in January, Hillary Clinton, John Edwards, Joe Biden,
and Barack Obama were all contenders. But then in Iowa, very white and
nonurban Iowa, Barack Obama won with 38 percent of the vote. The subsequent primaries were a hard-fought contest between Clinton and Obama,
as the other contenders gradually dropped out of the race. Even through
the fifth of February, or Super Tuesday, the day the greatest number of
state primaries are held, the race remained basically tied. It continued until early June, when Obama had amassed enough support from delegates
(determined by the caucuses and primaries) and also superdelegates (at-
large votes from party members in Congress, governors, and other leaders)
to the national convention to make a Clinton win impossible.

Meanwhile, in March 2008, John McCain had clinched the Republican Party nomination, and in that same month, the global investment
bank Bear Stearns collapsed. When I returned to many of the communities in April and May of 2008, the reality of the economic crisis was
dawning. In one logging community in northwestern Wisconsin, among

a group of men on their way to work (Group 6), one man explained, "Well, the company my brother works for, last summer they had eighty-six guys working. This winter they had forty-three or something. Now they're down to twelve, and they're having a hard enough time finding part-time work for twelve guys."

A year later, in the spring of 2009, all of the groups recognized the difficult economic times, although some still avoided the term "recession." In the central Wisconsin city I visited, the group of professionals who met every morning at a café showed the effects (Group 16). When I had first met them, in June 2007, it was difficult to find a space among the ten or so regulars. But in May 2009, the group had dwindled to three. The rest of the regulars had been fired or laid off and had stopped making the breakfast group a part of their workday routine.

But the groups in the small towns had not changed much, in composition or in attitude. When I returned to the loggers in northwest Wisconsin (Group 6) in April 2009, I asked, "What are the big concerns in [this town] or in the area these days?"

> JIM: Probably more jobs to lose. [The mill in town was about to lay off eighty people.]
> [. . .]
> FRED: The only good thing is we don't have enough money to leave town.

A little earlier in the year, in February, I was visiting with the folks at the diner counter in the northern tourist town (Group 9). I was surprised to hear them talk about the economy as not so bad.

> PETE: What's the rest of the state got to say that you've been adventuring around?
> KJC: Jobs, jobs, jobs. You know.
> PETE: Sure.
> COREY: See, that really hasn't hit here much . . . it really hasn't been that bad. People have been spending money, you know, just until now.
> DAVE: Construction is down.
> KJC: Is it down?
> DAVE: Well, it's not lost. I mean it's not lost. They have homes, or houses that they're working on. You know. All the guys I talk to are, you know, got a house that is going.

KJC: So it seems like, it seems like tourism has been down for a little while now, like a year and a half or so, right? But lately it's pretty much the same in winter?

DAVE: We really don't, yeah . . .

COREY: I think it's down, but there are so many homes that are here owned by, that are secondary homes, that's, it might get affected, but I don't think it's affected to where—

DAVE: You don't have resorts. It's all private homeowners.

KJC: So people kind of are gonna come here—

COREY: So they might not come eight times a year, they might come five or something.

[. . .]

DAVE: Well that's what I'm saying, where if you go to destinations like I said, Disneyworld or places like that, I bet they're probably seeing a bigger effect, than you would notice it here, not that it ain't happening, but . . .

KJC: Yeah.

DAVE: It's pretty cheap to come to [this town]. The prices are cheap. The restaurants are cheap. Compared to the big city.

[. . .]

DAVE: And even when gas was up. I mean, there's still people around here. I mean, everyone knows when you had [a local festival] or you had Fourth of July, I mean, you still had people here, you know, I mean, they're still here, you know.

KJC: Yeah.

PETE: The ones that are hurting are the ones living off the stock market. They're hurting.

It sounded to me like they were saying their economy was doing OK. So I asked directly:

KJC: For the most part, things for folks up here are stable?

COREY: They've never been great, so they're still not great. You know what I'm saying?

KJC: Yeah.

COREY: You're used to what you got, you know?

KJC: Yup, yup.

COREY: So when we hear about all those other people crying the blues, well we—that's life.

Making Sense of Who Is to Blame

Even though people in small towns did not perceive that the recession was making a big difference in their lives, they nevertheless frequently talked about the economy, just as they had before the Great Recession set in. As I listened to those exchanges, I listened to hear whom people blamed. I did this in all types of places, because whom people blame tells us something about the kinds of policies they will be willing to support.

You might expect that people generally blamed the recession on Wall Street and on financial institutions. But I heard very little discussion of banks or financiers, before or after the crisis, by groups in any type of location. Several groups did mention blame of corporations and wealthy chief executive officers—but I heard such mentions only three times in over eighty-eight visits to thirty-nine different groups. Also, only five groups mentioned economic inequality as the culprit of economic woes. For example, even after the crisis began, members of the dice game group in the central Wisconsin town refused to fault corporations. They nodded in agreement as one member said, "Well, on the other hand, you can't blame the corporations, they're responsible to their stockholders" (Group 11b, April 2008).

The government, in contrast, was a consistent and pervasive target of blame. Throughout my fieldwork, "the government" was not popular. Liberals and conservatives alike blamed the government for economic problems before, during, and after the crisis. In liberal-leaning groups, people complained that economic policy was flawed because the government was in cahoots with the rich as it leached off of ordinary taxpayers. Also, they complained that elections were about money and believed the playing field was clearly tilted toward the rich. Conservative groups, in contrast, complained that the government was too large and not run enough like a business. Groups that contained both liberals and conservatives displayed a mix of these ideas.

Once the crisis began, criticism of the government became even more common. For example, the group of loggers meeting in a Democratic-leaning northwestern community complained that the 2008 presidential race was all about money (Group 6, April 2009):

> SAM: Well, those outfits donate all that money and the congressmen vote to let them steal out of our 401(k)'s for all kinds of fees and, and just the

people with all the money control everything. [*pause*] Whoever makes the
big donations gets their way.

FRED: It's kinda hard to trust politicians to put it that way, no matter what
side you're on. You know.

KJC: Yeah. You think it's different today than it used to be?

FRED: No, it's just on a bigger scale.

SAM: More money involved.

[. . .]

RANDALL: Well, yeah, then you get this economist: "When them oil prices
start going more than four dollars, boy that isn't gonna bother the economy." Well, how can it *not* bother the economy? Jeez, how much BS do
you think we can swallow?

The group of folks at the diner counter in the northern tourist town
also claimed that the government and the private sector were in cahoots
against ordinary citizens (Group 9). They lumped Wall Street and the
secretary of the Treasury together as enemies of the public.

COREY: My whole point of that thing is that they're just throwing this money
to Wall Street and the banks right away, no questions asked. AIG goes
and has a hunting party in England, they go to a party down there and
Henry Paulson [then secretary of the Treasury] is gonna take care of the
whole thing. But you haven't even seen that guy, they gave him control of
three hundred billion dollars but you haven't seen nothing.

[. . .]

DAVE: Well the secretary of the Treasury. Just think, wow that guy didn't
pay his taxes . . . Well, you're putting a guy in there that cheated the government, that's stealing. How can he be the Treasury secretary? Just
ridiculous.

A common complaint was that government did not run more like a
business (see Gangl 2007). This came up often, and not just in predominantly Republican groups. For example, one small business owner in the
group of loggers in the northwestern town noted his own need to balance
a budget and lamented the lack of accountability in government spending (Group 6, April 2008). Other mixed-partisan groups blamed the government's lack of performance on the fact that government officials were
wealthy people with little experience in the real world. For example, in
April 2008, in the logging community in central Wisconsin, the regulars

in the morning dice game blamed the mortgage crisis on government deregulation (Group 11b):

> MARK: Nobody has any idea what real life is like. None of them work for a living. They're legislators. They don't have outside jobs. And they, they lose touch, they don't have to deal with it.
>
> HENRY: I mean I laugh now, you listen to all this thing now over the mortgage crisis. You could see this train wreck coming years ago.

Blaming the government happened in all types of places. But in small rural towns, people talked as if they had a special claim to those arguments. They talked as people living in an economy that was especially difficult and who were especially skeptical of government actions to improve it.

In the northern tourist town, in February 2009, the folks at the diner counter seemed supportive of government spending in the form of the stimulus package, but whatever willingness they had to support that kind of government program was tempered by their perspective as people from a rural community that was unlikely to feel the effects of a stimulus (Group 9).

> COREY: I mean, last week the government puts in their stimulus package. I mean, there you have, what, over 1.4 trillion dollars sitting there doing nothing, you know, and they all want to build new buildings and crap like that and I mean ridiculous, you know?
>
> KJC: What do you think they ought to do to jumpstart the economy? Or is it just kinda, nothing you can do?
>
> COREY: No, like I said earlier, you know, last summer we all got that stimulus check and—
>
> PETE: That's not enough.
>
> COREY: If you didn't buy a forty-two-inch flat screen TV with it, you know, there were sure a lot of them for sale for six hundred bucks. Paid off bills and, and actually, you know what we did, went to Canada, so we spent it all in Canada.
>
> PETE: Yeah.
>
> COREY: The three of us, you know.
>
> DAVE: It's not, it's not enough money to make a difference of nothing.
>
> COREY: But what I'm saying is that—
>
> DAVE: Well I think for a lot of people it did pay for your gas.

COREY: Right—

PETE: What was your stimulus package last time? Was bigger than mine . . .

COREY: But they took all this money that you're giving away now, and if they would use it, just give it to the American people. You know? Divide it up and give it to the American people you'd have a lot of cash to spend, you know? And you know, of course, a lot of people are gonna just do stupid stuff with it. Drink, buy their drugs, whatever, but I think other people—

DAVE: They'll still—

COREY: Pay some mortgages, you know.

DAVE: They're always gonna do that.

COREY: And then we'll be broke in a year anyways, all of us would be. But you know what I'm saying? Like I said earlier you give it to the car companies, you know, and you got the person making twelve bucks an hour, sixteen bucks an hour, twenty bucks an hour. OK, I'm gonna pay my taxes so you can give it to them so they can make *forty and sixty dollars an hour*? Wait a second. That does not make sense. It doesn't compute.

DAVE: Well that's where the union has to make the concessions. The unions have to make the concessions and they're not doing it.

COREY: Right. And it's terrible.

PETE: And I don't know what tax breaks they're giving us because after doing my taxes this year—

COREY: Well, they're talking about cutting them off, so, and I don't know how, and what do you mean, OK, now where are you gonna get the money from?

PETE: Yeah.

COREY: You know? Holy crike.

KJC: You wonder . . .

COREY: But you know the other day on the radio they said about the people that, they gave the figure of people that underpay on their taxes. And it was something billions of dollars, billions, it was a ton of money, every year, and it says like 5 percent. Holy crikes. And they got the money coming in. And you go take that times, what would that be then—twenty? Holy smokes. So they got the money coming in. So I mean there's a lot of dough, but to cut the taxes off, you need money to operate to give away all this money, you need money!

[*KJC laughs*]

PETE: And that's what they're doing and we all know that and there's no— buying it anymore. Well and—

COREY: There's money.

DAVE: Well, if you take northern Wisconsin here, there's no way to get a business in here. They'd have to hire people, so far to freight it back to the city.

COREY: Right, right it wouldn't make sense.

DAVE: It wouldn't make sense. Unless everybody's gonna live on one thousand dollars a year no matter what.

KJC: Yeah.

DAVE: They're loading the stuff up and taking it down to Milwaukee.

PETE: That's one of the reasons.

TREVOR: Ain't a "down there," up here.

COREY: It's cheaper here, that's why it was here. That's why they came here, they were only offering $5.25 an hour starting at that time.

KJC: To do what? Manufacturing?

PETE: When it was—

COREY: [Describes the kind of manufacturing this local plant does.] They've been here longer than me, but ten, twelve years ago they were paying eight bucks an hour. You can't live on that.

KJC: You can't.

COREY: You can't live on that.

KJC: Nope.

COREY: Nowadays it takes a thousand dollars a week for a family to live. You gotta have a thousand dollars a week, for a family to live.

KJC: Yeah.

COREY: That's a house payment, one car payment, maybe, insurance.

PETE: And a lot of people doing it on thirty, thirty-five [thousand], I don't know how.[1]

KJC: Trying to, right?

PETE: I don't know how about 80 percent of these people live, in town here. I really don't. I can't—I've never lived on what they do. I can't.

COREY: A lot of those people don't have any kind of insurance.

PETE: No, no.

COREY: But their wages—I can't . . .

To these folks, there was money in the economy, money to help people out. But they sure did not believe it resided in their community.

Except of course, among public employees. In the previous chapter, I described how many people in small towns perceived that public employees were the wealthy members of their community and were receiving higher salaries, plus health care and pensions, and the money to pay for all of that was coming from taxpayers like themselves.

In that framework, when the conversations came around to the Great Recession, it was common for people to blame public employees.

About ten months earlier, the group in the northern tourist town had expressed similar concerns about the impossibility of leading a normal life on the salaries available in their type of town. "How in the heck can you afford to do anything? Can't even afford to live," one man, Pete, said. During that visit, the conversation moved from the lack of manufacturing in the United States to government inefficiency, then government corruption, and finally to public employees, as Nelson piped in (with a laugh): "I think those people that work for the UW should take a pay cut," and at least one other nodded in agreement, adding, "professors— professors have student teachers" (implying professors are lazy).

During my February 2009 visit, Corey worried aloud about the ability for people to get by on the wages available, then suggested that there be a 10 percent sales tax across the board to try to generate some revenue. But Pete steered the conversation back to the way tax dollars were wasted on the bureaucracy, on public employees.

> COREY: I mean we could save us a lot of money if we could do 10 percent tax right across the board for everything. . . . You know, sales tax, 10 percent sales tax right across the board. Save a lot of things. Of course, I'm, you gotta keep smoking because they're gonna raise the, that's a lot of tax money, you know, if I quit that could be another . . . well let me figure out—
> PETE: Well, you gotta think how many people that you got down in Madison—
> COREY: Another three hundred dollars a year. Well whatever, you know, but—
> PETE: Secretaries, with secretaries, with secretaries.

And then Corey agreed that tax revenue is wasted on public employees in the cities:

> COREY: It's Madison's schools, it's everything, it's just getting pathetic you know.

Often, when people talked about the economy, someone would offer up public employees as a target of blame. And notice that, even though a portion of workers in all communities are public employees, in the outstate groups, "Madison" was often used as shorthand for public workers.

Making sense of the Great Recession through the lens of rural consciousness meant several things: that a recession was not big news and that blame went to the cities and to the government. Many people in rural communities looked around and saw themselves in a place perpetually stuck in disadvantage, and they resented public employees who seemed to be protected from hardship, all because of the hard work of people like themselves in small towns.

Reactions to Obama

When I started my fieldwork in the spring of 2007, Barack Obama was a contender for the Democratic nomination for the presidential election, but he had just come on the scene. He had been a state senator in Illinois, then a U.S. senator from that state, and a much talked-about speaker at the 2004 Democratic Party National Convention, but he was new to most people.

People everywhere were trying to make sense of him and whether the country was ready for an African American president. I heard that in my fieldwork, and I heard it in all types of places, not just rural ones.

But because of Obama's racial background, how people reacted to him can perhaps tell us something about the role race plays in rural consciousness. As I have mentioned before, when people in rural areas were expressing resentment against urban areas and perceiving that power and resources were unfairly focused on cities, race was embedded in those arguments.

The people I spent time with did not talk about Obama as a city person. It was not necessary. So many things about him conveyed that he was a city person: his party affiliation, his past political experience, and his occupation (he had represented Chicago, been a professor, and been an urban community organizer), as well as his race.

People referred to Obama's "otherness" in a variety of ways. In particular, they assumed that his base of support was either African American voters or young people.[2] When I asked the women in the northwest tourist town if they were surprised by Obama's success in the Iowa Caucus, they said (Group 2, January 2008):

ELAINE: Well, I guess I was surprised that a black person could do that well. In the heartland of our country, I mean I could see it on either coast

perhaps, but in Iowa? Wow. Maybe that was—it was, you know, it was—
heartening. I mean, it was uplifting.

KJC: Yeah.

SUE: I think that there's this huge amount of young people who have been so
disenfranchised from our political system—

[*Multiple "Yeahs."*]

SUE:—that is just wonderful to see them get out, I don't care who they elect,
and if they become part of it. And—and they are. Look at those faces.

In the southwest town on the Wisconsin River (Group 8, April 2008),
one man, Larry, explained Obama's likely success this way: "Obama's a
description of all, where all the young latte Democrat voters are, they're
gonna vote for him." And another (Glenn) explained simply: "Because
all the blacks will vote for him. All the Clinton-haters will vote for
him." Earlier in the year, in January 2008, another man, Dan, suggested
Obama's success in the primary elections was due to the overwhelm-
ing support he was getting among African American voters. "Like the
South Carolina results, where 85 percent of the blacks voted for Obama.
Big surprise. You know, and the only thing he's gonna do is keep Hillary
from getting 85 percent of the woman's vote. Because some of those
women are black."

I asked the men in the gas station in the west-central logging town
(Group 11a, January 2008), "Do you think Obama is unbeatable?"

WARREN: I think if he'd be a Democrat. I think if you're a Democrat, and you
have a pulse you're gonna win the election, presidential election unless
you're Hillary.

HANK: He'll have the African American votes. I do like him a lot better than
Hillary, if I had my choice.

These sentiments that Obama's support was mainly among African
Americans and young people were not unique to rural areas. In a Wisconsin suburb of Minneapolis (Group 13, January 2008), one man said,
"For the younger generation, he's a very popular candidate, I think."
A man in the group of professionals in the central Wisconsin city said,
"The young people want change, I mean that's it. Young people want
change and that's Obama" (Group 16a, April 2008). In a Milwaukee suburb, about the time of Obama's inauguration (Group 18b): "Oh and I'll
tell ya, the blacks would have never come out and voted if he wasn't a

black person. They would have sat at home and drank and did whatever they did. I'm sorry. That's my feeling."

The people I spent time with were aware of Obama's appeal, but few admitted that they themselves supported him. One notable exception was a relatively reserved woman in the breakfast group in the northwest tourist town (Group 2) stating bluntly, "I am an Obama Girl."

Usually, though, when people expressed support for Obama, they found it necessary to state that race was not a relevant factor. In the north-central tourist town, I was asking the group about Mike Huckabee, a maverick candidate in the Republican primary, but they turned their attention to the Democrats (Group 9, January 2008):

KJC: Yeah, how about that Mike Huckabee? Everybody says he seems so down-to-earth. What do you think?

DAVE: Big business won't allow him in. They'll pour the money into somebody else that will protect them.

PETE: Of course, he's flying pretty high right now. I don't think Hillary's gonna make it. I liked her up until she told us she was our girl, and I didn't like that.

KJC: She was what?

PETE: She was "our girl." OK, Hillary, goodbye. I think Obama has a really good chance.

DAVE: Well I think he's the best one, as far as the Democrats.

PETE: I really just, I have no problem with him.

KJC: Yeah? Were you surprised he won Iowa?

DAVE: I wasn't.

KJC: Yeah? How come?

DAVE: Because he's more down-to-earth as far as talking to the average person, and Hillary is up here, she's a multimillionaire. And her nose is turned this way, and the rest of them . . .

[*Laughter*]

KJC: Yeah, that's a good way of putting it.

DAVE: So she's not really the average person . . .

KJC: But Obama seems still kind of . . . ?

DAVE: Down-to-earth, yeah.

KJC: That would be interesting, wouldn't it? If he were president of the United States?

DAVE: Yeah. Well that wouldn't bother me. I can work with anybody. We've had good and bad in every color.

KJC: Right. Some people were saying there's no way he's gonna win Iowa, Iowa is 97 percent white, and, you know, it just didn't seem to matter a whole lot.

DAVE: No, no. That wouldn't be my criteria as far as . . . picking my president if he was the one going to do the best for the average person. You know, the millionaires don't need any help, because they're millionaires. They're OK. They might be able to send their kids to Madison.

I heard similar statements in the central Wisconsin city and in Milwaukee suburbs: "I don't have a problem with Obama at all." Several people who supported Obama also found it necessary to justify their stance with comments about Obama's intelligence and distinctiveness from Jesse Jackson and Al Sharpton. The type or size of community did not matter for the apparent need to justify voting for an African American man.

In general, white people across all types of communities seemed uncomfortable talking about the fact that Obama is African American. It was the kind of discomfort among whites that goes along with a lack of experience with African Americans and a lack of understanding or familiarity with anyone who is African American. Because Wisconsin is predominantly white and highly racially segregated in its urban areas, that lack of experience is not something exclusive to rural areas.

At the same time that people seemed uncomfortable with Obama's race and race as a concept in general, Obama's theme of change and unity resonated with people—or at least they believed it resonated with others. The professionals in central Wisconsin might have found it necessary to qualify his appeal as a certain "kind" of African American, but they also nodded as one man said, "He is the one with the best truth out there." I heard glimmers of hope that he was a different kind of politician, one not entrenched in Washington, and one who, especially compared to Hillary, was closer to the people.

In the gas station in the central-west logging town, here's the way the folks compared Hillary Clinton and Barack Obama in January 2008 (Group 11a):

TOBY: Well, I'm a Republican so I'd like to see the Republican win, and I think if Hillary would be the candidate, then a Republican would win . . . I want Hillary, you bet. Barack Obama, I think, is unbeatable.

HANK: It's between those two. Well, Barack is . . . I don't know what. We've already had Hillary in the White House, we don't want her no more. She was running the White House to start with. [*Turning to Jeremy*] Tell her the way you told us. "I got a woman at home. I don't want one telling me what I can do in the United States."

WARREN: Let it all out.

JEREMY: That is not true.

HANK: Oh, that wasn't you, that was Dave. "You guys think you have it bad at home just wait until a woman runs this country."

KJC: That's a good line. That was Dave?

WARREN: I just think a lot of people don't like her.

HANK: I don't like her. I just don't like her. I think she's a little . . .

WARREN: She's got that air around her. That aura. That "I'm better than you are." She doesn't seem genuine.

These references to Hillary being too distant and Obama having more appeal did not include any kind of rural-versus-urban tension. No one said to me that Obama was more appealing to people "in towns like ours" or "places like this," and so forth. But there seemed to be a kind of fascination that someone "like Obama" could have appeal in small places like their own.

That fascination came crashing down a bit in April 2008 when a citizen journalist told the world something Obama had said at a San Francisco fundraiser. He had said that working-class voters in old industrial towns "get bitter, they cling to guns or religion or antipathy to people who aren't like them or anti-immigrant sentiment or anti-trade sentiment as a way to explain their frustrations."

I visited the dice game in the central-west logging town just days after news of that remark broke (April 2008). Dave asked me, "You know, do you detect the bitterness that Barack Obama's talking about? Have you detected it yet?" His pal, Richard, said, "Yeah, we talked about it, some are going to religion and some are going to guns, and I haven't decided which one I'm gonna take up yet. If it's a gun in the end, you better stay home." They were mad—resentful, bitter even, and any aura of affinity between Obama and folks like themselves seemed to have worn off.

After Obama won the presidential election in 2008, the recession gained steam. Debate over health care escalated and the partisan camps on that issue became more clearly defined. After those events, I heard fewer comments that were supportive of Obama, even if that earlier support had been somewhat tepid. For example, in the diner in the northern tourist town (Group 9), in January 2008, several people had given him some support ("I have no problem with him" and "that would not bother me" if he became president.) But, a year later, in February 2009, one quickly offered: "But I don't care for Obama, I didn't vote for him." The professionals in the city in the middle of the state, who had talked about Obama's articulateness and intelligence, now said he was a media whore and exclaimed that he was spreading fear about the recession (Group 16a, Feb 2009). Across the groups, across types of places, there were increasing claims that Obama was not following through on his promises. Some people acknowledged that the context in which he found himself was particularly difficult for passing legislation.

In general, I did not see evidence that rural consciousness provided a distinctive interpretation of Obama initially. The way people talked about him in rural areas seemed very similar to what I heard in urban and suburban areas. That fact that Wisconsin is racially very homogenous and segregated makes it not that surprising that rural residents did not seem any more awkward than white suburban and urban residents when talking about race.

But the other reason that rural consciousness may not have made a big difference in the way people in small towns talked about Obama is because they tended to lump all politicians together. Rural consciousness is partly about the perception that people in power overlook and disregard rural areas. For a time, a few people seemed to be open to the possibility that Obama's racial distinctiveness meant that he might actually listen to people like themselves. But there seemed to be a collective sigh of, "Oh right, he's just like the rest of them," once it was clear Obama was not going to be able to unify the country, provide a magical solution to the health care quandary, or reverse their local economies.

The 2012 election returns showed a bit of this deflation. Although Obama won Wisconsin in 2012, he did considerably worse in the rural counties than he had in 2008. In figure 7.1, you can see the way the rural areas went from relatively Democratic (light grey) in the presidential election of 2008, to Republican (darker grey) in the gubernatorial election of 2010 and the 2012 recall, to lighter—but still darker than 2008—in the 2012 presidential election.

Reactions to Governor Scott Walker

Reactions to Scott Walker were different, though. How is it possible that this Republican was elected to the governorship in 2010, although

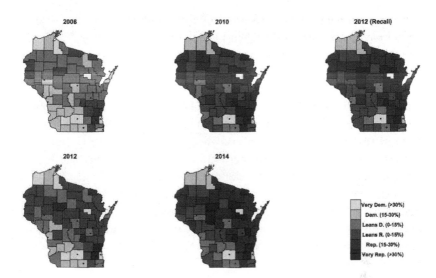

FIGURE 7.1. County margins separating Democratic and Republican votes across five presidential and gubernatorial elections (2008–2014). Sources: Wisconsin Blue Book, State of Wisconsin Legislative Reference Bureau (2008–2012 results) (http://legis.wisconsin.gov/lrb/pubs/bluebook.htm); Associated Press (2014 results) (http://wisconsinvote.org/election-results).

Obama won the state in 2008 and 2012? Part of the explanation is that the 2010 gubernatorial election was an "off-year" election, a less-publicized and -hyped election than a presidential election. Young people and racial minorities were a smaller share of the electorate that turned out to vote in 2010 than in 2008, and that meant less support for the Democratic candidate in 2010.[3]

Also, Scott Walker rode the wave of the Great Recession. In June before the election, 85 percent of Wisconsinites perceived that the state was in "bad times" economically (up from 40 percent in June of 2007), and 95 percent felt this way about the United States as a whole.[4] Walker campaigned on a Tea Party platform, vowing to balance the state's budget without raising taxes. He won with 52 percent of the vote.

When Walker took office on January 3, 2011, he used the context of the recession to implement Act 10, one of the most controversial legislative measures in Wisconsin history. The protests, fleeing Democratic state senators, and recall efforts that resulted constituted the most intense political uproar the state of Wisconsin had seen in decades, perhaps ever. The fact that Act 10 became law is all the more striking because Wisconsin had been home to the start of collective bargaining for government employees, back in 1959.

Walker not only made the most of the Great Recession—he also tapped into rural consciousness. I revisited eight rural groups, one out-state urban group, one suburban Milwaukee group, and one Madison group after the protests had erupted in Madison (seven visits to these groups in the spring and summer of 2011, eight visits in summer 2012, and one in fall 2012). Each of those groups was supportive of Walker's proposal to require public workers to pay more into their health and pension benefits. Given the perceptions of public employees I had been hearing from them for years, this was not a surprise. To people who perceived that public employee benefits came directly from their own pockets despite the "fact" that people in their town worked much harder than the overpaid desk workers in state government, Walker's proposals were not necessarily a victory for smaller government. They were a victory for small-town Wisconsinites like themselves.

To illustrate what I mean by rural consciousness structuring the way people made sense of Scott Walker and Act 10, I return to conversations among the members of two blue-collar groups, one in Madison and the other in the northwestern logging town. Both of these groups meet in predominantly Democratic areas of the state. Both contain many members who said they vote Democratic, but who often expressed moderate or conservative views. One group meets every morning at a diner in Madison (Group 22b), and the other is the one that meets every morning in a gas station in the northern logging town (Group 6). Both groups are composed of current or retired laborers; many in the Madison group are former union members. Most of the members of the rural group are currently working in the logging industry, as owners of small logging businesses. One of the members of that group is a current local elected official (a Democrat).

During my visits before 2011, members of both groups had complained that state employees have extravagant health care and pension benefits, are inefficient, and do not work very hard. However, rural consciousness made a difference in the way they talked about the ruckus in Madison after Walker came to power. When I revisited them in 2011, the Madison group talked about the protests at the state capitol and the budget issues involved by referencing their own work ethic and contrasting public and private employees. The rural group, conversely, discussed the protests and budget with use of their geography-based identity: through the lens of rural people governed by arrogant, out-of-touch urbanites.

Let's start with the urban (Madison) group first. On a February 2008 morning visit to the Madison group, I asked what the important concerns were in their community. They immediately blurted out their anger about public employee benefits. One man turned to me and asked, "How about wages for people? Ya educated people get all the money. . . . I worked, we worked in the trades, we don't get anywhere that kind of money that they get, and all the benefits they get." Then another man, Harold, turned to me and said, "That includes you, too. They bleed the rest of us to death."

When I visited this group shortly after the protests erupted in Madison in February 2011, there were six men present, four of whom were current or former private union members. One other owned a used-car dealership, and another, Harold, had been a member of the United Auto Workers, and also a union steward for a few years. (He quit because he believed the union was corrupt.) All of the members agreed state workers should pay more into their pensions and health benefits. But all of them except Harold were highly critical of Walker's attempts to eliminate most collective bargaining for most public employees (which was consistent with the tendency of people in union households in the state to disapprove of Walker's performance).[5]

Harold said to us all, "The teachers' union—they been in there—they were in there like the cat at the bowl of milk. Then they turned it to cream. And then they turned it to *ice* cream. And finally it's *gonna melt!*" And then one of the pro-union members said:

STU: Oh no, it's not only the teachers' union, it's all the unions—state employees.

HAROLD: You name me one thing that they've given up in the past forty-five years. It's nothing, nothing, nothing.

STU: It's not a matter of what they are giving up. It's taking away collective bargaining.

HAROLD: I'm sick of collective bargaining. And I'm a taxpayer. And you are too! And you sit here bellyaching about paying taxes and you don't want to—

STU: No, no, no, no!

[*"Time outs!" from some members.*]

KJC: I don't mean to start a fight here.

HAROLD: Let me tell you something. There is nobody that had a rougher childhood and place to stay than I did.

STU: I'm not—

HAROLD: Now wait a second. [*wagging his finger*] I used to work and swing a sixteen-pound maul. I built the first pier in front of The Edgewater [a lakeside hotel in town], see, and I was about twelve, thirteen years old and swinging a sixteen-pound sledge from the minute I got out of school until the sun went down . . . and I got a quarter a week *if* the guy got paid by the sorority house/fraternity house [behind which he also built piers] . . . I used to have to catch a hundred fish before breakfast if the whole family was going to eat that day. Clean 'em and skin 'em and sell them for a quarter a dozen or two cents apiece. *So I know what it is to be on the bottom.* And I would do it all over again. But the people at the top, they are just milking us dry on taxes. That's what it is. And 90 percent of 'em, up in that state office building or wherever the hell they are working, if they lost the job they got, they would lay down in the gutter outside here and die, since they don't know how to do anything else. There ain't very many of 'em that sweat. . . . I still know how to work. I'm eighty-two years old and I'm driving a semi!

Deservingness was important to Harold, as it was to many people I encountered in this study. Notice how he hinges his comments about who deserves to get more and who is getting more than their fair share on his personal identity as someone who has labored extremely hard his entire life. Comments about whether public employees were deserving were central to the way the members of this group evaluated Walker's budget proposals. They regularly made comments about how hard (or not) public employees worked and linked those judgments to whether they deserve the hard-earned dollars of taxpayers like themselves (Soss and Schram 2007).

After Harold exclaimed that he was eighty-two and still driving a semi, I pressed him a bit further:

KJC: So let me ask you this. You mentioned the people at the top milking the rest of us dry.

HAROLD: Yeah!

KJC: Is it the people at the top versus the rest of us, or is it the public employees versus the workers who aren't public employees? [*pause*] You know what I mean?

HAROLD: Hey—can you tell me why Lizard Doyle [Jim Doyle, the former governor] gave the guy the $252,000-a-year job and he just walked in the door and got it? Can anybody back that up and apologize for it with one word even if it means anything? Hell no! See it's just—on and on and on.

This is what is going on here: I tried to clarify whether Harold thought the big divide was between the haves and the have-nots or between public and private employees. His answer made it clear that, to him, public employees *are* among the haves. His comments convey the following understanding of the world:

people like me = hard-working people = nonpublic employees
versus
people not like me = people who don't work hard = public employees

I heard these perspectives in conversations throughout the state (and well before Walker was on the scene). But in rural areas, there was another component. Many people perceived that rural folks had a qualitatively different work ethic and orientation to public decision making than people in urban areas and perceived that public employees were at root urbanites, even if they lived in rural communities.

Their understanding of the world came across like this:

rural folks like me = hard-working people = nonpublic employees = deserving
versus
urbanites = people who don't work hard = public employees = undeserving

To clarify this, I'll contrast the conversations of the Madison group above with the group of loggers in northwestern Wisconsin (Group 6). The talk in the latter group was different. It was not their identity as workers that was central to their notions of deservingness but, instead, their sense of themselves as rural folks.

Their identity as people perpetually in economic hard times characterized their conversations long before Walker became governor, and it structured the way they talked about state politics once he was in office. When I revisited this group in May 2011, several months after the protests, just a few men were present, all self-proclaimed Walker supporters.[6] Two of them had recently gone to a Republican fundraiser at which Walker spoke in a nearby town. I asked them why they leaned Republican even though the surrounding area tended to vote Democratic. They said that they were both small business owners and their economic views better aligned with the Republicans.

I asked Ron why the prevailing economic divide pitted public workers against private workers, rather than the people versus big business. His response is contained in the following conversation. Part of what gets discussed here is a controversy over a proposed nearby iron ore mine that was alleged to pose major environmental impacts yet provide an estimated eight hundred jobs for fifteen years.

> KJC: What do you say then to people who say, "Ok, why has it become pub-
> lic workers versus private workers? Why aren't we all arguing against, say,
> the Koch brothers or whoever big money people are and say, '*Everybody*
> should be getting a pension like this, *everybody* should be getting' health
> care?'"
>
> RON: How can everybody get it? Because who's gonna pay the tab?
>
> KJC: Well the, the argument people say is, the Koch brothers—
>
> RON: But the thing is—
>
> KJC: And, "Why don't we tax the corporations more," you know?
>
> RON: The Koch brothers [major funders of Walker and other conservative
> candidates nationwide], they're private individuals, private businesses.
> OK? The only ones that are paying, they're charging their customers like
> you or I whatever you're using. They're dumping all that expense onto
> their customers, the consumer. And the, and the, and the whole ball of
> wax, the consumer is paying, one way or the other. But, like, Koch broth-
> ers or whatever they're into, they are creating jobs that are producing
> something that is beneficial, like, whatever they're, like electricity or what-
> ever, you know? So you—just tell me, how can I put this politely?
>
> KJC: Oh, you don't have to!
>
> RON: No, no, I'm just saying—
>
> KJC: You don't have to put it politely.
>
> RON: How can you, I mean state employees, I mean you've got lots of, lots
> of divisions in the state that are just, just take like the [Department of
> Natural Resources], OK? You've got the DNR with all this environmental
> bullshit, we got a job, seven hundred good-paying jobs if this mine starts
> up. They're all fighting it. . . . Because of the water pollution and the air
> pollution and everything else. But it's, the chances of [pollution] happen-
> ing are so slim that it's, you know, because they're gonna be so dictated to,

what they can do and what they can't, but [the politicians and state workers] are not worried about the seven-or-eight hundred jobs, they already got their jobs with their benefits and everything else. . . . They got their pockets full already but they're not worried about the younger generation like Johnny or anybody else in this area. Can you imagine what seven hundred, eight hundred good-paying jobs would, and the runoff of *that*?

KJC: Yeah.

RON: They might have a little runoff on the water for pollution but the runoff of money that would be created by this mine.

KJC: That would be amazing.

RON: It would be awesome. I mean . . .

KJC: Yeah.

RON: It, there is not seven/eight hundred good-paying jobs in this whole county.

KJC: I know. I know.

RON: The only ones that are, gotta have good-paying jobs are the people that work for the government, the power companies, you know.

We kept on talking for a while. As I was about to leave, another logger arrived. I said that I was aiming to be back within the year, and he mentioned the mine issue, unaware that others in the group had talked about it earlier.

LUKE: Come back if they shoot down this mining. Then we'll really be mad.

RON: Well, the thing is, if they do it the way it's set up right now it would take ten years to get all the permits and. . . . We need jobs now, not ten years from now.

LUKE: Well in ten years, this probably won't be here probably [*motions to the town outside*].

RON: Yeah, we won't be here in ten. You know, I mean we need 'em now. And the local people are, truthfully, 90, probably 98 percent of the local people are for this mining, you know, but you got these small groups that, you know, every day you look in the paper there's somebody writing articles against it, you know. . . . We need good-paying jobs. Simple as that. . . . We can't afford to lose them up here. People down south have good, basically have some good advantages, getting some good-paying jobs. . . . They have no clue, other people don't have no clue what's going on up here.

LUKE: No.

RON: Down in the cities, they don't even know their neighbors most of 'em!

KJC: Well yeah, I just meant—

LUKE: What I, what I get a kick out of is now, with this going on, is now it's garnering like national attention and everybody from out of the area rushes up here and says how great and wonderful it is and how much they love it up here. They probably never been here before in their life. But they want to save it. Well, where that mine is gonna go is where my deer stand is. . . . But, for the general good of my grandchildren, and the other children and the people that live in this area who've been struggling to get by their whole life—hey, put the mine in.

RON: Yeah.

LUKE: Let's get some, let's get some life in this area.

RON: Yeah.

LUKE: Let's re-, let's rejuvenate our future.

RON: Our lights are just about shot.

LUKE: Yeah. . . . They all have their big jobs and their big fancy cars.

RON: Yeah.

LUKE: And their lifestyle and they come up here and tell us how to live.

RON: Yeah, yeah.

Like Harold in the Madison group, these men have been "struggling to get by their whole life." But in contrast to Harold, they treat their economic circumstances as inseparable from their identification as people of a certain type of place. Harold's attitudes about benefits to public workers flow from his life experience, but for the men in this rural group, their attitudes flow from their experience with life in a rural town. Because their rural consciousness is a lens through which they view the world as people with less income and less power than folks "down south," they screen out the possibility that public workers are people like themselves. They view those workers as out-group members, as urban, wealthier people with different values and interests that are inconsistent with and contrary to their own.

Given those views, it is not surprising that the people I encountered in small-town Wisconsin typically did not look favorably on the protestors down in Madison. To me, a Madison resident, the protests at the capitol seemed to be a remarkable eruption of political activity. Madison is a hyperengaged city, but these protests were off the charts in terms of intensity and numbers of citizens participating. At the same time, they were remarkably peaceful. Thousands of people were sharing a relatively small space under tense political conditions, for days. People occupied the capitol for two weeks, sleeping on makeshift beds in the rotunda in close quarters. A pizza joint on State Street (the street that runs between the capitol and the university) donated free food to protestors. The word in Madison was that the atmosphere was more festive than frightening.

But in the rural places I visited after the protests, the word was different. Many of those folks had a visceral, negative reaction to the protests. To them, this was not a display of Wisconsinite ingenuity and collectiveness but of urban excess and arrogance.

When I visited the people at the diner counter in the northern tourist town in June 2011 (Group 9), they were downright resentful of the protestors. Even Dave, the former Democratic elected official in the group, thought that the thousands of protestors at the state capitol were not representative of people in the state, especially rural Wisconsin. "Those folks downstate have little understanding of what life is like up here." "Enough is enough," he said. "Public employees gotta pay their share."

Rural consciousness made resentment toward public employees commonsense knowledge and provided fertile ground for support for Scott Walker. But the way that groups made sense of the ruckus in Madison reveals that support for Walker, a devout small-government politician, was not inevitable. The rural groups I visited after Walker came to power expressed a desire for the government to spend what was necessary to keep their small towns alive, while at the same time giving voice to skepticism that increased government spending would help their locally owned businesses and communities.

Take the Downtown Athletic Club, for example. This is the group of working and retired men who met every morning at a service station in a hamlet in central Wisconsin (Group 1). The group contained several men who had been public school teachers in the local district, and they were often supportive of government spending. When I first spent time with the members of this group in May 2008, they had complained about the state school-funding formula and said it disadvantaged small towns in Wisconsin. The retired teachers offered a remedy: raise taxes on agricultural land, of which there was an abundance in their county.

But the group also contained several small business owners (including the station owner), and they often squabbled with those former public workers about politics. When I returned in April 2011 after the protests in Madison, the small business owners in the group complained that public workers had received too much money, at great taxpayer expense. One man said simply, "Too many people get too much for nothing." The conversation that day was largely in favor of Walker's proposals. Those who spoke up argued that, in these tough economic times, in a small community that was "drying up and blowing away," taxpayers simply could not afford to foot the bill for public workers the way they had in the past.

FRED: We're just tryin' to figure out where the money tree is so we can find it. A private business or whatever, you've got a pool of money here and when it runs out there's no other coffer to keep digging into. The state and government can seem to have that pile where they can just keep grabbing and seem to come up with it.

BEN: All I know is what our fathers gave us is way better than what we're giving our kids. Our kids are gonna pay for this the rest of their life. They aren't gonna have the life we had. No way. With the taxes. I mean, look what our fathers did, they built all these roads. They built all these schools and all that. Now they can't even fix 'em. Where's all that tax money going? . . . And our insurance, my union insurance just went up eight hundred bucks yesterday. Just for that reason. So I mean, uh, we as a working person can't keep this up, there is no more money. There is no more money. Taxes are going up next year again on property taxes—where's that all gonna add up? There's no more money.

RONNY: Where'd the money go in the first place? [*laughs*] Where'd it go? [*laughs*]

BEN: I know it got out of hand. Government got out of hand. They're twice as big, they could cut that right in half. All government agencies, counties, everything, cut that right in half. And they'd be just fine. Forest County especially. Counties are getting bigger, I was in road construction for fifty years and the county's doing half of what I used to do. The counties got bigger. Buying road machinery and everything. Put us all out of business.

KJC: Yeah?

BEN: Can't stop 'em.

RONNY: Government's running private sector out of business.

BEN: Yep.

RONNY: They're doing it themselves.

BEN: Government wants it all, that's why they want health care. They want to handle that too. . . . All the government does is pass laws, pass laws, and every time they pass laws all that does is take jobs. Takes jobs. . . . I don't care if its drunk driving or whatever it is. I just talked to a guy roofing, he's got two hundred more rules this year than he had last year from OSHA [Occupational Safety and Health Administration]. Roofing contractors. You know what Mike's gonna do? He knows her too, he's gonna sell off quick. He says "I can't have it no more, I can't pass it on anymore." He's selling his business.

FRED: You know who OSHA's targeting right now? Farmers. Dairy farmers with over ten employees. OSHA's gonna go after—that's their new target they're going after this year, dairy farms with over ten employees. They said they're gonna lay heavy fines now in that.

STU: My youngest son's a dairy farmer, milking forty some cows. He makes enough to pay expenses. That is, he has to have a good year to pay expenses. It just don't keep going. And these guys doing it all themselves, he's got one hired man part time, but—

BRAD: DNR isn't helping the state either. Passing all these rules. We got way poorer hunting than we used to have here in the seventies and eighties. Fishing—it's all worse. All because they pass all these catch-and-release and all this stuff, ruined it all. Ruined the deer hunting. . . . DNR spends our money worse ways than that, too. It seems like now, right now, if you ain't workin' for the government in the next few years, you ain't gonna have nothing.

FRED: Well, I can tell you that I ask this question—

BRAD: Force you to sell your land.

FRED:—to these guys all the time, I've got two kids that are eleven and twelve, what do you tell them to go to college for? To get a job on their degree after they get out and have job security afterwards? The only thing I can tell 'em is you've gotta figure out some way to get in and get a government job because then you're taken care of. If you don't there is no other job security out there in anything. Or where you can make enough money to pay back your $300,000 to $200,000 college debt you incur to go to college. It's tough.

KJC: It is tough. How do you think about the future of [this town]?

GARY: Small towns are in trouble. They're in big trouble.

BEN: Small businesses are all in trouble. All businesses are in trouble unless you're a Walmart or a big—that's what it's gonna be.

STU: Walmart's taking over.

BEN: Lowe's is in trouble. Gander Mountain's in trouble.

GARY: We lose that school, the whole town might just shut down.

KJC: Is there talk of closing it? Consolidating or . . .

GARY: No, but you hear it everywhere else.

KJC: Right.

GARY: It's what happens with finance in the schools. It's hardest on small schools because, you know, when you have to cut money in a school if you have multiple teachers of the same subject area you might be able to cut a science teacher, if you have one high school science teacher, you still have to offer the programs so with all the demands and again . . .

STU: [One school] just laid off an art teacher or something.

FRED: Basically one of our famous sayings is they've kicked the can down the road for so long, it's spiraled downhill it's hard to stop it now. Where do you start to stop it?

BEN: They're gonna kick it again, too.

Another man arrives, then after a few moments, Ben picks back up on government spending.

BEN: The government just doesn't spend our money where it's supposed to be going . . .

KJC: Where would you spend it?

BEN: The government should be cut right in half. All businesses. What the people are going to do I don't know, we can't afford 'em anymore. We can't afford 'em anymore, our property tax, on me, my business, I was in about a 80 percent tax bracket my whole life. Income tax, sales tax, property tax, business tax, right there. Sold out, 80 percent tax bracket what I paid in my lifetime. Capital gains, anything, take care of your machinery then you pay for that when you sell it.

FRED: Government makes you . . . If you make money, they make you spend it. Or pay taxes or spend it. For me, owning my own [descriptor deleted] company, if I have money at the end of the year, I can't go buy [inventory] and have 'em stocked to use the next year cause then that's inventory, that's considered income, so you've still gotta pay tax on it, but you can go buy a new car, which you don't need, but then you don't have to pay tax on that money either. Stupid. You can't do it wisely. Sticking it back in your business is, you've still gotta pay tax on it then.

BEN: Liability and insurance for businesses. They're quitting as we speak. I just spoke, felt so sad for Milo last night, said "I've been in business for thirty years," he says. "I can't take it no more. . . ." He's quitting.

In this conversation you see some push and pull over what ought to be done about the economy, and whether Walker is doing the right thing. You have a mix of public and private employees here, and it shows in the way they try to collectively make sense of doing the right thing.

Notice how important their identities as rural folks are for this task of trying to make sense of it all. Much of this conversation could have taken place anywhere in the state. The concerns about keeping a small business afloat, the idea that government regulation is excessive—those attitudes are not just found in rural places. But in this group, the identities expressed were not just those of small business owners or former public school teachers but of small business owners and public school teachers in a tiny, dying town, working in the only types of jobs available in those places. Through those lenses, the question of government spending and the nature of their community were inseparable.

I want to provide one more thorough example of this phenomenon of people using the lens of rural consciousness as they struggled to make sense of the events in Madison. Let's reexamine the dice game. I visited this group as well after the protests erupted in 2011. In the following excerpt from that conversation, there is no overt reference to place. But remember that their resentment toward Madison and places south of what they called the Mason-Dixon Line was so strong that they could easily joke about it (e.g., telling me to buy just the front end of a horse "because they got the back end in Madison"). Those resentments were accepted wisdom in this group. Their resentment toward public employees underpins their understanding of Walker and Act 10, but those attitudes look different when you realize they are rooted in a sense that public employees—the policies and regulations that drive their jobs, as well as the compensation they get for doing them—are part of a broader perceived injustice against rural places.

When I went back to this group after the protests, in April 2011, I walked through the curtain to join them, and they told me right away that they had agreed that they were not going to talk about Walker or the protests because their group contained people on both sides and they wanted to keep getting along. One small business owner acknowledged that public employees in their group and in the community were feeling "down on the dauber" and feeling attacked.[7] But he said that there were a lot of people in the community who were in favor of what Walker did but they were intimidated against speaking out about it:

Well, you know, you see all those people protesting down in Madison and there aren't a whole lot of people who are in favor of it showing up down there [at the protests] so we're kind of intimidated about speaking out. But . . . people are pretty conservative around here so there's a lot of people in favor of what he's doing but they're intimidated about speaking up about it. . . . I have two kids in the public sector, one who works, daughter who works to register deeds and another who's a public school teacher in a nearby district and they're gonna be hit by it, but it's not devastating. . . . Teachers were already paying in 10 percent to their health care so they'd only have to pay in 2 percent more . . . and that's not devastating.

He then contrasted the shoddy work ethic of public employees against that of hard-working private employees: "You know, who're all those people protesting during the week? I mean, all the big crowds showed up on the weekends and who're the people that are protesting during the week? Well the people showing up on the weekends were people in the private sector. The people during the week were the people calling in sick, public employees and you know, why were the private-sector people showing up only on the weekend? That's because if they'd called in sick to their employer they would have been fired."

I returned to this group on the day of Walker's recall election, June 5, 2012. Although the members had been reluctant to talk a year earlier, on this day they launched right in to a good-natured argument.

RICHARD: You know, you can't blame the public employees for being upset, because they're having something taken away from them that they had and people are going to get upset about that.

KJC: Right.

RICHARD: But where's the equalization here? Why should 318,000 people in this state [the public employees] have such an increased better deal than the other two million?

DALE: Why don't the—instead of the other two million putting the other 318,000 down, why don't they raise themselves up to what that . . .

RICHARD: What you're saying . . . that's socialism.

DALE: No it ain't.

RICHARD: Everyone in Europe has tried that shit.

DALE: No it ain't.

RICHARD: What you're saying is that all the private companies should pay the same thing so the public . . . Who the hell is running our government then? It ain't our elected officials running our government. It's the unions!

DALE: They don't know. It's the God damn—

RICHARD: It's the unions.

DALE: It's the companies!

RICHARD: It's the unions! That's why it's such a bitter battle, and there's so much money involved because you know how much money this loss of, you know, collective bargaining is for the unions, you know. This is big bucks. We're talking big money.

DALE: Put it the other way, you know how much money these companies are going to make by screwing people out of their wages.

RICHARD: How are they screwing them out of their wages? When you take a job, you know what it pays. You know what it's going to pay three years from now.

DALE: They're going to keep on cutting wages as long as the unions don't get a raise for the public employees, the other ones are going to stay stagnant. Hey look it up here.

RICHARD: Why do you think the unions put all their effort into public employees? They don't go out looking for private-sector unions that much. You know you got—that's where the money is.

DALE: The money is from companies that want to favor the governor and the president and all that kind of stuff. That's where the big money comes from.

RICHARD: I wish I knew what the comparison was, Dale. I don't know . . .

Someone else chimed in at this point, perhaps sympathetic to public employees, but critical of their "special" benefits nonetheless.

ERNIE: The only thing I don't like about it is the retirement age at fifty-seven for teachers. That stinks.

RICHARD: *Fifty-seven*? Fifty-five.

ERNIE: Fifty-five.

RICHARD: If you got thirty years of service in at fifty-five, you get your insurance paid for nine years. They're starting to back off of that now, but that varies from district to district. That wasn't everybody.

ERNIE: That part just stinks.

RICHARD: I see people ten years younger than I am, they're walking around town, doing exercise in the morning. They don't have a Goddamn thing to worry about. Life is good so—I don't know.

DALE: Yeah, but you're in private business. You sold it all away so you would never.

RICHARD: I would never say, Dale, that you live in a dream world, because I know better than that, but . . .

[*Laughter*]

ERNIE: You know what, I take it you two aren't going to vote the same way today. You might as well both stay home because neither of you are going to count.

KJC: There you go. There you go. Cancel each other out.

ERNIE: They should just stay home.

KJC: Take each other to lunch instead.

[*Laughter*]

RICHARD: I know how hard it is for the old to get around so I offered to go out and vote for him.

The group laughed and then moved on to another topic.

Later in the day, after leaving the dice game, I had lunch in a restaurant at the other end of Main Street with a group of women who get together once a week (Group IIc). It was my first time meeting with them. Unlike the dice game fellows, these women did not know whether I was familiar with rural perspectives, and so soon after we sat down, they filled me in.

I started out asking them, "I just want to know what your big concerns are in [this town] these days." They brought up the economy, social security, the fact that "senators and congressmen . . . have no idea what small, rural America is like," their lack of trust in politicians, their belief that the recall was a waste of taxpayer money, and their belief that we need more women running things. Then I asked:

KJC: Well, this is not a loaded question. Do you feel that either political party is better at representing your concerns, Republicans or Democrats? I mean . . .

DOLORES: Probably not.

KJC: I know it's a pretty Republican area . . .

BEVERLY: I don't think so [referring to whether either party is better at representing concerns].

KJC: Well that really stinks.

BEVERLY: We don't know who we're going to vote for if we do go vote. I think it's just going to stay the same way it's going to be—

SANDY: Or get worse.

BEVERLY: They promise us a lot, but once they get voted in the system?

SANDY: Do you want Walker to do more of the things he said he was going to do?

DOLORES: And that's why people are upset.

SANDY: Now all you get [are] all the bag ladies out there crying, because he didn't do what they wanted.

GLADYS: Did he do the financials he said he was going to do? Are we supposed to be out of debt now because of him?

BEVERLY: Walker . . . yeah?

SANDY: I don't think he did the full amount, but he did a lot in the short while he was there.

GLADYS: Oh.

DOLORES: I think . . . I don't know. I do not know if much will change, if anything, if the other party gets in, but Barrett is known for not doing a whole lot, you know, for our type of community. You know he's for the big city; he's from the big city. And he's taken Milwaukee right down the tubes, why would we want him in here, running the whole state, *when he can't run a city*? I think in that way, I give Walker a lot of credit for standing up for what he believes and saying this is what I told you I was going to do and this is what I have done. Now he may have not gone about it the real, ethical right way, but at least he made an effort to do something. You know, so many of these governors and they are wishy-washy is what they are. They don't care about what they told people, you know.

These women understood themselves as people from rural Wisconsin. Maybe neither party represented their concerns, but they sure were not going to vote for Barrett, because they saw him as a city guy who did not understand places like their town. It is a big leap, however, to go from there to the conclusion that people in small towns prefer small government. It makes more sense to me to conclude that people in small communities find small government appealing because they perceive that government is not of or about communities like their own.

Like many of the men in the rural groups, the women in this group expressed a belief that government employees operate in ways that suggested they were clueless about rural life. After our food arrived, one woman brought up the DNR.

GLADYS: That brings me to our son, who is quite the fisherman, and his wife are quite good at fishing, and he had seventy people in one night and they were frying up fish and they were afraid of the DNR coming up and looking in his freezer. That shouldn't be. That's a police state. If they can't catch him fishing, doing it illegally when he's fishing, what you have in your freezer should be private property and they shouldn't have no right to come in there.

KJC: Does that happen around here? Do they inspect people's freezers? I heard that, too, especially in north Wisconsin . . .

GLADYS: I'm sure he knows, but I don't know about anyone—

KJC: But he's concerned about it?

GLADYS: Yes, concerned yes. And this is his recreation and then to be concerned because you have too many pieces in your freezer. I think that is not a good situation for our country.

SANDY: I think the DNR has more power than any governor . . . the DNR has too much power.

GLADYS: And when did that start?

SANDY: It's been going on forever. The DNR shouldn't even exist, I think.

DOLORES: I think everyone feels like that.

Later on in the conversation, I had an opportunity to ask bluntly about the rural-versus-urban divide in Wisconsin. Sandy asked me, "So what is this information you're collecting actually used for? To help the economy? To help the government or the people or . . . ?" I explained that I had been using the information to help set the agenda for a statewide public opinion poll, to gather information on views toward the university, and to research political understanding. I then asked them bluntly for feedback on my perception that many people in outstate Wisconsin felt ignored by Madison and Milwaukee. I asked them to tell me more about "this thing that you all talked about today that I hear everywhere in the state, outside of Madison, Milwaukee, people do not feel listened to. They feel as though nobody really is taking into account their concerns, you know, I hear that in [this town], too, and it's sad."

DOLORES: It is.

KJC: And it's been shocking. It's been really shocking to me how widespread that is and how kind of tone deaf people in Madison are.

DOLORES: Almost as if the outlaying areas, people are not intelligent enough to know what is going on.

KJC: Right.

DOLORES: "We can't take their opinion as anything serious. They're all frivolous. They just don't care." I heard someone said once, and I worked in the school system, that you can't expect much of farm kids, because they don't excel in the sciences and all of that.

KJC: Oh my.

GLADYS: I worked with a girl like that.

DOLORES: I just about dropped my teeth and I thought, the expectation should be the same for these children as it is for any other child anywhere else in the state. And I was getting that from someone who should have known better.

KJC: And that was someone teaching here? My goodness.

DOLORES: Yeah. Yeah. Local school system, who said that. I was not expecting them to do that. I was just appalled.

GLADYS: But then some managers will hire farm children before other children because they know how to work.

DOLORES: They know how to work.

On the day of the recall election, these women made sense of the tumultuous politics of their state through their sense of themselves as rural people whose communities are disrespected, ignored, and left to fend for themselves. They also perceived that government workers, especially DNR employees, impose unfair regulations. And to top off their sense of injustice, they believe that there is nothing like the hard work that is required in a rural community like their own.

When you look at the world this way, it makes sense to support a politician who conveys that finally someone is paying attention to smalltown folks like you. It makes sense to vote for a person who has taken measures—even controversial measures—to scale back the resources going to public employees. We can lean back and wonder why anyone who can hardly afford to pay for health care, whose local schools are struggling, and who teeters on the edge of needing welfare assistance would vote for a candidate who openly pledges to roll back government spending. Or we can sit up, listen closely, and notice that having a worldview that rural people are treated unjustly leads in an understandable way to support for a politician like Scott Walker.

Tapping into These Understandings

We have a politics of resentment when political actors mobilize support for cutting back government by tapping into resentment toward certain groups in society. I have laid out in some detail how a place- and class-based identity like rural consciousness provides fertile ground for resentment-based arguments to flourish. But what does such mobilization look like?

It looks, at times, like a train. A high-speed train, to be exact. Under Democratic Governor Jim Doyle, Walker's predecessor, Wisconsin had successfully applied for federal stimulus money to build a high-speed rail system between Madison and Milwaukee. On a good day, this is a ninety-minute, boring drive on Interstate 94, and it is uncharacteristically ugly for Wisconsin. It is also heavily used. Undoubtedly, some of the people who make the drive would have used this rail system. But these users would have been predominantly "city people" living in the Madison and Milwaukee metro areas.

Walker took on the train as a major symbolic element of his 2010 gubernatorial campaign. He portrayed it as an $810 million "boondoggle" that would create only fifty-five permanent jobs.[8] "That's more than fourteen and a half million dollars per job."[9] He argued that it was an excessive government program that taxpayers could not afford. He accused proponents of treating it as if it were free, reminding people that no government program is free but is instead paid for by taxpayers.

He gave people many reasons to support his decision to give back the $810 million to the federal government as he refused to let the construction on the rail system go forward. But he especially focused on reasons that would resonate with those with a rural consciousness. He talked about the train as an expensive mode of transportation that most Wisconsinites would not ride.[10] He asserted that spending money on this project would directly take money away from regions of the state outside the Madison and Milwaukee metro areas. Here is an example of his talking points, from the first debate in the gubernatorial primary:

> If you look at what Jim Doyle and Tom Barrett [Walker's Democratic opponent] have put on the table, in spending $810 million on a high-speed train line between Milwaukee and Madison with no assurance that it will go to Eau Claire or La Crosse or anywhere else—it's just about those two areas—and it's about taking that money, money that will cost . . . the citizens of Wisconsin up to $10 million per year—according to their numbers, I think it will actually be much more—that's $10 million that doesn't go to fix the road that goes up from West Salem through the cutout up to Black River Falls, it doesn't fix

streets in La Crosse . . . that's money that's taken away from our local roads and our bridges and our other transportation needs today.[11]

He made a similar claim in the first debate of the general election:

This is a classic example of runaway government spending. I mean it's not only the $810 million of taxpayers' money—it's not free money, it's our money, it's the taxpayers' money—but on top of that the federal government, not my numbers, not the Republican Party's numbers, but the federal government numbers point out it will cost us at a minimum seven and a half million dollars or more per year, particularly with the cost overruns you alluded to, but seven and a half million dollars, presuming there are none, each year out of the state transportation fund—money we all paid as state taxpayers. That's money that comes out of important highway and bridge projects all across the state of Wisconsin.[12]

The rail system was not the only way Walker mobilized rural consciousness in support of small government. He used anti-city rhetoric in other ways, too. Walker had been county executive of Milwaukee County itself. But he was running against the mayor of Milwaukee, and so used his experience not as evidence that he identified with the people of Milwaukee but as evidence that he could successfully take on the city and its demons. He said that he was taking on "the political machine *down* in Madison" (emphasis added here, because he was in Milwaukee when he said this, which is not north of Madison).[13] But he also said he was taking on the political machine in Milwaukee:

Eight years ago, I took on the political machine here in Milwaukee County. . . . In the end, I needed to fix a problem, not just for myself but for my two sons, Matt and Alex, and for future generations. We've taken on those challenges and proved that we could take on the political machine in Milwaukee County. I'm proud of that. And I think that's one of those things, when I tell that story across the state of Wisconsin—tell what we inherited: the big pension scandal, the out-of-control spending, the taxes that had gone up under my predecessor and really the total lack of confidence in government—they see many of the same challenges we face today all across this state.[14]

Opposing the train and the Milwaukee machine were obvious attacks on the "M & Ms." But Walker invoked animosity toward the cities, especially Madison, in more subtle ways as well. Take, for example, these remarks about his tenure as county executive, made during a question-and-answer session at the American Enterprise Institute, a conservative think tank, on January 6, 2012:

> We were able to rein-in abuses of things like overtime and other excesses *out there* by no longer having opportunities where, in our case, some of our state employees could literally call in sick on their shift and then come back to work the next shift on overtime. *Or bus drivers in places like Madison that made $150,000 or more because of overtime.*
>
> Those things have all changed. And now the power is back in the hands of local officials and ultimately the taxpayers of our state. And so that's ultimately what we did. It seems pretty reasonable when you hear us talk about it.

I added the emphasis here to highlight the way he equates overpaid public employees with employees in "places like Madison."

Walker not only portrayed himself as "taking on" Madison and Milwaukee, he also demonstrated that he identified with small-town Wisconsin. He campaigned on a brown-bag theme, in which he described packing himself a brown bag lunch every day in order to cut back, just as governments have to learn to do. In an appearance on the television show *Fox and Friends*, he said "I grew up in a small town" and asserted that such a background gave him "a little bit of that brown-bag common sense."[15]

A Wisconsinite did not need to look at the world through the lens of rural consciousness for these arguments to resonate. They could hear Walker pledge to take on the political machines in Madison and Milwaukee and could cheer that someone was finally going to get government to listen to hard-working taxpayers like themselves. But for people who had an identity with places beyond the orbit of resources and power called Madison and Milwaukee, calling into question the high salaries of bus drivers *down* in Madison and reminding people of the good values of small-town Wisconsinites likely had an extra appeal.[16]

Conclusion

The ways in which the people in the groups I spoke with reacted to the uproar in Madison are instructive as to how they see themselves as distant from such incidents—see themselves as people who are never really in on the big events and power struggles anyway. But interestingly for me, this did not lead them to a perception that the main divide was between the people in power versus the people of the state. Instead, a large part of the conversations centered on Wisconsin-residents-like-me versus Wisconsin-residents-unlike-me. At the same time that people complained about "the government," I witnessed a lot of people focusing their resentment on other residents of their state.

I began this book with a story about ordinary people treating each other badly at the gas pump. And that is the dynamic that has troubled me throughout working on this book. I grew up in Wisconsin and have always taken pride in "Wisconsin nice"—a way of being in which people are kind to each other, sometimes to a fault. But the Wisconsin I know now is something different, something divided. The divide is partly about Republican versus Democrat, but it is about something more to most people, and something, unfortunately, much more meaningful to their lives.

The Great Recession, the candidacy and administration of Barack Obama, and the ascendance of Scott Walker—all of that has been a lot to take in a relatively short amount of time. The Wisconsinites I observed in rural areas waded through these things through the lens of rural consciousness. They tried to figure out what the Great Recession meant for them, and for the most part, they concluded it meant very little, given the already sorry state of their local economy. The Great Recession did do one thing, though. It honed their resentment toward public employees.

I heard people struggling and visibly uncomfortable with, but at the same time hopeful about, Barack Obama. What kind of a politician was this? And what did his race mean? People in rural areas did not seem to weigh race more or differently than people in other types of places, but their lack of faith in government meant Obama turned out to be less a beacon of hope than a threat of government gluttony.

Scott Walker arrived at the right place at the right time. His candidacy and programs have tapped into the economic anxiety and dread that mark this point in history. Walker's platform has also made use of the desire for people to make sense of their world, to figure out who is to blame and identify boundaries that clearly show that those who are to blame are not one of us.

CHAPTER EIGHT

We Teach These Things
to Each Other

When Wisconsin Governor Scott Walker won his recall election in June 2012, the city of Madison went into shock. The protests that had lit up the capitol square for week after week were a visible, tangible sign of the animosity toward Walker and his budget repair bill, Act 10. Many people in the Madison area had been directly affected. Among residents of Dane county, where Madison is located, 22 percent were employed by some level of government at the time and, therefore, had been part of unions that lost collective bargaining rights and were also were now contributing substantially more of their paychecks to their pensions and health care insurance. "RECALL WALKER" bumper stickers and yard signs were everywhere in Madison.

People expected to stay up late until the results were final. They expected a close race. But instead, it was over by 10 P.M. Many people living in Madison could not quite believe the outcome (see Knisely 2013). "Who were the 53.1 percent who voted for him?" many asked. "What were they thinking?"

Although many in Madison found it hard to believe that Walker would survive the recall effort, things looked different in rural parts of the state. I have never seen so many political yard signs, and the vast majority said "STAND WITH WALKER." The election was bitterly fought in the Madison and Milwaukee metro regions, but it was won in large part in rural areas. One keen observer called it the "rural landslide" (Gilbert 2012a).

The shock that people in Madison expressed when Walker won reminded me just how unfamiliar the perspectives of people in outstate

Wisconsin are to those living in Madison and perhaps in Milwaukee as well. When I gave talks in Madison about the anti–public employee sentiment I had observed in my fieldwork all the way back to 2007, people were surprised. They still are.[1] Walker's win in 2014 again shocked people in Madison.[2]

My hope is that this book helps to lessen that surprise and increase understanding of public opinion in our contemporary context. When we start to ask why people vote against their interests, we need to acknowledge that interests are subjective. In a simplistic view, this means that interests are not necessarily what we as observers would predict based on objective facts, such as a person's income. But in a more useful view, this means that interests are interpretations that people arrive at through thinking about the world as particular types of people—people with identities. The simplistic view paints voters as ignorant. The latter view acknowledges their humanity.

The particular puzzle I focus on in this book is why people prefer less government when they might seemingly benefit from more of it. This study shows how people can arrive at the interpretation that less government is better on the basis of perspectives with class- and place-based resentments at their core.

I used observations of conversations among thirty-nine groups in twenty-seven different Wisconsin communities to illuminate the way people arrive at preferences for less government by making sense of politics through perspectives rooted in social identities and perceptions of distributive justice. I visited these groups repeatedly across a contentious five-year period in a state that exemplified national debates over the role of government.

I did not expect to hear it, but many of the people I listened to in rural areas exhibited a multifaceted resentment toward urban areas. That resentment was part of a perspective I call rural consciousness. It is a perspective rooted in place and class identities that convey a strong sense of distributive injustice. Many of the people I listened to in rural areas identified strongly as rural people and took it as a given that rural areas do not get their fair share of political attention or decision-making power or public resources and have a fundamentally different set of values and lifestyles, which are neither understood nor respected by city dwellers.

One can view as misinformation or ignorance the perception among rural folks that they are the victims of distributive injustice, but the conclusion that people vote the way they do because they are stupid is itself pretty shallow. It overlooks that much of political understanding is not about facts; it is about how we see those facts (Bartels 2008, chap. 5; Nyhan and Reifler 2010). Support for less government among lower-income people is often derided as the opinions of people who have been duped. But the stands taken in favor of small government delineated in this book are rooted in views of the world that carry a great deal of meaning for the people that hold them. Listening in on these conversations, it is hard to conclude that the people I studied believe what they do because they have been hoodwinked. Their views are rooted in identities and values, as well as in economic perceptions; and these things are all intertwined. Economic interests *do* matter here. But they are a function of the complex meaning that people give to their lives.

Studying the act of making sense of politics in Wisconsin proved fruitful as Wisconsin became a focal point for debates about the role of government. Political commentators treated the 2012 gubernatorial recall election as a proxy test for the national debate between two visions of government: government as an essential safety net and guarantor of a healthy society versus government as an obstacle and bloated resource suck.

Wisconsin is a microcosm of the nation in another respect. What happened there is symptomatic of the role of divisiveness in contemporary politics, both in the public mind and in the manner in which politicians are actively using this divisiveness for political gain.

The contentiousness of our times is not exclusive to the urban versus rural divide. It occurs in the context of broader political polarization, in which our national and state-level political leaders are increasingly far apart on a range of issues (Layman et al. 2006; McCarty et al. 2008; Shor 2014). Members of the public have also sorted themselves into partisan camps (Fiorina et al. 2010), which are distinctly different in fundamental cultural ways (Dionne 2006; Abramowitz 2014).

This study and events in Wisconsin in the past few years suggest these divides are not just political disagreements, but are actually intensely personal for many people. When Walker proposed Act 10, public employees felt personally attacked. And they were, at times.[3] Walker opponents were not innocent of this incivility either.[4] The personal nature of politics did not just involve tearing down each other's yard signs (Knisely 2013, 72–74) or name-calling. In a surprising number of cases, the basic act of talking to one another seemed to become impossible. A week after the recall vote, 31 percent of Wisconsinites reported that they had stopped talking with someone about politics due to the attempted recall of Scott Walker.[5] The story I told of Tom the Prius driver at the beginning of this book is a related case in point.

A politics of resentment stems from and reinforces political differences that have become personal. In a politics of resentment, we treat differences in our political points of view as fundamental differences in who we are as human beings.

I have focused on rural consciousness as one perspective through which the politics of resentment can operate. The work of rural consciousness that I have revealed in this study is evidence that support for small government can come from something more visceral, though certainly not less serious, than political principles: our sense of who is on the side of good and who is on the bad.

There are other dimensions along which a politics of resentment can operate. On a national scale, the United States has experienced a great many divisions—Northerners versus Southerners and people in favor of equal rights for women versus those in favor of traditional roles for women, just to name a few. Other forms of resentment could feed a politics of resentment if they they tap into salient identities that coincide with perceptions of injustice that encompass both economic and cultural considerations—namely, a perception that people on opposite sides of the battle lines have unequal shares of power and resources and that they live different lifestyles according to different values. These battle lines do not need to coincide with geography, but they likely do, given the way Americans have segregated themselves socioeconomically.

Beyond garnering the insight that people use social identities to think about politics, this book also shows how social group divides can operate as the central narrative by which people understand the political landscape and by which they structure their ideas about which candidates to support. In this politics of resentment, when we tell ourselves and others about the reasons behind how events have unfolded, the stories hinge on blaming our fellow citizens. What I am calling the politics of resentment is a political culture in which political divides are rooted in our most basic understandings of ourselves, infuse our everyday relationships, and are used for electoral advantage by our political leaders.

A review of what the work of rural consciousness teaches us about the politics of resentment may be helpful at this point. In chapter 3, I explored, using conversational data, the ways in which rural consciousness is a perspective rooted in identity—specifically, the belief that rural folks are the victims of distributive injustice in terms of resources, power, and also cultural respect.

Chapter 4 provided empirical support for these perceptions. However, evidence that rural people are the victims of distributive injustice is not straightforward. Nevertheless, there are a variety of solid reasons that people living in rural areas would perceive that their type of community is under attack. I also argued that these perceptions are likely the result of social interaction, not simply the parroting of facts, and that matters for how people use them to interpret politics.

In chapter 5, I detailed how rural consciousness structures attitudes toward public employees and public institutions, especially with respect to the University of Wisconsin–Madison. I found that people in rural Wisconsin felt distant from the university and believed that people in their community were at a disadvantage in terms of accessing it. They believed that university sorts looked down on their type of wisdom—a commonsense wisdom—and generally viewed public employees as lacking such wisdom. They also regarded those affiliated with the university as people who were driven by urban policies and urban priorities that were antithetical to the hard-work ethic and values among rural people like themselves. They saw public employees enjoying high salaries and great benefits, while not really working hard like rural folks. They resented public employees because they viewed them as undeserving recipients of rural folks' hard-earned taxpayers' dollars.

I clarified how the rural consciousness perspective and the views of public employees it fostered were connected to support for small government in chapter 6. After a review of the history of public opinion toward property taxes and social welfare, I argued that what elites have construed as support for limited government in general is often support for (or opposition to) something more specific. This is in line with decades of research suggesting that individuals' opinions are more often formed on the basis of attitudes toward social groups rather than on the basis of ideology (following Converse [1964]). We see in the conversations I presented here the ways championing small government policies is not support for the principle of small government but, rather, support for or opposition to a particular social group.

For example, my observations documented some rural residents opposing higher taxes in order to fund education. They were often proud of and concerned about their local public schools and weren't opposed to paying more taxes if that money would improve education. But they perceived their tax dollars going instead to urban and suburban schools or to undeserving public school teachers. It was not more money for education that they opposed; instead, they resented the perceived recipients and that fueled their desire for limiting this aspect of government.

Part of my argument in that chapter is that lack of trust in government is not the same as wanting less of it. I focused on conversations about health care and education to emphasize three ways that rural consciousness among people in small towns brought together their distaste for government with support for small government policies and candidates. Rural consciousness fed the argument that people in small towns simply cannot afford higher taxes. It fed an attitude that government regulations are out of touch with rural life, causing rural inhabitants to want less regulation. Rural consciousness also structured talk about government programs such that people said they were willing to pay higher taxes in principle but were resistant to do so in practice because they believed those tax dollars would not return to the people of their community.

These arguments were rooted in rural identity and perceptions of the rural economy and rural life and values. In other words, although I was able to identify resentment toward public employees in conversations among urban and suburban groups, too, the resentment among rural people was special in the way it wove together place and class identities, making preferences for less government logical.

The economic woes people communicated to me through the lens of rural consciousness were interlaced with their sense of who they are, who is a part of their community, what their values are, who works hard in society, who is deserving of reward and public support, and how power is distributed in the world. This complex set of ideas is the product of many years of political debate at the national level as well as generations of community members teaching these ideas to each other. This entwined set of beliefs was not something that any one politician instilled in people overnight—or even over a few months.

In chapter 7, I examined how people used rural consciousness to make sense of politics by focusing on their conversations about the Great Recession, Barack Obama, and Scott Walker. People in small towns treated the Great Recession as unremarkable since they perceived their rural economy as having been bad off prior to then. Assigning blame to certain fellow citizens—public employees—became the centerpiece of the stories people told to explain the economic downturn. People in small towns were uncomfortable talking about Obama and race—much the case with people throughout Wisconsin—but they were initially supportive of him. However, they eventually came to talk about Obama as just as aloof to rural concerns as other politicians. Scott Walker made a bigger splash. Many people in the rural places believed that here, finally, was someone on the side of small town Wisconsinites. And a look at Walker's rhetoric shows he overtly attempted to foster that image.

Scott Walker's public comments are suggestive of how our leaders mobilize resentment for electoral and legislative gain. Mobilizing resentment toward public employees, for example, is not simply the act of persuading ignorant, unsophisticated voters that the real enemy is public school teachers. Tapping into these resentments works because members of the public have complex interpretations that are ripe for tapping into, as the analyses in this book collectively demonstrate.

Lessons from Listening

Researchers do not usually study American public opinion by inviting themselves into conversations in gas stations. Those used to reading positivist research will wonder about the generalizability of the results of this study. And as discussed in chapter 2, I agree that it would have been optimal if there were enough of me that I could have spent time in enough groups, in enough places, at enough times that I would have had a truly representative sample of Wisconsinites, or even of people in the United States. I would be able to describe urban-rural divides generally.

But my purpose was to better understand how people in particular places ascribed meaning to their political world. This study should be judged, therefore, not on the basis of whether the results are sufficiently generalizable to a broader population but, rather, whether I have provided results that are "sufficiently contextualized so that the interpretations are embedded in, rather than abstracted from, the settings of the actors studied" (Schwartz-Shea and Yanow 2012, 47).

Though my intent was not to generalize to all people in the United States or even all Wisconsinites, the fact that the vast majority of the people I observed were middle-aged or older raises a question of whether the perspectives encountered here reflect a generational divide rather than simply a rural-urban divide. Would my findings have differed if I had spent time with additional younger people?

I spent much time in these pages dissecting resentment toward public employees. It is possible that older folks in particular are more resentful toward public employees—especially public school teachers. Their kids are no longer in school but older people nevertheless have to pay rising tax bills, and they are especially sensitive to those increases because they are often living on fixed incomes. High school students in the conversations I observed in 4-H groups did exhibit less resentment in general than did older folks. Mass sample survey studies show that younger people are actually no less willing to pay for older folks' social welfare benefits like social security than are older people (Campbell 2009). However, there is evidence of an increasing generational divide in terms of attitudes toward government spending in general, especially between older white Americans and younger nonwhite folks. This is sometimes called the gray-brown divide. Older white voters are more likely to prefer smaller government than are younger people of color (Brownstein 2010; Skocpol and Williamson 2012, 204; see also Leonhardt 2012).[6]

The in-depth view I provide of older citizens' understandings helps explain why the gray-brown divide has power. It may manifest itself as a divide over the role of government, but it is likely rooted in social identities and resentments against particular types of people. Even if younger generations are less resentful, getting rid of the politics of resentment will require political leaders who do not foment divides but, instead, try to bridge them.

Questions about the way younger people interpret politics and fit into the politics of resentment are among those this book leaves unanswered. Many of my claims about the manner in which politicians actively tap into these resentments are as yet untested. It would be useful for future research to examine the relationships between everyday conversations and the rhetoric of political actors and news media outlets to better understand how the connections we see in the public and those among political elites reinforce one another. Experiments would undoubtedly aid our understanding of causal effects. Some additional historical perspective of the arguments that have been used over time to cultivate support for small government is also necessary, as is an understanding of the nature of arguments political actors are using in the contemporary period.

One of the benefits, however, of approaching the study of public opinion in the manner I have used here is that it illuminates our understanding of public opinion in ways other methods cannot. It can help improve our poll-based positivist analyses in numerous ways. First, this study suggests that although measures of preferences for limited government are useful predictors of political opinions, there is much to learn about what predicts those preferences.[7] On what basis do people believe "the less government, the better"? We might interpret such a question as an indicator of libertarianism. But the conversations in this book suggest it may instead reflect primarily resentment. The distinction matters. If we conceptualize limited government measures as tapping an ideological principle, that seems to ignore the decades of research reinforcing Converse's insight (1964) that the vast majority of people do not reason on an ideological basis (Kuklinski and Peyton 2007). If, instead, it is an indicator of resentment toward public employees, or something else entirely, we could more accurately model opinion by asking directly about such sentiments, delving into the complexities of attitudes toward different levels of government and how those change depending on who is in office.

Second, this study suggests that consideration of external efficacy ought to take into account not just whether people believe government is responsive to "people like me" but also whether it is responsive to "people in my community." We see in these analyses people thinking about government through the lens of their geographic community. Which geography people have in mind when they think about "my community" matters for their perceptions of racial context and resentment toward racial groups (Wong et al. 2012). Given that, it seems our understanding of individuals' orientations to government would be improved with attention to perceptions of geography.

The approach I use in this study suggests not only new avenues for positivist research or refinements of existing measures but also answers to some of the puzzles raised in positivist studies. Returning, for example, to the question of why white working-class people tend to vote for Republican candidates, hard data show that this is a common misperception. The majority of lower-income whites actually side with Democrats—and pretty consistently so ever since income inequality has started to rise (Bartels 2008, 73). Yes, higher-income states do lean Democratic, while lower-income states tend to vote Republican these days. However, the relationship between higher income and Democratic votes does not hold on the individual level.

But what about those red and blue electoral maps that pop up during elections showing rural areas within states—which tend to be lower income—as red (Republican)? Yes, rural America increasingly leans Republican (Gimpel and Karnes 2006, 467). But again, behavior at the aggregate level is not consistent with individual-level behavior. Within states, lower-income people still side with the Democrats (Gelman et al. 2008).

A mystery, though, is why lower-income areas within blue or Democratic-leaning states are more likely to vote Republican than higher-income areas (Gelman et al. 2008, e.g.). This study offers one possible explanation. Let's assume that some version of rural consciousness exists outside of Wisconsin. It may be, then, that rural places in blue-leaning states are places in which many people hold a perspective that is conducive to small-government arguments. In that respect, people in rural, low-income areas in blue states might be more likely to vote Republican, even though the relationship between low-income and Democratic votes holds nationwide.

Which party people vote for is obviously important. But this study provides a significant caution for our continued reliance on partisanship as the most important predisposition in the study of political opinion. There is no denying that partisanship performs well as a predictor of votes and policy preferences. But what is that actually telling us? If the main divide that people see in the political world is not Democrats versus Republicans but, instead, us versus the government, or people with my work ethic versus people without it, shouldn't we spend more time measuring identities that are more meaningful to people than partisanship?

One possibility suggested by this study is place identity. For at least some people, place matters more than just as a proxy for which partisans are where. It is a part of at least some voters' fundamental sense of self. One can imagine many other perspectives rooted in the intertwined identities of place and class that matter for politics. Neighborhood- or municipality-based identities in urban politics and region-based identities in national politics are some examples. Our tendency to use national-level survey data leads us to overlook the manner in which respondents' perceptions about their immediate geographic context matter for their political preferences. Voters' sense of *where* resources are going may often be intertwined with partisanship, or as important for understanding the shape of public opinion as partisanship.

This study also highlights the importance of place with respect to class. The way many people in these conversations imbued geography with economic and distributive meaning suggests that whether we are interested in class identity or the social construction of identity in the Bourdieuian sense, attention to place can be useful. For many people in this study, geographic place of residence was a central consideration in their subjective sense of their place in society. Alongside indicators like income, occupation, and education, whether one is rural or urban was part of the way they constituted their own position with respect to wealth, resources, and authority.

The manner in which people intertwined place and class in these conversations reminds us that social class is a social science concept. It is not an everyday, readily familiar concept. The people in this study did not refer to themselves as white working class, or working class, or even any "class" unless I encouraged them to do so. But they did talk about themselves in more specific but nonetheless meaningful categories (e.g., rural folks) that convey a perception of relative wealth and power.[8] In other words, even though people do not readily use the terminology of "class," this does not mean that people do not think about how they compare to others in terms of power and resources. Whether we call this act of comparison "status," "class," "social location," or something else does not really matter. What matters is that we recognize that these comparisons to other people in terms of haves and have-nots are very much a part of our politics.

These insights with respect to social class are an additional indication that poll-based analyses of opinion ought to be accompanied not just by focus groups or in-depth interviews but also by listening methods that expose us to the conversations and contexts of everyday life. People use people they know and the physical surroundings they are familiar with to make sense of politics. When we study them independent of these things, we treat them like particles, not people. If we wish to know the social bases of politics, we would do well to open the study of opinion to a wider range of methods and methodological approaches that enable us to see these social tools at work.

My focus in this book has been on public opinion among ordinary people, not so much on the strategies that politicians use to influence these opinions. But the lessons of this book nonetheless speak to a conception of public opinion in which top-down as well as bottom-up forces matter. Some critics of Governor Walker have reflected on the events in Wisconsin and argued that it was the budget legislation he proposed that created a divide in Wisconsin between public workers and the rest of the public (Lueders 2011). However, the discussions in this study show that the seeds of this public-versus-private-worker divide predated the 2011 legislation, and even the 2010 election that brought Walker to power.

Undoubtedly, these battle lines are adopted to a degree from mass media.[9] Walker may not have created these divisions, but his policies exposed them and made them readily available for people to grasp onto as legitimate categorizations and targets of blame. The current animosity toward public unions is arguably part of a decades-long battle against unions among conservative and Republican elites (Zernike 2011). But again, it is the bottom-up process of people teaching in-group/out-group categorizations to each other, including the many layers and associations that those distinctions contain, that clarifies, reinforces, and keeps alive these divisions that politicians can then exploit. In chapter 4, I presented evidence from an analysis that showed animosity toward urban areas was not present in daily newspapers serving areas outside Madison and Milwaukee. If this and other aspects of rural consciousness are not prominent in daily news outlets in the communities where people are expressing anti-urban opinions, then how else are such positions communicated? Interpersonal interaction is likely an important part of the process.

As people tried to make sense of the economic crisis they experimented with various scapegoats. However, Walker's budget bills (like the budget bills offered by Republican governors in numerous other states in 2011, such as Ohio, Indiana, New Jersey, and Florida) put two particular targets of blame front and center: public employees and the unions through which they organize. And as my findings in this study indicate, public opinion and the political process are driven neither by elites nor from the bottom up. Rather, politics occurs at the confluence of these forces. In order to fully understand the origins of mass opinion at a given point in time, we need to acknowledge processes taking place among members of the mass public as well as the messages coming from political elites.

Implications for Democracy

I do not know if the politics of resentment is increasing in the United States. Democracy, for good reason, has contention built into it. The United States' form of government was designed on the assumption that people do not automatically agree about the best way forward. We are supposed to have competitive elections. We are supposed to have debate in and outside of government. The system, in theory, privileges the voicing of disagreement, rather than its suppression.

But contentiousness is not necessarily resentment. My fear is that democracy will always tend toward a politics of resentment, in which savvy politicians figure out ways to amass coalitions by tapping into our deepest and most salient social divides: race, class, culture, place. This does not exactly make for a pleasant public life. When we get to a point where we do not actually have a public life, when we turn away from politics because it brings resentment rather than hope to the surface, democracy ceases to exist.

The trick, then, would seem to be finding some way to prevent resentment from dominating the perspectives through which people make sense of politics. The question is, what is that fix? What is the change that needs to take place to ensure that democratic debate is fueled by something other than resentment? Is it institutional? Is it the act of encouraging the public to get along despite our leaders' proddings to the contrary? Is it a move toward greater economic equality?

As we ask ourselves these questions, we should also question the quality of representation that takes place in a politics of resentment. In this study, we see politicians tapping into divides and nourishing resentment and then claiming that electoral support is evidence that the public has a principled stance on the role of government. The conversations I observed suggest that what gets sold as support for small government is often something quite different.

Even support for the Tea Party is perhaps not best understood as support for small government. Support for the Tea Party may be a manifestation of simmering resentment toward social groups in the majority culture, though its most devout adherents may themselves be ideological extremists (Barreto et al. 2011). Moreover, the charge of Tea Partyers to "take back our country" seems an enticing call to a seemingly broad swath of people who believe their lives are buffeted by forces beyond their control that they can't even observe. Is this support for limited government? Or support for a kind of government that listens to "people like me"? Tea Partyers' pro-small-government arguments are often not based in libertarian principles but are instead rooted in a sense of injustice (Williamson et al. 2011; Skocpol and Williamson 2012).

Nevertheless, we can expect that political elites who are small-government proponents will continue to claim a mandate for limited government policies. That certainly has been the case in Wisconsin, as small-government proponents have taken center stage. Governor Walker has survived a recall and a closely fought reelection campaign and was for a while in mid-2015 a serious contender for the Republican presidential nomination. Congressman Paul Ryan, an Ayn Rand devotee, was a vice-presidential nominee. Since the November 2012 elections, both houses of the state government have been controlled by the Republican Party. As long as public workers continue to be portrayed as less hard-working and as undeserving of the pay and benefits they receive, there is leeway for an antigovernment stance to serve as a viable campaign strategy.

One might say that even if Tea Party politicians are tapping into negative attitudes toward particular social groups in order to win, they should be applauded for giving people a sense that finally someone in government is listening to people like them. Many of the people I spent time with who expressed support for Act 10 and Walker conveyed a sense of gratitude that finally someone in power was recognizing the burdens they faced. To them, someone was finally acknowledging the injustice of their hard-earned money being shunted toward the undeserving.

But what about the people in rural areas that complained about being ignored? Was Scott Walker representing them? One simple way of addressing this is to examine how he has spent his time in office (Hall 1996). Has he spent time in rural areas in the state? According to the Wisconsin Center for Investigative Journalism (a center housed at the UW–Madison and supported in part by funds from liberal groups), the answer is no. Their analysis of Walker's official calendar from his first thirteen months in office shows just sixteen public appearances in the northern third of the state (the most rural portion of the state), as compared to 778 appearances in the southern two-thirds of the state.[10] If Walker had made visits in proportion to the distribution of population, he would have made four times as many visits to northern Wisconsin. Unfortunately, even if many rural Wisconsinites perceive that Scott Walker understands the concerns of people like them, it does not appear that he is going out of his way to listen to them, at least not in person in the first year he was in office.

Moreover, we still have the broader problem of lack of representation with which I began this book. We live in a time of increasing economic inequality, and yet voters continue to elect politicians whose policies respond very disproportionately to the preferences of affluent people. In that respect, the issue is not why is the white working class getting it wrong, but why is nearly every voter getting it wrong?

I have resisted the terminology of "getting it wrong" throughout this book to try as much as possible to listen openly to the views of people and set aside my own predispositions. I could provide an argument that says each person has the right to define his or her interests and that no academic should be so arrogant to judge what people "ought" to think.

It is not the case that people have been hoodwinked into voting for Republicans by being distracted from economics by social and cultural issues (as Frank 2004 argues). In the conversations that I observed, economics are very much a part of the conversation. Bartels' analysis of survey data also shows that economics are of as much importance, if not more importance, than social and cultural issues in recent presidential votes (2008, 86). But consideration of economic issues is not devoid of social and cultural issues, either. I observed people making sense of economics by pitting themselves against their fellow citizens along social and cultural lines.

So the problem, for me, is this. We are in a time of increasing economic inequality and of stark policy bias in favor of the affluent, and yet the politics of resentment draws our attention to our animosity toward each other rather than the ways in which the political system is not working for anyone but the very few.

In more partisan terms, why do people vote for the Republican Party when it is that party that is especially likely to represent the policy preferences of the affluent and ignore those of everyone else? The conversations in this study suggest that it is not because a wide swath of people identify as affluent or believe that they will be affluent someday. Instead, the conversations suggest that the Republican Party has been very successful at tapping into existing resentments toward particular targets. In the frameworks they provide, the demons are not affluent people but, rather, the government, the people that work for it, and urban areas that are home to liberals and people of color. The manner in which these understandings hinge on notions of hard work and deservingness means that social and cultural issues are important considerations, as are economic concerns. The "them"—the "haves"—is defined not by affluence but by culture. In these narratives, people are telling each other that there are people that do not value what we value, do not work as hard as we do, and are actively sucking away the livelihoods we have worked so hard to create. While some people point to the government as a source of assistance, others—such as those just described—do not believe claims that government programs will help. They have been hurting economically for generations, and in their eyes government programs do two things: they help the undeserving, and they require an increase in taxes. Even though they perceive that their towns are about to dry up and blow away, they want government to just leave them alone.

The 2012 presidential election demonstrated a limit to the ability of the Republican Party to capitalize on such arguments. Mitt Romney's personal wealth and plutocratic lifestyle proved to be a liability for the Republican Party. Bartels (2013a) has demonstrated that Romney turned voters off because he appeared to care more about those with wealth than those without. In that light, it seems the Republicans' ability to paint the haves as social groups other than the wealthy is limited.

In other words, it is not inevitable that rural residents will remain attracted to the Republican Party. The Romney candidacy demonstrates this, and so does the lack of enthusiasm that I observed for either party. If the conversations I observed are at all representative of conversations among white working people elsewhere in the country, this is a demographic that displays considerable ambivalence about, not solid allegiance to, the Democratic and Republican Parties. When these folks expressed support for small government, it was typically rooted neither in political principles nor in identification as Republicans but in a perception that services were not benefiting people who deserve them: hardworking Americans, like themselves.

What the rural voters I observed wanted in their politicians are people who understand and respect the way rural folks live and their daily concerns and desires. It is not obvious to me that Republican candidates are innately better suited to provide this understanding and respect.[11]

What Is to Be Done?

One straightforward response to the concerns I have raised in this book might be for policy makers to reassess what is going on in rural places and reconsider the policy responses they have made to date. As I documented in chapter 4, rural communities in Wisconsin are receiving significant amounts of resources—and not necessarily less than their fair share, as many of them believe. However, the depth of the resentment toward cities and policy makers suggests three possible alterations to public policy targeted toward rural areas.

First, it is possible that the resources rural communities are receiving are not effectively addressing the needs of rural communities. Perhaps state, federal, and even county legislation is too often applied to all types of places equally. Maybe more programs should be tailored specifically for rural needs and crafted with recognition that not all rural areas are the same. When such programs are developed, they have to be approved by legislative bodies that include representatives from urban, suburban, and rural areas. We need geographic cooperation as well as bipartisanship. Within state legislatures, something as simple as an exchange program, in which representatives from urban districts spend time in rural districts and vice versa, could help improve empathy for the needs of people outside one's own type of district.[12]

The second thing rural resentment toward the cities suggests about public policy is that some of the resources rural communities are receiving are invisible to the people who live there. Many of the government benefits that a wide variety of people receive are part of the "submerged state"—government programs that are as expensive as welfare but less often acknowledged (Metler 2011). How many of us, when asked, admit that we have "ever used a government social program, or not?" Most—56.5 percent—say we have not. But 60 percent of those who say they haven't used any government social programs do admit that they have received a tax deduction for paying a mortgage, for example (Metler 2011, 37–38). A similar kind of invisibility likely applies to the benefits that rural residents receive.[13]

The third thing this book suggests about public policy is that the manner in which policy is created and delivered is important for whether people perceive it as meeting their needs or being in their interests. If the people I spent time with had perceived that policy makers had listened to the concerns of rural residents before creating government programs, would they have felt differently about those programs? If they had perceived that UW–Madison researchers were going out of their way to ask locals for their insights on the projects they were pursuing in their small towns, would they have felt more supportive of that work? A team of archaeologists who have invited community members to be a part of the research process in Trempealeau, Wisconsin, for example, suggests the answer is likely yes.[14] I recognize that this is easier said than done. The Department of Natural Resources has gone to great lengths to listen to community members, live alongside them, and deliver policy in ways that meet people where they are in the course of their daily lives (such as delivering information at boat landings), yet still bears the brunt of a great deal of criticism in small-town Wisconsin.

At root, my hope in writing this book is that more and more people redirect the energy they use to engage with public issues away from criticizing their fellow citizens and toward improving the policy process to ensure that it is responsive to the needs of all people. That is asking a lot. In an atmosphere of resentment, it is tough to take the high road and operate on a belief that all people are, at root, good and deserving of respect. Our current politics give little incentive for elected officials to pursue such behavior. It is time that those of us with the power to vote demand it of them.

County Map of Wisconsin

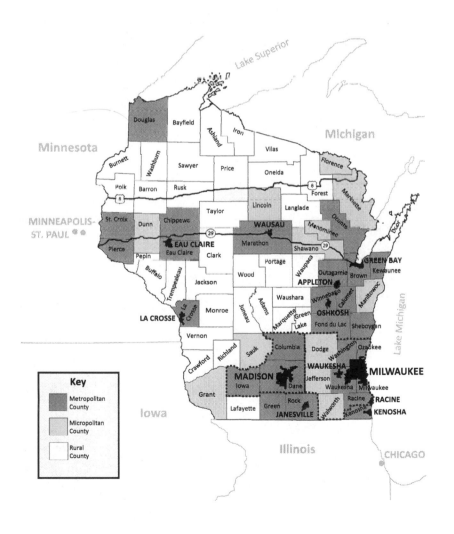

Descriptions of Groups Observed and Municipalities in Which They Met

Group No.	Municipality Description	Group Type	Municipality Population (2010)	Median Annual Household Income (2012)	2010 Republican Gubernatorial Vote (%)	Dates of Site Visits (Month/Year)
1	Central hamlet	Daily morning coffee klatch, local gas station (employed, unemployed, and retired men)	500	35,000	55	5/08, 4/11, 11/12
2	Northwestern village	Weekly morning breakfast group, restaurant (women, primarily retired)	500	34,000	25	6/07, 1/08, 4/08, 4/09, 5/11, 5/12
3	Northwestern hamlet	Weekly morning coffee klatch, church (mixed gender, primarily retirees)	500	39,000	50	6/07, 1/08
4a_1, 4a_2	North-central village	Group of library volunteers at library (mixed gender, retirees)	500	42,000	70	6/07, 5/12
4b	North-central village	Daily coffee klatch of male local leaders meeting in the municipal building	500	42,000	70	1/08, 6/08
5	Northeastern resort village	Group of congregants after a Saturday evening service at a Lutheran church (mixed gender)	1,000	62,000	45	6/07
6	Northwestern village	Daily morning coffee klatch, gas station (employed, unemployed, and retired men)	1,000	32,000	35	6/07, 1/08, 4/08, 4/09, 5/11
7	Northern American Indian reservation	Group of family members, during a Friday fish fry at a gas station/restaurant (employed and retired, mixed gender)	5,000	54,000	50	6/07
8	South-central village	Daily morning coffee klatch, gas station (mixed gender, employed, and retired)	1,500	35,000	50	6/07, 1/08, 4/08, 4/11
9	North-central village	Daily morning breakfast group, diner (employed and retired, mixed gender)	2,000	41,000	65	6/07, 1/08, 4/08, 2/09, 6/11, 5/12
10a	South-central village	Women's weekly morning coffee klatch at diner	2,500	58,000	40	6/07
10b	South-central village	Daily morning coffee klatch of male professionals, construction workers, retirees	2,500	58,000	40	2/08, 7/08
11a	Central-west village	Daily morning coffee klatch of men at gas station (employed and retired)	2,500	38,000	60	5/07, 1/08, 4/08
11b	Central-west village	Daily morning coffee klatch of men at diner (employed and retired)	2,500	38,000	60	5/07, 1/08, 4/08, 4/11, 6/12

11c	Central-west village	Weekly lunch group of women at restaurant (employed and retired)	2,500	38,000	60	6/12
12a	Central-east village	Kiwanis meeting (mixed gender, primarily retirees)	3,500	46,000	55	6/07
12b	Central-east village	Daily morning coffee klatch of male retirees at fast food restaurant	3,500	46,000	55	5/08
13	Suburb of Minneapolis/St. Paul, Minnesota	Daily morning coffee klatch of male local business owners, lawyers, retirees at diner	3,000	61,000	55	6/07, 1/08, 4/08
14	Milwaukee northern suburb	Daily morning coffee klatch of male retirees and construction workers	7,000	58,000	70	6/07, 1/08, 5/08
15	South-central city	Middle-aged man and woman taking a midmorning break at café	11,000	40,000	50	6/07
16a	Central city	Daily morning coffee klatch of middle-aged professionals and a few retirees, mixed gender, at café	55,000	42,000	50	6/07, 1/08, 4/08, 2/09, 5/09, 7/12
16b	Central city	Gathering of women who attend church together, in a café	55,000	42,000	50	7/12
17	East central city	Daily morning coffee klatch, gas station (retired men)	45,000	45,000	60	6/07, 1/08, 4/08, 1/09
18a	Milwaukee suburb (western edge)	Group of teachers and administrators at high school (mixed gender)	45,000	69,000	50	6/07, 6/12
18b	Milwaukee suburb (western edge)	Daily lunch group of employed and unemployed middle-aged men	45,000	69,000	50	4/08, 1/09 (twice), 2/09
18c	Milwaukee suburb (western edge)	Daily morning breakfast group of male and female small business owners and retirees	45,000	69,000	50	1/09, 2/09 (twice)
19	Western city	Daily morning coffee klatch, café (middle-aged professionals and retirees; mixed gender)	50,000	39,000	40	6/07, 1/08, 4/08
20	Southeastern city	Weekly morning breakfast group, diner (mixed gender, retirees and employed)	72,000	39,000	40	7/08

Group No.	Municipality Description	Group Type	Municipality Population (2010)	Median Annual Household Income (2012)	2010 Republican Gubernatorial Vote (%)	Dates of Site Visits (Month/Year)
21a	Northeastern city	Daily morning breakfast group, diner (employed and retired men)	104,000	43,000	50	6/07
21b	Northeastern city	Daily morning breakfast group, diner counter (employed and unemployed, mixed gender)	104,000	43,000	50	5/08
22a	Madison	Middle-aged, female professionals' book club	233,209	53,958	20	7/07
22b	Madison	Daily morning coffee klatch of male and female retirees at bakery	233,209	53,958	20	2/07, 3/07, 2/08, 7/08, 2/11
22c	Madison	Female resident volunteers in food pantry in low-income neighborhood (employed and unemployed)	233,209	53,958	20	Multiple visits, fall 2006
23a	Milwaukee, northern neighborhood	Activist group meeting after services in a Baptist church (mixed age and gender, employed)	594,833	35,823	25	7/07
23b	Milwaukee, southern neighborhood	Mexican immigrants waiting at a pro bono health clinic (mixed age and gender, employed and unemployed)	594,833	35,823	25	6/07
24	Southwestern village	4-H group (mixed gender)	5,000	50,000	45	2/10
25	Central village	4-H group (mixed gender)	10,000	40,000	50	3/10
26	Southeastern city	4-H group (mixed gender)	31,000	55,000	70	4/10
27	Central-east village	4-H group (mixed gender)	4,000	51,000	60	4/10

Note: Population and income figures have been rounded to preserve confidentiality of groups observed. Vote figures are rounded to nearest 5 percent.

Questions Used during Observations

Initial Visit Protocol[1]

Most important issues:

What do you think are the major issues facing people in [name of munici-pality] these days? Which of these issues are of special concern to you all personally?

[*If issues include taxes, health care, or immigration, skip to relevant ques-tions below.*]

What do you think should be done about this?
Why do you think this has been overlooked?
Whom does the current policy benefit?

Taxes [if not addressed above]:

With respect to property and income taxes, do you think people similar to yourself currently pay a fair share?
Whom do you think benefits from our current tax policies?

Health care [if not addressed above]:

Now I would like to talk about health care for a few moments. Do you feel that you have been able to obtain adequate health care for you and your families?
Are there people in your community who don't/do have adequate health care? Why do you think that is the case?

1. Protocols were adjusted to be relevant for 4-H groups.

Immigration [if not addressed above]:

> Is immigration an issue in this community? How does it affect you? How do you think immigration is affecting life in [this state] in general?

Self-description (identity and occupation):

> How would you describe the kind of people that are a part of your group to outsiders like me?
> Do any of you work outside the home? What kind of work do you do?

Children, activities, and education:

> Do you have children? How old are they?
> What kinds of activities are they involved in after school?
> For those of you with kids still in school, do you think they will go on to obtain some kind of post–high school education?
> Would you want them to attend UW–Madison? Why/why not?
> Did any of you attend school after high school? Did any of you attend UW–Madison, or another state public university system school? [If the latter:] Which one?

University of Wisconsin–Madison

> What, in your opinion, does UW–Madison currently do well?
> What, in your opinion, can UW–Madison do better?
> What *should* UW–Madison be doing in your community?
> Whom do you think the UW–Madison currently benefits?
> When you think about the students who attend UW–Madison, and the faculty and staff who work there, what comes to mind?

Financial security:

> Thinking about your overall situation here in [name of municipality], would you say that you struggle to make ends meet, or do you live comfortably?

Success and deservingness:

> In America today, some people have better jobs and higher incomes than others do. Why do you think that is — that some Americans have better jobs and higher incomes than others do?

[Here are some reasons other folks have stated—how important do you think these reasons are?]

> Because some people have more in-born ability to learn.
> Because discrimination holds some people back.
> Because some people don't get a chance to get a good education.
> Because some people just choose low-paying jobs.
> Because government policies have helped high-income workers more.
> Because God made people different from one another.
> Because some people just don't work as hard.

What does the term "hard work" mean to you?
I'm going to give you a list of occupations. Tell me which of these folks work hard for a living, and why you think that's the case: lawyers, construction workers, waitresses, public school teachers.

Second Visit Protocol

During my last round of visits with groups like this around the state, I found that many people were concerned about health care, higher education, and issues related to water. I would like to ask more about your thoughts on these topics.

Health care:

> What *are* your concerns about health care?
> Do you think people here in your community are better or worse off with respect to health care than people in other parts of the state? Why? The country? Why?
> [A statewide public opinion poll conducted by UW–Madison] asked people which of four health care reform solutions they support. Let me describe these and then ask for your opinions. [Describe four alternatives, based on following question wording:] A number of proposals have been made about ways to change the health care system in Wisconsin. I am going to read some of these proposals and for each please tell me whether you strongly oppose it, somewhat oppose it, somewhat favor it, or strongly favor it.
>
> [In the poll, the four questions below were randomized]
> A. What about consolidating all the money and resources now being spent by employers, individuals, the state government, and insur-

ance companies to operate the current health insurance system and replace it with a new system, administered entirely by state government and covering all residents of Wisconsin?

B. How about expanding the eligibility of existing state government health insurance programs for low-income people, such as Badgercare and Medicaid, to provide coverage for more people without health insurance?

C. What about requiring every resident of Wisconsin to have health insurance, either from their employer or another source, and offer government subsidies to low-income residents to help them pay for it?

D. How about encouraging individuals to put money into a tax-free health savings account that they would use to pay for their regular health care bills and accompany this with a catastrophic insurance plan they must also purchase to help pay for major medical bills?

Higher education:

In what ways is higher education a big issue for people here in your community?

Is higher education more of a pressing concern for people here than in other parts of the state?

In general, whom do you think UW–Madison benefits? Whom do you think higher education in general benefits in this country?

Do you have children? Do/did you want your kids to go to college? Why/why not?

Water:

Taking care of [name issue related to water mentioned in previous visit] will likely require broad support in the state legislature. Do you think it's possible to get that support? Why/why not?

Is this an issue that all Wisconsinites should be concerned about? How would you sell that to the broader Wisconsin public?

Presidential race:

Which of the candidates would be most attentive to the concerns of people here in your community. Why? Most attentive to concerns of people in Wisconsin? Why?

What are your hopes for this presidential race?

Higher education:

[Repeat questions from first round]

Social class identity:

People talk about social classes such as the poor, the working class, the middle class, the upper-middle class, and the upper class. Which of these classes would you say you belong to?

Third and Additional Visits Protocol

Most important issues:

What are the major issues facing people in this community?
What do you think should be done about this?
Why do you think this has been overlooked?
Whom does the current policy benefit?

Power and authority:

How would you describe your group to an outsider like me? How do you think you compare to the rest of the community?
Who do you think has power in your community? In the state? The nation? Do you tend to feel or not feel that most people with power try to take advantage of people like yourself?
How has this community changed over time?

Political parties:

Which party do you feel is more attentive to the concerns of people like you? Why?
Is it fair to say that Republicans are for the rich, and Democrats are for the lower income?
Which party do you trust to handle the economy? Why?

Attitudes toward government:

How much attention do you feel the government pays to what the people think when it decides what to do—a good deal, some, or not much?"
Would you say the government is pretty much run by a few big inter-

ests looking out for themselves or that it is run for the benefit of all the people?

[Agree/disagree:] People like me don't have any say about what the government does.
[Agree/disagree:] Public officials don't care much what people like me think.

News use:

Over the past seven days, which of the following have you used to obtain news?

A. Read a newspaper
B. Read magazines like *Newsweek*, *Time*, or *U.S. News and World Report*
C. Watched the national news on television
D. Watched the local news on television
E. Listened to the news on radio
F. Read news on the Internet

Higher education:

[Repeat questions from first round]
Where do you usually get your news about the UW–Madison?

Notes

Chapter One

1. Quoted in American Federation of State, County and Municipal Employees, Wisconsin Legislative Council 11, Legislative Report, March 15, 2013, http://www.wiafscme.org/index.cfm?action=article&articleID=D0C7B705-A90A-4BB9-ADC9-1A462E5B242C.

2. The state election board—i.e., the Government Accountability Board—certified recall petitions for six Republicans and three Democrats. Two of the Republicans were defeated, and the other incumbents retained their seats.

3. The top one hundredth of the top 1 percent earned an average $25,726,965 that year (Winters and Page 2009, 735).

4. This estimate is from Bartels (2013b), reflecting on Pfeffer, Danziger, and Schoeni (2013), fig. 2a. See also Saez 2013.

5. This study was conducted using data gathered between 1988 and 1992.

6. See Hacker and Pierson (2010), 7, for a similar question (and also Bartels 2013a, 1).

7. Please see app. B.

8. Throughout, I use the term "place identity" to refer to residents' conceptions of themselves as the type of people who live in a particular place or type of place. I distinguish this from "sense of place," which is the way people invest their geographic surroundings with meaning and also confer psychological attachment to a geographic place (Williams et al. 2010, 906). My intent is to follow in the tradition of social identity theory and conceptualize how place enters into the way people carve up the world into in-groups and out-groups, rather than focus on how attached people are to a particular place.

9. For a quick recap of the partisan composition historically, see "Wisconsin State Senate," BallotPedia: An Interactive Almanac of U.S. Politics, charts in the sec. titled "Senators," http://ballotpedia.org/wiki/index.php/Wisconsin_State_Senate.

10. I grew up in Grafton, Wisconsin, which is twenty-two miles north of Milwaukee.

11. I explain in more detail in chap. 3 what I mean by rural. Briefly, I acknowledge that rural can be defined in many ways. In this study, perceptions are central. Therefore, when the rurality of a place is not clear, I consider it to be rural if the residents I am talking with define it as such. Generally, I consider a place to be rural if it is located outside a census-designated metropolitan area (while recognizing that even counties typed as metropolitan can contain rural communities). In practice, what I am calling rural areas tended to be sparsely populated areas with abundant green space and few if any stoplights.

12. A focus on place identity could be considered a little antiquated; some say distinctions between places are fading and becoming less relevant to social life (Knoke and Henry 1977). But I disagree. Modern life has not erased the importance of place (Agnew 1987). It may have, instead, increased the need for people to draw boundaries, to more crisply define their geographic community (Cohen 1985; Bell 1992), and to behave in ways that signal their place-related identities, such as speech patterns. In Wisconsin, almost half of the residents have some amount of German background in their heritage (43 percent claimed German ancestry in the 2000 U.S. Census). You might think that things like cable TV, Skype, and cell phones would be quickly erasing the German-influenced dialects that have persisted for decades. But in fact, those dialects are strongest among younger generations (Purnell et al. 2005). People are often proud of where they are from, and they continue to want you to know it. (See Bell [1992] and Mellow [2005] with respect to rural identity in particular.)

13. Gelman et al. 2008 asserts that the main culture war is among upper-income people, reinforcing the idea in Wisconsin that the main battle is Dane versus Waukesha County (the county home to Madison versus one of the strongly Republican Milwaukee suburban counties, respectively).

14. Wisconsin has seventy-two counties, and forty of them were designated as metropolitan (twenty-six) or micropolitan (fourteen) by the 2010 Census. Eight of these comprise the Milwaukee metropolitan area. (Technically, according to the 2010 Census, this is the Milwaukee-Racine-Waukesha metropolitan area and is composed of the metropolitan counties of Milwaukee, Ozaukee, Washington, Waukesha, and Racine, along with the micropolitan counties of Dodge, Jefferson, and Walworth). An additional three comprise the Madison metropolitan area. (The Madison combined statistical area is Dane, Iowa, and Columbia counties.)

When people referred to the Madison and Milwaukee metro areas, they were referring roughly to the southeastern portion of the state, the fourteen-county area in the southeastern corner of the state that is made up of the Madison and Milwaukee metropolitan areas, plus the two counties to the south of the Madison combined statistical area (Green and Rock) and the one county to the south of the Milwaukee combined statistical area (Kenosha) that are technically part of other metro areas. Unless I state otherwise, that is the area I am referring to when I refer to the Madison and Milwaukee metro areas. I will at times use the shorthand terms major metro and nonmajor metro to refer to the Madison and Milwaukee metro areas and places outside these areas, respectively. Throughout this book, I label a place as rural if the people I studied considered that place as nonmetro, unless I note otherwise. I also use the term "small community" interchangeably with this definition of rural.

Beyond the Milwaukee and Madison metropolitan areas, most of the other metropolitan and micropolitan counties are in the southern or eastern portions of the state. Two counties to the south of the Madison metro area are part of the Janesville-Beloit metropolitan statistical area, and one county to the south of the Milwaukee metro area is part of the Chicago combined statistical area. Twelve others to the north of Milwaukee comprise the Fox Valley, Green Bay, Sheboygan and Fond du Lac metro areas. There are several other population centers in the state outside the Madison and Milwaukee metro areas. There is one metro county in the center of the state, which is the location of the city of Wausau. There is another in the far northwest, which is part of the Duluth (Minnesota)/Superior (Wisconsin) metro area. La Crosse County on the western border of the state on the Mississippi River is part of the La Crosse metro area, and five counties north of there are part of the Eau Claire/Chippewa Falls and Minneapolis/Saint Paul metropolitan areas.

15. Many people observe that Wisconsin has a strong independent streak in general. The state's political institutions have long been structured in ways that convey "confidence in the independent and more or less self-informed citizen" (Epstein 1958, 310). For example, the state has open primaries, which allow voters to remain independent until receiving a ballot on primary election day, nonpartisan municipal elections, and until the recent passage of voter identification legislation, very lenient voting registration laws (Epstein 1958, 22–32).

A University of Wisconsin–Madison Survey Center Badger Poll, a statewide public opinion poll of Wisconsin, conducted June 17–July 10, 2011, found 42 percent identifying as Independents or leaners, 55 percent among those identifying as rural calling themselves Independents or leaners, and 45 percent among those identifying as urban or suburban calling themselves Independents or leaners ($\chi^2 = 2.58, p = 0.108$)

16. Milwaukee's suburbs may be particularly white and Republican after redistricting of congressional and state legislative districts following the 2010 Census, conducted by a Republican majority state legislature.

17. There are some scholars, even in the field of geography, who disagree that class and place are linked (see discussion in Dowling 2009, 835). In particular, there are contentious arguments around whether globalization has increased or diminished the importance of physical space for the way people organize social

life across urban areas. For example, Castells argues that globalization means that now most major systems are not organized around the "space of places" but instead around the "space of flows" or global information networks (2000, 14).

18. In recent scholarship, prominent examples of work defining class according to objective indicators include Eric Olin Wright's Marxian approach (1997), which conceptualizes social class as individuals' relationship to the means of production (skill-level, self-employment and authority). There are other approaches to social class that focus on objective indicators, such as a focus on the socioeconomic characteristics of income, education, and occupational prestige (Hauser and Warren 1997).

19. Bourdieu resists linking social space with physical space and gives little attention to physical space in his consideration of social class (Blokland and Savage 2001, 222; Veenstra 2007). He argues that people of varying class positions can and often do occupy the same physical space and that physical proximity often masks the social differentiation going on (Bourdieu 1989). However, I find Bourdieu's theory quite useful for conceptualizing the relationship between place and social class, as have others (Pred 1984; Veenstra 2007).

20. Technically, populism is "a mass movement led by an outsider or maverick seeking to gain or maintain power by using anti-establishment appeals and plebiscitarian linkages" (Barr 2009, 38). Breaking this down a bit, we see that (1) populism is a mass movement (meaning a political organization or set of arguments that gains a following from a large part of the public); (2) populist movements are led by a person who has risen to power outside the existing, dominant party organizations or has risen up through them and then formed his or her own independent party; (3) populism operates through an us-versus-them approach, divisions that basically map onto a divide between people versus the powerful elite; and (4) populist politicians make appeals to extreme accountability in which direct democracy, public opinion polls, or demonstrations are taken as manifestations of what the public wants and therefore what this politician will enact.

21. Margaret Canovan defines populism this way: "Populism in modern democracies is best seen as an appeal to 'the people' against both the established structure of power and the dominant ideas and values of society" (1999, 3).

22. On the borderline are people who are local-level elected officials. I spoke with many local-level elected officials in my travels who talked about themselves and were treated by others in their group as ordinary folks.

23. When I claim that a perspective is influential for the way people think about politics, isn't that a claim about causation? If I am not taking a positivist approach, then why am I talking about explaining? If by explaining, we mean establishing causation in the traditional positivist sense, then I am overstepping my bounds. But if by explaining we mean identifying and clarifying the resources and reasoning processes people use to make sense of politics, then explanation is the business of a constitutive approach like this, too.

Chapter Two

1. I use these numbers throughout the manuscript to identify each group in the study. See app. B for more detail.

2. For example, one hand-painted sign posted on a deer stand along a major highway read, "Walker Fixed It. Don't Falk it Up. Wisconsin Couldn't Barrett." The references are to two candidates in the primary campaign for the Democratic spot on the recall ballot, Kathleen Falk and Tom Barrett.

3. With respect to yard signs, see Knisely (2013). With respect to talking to one another, see Marquette Poll results June 2012, discussed in chap. 8 (https://law.marquette.edu/poll/). As far as running each other over, see Garza (2012). Thanks to Larry Bartels for sending news of that incident to me with the subject heading "Unobtrusive measurement of political affect."

4. See Soss (2006), 319, for a discussion of the value of these surprise reactions in interview research.

5. A related issue is that as a representative of a resource-rich institution, people often perceived that I could provide them with things or access to powerful people. For example, people in several different communities asked me if I could get the UW Marching Band to come to their town. In such cases, I felt a duty to do what I could to connect people with the appropriate resources. (In one case, part of the marching band *did* march in that town's Fourth of July Parade, to my delight.) But I was very cautious about promising more than I could deliver. Wrecking expectations would have just exacerbated the distance from UW–Madison and other power holders in Madison that many people reported feeling.

6. As challenging as witnessing these conversations firsthand could be at times, one of the many upsides is that I was able to pay close attention to the way my presence affected the conversations. All kinds of measurement, including mass sample surveys, affect whatever it is researchers are trying to study. Survey interviewers affect many aspects of the survey response, from the answers themselves to whether people sampled choose to participate (e.g., Durrant et al. 2010).

7. I conducted some preliminary (practice) fieldwork in Madison in late 2006 and early 2007 (with Groups 22b and 22c).

8. More specifically, according to the 2010 U.S. Census, Wisconsin was 6.2 percent non-Hispanic African American; 5.9 percent Hispanic of any race; 0.9 percent non-Hispanic American Indian; 2.3 percent non-Hispanic Asian American; and 1.5 percent non-Hispanic Pacific Islander, non-Hispanic and another race besides those listed, or non-Hispanic and two or more races.

9. I changed my name back to my maiden name, Kathy Cramer, after concluding fieldwork.

10. Based on what I learned during the first round, I asked the Wisconsin

Alumni Association if I could pass out materials that said the University of Wisconsin–Madison rather than Wisconsin Alumni Association. There is a strong sense of ownership of the flagship university in the state even among people who have never gone to school or worked there, but giving alumni materials to non-alumni seemed to convey a kind of Madison-centric arrogance I wanted to avoid.

11. On one occasion (Group 17, January 2008) a latecomer complained that "I didn't know you were taping us" and scolded me for not announcing so, despite the presence of my recorder in the center of the table. I apologized profusely, the other group members defended me, and he said it was OK for me to stay.

Chapter Three

1. This notation indicates several comments omitted for brevity.

2. Stevens Point and Wisconsin Rapids are small cities in adjacent counties.

3. Jeremi Suri, "The New McCarthyism?" March 13, 2011, http://jeremisuri .net/archives/tag/tea-party; and see also Knoke and Henry (1977), 50; but see Fowler (2008), 161–62.

4. There are many different ways to define technically what constitutes a rural area. Even government agencies such as the U.S. Department of Agriculture have numerous different definitions, on which huge allocations of public dollars depend (see Economic Research Service, "Rural Classifications," U.S. Department of Agriculture, last updated December 30, 2013, http://www.ers.usda.gov/topics/rural-economy-population/rural-classifications.aspx). Even residents often say they live in a certain type of area (rural, urban, or suburban) when survey analysts or other social scientists claim they live in another. A Badger Poll of Wisconsin included a subjective measure of residency in a rural area: "Would you describe the place where you live as urban, suburban, or rural?" When necessary, interviewers used this prompt: "Urban is a big city like [examples of metro areas given]. Suburban is a built-up place close to a big city and Rural is less built up with fewer people and further away from a big city.") Respondents' classifications were consistent with standard Survey Sampling International classifications just 58 percent of the time (Badger Poll 30, June 9–July 10, 2010, http://uwsc.wisc.edu/badger-poll.htm). On perhaps the simplest level, by "rural" I do not mean "farming." There are many rural places that do not have great cropland (e.g., Gough 1997). Even in so-called farming communities, many people do not work in a job related to agriculture. In Wisconsin, for example, the two counties most dependent on agriculture jobs had approximately just one in two people working in an agriculture-related industry in 2008 (54 percent and 46 percent, respectively [Jones 2012]). In small communities with farming,

farmers and businesspeople might not even interact much (Varenne 1977). Even small communities have internal diversity (Carr and Kefalas 2009).

5. This includes some that met in census-designated metropolitan (eleven) and micropolitan (four) counties, yet were beyond the Madison and Milwaukee metro areas.

6. Even some people who live in rural areas of the Madison metro area think of themselves as rural residents and contrast themselves against Madison (Group 10a).

7. This perception was volunteered (i.e., I did not ask whether people agreed with such a statement). Unless otherwise specified, that is the case for all other findings reported.

8. This was a common allegation of fraud after the 2012 election. See http://www.snopes.com/politics/ballot/2012fraud.asp.

9. This is one of those notes that, if allowed to grow, could be a book in itself. Scholars of power will recognize yet another "face" of power here: a third face in which the relationships of power influence the conceptions that people have of their own powerlessness and the utility of challenging relationships of power (Lukes 1974; Gaventa 1980; Hayward 2000). That face of power is quite relevant to the understandings I uncover in this book. A useful extension of the present study would involve an examination of the manner in which the exercise of power affects the understandings I am examining here. What is the process by which people come to blame certain entities for their perceived distributive inequality? How does the exercise of power cause people to blame the government and not other actors in society? I am fascinated by these questions but am restricting my attention in this book to what the conceptions of inequality and power among the people I studied look like and how they work to affect interpretations of politics.

10. By public decision makers, I mean government and university employees and elected officials.

11. I assessed partisanship via listening to volunteered identities, responses to questions about voting history, and perceptions of attentiveness of the parties to concerns of "people like you" and also by bluntly inquiring about partisanship. If such direct prompts were not fruitful, I did not classify groups as leaning toward one or the other party.

12. The game is played with five dice. On a given turn, you have three rolls. You have to shake a six, a five, and a four, in that order, and then the total on the remaining two dice gives you your score.

13. The percentage of African Americans living outside the Madison and Milwaukee areas was calculated with data from 2010 U.S. Census, factfinder2.census.gov.

14. Examples of when hostility toward Native Americans arose include my conversations with Group 6 (May 2011) and Group 2 (January 2008).

Chapter Four

1. State spending data is derived from the 2010 report by the Wisconsin Department of Revenue, "State Taxes and Aids by Municipality and County for Calendar Year 2010," available here: http://www.revenue.wi.gov/ra/10StateTaxesAndAidsByMuniCo.pdf. Federal expenditures are reported by the Census Bureau in its "Consolidated Federal Funds Report for Fiscal Year 2010," available here: http://www.census.gov/prod/2011pubs/cffr-10.pdf. County population and percentage of rural areas are also derived from Census data (http://www.census.gov/did/www/saipe/data/statecounty/data/2010.html) and the "2010 Census Urban and Rural Classification and Urban Area Criteria" (http://www.census.gov/geo/reference/ua/urban-rural-2010.html).

2. The two excluded outliers are Menominee and Winnebago counties. All but 1 percent of Menominee County's population are tribal members from the Menominee nation, who have struggled with poverty rates double the state average. Winnebago County is home to the tenth largest federal contractor in the United States, the Oshkosh Corporation, which designs and builds trucks and military vehicles. As a result, despite Winnebago being home to less than 3 percent of Wisconsin's total population, the county received two-thirds of all the federal procurement dollars received by the state in fiscal year 2009 (Pinkovitz 2011; Siewert 2014).

3. State tax revenue data derived from the 2010 report by the Wisconsin Department of Revenue, "State Taxes and Aids by Municipality and County for Calendar Year 2010," available here: http://www.revenue.wi.gov/ra/10StateTaxesAndAidsByMuniCo.pdf. County-level federal tax revenue was reported by the Internal Revenue Service in 2011, "Total Tax Liability," available here: http://www.irs.gov/uac/SOI-Tax-Stats-Individual-Income-Tax-Statistics-ZIP-Code-Data-(SOI).

4. I am sincerely indebted to Ben Toff for these analyses and to Sarah Niebler for a similar set of analyses in the early stages of this project.

5. Rural poverty rates outpace urban poverty rates, especially among children, at least according to census data from 1970 through 2000 (Lichter and Johnson 2006). Specifically, most counties with high poverty (more than 20 percent of the population below the poverty line) are in nonmetro areas. Also, people who live in nonmetro areas are more likely to live in high-poverty areas. Finally, when it comes to persistent poverty, measured as the incidence of 20 percent or more of the population living in poverty from 1970 to 2000, 90 percent of such counties are nonmetro. Out of the 730 counties identified as having persistent poverty among people younger than eighteen, 82 percent were nonmetro counties (Lichter and Johnson 2006). Also, per capita income was lower in nonmetro than in metro areas from 1969 through at least 2005 (Miller 2008). Thank you to Ben Toff for help with this research.

6. For an earlier assessment to the contrary, see Knoke and Henry (1977). Also, Ansolabehere and Snyder note that urban voting blocks that some feared would develop did not do so. As of 1980, if anything, rural areas received more public funds than urban areas on a per capita basis (2008, 207).

7. This history is drawn primarily from Robert Gough's *Farming the Cutover* (1997).

8. Gough 1997, 227, quoting Glad 1990.

9. But this tends to be the case because in rural areas the highest income earners do not earn as much as their counterparts in urban areas. See Gallardo and Beaulieu (2011).

10. Geographic classifications are based on respondents' self-classifications. $N = 556$ for full sample, $N = 547$ on this item. $\chi^2 = 26.43$, $p = .001$. Poll conducted June 17–July 10, 2011. See Badger Poll 32, http://www.uwsc.wisc.edu/bpoll .php.

11. Badger Poll 32, June 17–July 10, 2011. "How well does the state government in Wisconsin represent the values of the people in your community: not at all, only slightly well, somewhat well, very well or extremely well?"

12. Ibid. Of self-described rural and also urban respondents, 43 percent responded "not at all" or "only slightly well," compared to 34 percent of suburban respondents.

13. Thanks to Alexander Shashko for making this point.

14. We sampled content from the following newspapers: *Appleton Post Crescent, Ashland Daily Press, Chippewa Herald, Eau Claire Leader-Telegram, Fond du Lac Reporter, Green Bay Gazette, La Crosse Tribune, Lakeland Times, Marshfield News Herald, Milwaukee Journal Sentinel, Monroe Times, Oshkosh Northwestern, Sheboygan Press, Stevens Point Journal, Wausau Daily Herald,* and the *Wisconsin State Journal.* The *Lakeland Times* and the *Ashland Daily Press* are published in noncore counties, and the *Marshfield News Herald* is published in a micropolitan county. The others are each published in counties the 2010 census designates as metropolitan.

15. We coded up to twenty actors per article. A complete codebook is available on request. To increase the reliability of our coding, we conducted interrator reliability tests throughout. Reliabilities (Cronbach alphas) were consistently at 80 percent agreement or better on each variable (and often at 100 percent). The exceptions were coding of actor actions (coded at 56 percent agreement). We exclude those variables from these analyses.

16. Thus, an article whose coverage of a statewide actor focused on county officials' criticism of the state actor was coded as negative as was an opinion piece in which a paper's editorial board directly condemned a state actor's behavior.

17. We create an index for tone in which mixed tone and neutral/not clear mentions were combined into a middle category ($r = .07$, $p = .01$).

18. Twelve percent of the articles about state government published in the

Madison and Milwaukee papers covered the economy, but 18 percent of the state articles did so ($\chi^2 = 5.16, p = .02$).

19. Another way of thinking about news content is to take into account the fact that journalists see the world through a particular cultural perspective, just as their readers do (Kahn 1996, chap. 4; Gilens 1999; Schudson 2002). Thus, the journalists' own perspectives might matter. If a journalist grew up in a rural area, her coverage might be different from a journalist who was raised in a major city. Unfortunately, for this analysis we do not have data on the backgrounds of the journalists. As a proxy, we compared stories written by staff writers at the smaller papers to those attributed to wire services but found no differences (perhaps because those wire articles are often written or contributed to by local newspaper staff).

20. The *Lakeland Times* is a well-known biweekly in northern Wisconsin. (Print circulation is approximately 10,500 and online readership is about 30,000 unique hits per month, according to self-reported figures in the February 26, 2010, article "Lakeland Times Staff Earns Eight WNA Awards," http://www.lakelandtimes.com/main.asp?SectionID=9&SubSectionID=9&ArticleID=11010. Circulation figures were not available via Alliance for Audited Media.) One indicator of its popularity is that people in a central city in Wisconsin (Group 16a) told me about an article published in the *Lakeland Times* in spring 2008 that I would be interested in and called the paper "the biggest gossip sheet in Northern Wisconsin."

21. One of the best examples of this is what scholars call the hostile media effect. People who have a strong opinion on an issue are likely to interpret news coverage as biased against their point of view, even when it is not (e.g., Gunther and Schmitt 2006).

22. One might say letters to the editor, rather than news content, are a better indicator of what is on the mind of people in a particular community since it is residents of the communities within the circulation area that typically write the letters. While it is true that these letters are usually screened by editors and that their writers tend to be older than the average resident of a place (Hart 2001), they are nevertheless an indicator of community sentiment and are relatively unfiltered compared to other local news content.

I turned to letters to the editor to try to get a sense of the historical nature of rural consciousness, that is, how long it has been around and when it emerged. An undergraduate student working with me, Helen Osborn, coded 302 letters to the editor from six daily newspapers printed in or near communities I studied. These papers were the *Ashland Daily Press, Green Bay Gazette, Fond du Lac Reporter, La Crosse Tribune, Marshfield News Herald,* and *Wausau Daily Herald.* The *Ashland Daily Press* is published in a noncore county, and the *Marshfield News Herald* is published in a micropolitan county, while the Green Bay, Fond du Lac, La Crosse, and Wausau papers are published in metro counties (though all outside the Madison and Milwaukee metro areas). We sampled six dates per decade since 1950 and then collected all letters to the editor printed on those dates. We looked for whether the letters mentioned place (Madison, Milwaukee, "metro areas," "rural areas," "up north," "outstate," or any other reference to a place such as "central Wisconsin communities"), a government entity such as a particular public official or a government organization such as an agency or department, and the types of issues on which the writers focused.

Only a few of these letters (fourteen) mentioned Madison or Milwaukee specifically. So in general, antiurban sentiment was not prominent in these letters. The percentage of letters each decade that referred to place as well as mentioned public employees or a government-related entity (person or organization) varied over time in interesting ways, however. In the 1950s, over half of the letters made such mentions, and then these references declined to about 30 percent in the1980s, then rose to about 40 percent in the 2000s. The higher rate of references to geography decades ago suggests that the relevance of place to politics in Wisconsin is not new. However, the recent resurgence of these mentions leaves open the possibility that its shape is different now than in the past.

Chapter Five

1. In particular, Peyton Smith pushed me to ask questions about perceptions of the University of Wisconsin–Madison and made it possible for me to receive an Ira and Ineva Reilly Baldwin Wisconsin Idea Endowment Grant to do this work.

2. There is a great deal of pride in the UW System as a whole. A March 2012 survey of Wisconsin adult residents conducted for the UW System found that 80 percent feel a sense of pride about the education people can receive at UW System schools and at Wisconsin technical colleges. Pride in K–12 education in the state was lower, at 65 percent.

3. That figure includes undergraduate, professional, and graduate students. Wisconsin resident enrollment data is from the 2012–13 UW System *Fact Book*, http://www.uwsa.edu/cert/publicat/factbook.pdf.

4. The Wisconsin Alumni Association reports (as of June 2015), that 146,810 UW–Madison alums lived in Wisconsin (http://www.uwalumni.com/about/facts/).

5. Among Wisconsin residents, students from rural high schools are in fact less likely to apply to UW–Madison than students from urban high schools (Huhn 2005). This seems to be part of a more general trend across the United States. Rural youth are less likely to obtain a college degree than are others; this is a function, in part, of lower socioeconomic status and in part of lower parental expectations (Byun et al. 2012).

6. I did not have the guts to admit in this context that my parents generously paid for my college education.

7. In the 2007–8 academic year, in-state tuition at UW–Madison was $6,330 for two semesters.

8. In the 2007 college football season, Ohio State won the Big 10 championship for the second year in a row.

9. Names of these lakes have been changed to protect confidentiality.

10. The College of Agriculture and Life Sciences at the UW–Madison has a 125-year history of running "short courses" for people preparing for careers in farming and related businesses (Farm and Industry Short Course, http://fisc.cals .wisc.edu/).

11. Over three-quarters of Wisconsin's 283,000 public workers are employees of local governments and school districts and thus a majority are not urbanites (Wisconsin Taxpayer Alliance report, March 2010, www.wistax.org/news _releases/2010/1002.html).

12. It is not necessarily the case that resentment toward public employees was stronger in rural areas. For example, in a June 17–July 10, 2011, Badger Poll, the percentage of self-reported rural respondents answering that public employees had "too much influence" was statistically indistinguishable from self-reported suburban and urban residents. ("Some people think that certain groups have too much influence in Wisconsin life and politics, while other people feel that certain groups don't have as much influence as they deserve. For each of the groups that I read to you, tell me whether you think this group has too much influence, just about the right amount of influence, or too little influence . . . Do public employees have too much influence, just about the right amount of influence, or too little influence?") Rural residents ($N = 226$): 29 percent, suburban residents ($N = 202$): 25 percent, urban residents ($N = 128$): 28 percent.

13. Specifically, we conducted analyses using American Community Survey five-year estimates from data collected 2006–10 and analyzed it by Public Use Microdata Area. Such areas are geographic zones into which each state is carved, each containing at least a hundred thousand people. We compared average total income among employees who reported working for a state, local, or federal government against average total income for employees who did not. Thresholds for low-income and high-income regions correspond to the bottom and top third of all Public Use Microdata Areas in the state ranked according to average income. Thanks to Ben Toff for these analyses.

14. My sincere gratitude to Ben Toff for these analyses and figures.

15. This comment was reported here: http://www.nytimes.com/2011/01/04/ business/04labor.html.

16. Data obtained from the online database *Polling the Nations* ([Silver Spring, MD: ORS Pub., 1997–]), http://poll.orspub.com/. Enrollment levels suggest that a sizable segment of the public perceives that for-profit higher educa-

tion institutions are more efficient and more attentive to needs of the public (see Coleman and Vedder 2008).

17. I am deeply grateful to Ben Toff for excellent research on this history.

18. American Federation of State, County and Municipal Employees 1936. Thank you to Alexis Walker for bringing this document to my attention.

19. Badger Poll 32, June 17–July 10, 2011, $N = 556$. See n. 12, this chapter, for question wording regarding influence. The Tea Party question was: "Do you consider yourself to be a supporter of the Tea Party movement or not?"

20. Thank you, Larry Bartels, for raising this point.

21. Badger Poll 32 conducted in summer 2011 estimated that 44.84 percent of men in the state believed that public employees have "too much influence," almost identical to the 44.85 percent of women. See n. 79 in the poll. $\chi^2 = .06, p = .81$.

22. "Wisconsin Recall Exit Polls: How Different Groups Voted," June 5, 2012, http://www.nytimes.com/interactive/2012/06/05/us/politics/wisconsin-recall-exit-polls.html

23. "America's Choice, 2014 Election Center—Governor: Wisconsin (Walker vs. Burke)," CNN Politics, November 5, 2014, http://www.cnn.com/election/2014/results/state/WI/governor.

Chapter Six

1. I do not mean to claim, in this chapter, that small-government views are more common in rural areas or among people who label themselves as living in a rural area than they are in suburban areas. (Suburban areas tend to lean conservative. See McGirr [2002]; Gelman et al. [2008]; Peck [2011]; and Cho, Gimpel, and Shaw [2012], 120.) Instead, I will demonstrate what support for small government looks like among rural folks, a population of people who define themselves by their residence in rural areas, which they view as places facing rough economic times. These are also people who are commonly described as getting it wrong (e.g., Frank 2004). With respect to the nation as a whole, survey respondents who called themselves rural (rural farm or rural town) are, if anything, only marginally more likely to express small-government views than suburbanites but are distinctive from urban dwellers. The following are the percentages of rural, suburban, and urban respondents (based on self-reported type of place) expressing small-government views in response to the three relevant items in the 2012 American National Election Studies (see fig. 6.1; question wording is identical to Badger Poll wording quoted below). Percentage saying government is involved in things people should do for themselves: 51.7 percent—rural; 50.0 percent—suburban; and 35.7 percent—urban. Percentage saying the free market is better at solving problems: 33.5 percent—rural; 34.87 percent—suburban; and 28.4 percent—urban. Percentage saying the less government, the

better: 50.0 percent—rural; 49.5 percent—suburban; and 37.3 percent—urban. In Wisconsin (using statewide data from Badger Poll 30, June 2010, http://uwsc.wisc.edu/badger-poll.htm), self-reported rural respondents are less conservative with respect to small-government views than are self-reported suburban respondents (where small-government views are measured with the following three items: "Please tell me which of the following two statements come closer to your thoughts. [1] The main reason government has become bigger over the years is because it has gotten involved in things that people should do for themselves; OR the government has become bigger because the problems we face have become bigger. [2] We need a strong government to handle today's complex economic problems; OR the free market can handle these problems without government being involved. [3] The less government, the better; OR there are more things that government should be doing?")

2. What accounts for the discrepancy between claims about level of public support for welfare in the 1970s and early 1980s? One reason is technical—the overreliance on a particular question fielded in the General Social Survey by the National Opinion Research Center that asked about support for "welfare." The question read, "Do you think we spend too much money on welfare, too little money, or about the right amount on welfare?" (Cook and Barrett 1992, 25). Since "welfare" is such a stigmatized term, the question may not accurately gauge how willing people are to support programs that provide for people in poverty. Cook and Barrett report findings from Smith (1987) that when a 1984 National Opinion Research Center survey asked about welfare in different ways, in terms of "assistance to the poor" or "caring for the poor," public support at the same point in time was about 44 percent and 39 percent higher, respectively (Cook and Barrett 1992, 27). Another problem with using responses to support for "welfare" is that there is (and there was) no such program as "welfare." When asked about specific programs (Aid to Families with Dependent Children, Social Security, and Medicaid), a majority of the public is supportive of these programs (Cook and Barrett 1992, 61–60).

Larry Bartels, in personal communication, points out another problem with these questions: they are sensitive to perceived levels of welfare spending and do not respond to actual spending levels. When Reagan became president, people perceived government cutbacks and started asking for more spending. The reverse happened when Barack Obama became president.

3. Please see n. 1, this chapter. The Badger Poll used question wordings for these three items identical to those used in the American National Election Studies.

4. When I waded into the conversation data to learn more about how people connect antigovernment attitudes with small-government attitudes, I looked for attitudes with respect to small government, as well as attitudes toward government in general, and instances in which people connected the two. And I looked

for these attitudes and connections in conversations in all types of places—rural, as well as urban and suburban—and examined the differences across type of place to understand the particular work of rural consciousness.

5. Wisconsin Association of School Boards, "School Finance 101," 2012, http://www.wasb.org/websites/communications/File/school_finance_101_web.pdf.

6. This is one example of misunderstanding. Property taxes are not diverted to Madison to pay for education. It is income taxes that are collected and then reallocated across the state in an attempt to guarantee a "basic educational opportunity" to each student. Wisconsin Association of School Boards, "School Finance 101."

7. The "Mason-Dixon line" is their term for Highway 21, which cuts east-west across the state from Sparta to Oshkosh and provides a marker between the metro areas in the southern tier from the rest of Wisconsin.

8. Just because blatantly racist statements did not appear in the conversations I observed in rural areas does not mean that racism does not exist in those places. Badger Poll data do suggest that self-identified rural residents are more likely to think that minorities have too much influence than are self-identified urban or suburban residents. (In response to the question "Do minorities have too much influence, just about the right amount of influence, or not enough influence?" 21 percent of rural residents said "too much," while just 13 percent of nonrural residents said so. $\chi^2 = 9.32$, $p = .009$, Badger Poll 32, June 17–July 10, 2011, $N = 516$).

9. I did indeed observe conversations in which people openly displayed racial resentment as part of their justification for small government, but these always took place in urban and suburban areas. Numerous examples come from the consistently conservative group in suburban Milwaukee (Group 18c). One member was a former teacher in the Milwaukee public school district, and she complained about students in the district taking the free lunch program as a given, when hard-working people like herself have to pay for that program via their tax dollars. She did not state outright that the students she was talking about were racial minorities, but approximately 84 percent of the students in the Milwaukee Public School district are racial minorities (National Center for Education Statistics, "Characteristics of the 100 Largest Public Elementary and Secondary School Districts in the United States: 2007–08," table A9, July 2010, http://nces.ed.gov/pubs2010/100largest/tables/table_a09.asp). She also complained that a double standard was applied to white staff at the school versus employees of color. Other comments in that group conveyed that, in their eyes, racial minorities were getting more than their fair share. These comments convey a belief that scaling back government is desirable because currently government gives benefits to the wrong people, not necessarily because limited government is preferable in general.

In other groups, people supported small government with less overt mention of racial minorities. Among consistently conservative groups in particular, arguments for less government sometimes hinged on perceptions of government inefficiency (Groups 13 and 12b), the failure of government officials to understand rural wants and needs (Groups 3 and 16a), or a desire for organizations, especially churches, to provide a social safety net rather than for government to do so (Groups 12b and 25).

10. The ubiquity of subconscious racial prejudice, even among people who consciously express racial tolerance (Devine 1989), underscores this possibility. Many scholars argue that, in the contemporary context, racism is often "symbolic racism" or racial prejudice rooted in moral values rather than perceived threats to one's self interest. One of the main measures of such racism since it was conceptualized in the early 1970s has been agreement with the idea that black Americans do not work hard enough to make ends meet (see Sears and Henry 2005).

Chapter Seven

1. Their astonishment that people could live on less than a thousand dollars a week means that their own household income was higher than the median in their community, which when rounded off for confidentiality purposes is approximately thirty-eight thousand dollars per year.

2. One man, in the town hall group in the northern tourist group, told me that Obama had pledged to stand by his Muslim brothers (Group 4b, June 2008).

3. See exit poll results at "Election Center 2008: Exit Polls," CNN Politics, http://www.cnn.com/ELECTION/2008/results/polls/#val=WIP00p1 and "Election Center," CNN Politics, http://www.cnn.com/ELECTION/2010/results/polls/#WIG00p1.

4. University of Wisconsin–Madison Survey Center Badger Poll 30, conducted between June 9 and July 10, 2010 ($N = 500$) and Badger Poll 24, conducted between June 7 and June 15, 2007 ($N = 502$), http://uwsc.wisc.edu/badger-poll.htm.

5. In Badger Poll 32 conducted between June 17 and July 10, 2011, 77 percent of people in union households answered "disapprove" to the question: "Overall, do you approve or disapprove of the way Scott Walker is handling his job as Governor of Wisconsin?" ($N = 556$); 51 percent of people in nonunion households did so.

6. When I first arrived, there were three men present, but over the course of my hour-long visit, attendance ebbed and flowed between one and four people.

7. "Down on the dauber" is a colloquial saying meaning in low spirits.

8. "Scott Walker Ad: 'Yes We Can!'" uploaded on August 15, 2010, YouTube video, 1:00, http://www.youtube.com/watch?v=HcQ7hwRhKIs&.

9. Statement made during first debate of general election, September 24,

2010, Milwaukee, Wisconsin, http://www.c-span.org/video/?295644-1/wisconsin
-gubernatorial-debate.

10. "Scott Walker Ad: 'Yes We Can!'"

11. "Wisconsin Governor Republican Primary Debate," August 27, 2010, Milwaukee, Wisconsin, http://www.c-span.org/video/?295182-1/wisconsin-governor
-republican-primary-debate.

12. "Wisconsin Gubernatorial Debate," September 24, 2010, Milwaukee, Wisconsin, http://www.c-span.org/video/?295644-1/wisconsin-gubernatorial-debate.
He also claimed in that debate that constructing the train would give jobs to
Spain and take them away from Sheboygan, a Wisconsin city: "As I said to the
folks in Sheboygan about a year and a half ago when Jim Doyle was over working on getting that train from Spain, instead of focusing on Thomas Industries
[a vacuum pump and air compressor manufacturer in Sheboygan that closed in
2009]—there will never be a time in this state when any worker, not just employer, will have to look their governor in the face and say he didn't do everything in his power to keep my job in the state of Wisconsin."

13. During the first general election debate he said, "There's no doubt we can
take on the political machine down in Madison and win for all the taxpayers in
this state." And in a campaign ad, he said: "Together, we can take on the political machine down the way in Madison and win for all the taxpayers" ("Scott
Walker: 3 Months to Victory," uploaded August 2, 2010, YouTube video, 1:48,
http://www.youtube.com/watch?v=bDhOrxhftE0).

14. "Wisconsin Gubernatorial Debate," September 24, 2010.

15. "Scott Walker on 'Fox and Friends,'" uploaded on September 20, 2010,
YouTube video, 3:55, http://www.youtube.com/watch?v=aZZSnhsGJyE.

16. Walker's success in rural areas of the state in the 2010 election suggests he
was able to tap into anti-Madison sentiment (see Fanlund 2010) as well as anti-
Milwaukee sentiment (Fanlund 2011). Whereas the previous Republican candidate for governor had carried only twenty-four of the sixty-four counties outside
the Milwaukee combined statistical area or the Madison metropolitan statistical
area, Walker carried fifty-six of sixty-four. Walker picked up almost 87,000 more
votes in the counties outside those two metro areas in 2010 than the previous Republican gubernatorial candidate in 2006 (667,643 votes compared to 580,722 in
2006.) This is especially impressive, given that turnout in those counties declined
between 2006 and 2010. He did pick up votes in the two main metro areas, too,
but not as many as in the other counties (a 63,000 gain in the Madison and Milwaukee metro areas).

Chapter Eight

1. A year after the gubernatorial recall election, I was a guest on a Wisconsin Public Radio call-in show. A caller expressed disbelief that anyone could

perceive public employees as among the "haves." "Urban vs. Rural Wisconsin," July 31, 2013, http://www.wpr.org/shows/urban-vs-rural-wisconsin-shakespeare -star-wars.

2. The surprise was due in part to polls showing the race was a dead heat even until less than one week before the election.

3. Take, for example, Rush Limbaugh attacking a Wisconsin public school teacher on air as "an idiot" and a "glittering jewel of colossal ignorance" for her comment that we have lost "the sense of democracy" (Lueders 2011).

4. For example, according to the conservative news website Newsmax.com, Walker claimed that his mother and sons were yelled at while shopping and that his sons were attacked on Facebook ("Wis. Gov. Walker: Opponents Attacking My Family," *Newsmax*, April 5, 2012 http://www.newsmax.com/Newsfront/ Wisconsin-Recall-Governor-Walker/2012/04/05/id/434935).

5. Marquette Poll, fielded June 13–16, 2012, $N = 707$. "Is there anyone you have stopped talking with about politics due to disagreements over the re-call elections or Scott Walker?" (https://law.marquette.edu/poll/wp-content/ uploads/2012/09/MLSP11_Toplines.pdf).

6. Brownstein 2010.

7. See n. 1, chap. 6, for standard measures of preferences for limited government.

8. Thank you to John Zaller for observing during a book conference on revisions to *Unequal Democracy* (Bartels 2008) that "maybe the reality [of how people understand themselves] is closer to more discrete concepts like 'I'm a rural Wisconsin person,' as opposed to, 'I'm white working class.'"

9. It is notable that the most ideologically consistent group in my sample, the group of conservatives meeting for breakfast every day in a Milwaukee suburb, were also the ones who most openly pledged an allegiance to a specific news source, Fox News. At one point one woman said, to nodding heads, "The people who vote are not informed. The only source we trust is Fox News." I was able to trace many of their claims back to Fox News, such as an assertion that Obama was a hypocrite because he urged Americans to conserve energy while at the same time keeping the Oval Office very warm ("Obama Getting Heat for Turning up the Oval Office Thermostat," Fox News: Politics, February 3, 2009, http://www.foxnews.com/politics/2009/02/03/obama-getting-heat-turning-oval -office-thermostat/). I could have likely done the same with claims made by devout MSNBC watchers, but no one in my sample reported watching that channel consistently.

10. See map of visits and study details at WisconsinWatch, "Interactive Graphics: The Walker Calendar Files—Part Two," Money and Politics, May 16, 2012, http:// wisconsinwatch.org/2012/05/interactive-graphics-the-walker-calendar-files -part-two/. According to U.S. Census 2011 population estimates, 8.25 percent of the population lived in the northern third of Wisconsin counties.

11. In an analysis of the influence of various candidate traits on presidential votes, the trait that seemed to matter most is to what extent each candidate "really cares about people like you" (Bartels 2002, 61–66).

12. One example is the Rural-Urban Leadership (RULE) program, run by the Penn State Extension, which trains leaders from many sectors, not just elected officials (http://extension.psu.edu/community/rule/about). Another type of program is the Adopt-a-Legislator program run by farm bureaus in a variety of states (e.g., Illinois, http://www.ilfb.org/get-involved/get-political/adopt-a-legislator-program-original.aspx), in which urban state legislators are paired with farmers in order to educate the legislators on agricultural concerns. Many of these examples are focused on exposing urbanites to rural concerns. That is desirable, but only part of what I am recommending. There is a need for rural residents to better understand urban concerns as well.

13. See related arguments about the need for more visible forms of taxation in Campbell (2011).

14. See a brief story on archeologist Danielle Benden's work on the dig of mounds made by humans approximately a thousand years ago (Tenenbaum 2014).

References

Abramowitz, Alan I. 2013. *The Polarized Public? Why American Government Is So Dysfunctional.* Upper Saddle River, NJ: Pearson.

———. 2014. "How Race and Religion Have Polarized American Voters." *Washington Post,* January 20. http://www.washingtonpost.com/blogs/monkey-cage/wp/2014/01/20/how-race-and-religion-have-polarized-american-voters/.

Achenbach, Joel. 2012. "Wisconsin, the Land of Persuadable Voters." *Washington Post,* October 15. http://www.washingtonpost.com/politics/decision2012/wisconsin-the-land-of-persuadable-voters/2012/10/15/db93c9d8-0f32-11e2-bb5e-492c0d30bff6_story.html.

Agnew, John A. 1987. *Place and Politics: The Geographical Mediation of State and Society.* Winchester, MA: Allen & Unwin, Inc.

Alesina, Alberto, and Edward L. Glaeser. 2004. *Fighting Poverty in the US and Europe: A World of Difference.* Oxford: Oxford University Press.

American Federation of State, County and Municipal Employees. 1936. Government Research and the A.F.S.C. and M.E.: Report from the First Biennial Convention of AFSCME in 1936. Wisconsin Historical Society. Shelf M72–226, Box 43, Folder A.F. Of S.C. + M.E.

Ansolabehere, Stephen, and James M. Snyder. 2008. *The End of Inequality: One Person, One Vote and the Transformation of American Politics.* New York: W. W. Norton.

Axelrod, Robert. (1984) 2006. *The Evolution of Cooperation.* rev. ed. Cambridge, MA: Basic Books.

Bachrach, Peter, and Morton Baratz. 1962. "Two Faces of Power." *American Political Science Review* 56:947–52.

Barber, Michael, and Nolan McCarty. 2013. "Causes and Consequences of Polarization." In *Task Force on Negotiating Agreement in Politics,* ed. Jane Mansbridge and Cathie Jo Martin, 19–53. Washington, DC: American Political Science Association.

Barr, Robert R. 2009. "Populists, Outsiders and Anti-Establishment Politics." *Party Politics* 15 (1): 29–48.

Barreto, Matt A., Betsy L. Cooper, Benjamin Gonzalez, Christopher S. Parker, and Christopher Towler. 2011. "The Tea Party in the Age of Obama: Mainstream Conservatism or Out-Group Anxiety?" *Political Power and Social Theory* 22:105–37.

Bartels, Larry M. 2002. "The Impact of Candidate Traits in American Presidential Elections." In *Leaders' Personalities and the Outcomes of Democratic Elections*, ed. Anthony King. Oxford: Oxford University Press.

——. 2008. *Unequal Democracy: The Political Economy of the New Gilded Age*. New York: Russell Sage Foundation; Princeton, NJ: Princeton University Press.

——. 2013a. "The Class War Gets Personal: Inequality as a Political Issue in the 2012 Election." Paper presented at the Midwestern Political Science Association annual conference, Chicago, April 11–14.

——. 2013b. "Power to (Altruists Concerned with?) the Poor." *The Monkey Cage* (blog). August 13. http://themonkeycage.org/2013/08/13/power-to-altruists-concerned-with-the-poor/.

Bell, Michael. 1992. "The Fruit of Difference: The Rural-Urban Continuum as a System of Identity." *Rural Sociology* 57 (1): 65–82.

Bennett, W. Lance. 1989. Toward a Theory of Press-State Relations. *Journal of Communication* 40 (2): 103–25.

——. 2011. *News: The Politics of an Illusion*. 9th ed. New York: Longman.

Blalock, Hubert M. 1967. *Toward a Theory of Minority-Group Relations*. New York: Wiley.

Blokland, Talja, and Mike Savage. 2001. "Networks, Class and Place." *International Journal of Urban and Regional Research* 25 (2): 221–26.

Blumer, Herbert. 1948. "Public Opinion and Public Opinion Polling." *American Sociological Review* 13 (5): 542–49.

Bobo, Lawrence D., and Mia Tuan. 2006. *Prejudice in Politics: Group Position, Public Opinion, and the Wisconsin Treaty Rights Dispute*. Cambridge, MA: Harvard University Press.

Bourdieu, Pierre. (1979) 1984. *Distinction: A Social Critique of the Judgement of Taste*. Translated by Richard Nice. Cambridge, MA: Harvard University Press.

——. 1989. "Social Space and Symbolic Power." *Sociological Theory* 7 (1): 14–25.

Brewer, Marilynn. 1999. "The Psychology of Prejudice: Ingroup Love or Outgroup Hate?" *Journal of Social Issues* 55 (3): 429–44.

Brewer, Marilynn, and Norman Miller. 1984. "Beyond the Contact Hypothesis: Theoretical Perspectives on Desegregation." In *Groups in Contact: The Psy-*

chology of Desegregation, ed. Norman Miller and Marilynn B. Brewer, 281–302. Orlando, FL: Academic Press.

Brooks, Clem, and Jeff Manza. 2007. *Why Welfare States Persist: The Importance of Public Opinion in Democracies*. Chicago: University of Chicago Press.

Brownstein, Ronald. 2010. "The Gray and the Brown: The Generational Mismatch." *National Journal*, July 24, http://www.nationaljournal.com/magazine/the-gray-and-the-brown-the-generational-mismatch-20100724.

Bryce, James. 1913. "The Nature of Public Opinion." In *The American Commonwealth*, 2:251–376. New York: Macmillan.

Burghart, Devin, and Leonard Zeskind. 2010. *Tea Party Nationalism: A Critical Examination of the Tea Party Movement and the Size, Scope, and Focus of Its National Factions*. Kansas City, MO: Institute for Research and Education on Human Rights.

Burrows, Roger, and Nicholas Gane. 2006. "Geodemographics, Software and Class." *Sociology* 40 (5): 793–812.

Byun, Soo-yong, Judith L. Meese, and Matthew J. Irvin. 2012. "Rural Nonrural Disparities in Postsecondary Educational Attainment Revisited." *American Education Research Journal* 49 (3): 412–37.

Campbell, Andrea L. 2009. "Is the Economic Crisis Driving Wedges between Young and Old? Rich and Poor?" *Generations* 33 (3): 47–53.

———. 2011. "The 10 Percent Solution." *Democracy* 19:54–63.

Campbell, Angus, Philip E. Converse, Warren E. Miller, and Donald E. Stokes. 1960. *The American Voter*. Chicago: University of Chicago Press.

Canovan, Margaret. 1999. "Trust the People! Populism and the Two Faces of Democracy." *Political Studies* 47:2–16.

Carnes, Nicholas. 2013. *White-Collar Government: The Hidden Role of Class in Economic Policy Making*. Chicago: University of Chicago Press.

Carr, Patrick J., and Maria J. Kefalas. 2009. *Hollowing Out the Middle: The Rural Brain Drain and What It Means for America*. Boston: Beacon Press.

Carsey, Thomas M., and Geoffrey C. Layman. 2006. "Changing Sides or Changing Minds? Party Identification and Policy Preferences in the American Electorate." *American Journal of Political Science* 50 (2): 464–77.

Castells, Manuel. 2000. "Materials for an Exploratory Theory of the Network Society." *British Journal of Sociology* 51 (1): 5–24.

Chi, Michelene T. H., Paul J. Feltovich, and Robert Glaser. 1981. "Categorization and Representation of Physics Problems by Experts and Novices." *Cognitive Science* 5:121–52.

Cho, Wendy K. Tam, James G. Gimpel, and Daron R. Shaw. 2012. "The Tea Party Movement and the Geography of Collective Action." *Quarterly Journal of Political Science* 7:105–33.

Cohen, Anthony P. 1985. *The Symbolic Construction of Community*. London: Ellis Horwood.

Coleman, James, and Richard Vedder. 2008. *For-Profit Education in the United States: A Primer*. Policy Paper, Center for College Affordability and Productivity, Washington, DC. research.policyarchive.org/20592.pdf.

Conn, Steven. 2014. *Americans against the City: Anti-Urbanism in the Twentieth Century*. New York: Oxford University Press.

Conover, Pamela Johnston. 1984. "The Influence of Group Identifications on Political Perception and Evaluation." *Journal of Politics* 46:760–85.

———. 1988. "The Role of Social Groups in Political Thinking." *British Journal of Political Science* 18:51–76.

Converse, Phillip E. 1964. "The Nature of Belief Systems in Mass Publics." In *Ideology and Discontent*, ed. D. E. Apter, 206–61. New York: Free Press.

Cook, Fay Lomax, and Edith J. Barrett. 1992. *Support for the American Welfare State: The View of Congress and Public*. New York: Columbia University Press.

Cook, Timothy E. 1998. *Governing with the News: The News Media as a Political Institution*. Chicago: University of Chicago Press.

Cooper, Zachary. 1994. *Black Settlers in Rural Wisconsin*. Madison: State Historical Society of Wisconsin.

Corbett, Julia B. 1995. "When Wildlife Make the News: An Analysis of Rural and Urban North-Central U.S. Newspapers." *Public Understanding of Science* 4:397–410.

Cramer, Katherine J. 2014. "Political Understanding of Economic Crises: The Shape of Resentment Toward Public Employees." In *Mass Politics in Tough Times: Opinions, Votes, and Protest in the Great Recession*, ed. Nancy Bermeo and Larry M. Bartels, 72–104. Oxford: Oxford University Press.

Cramer Walsh, Katherine. 2004. *Talking about Politics: Informal Groups and Social Identity in American Life*. Chicago: University of Chicago Press.

———. 2007. "Studying the Role of Social Class Identity in Political Understanding: A Proposed Method." Paper presented to the University of Michigan Ford Fellows' Reunion, Ann Arbor, May 12.

———. 2009. "Scholars as Citizens: Studying Public Opinion through Ethnography." In *Political Ethnography*, ed. Ed Schatz, 165–82. Chicago: University of Chicago Press.

———. 2011. "Get Government Out of It: Heterogeneity of Government Skepticism and Its Connection to Economic Interests and Policy Preferences." In *Who Gets Represented?* ed. Peter Enns and Christopher Wlezien, 129–59. New York: Russell Sage.

———. 2012. "Putting Inequality in Its Place: Rural Consciousness and the Power of Perspective." *American Political Science Review* 106 (3): 517–32

Cramer Walsh, Katherine, M. Kent Jennings, and Laura Stoker. 2004. "The Effects of Social Class Identification on Participatory Orientations toward Government." *British Journal of Political Science* 34: 469–95.

Creed, Gerald W., and Barbara Ching. 1997. "Recognizing Rusticity." In *Knowing Your Place: Rural Identity and Cultural Hierarchy*, ed. Barbara Ching and Gerald W. Creed, 1–28. New York: Routledge.

Dahl, Robert A. 1961. *Who Governs? Democracy and Power in an American City*. New Haven, CT: Yale University Press.

Davidson, Osha Gray 1996. *Broken Heartland: The Rise of America's Rural Ghetto*. Iowa City: University of Iowa Press.

Delli Carpini, Michael X., and Scott Keeter. 1996. *What Americans Know about Politics and Why It Matters*. New Haven, CT: Yale University Press.

DeSante, Christopher D. 2013. "Working Twice as Hard to Get Half as Far: Race, Work Ethic, and America's Deserving Poor." *American Journal of Political Science* 57 (2): 342–56.

Devine, Patricia. 1989. "Stereotypes and Prejudice: Their Automatic and Controlled Components." *Journal of Personality and Social Psychology* 56:5–18.

Dewees, Sarah, Linda Lobao, and Louis E. Swanson. 2003. "Local Economic Development in an Age of Devolution: The Question of Rural Localities." *Rural Sociology* 68 (2): 182–206.

Dionne, E. J., Jr. 2006. "Polarized by God? American Politics and the Religious Divide." In *Red and Blue Nation? Characteristics and Causes of America's Polarized Politics*, ed. Pietro S. Nivola and David W. Brady, 175–205. [Stanford, CA]: Hoover Institution on War, Revolution, and Peace; Washington, DC: Brookings Institution Press.

Domina, Thurston. 2006. "What Clean Break? Education and Nonmetropolitan Migration Patterns, 1989–2004." *Rural Sociology* (71) 3: 373–98.

Dowling, Robyn. 2009. "Geographies of Identity: Landscapes of Class." *Progress in Human Geography* 33 (6): 833–39.

Durrant, Gabriele B., Robert M. Groves, Laura Staetsky, and Fiona Steele. 2010. "Effects of Interviewer Attitudes and Behaviors on Refusals in Household Surveys." *Public Opinion Quarterly* 74 (1): 1–36.

Epstein, Leon. 1958. *Politics in Wisconsin*. Madison: University of Wisconsin Press.

Fanlund, Paul. 2010. "Madison 360: Mayor Dave Ponders Response to Attacks on Madison." *Capital Times*, December 15. http://host.madison.com/ct/news/local/madison_360/article_936be31e-07c0-11e0-8418-001cc4c03286.html.

———. 2011. "Barrett Steps up, but for Another Shot at Walker?" *Capital Times*, May 18, 5.

Feather, Norman T. 1999. *Values, Achievement, and Justice: Studies in the Psychology of Deservingness*. New York: Kluwer.

Feather, Norman T., and Katherine Nairn. 2005. "Resentment, Envy, *Schadenfreude*, and Sympathy: Effects of Own and Other's Deserved or Undeserved Status." *Australian Journal of Psychology* 57:87–102.

Feather, Norman T., and Rebecca Sherman. 2002. "Envy, Resentment, *Schadenfreude*, and Sympathy: Reactions to Deserved and Undeserved Achievement and Subsequent Failure." *Personality and Social Psychology Bulletin* 28 (7): 953–61.

Feldman, Martha S. 1995. *Strategies for Interpreting Qualitative Data*. Thousand Oaks, CA: Sage.

Fenno, Richard. 1978. *Home Style: House Members in Their Districts*. Boston: Little Brown.

Fiorina, Morris P., Samuel J. Abrams, and Jeremy C. Pope. 2010. *Culture War? The Myth of a Polarized America*. 3rd ed. Boston: Longman.

Fishman, Mark. 1980. *Manufacturing the News*. Austin: University of Texas Press.

Flavin, Patrick. 2012. "Income Inequality and Policy Representation in the American States." *American Politics Research* 40 (1): 29–59.

Fowler, Booth. 2008. *Wisconsin Votes: An Electoral History*. Madison: University of Wisconsin Press.

Frank, Thomas. 2004. *What's the Matter with Kansas? How Conservatives Won the Heart of America*. New York: Metropolitan Books.

Frey, William H. 2010. "Census Data: Blacks and Hispanics Take Different Segregation Paths." http://www.brookings.edu/research/opinions/2010/12/16 -census-frey.

Gallardo, Roberto, and Bo Beaulieu. 2011. "Inequality Rising in Rural and Urban America." *Daily Yonder*, April 21. http://www.dailyyonder.com/about -daily-yonder.

Gangl, Amy. 2007. "Examining Citizens' Beliefs that Government Should Run Like Business." *Public Opinion Quarterly* 71 (4): 661–70.

Garza, Jesse. 2012. "Wife Hits Husband with SUV after Argument over Recalls." *Milwaukee Journal Sentinel*. May 8. http://www.jsonline.com/news/ wisconsin/wife-drives-into-chippewa-falls-man-after-vote-argument -ke5bdap-150697635.html.

Gaventa, John. 1980. *Power and Powerlessness: Quiescence and Rebellion in an Appalachian Valley*. Urbana: University of Illinois Press.

Geertz, Clifford. 1973. "Thick Description: Toward an Interpretive Theory of Culture." In *The Interpretation of Cultures: Selected Essays*, 3–30. New York: Basic Books.

Gelman, Andrew, with David Park, Boris Shor, Joseph Bafumi, and Jeronimo Cortina. 2008. *Red State, Blue State, Rich State, Poor State*. Princeton, NJ: Princeton University Press.

Gilbert. 2012a. "Dominance in Rural Areas Ensured Walker's Recall Win."

The Wisconsin Voter (blog), *Milwaukee Journal Sentinel*, June 16. http://www
.jsonline.com/blogs/news/159318735.html.

———. 2012b. "Swing Voters to Watch in Wisconsin: Those Who Approve of
Both Walker and Obama." *The Wisconsin Voter* (blog), *Milwaukee Journal
Sentinel*, October 6. http://www.jsonline.com/blogs/news/1729183711.html.

Gilens, Martin. 1999. *Why Americans Hate Welfare: Race, Media, and the Politics of Antipoverty Policy.* Chicago: University of Chicago Press.

———. 2005. "Inequality and Democratic Responsiveness." *Public Opinion
Quarterly* 69 (5): 778–96.

———. 2012. *Affluence and Influence: Economic Inequality and Political Power
in America.* New York: Russell Sage Foundation; Princeton, NJ: Princeton
University Press.

Gillett, Sharon E., William H. Lehr, and Carlos Osorio. 2004. "Local Government Broadband Initiatives." *Telecommunications Policy* 28 (7–8):
537–58.

Gimpel, James G., and Kimberly A. Karnes. 2006. "The Rural Side of the Rural-
Urban Gap." *PS: Political Science and Politics* 39 (3): 467–72.

Gimpel, James G., and Jason E. Schuknecht. 2003. *Patchwork Nation: Section-
alism and Political Change in American Politics.* Ann Arbor: University of
Michigan Press.

Glad, Paul W. 1990. *History of Wisconsin*, vol. 5: *War, a New Era, and Depression.* Madison: Wisconsin Historical Society Press.

Goren, Paul. 2005. "Party Identification and Core Political Values." *American
Journal of Political Science* 49 (4): 881–96.

Gough, Robert. 1997. *Farming the Cutover: A Social History of Northern Wisconsin, 1900–1940.* Lawrence: University Press of Kansas.

Green, Donald, Bradley Palmquist, and Eric Schickler. 2002. *Partisan Hearts
and Minds: Political Parties and the Social Identities of Voters.* New Haven,
CT: Yale University Press.

Grieve, P. G., and M. A. Hogg. 1999. "Subjective Uncertainty and Intergroup
Discrimination in the Minimal Group Situation." *Personality and Social Psychology Bulletin* 8:926–40.

Gunther, Albert C., and Kathleen Schmitt. 2006. "Mapping Boundaries of the
Hostile Media Effect." *Journal of Communication* 54 (1): 55–70.

Hacker, Jacob S., and Paul Pierson. 2010. *Winner-Take-All Politics: How Washington Made the Rich Richer—and Turned Its Back on the Middle Class.* New
York: Simon & Schuster.

Haidt, Jonathan, and Marc J. Hetherington. 2012. "Look How Far We've Come
Apart." *Campaign Stops* (blog), *New York Times*, September 17. http://
campaignstops.blogs.nytimes.com/2012/09/17/look-how-far-weve-come
-apart/.

Hall, Richard L. 1996. *Participation in Congress.* New Haven, CT: Yale University Press.

Hart, Roderick. 2001. *Campaign Talk: Why Elections Are Good for Us.* Princeton, NJ: Princeton University Press.

Hatemi, Peter K., and Rose McDermott. 2011. *Man Is by Nature a Political Animal: Evolution, Biology, and Politics.* Chicago: University of Chicago Press.

Hauser, Robert M., and John Robert Warren. 1997. "Socioeconomic Indexes for Occupations: A Review, Update, and Critique." *Sociological Methodology* 27 (1): 177–298.

Hayward, Clarissa Rile. 2000. *De-Facing Power.* Cambridge: Cambridge University Press.

Herbst, Susan. 1998. *Reading Public Opinion: How Political Actors View the Democratic Process.* Chicago: University of Chicago Press.

Herman, Edward S., and Noam Chomsky. 1988. *Manufacturing Consent: The Political Economy of the Mass Media.* New York: Pantheon.

Hetherington, Marc J. 2009. "Review Article: Putting Polarization in Perspective." *British Journal of Political Science* 39 (2): 413–48.

Hibbing, John R., and Kevin B. Smith. 2007. "The Biology of Political Behavior: An Introduction." *Annals of the American Academy of Political and Social Science* 614 (1): 6–14.

Hochschild, Jennifer L. 1981. *What's Fair: Americans' Beliefs about Distributive Justice.* Cambridge, MA: Harvard University Press.

Huber, Gregory A., and John S. Lapinski. 2006. "The 'Race Card' Revisited: Assessing Racial Priming in Policy Contexts." *American Journal of Political Science* 48 (2): 375–401.

———. 2008. "Testing the Implicit-Explicit Model of Racialized Political Communication." *Perspectives on Politics* 6 (1): 125–34.

Huddy, Leonie. 2003. "Group Identity and Political Cohesion." In *Oxford Handbook of Political Psychology,* ed. David O. Sears, Leonie Huddy, and Robert Jervis, 511–58. New York: Oxford University Press.

Huddy, Leonie, and Stanley Feldman. 2009. "On Assessing the Political Effects of Racial Prejudice." *Annual Review of Political Science* 12 (2009): 423–47.

Huhn, Claire. 2005. *High School Characteristics and Early Academic Performance at UW–Madison.* Madison: Academic Planning and Analysis, Office of the Provost, University of Wisconsin–Madison. https://apir.wisc.edu/admissions/Analysis_of_School_Characteristics.pdf.

Hurwitz, Jon, and Mark Peffley. 2005. "Playing the Race Card in the Post-Willie Horton Era." *Public Opinion Quarterly* 76 (2): 99–112.

Jackman, Mary R., and Robert W. Jackman, 1983. *Class Awareness in the United States.* Berkeley: University of California Press.

Jacobs, Lawrence, and Robert Y. Shapiro. 2000. *Politicians Don't Pander.* Chicago: University of Chicago Press.

Jacobson, Gary C. 2010. *A Divider, Not a Uniter: George W. Bush and the American People*. 2nd ed. London: Routledge.

Jarosz, Lucy, and Victoria Lawson. 2002. "'Sophisticated People vs. Rednecks': Economic Restructuring and Class Differences in America's West." *Antipode* 34 (1): 8–27.

Johnson, Kenneth M., John P. Pelissero, David B. Holian, and Michael T. Maly. 1995. "Local Government Fiscal Burden in Nonmetropolitan America." *Rural Sociology* 60 (3): 381–98.

Jones, Bruce. 2012. "Wisconsin Food Production and Agricultural Economy." Presentation to the Wisconsin Ideas Scholars Program, Wisconsin Rapids, Wisconsin, September 21.

Kahn, Kim Fridkin. 1996. *The Political Consequences of Being a Woman: How Stereotypes Influence the Conduct and Consequences of Political Campaigns*. New York: Columbia University Press.

Kandel, William, and John Cromartie. 2004. *New Patterns of Hispanic Settlement in Rural America*. Washington, DC: U.S. Department of Agriculture, Economic Research Service.

Kaufman, Dan. 2012. "How Did Wisconsin Become the Most Politically Divisive Place in America?" *New York Times Magazine,* May 24. http://www.nytimes.com/2012/05/27/magazine/how-did-wisconsin-become-the-most-politically-divisive-place-in-america.html.

Kelly, Nathan J., and Peter K. Enns. 2010. "Inequality and the Dynamics of Public Opinion: The Self-Reinforcing Link between Economic Inequality and Mass Preferences." *American Journal of Political Science 54* (4): 855–70.

Kenworthy, Lane, and Jonas Pontusson. 2005. "Rising Inequality and the Politics of Redistribution in Affluent Countries." *Perspectives on Politics* 3 (3): 449–71.

Key, V. O., Jr. 1949. *Southern Politics in State and Nation*. New York: A. A. Knopf.

———. 1961. *Public Opinion and American Democracy*. New York: John Wiley.

Kinder, Donald R., and Cindy D. Kam. 2009. *Us against Them: Ethnocentric Foundations of American Opinion*. Chicago: University of Chicago Press.

Kinder, Donald R., and Lynn M. Sanders. 1996. *Divided by Color: Racial Politics and Democratic Ideals*. Chicago: University of Chicago Press.

Knisely, Sandra M. 2013. "Division in Dairyland: Community Structure, Social Identity, and News Frames during the Wisconsin Gubernatorial Recall Election." Master's thesis, University of Wisconsin–Madison.

Knoke, David, and Constance Henry. 1977. "Political Structure of Rural America." *Annals of the American Academy of Political and Social Science* 429:51–62.

Korpi, Walter. 1983. *The Democratic Class Struggle*. London: Routledge and Keagan Paul.

Kuklinski, James H., and Buddy Peyton. 2007. "Belief Systems and Political Decision-Making." In *Oxford Handbook of Political Behavior, ed.* Russell J. Dalton and Hans-Dieter Klingemann, 45–64. Oxford: Oxford University Press.

Lamont, Michèle. 2000. *The Dignity of Working Men: Morality and the Boundaries of Race, Class, and Immigration.* New York: Russell Sage; Cambridge, MA: Harvard University Press.

Lane, Robert E. 2001. "Self-Reliance and Empathy: The Enemies of Poverty— and the Poor." *Political Psychology* 22 (3): 473–92.

Lareau, Annette. 2008. "Introduction: Taking Stock of Class." In *Social Class: How Does It Work? ed.* Annette Lareau and Dalton Conley, 3–24. New York: Russell Sage.

Lawson, Victoria, Lucy Jarosz, and Anne Bonds. 2010. "Articulations of Place, Poverty and Race: Dumping Grounds and Unseen Grounds in the Rural American Northwest." *Annals of the Association of American Geographers* 100 (3): 655–77.

Layman, Geoffrey C., Thomas M. Carsey, and Juliana Menasce Horowitz. 2006. "Party Polarization in American Politics: Characteristics, Causes, and Consequences." *Annual Review of Political Science* 9:83–110.

Lazarsfeld, Paul F., Bernard Berelson, and Hazel Gaudet. 1944. *The People's Choice: How the Voter Makes up His Mind in a Presidential Campaign. 2nd ed.* New York: Columbia University Press.

Leonhardt, David. 2012. "Old vs. Young." *New York Times,* June 22. http://www.nytimes.com/2012/06/24/opinion/sunday/the-generation-gap-is-back.html.

Lichter, Daniel T., and Kenneth M. Johnson. 2006. "The Changing Spatial Concentration of America's Rural Poor Population." National Poverty Center Working Paper Series, no. 06-33. National Poverty Center, University of Michigan, Ann Arbor.

Lobao, Linda, and David S. Kraybill. 2005. "The Emerging Roles of County Governments in Metropolitan and Nonmetropolitan Areas: Findings from a National Survey." *Economic Development Quarterly* 19 (3): 245–59.

Lueders, Bill. "Scott Walker's War." 2011. *Isthmus,* February 24. http://www.thedailypage.com/isthmus/article.php?article=32445.

Lukes, Steven. 1974. *Power: A Radical View.* London: Macmillan.

Lupia, Arthur. 2006. "How Elitism Undermines the Study of Voter Competence." *Critical Review: A Journal of Politics and Society* 18 (1–3): 217–32.

Lupu, Noam, and Jonas Pontusson. 2011. "The Structure of Inequality and the Politics of Redistribution." *American Political Science Review 105* (2): 316–36.

MacGillis, Alec. 2012. "Why Walker's Urban-Crime Scare Ad Might Work." *New Republic,* June 1. http://www.newrepublic.com/blog/plank/103842/why-walkers-urban-crime-scare-ad-might-work.

Macgregor, Lyn C. 2010. *Habits of the Heartland: Small-Town Life in Modern America.* Ithaca, NY: Cornell University Press.

Manna, Paul. 2000. "How Do I Know What I Say I Know? Thinking about *Slim's Table* and Qualitative Methods." *Endarch: Journal of Black Political Research* (Spring), 19–29.

Martin, Isaac William. 2008. *The Permanent Tax Revolt: How the Property Tax Transformed American Politics.* Stanford, CA: Stanford University Press.

McCann, Michael. 1996. "Causal versus Constitutive Explanations (or, On the Difficulty of Being so Positive . . .)." *Law and Social Inquiry* 21 (2): 457–82.

McCartin, Joseph. 2011. *Collision Course: Ronald Reagan, the Air Traffic Controllers, and the Strike That Changed America.* Oxford: Oxford University Press.

McCarty, Nolan M., Keith T. Poole, and Howard Rosenthal. 2008. *Polarized America: The Dance of Ideology and Unequal Riches.* Cambridge, MA: MIT Press.

McChesney, Robert W., and John Nichols. 2010. *The Death and Life of American Journalism: The Media Revolution That Will Begin the World Again.* New York: Nation Books.

McClosky, Herbert, and John Zaller. 1984. *The American Ethos: Public Attitudes toward Capitalism and Democracy.* Cambridge, MA: Harvard University Press.

McGirr, Lisa. 2002. *Suburban Warriors: The Origins of the New American Right.* Princeton, NJ: Princeton University Press.

Meckler, Laura, and Dante Chinni. 2014. "City vs. Country: How Where We Live Deepens the Nation's Political Divide." *Wall Street Journal,* March 21.

Medin, Douglas L., and John D. Cooley. 1998. "Concepts and Categorization." In *Perception and Cognition at Century's End,* ed. Julian Hochberg. San Diego, CA: Academic Press.

Mellow, Muriel. 2005. "The Work of Rural Professionals: Doing the *Gemeinschaft-Gesellschaft* Gavotte." *Rural Sociology* 70 (1): 50–69.

Mendelberg, Tali. 2001. *The Race Card: Campaign Strategy, Implicit Messages, and the Norm of Equality.* Princeton, NJ: Princeton University Press.

Metler, Suzanne. 2011. *The Submerged State: How Invisible Government Policies Undermine American Democracy.* Chicago: University of Chicago Press.

Milbourne, Paul. 2004. *Rural Poverty: Marginalisation and Exclusion in Britain and the United States.* London: Routledge.

Miles, Matthew B., and A. Michael Huberman. 1994. *Qualitative Data Analysis: An Expanded Sourcebook,* 2nd ed. Thousand Oaks, CA: Sage Publications, Inc.

Miller, Arthur H., Patricia Gurin, Gerald Gurin, and Oksana Malanchuk. 1981. "Group Consciousness and Political Participation." *American Journal of Political Science* 25:494–511.

Miller, Kathleen. 2008. "Nonmetro America: Conditions and Trends." Rural Policy Research Institute. Report presented to the Agriculture Chairs Summit, St. Louis, Missouri, January 18–20.

Mullin, B.-A., and M. A. Hogg. 1999. "Motivations for Group Membership: The Role of Subjective Importance and Uncertainty Reduction." *Basic and Applied Social Psychology* 21:91–102.

Nelson, Thomas E., and Donald R. Kinder. 1996. "Issue Frames and Group-Centrism in American Public Opinion." *Journal of Politics* 58:1055–78.

Nyhan, Brendan, and Jason Reifler. 2010. "When Corrections Fail: The Persistence of Political Misperceptions." *Political Behavior* 32:303–30.

Parker, Christopher, and Matt A. Barreto. 2013. *Change They Can't Believe In: The Tea Party and Reactionary Politics in America.* Princeton, NJ: Princeton University Press.

Patterson, Thomas E. 1993. *Out of Order.* New York: Knopf.

Peck, Jamie. 2011. "Neoliberal Suburbanism: Frontier Space." *Urban Geography* 32, no. 6 (2011): 884–919.

Petro, Sylvester. 1974–75. "Sovereignty and Compulsory Public-Sector Bargaining." *Wake Forest Law Review* 10:25–165.

Pfeffer, Fabian, Sheldon Danziger, and Robert F. Schoeni. 2013. "Wealth Disparities Before and After the Great Recession." Unpublished manuscript, University of Michigan.

Piketty, Thomas, and Emmanuel Saez. 2003. "Income Inequality in the United States, 1913–1998." *Quarterly Journal of Economics* 118 (1): 1–41.

Pinkovitz, Bill. 2011. "Federal Procurement: A $9.5 Billion Business in Wisconsin." *UW Extension Econ Quiz. http://fyi.uwex.edu/econquiz/2011/07/29/ federal-procurement-a-9-5-billion-business-in-wisconsin/.*

Popkin, Samuel. 2007. "Public Opinion and Collective Obligations." *Society* 44:37–44.

Pred, Allan. 1984. "Place as Historically Contingent Process: Structuration and the Time-Geography of Becoming Places." *Annals of the Association of American Geographers* 74 (2): 279–97.

Provasnik, Stephen, Angelina Kewal Ramani, Mary McLaughlin Coleman, Lauren Gilbertson, Will Herring, and Qingshu Xie. 2007. *Status of Education in Rural America.* NCES 2007-040. Washington, DC: U.S. Department of Education, National Center for Education Statistics, Institute of Education Sciences.

Pucher, J., and J. L. Renne. 2004. "Urban-Rural Differences in Mobility and Mode Choice: Evidence from the 2001 National Household Transportation Survey." New Brunswick, NJ: Bloustein School of Planning and Public Policy, Rutgers University.

Purnell, Thomas, Joseph Salmons, Dilara Tepeli, and Jennifer Mercer. 2005.

"Structured Heterogeneity and Change in Laryngeal Phonetics: Upper Midwestern Final Obstruents." *Journal of English Linguistics* 33 (4): 307–38.

Putnam, Robert D. 2000. *Bowling Alone: The Collapse and Revival of American Community.* New York: Simon and Schuster.

Quadagno, Jill, and Debra Street. 2005. "Ideology and Public Policy: Antistatism in American Welfare State Transformation." *Journal of Policy History* 17 (1): 52–71.

Reeder, Richard J. 1985. *Rural Governments: Raising Revenues and Feeling the Pressure.* Washington, DC: U.S. Department of Agriculture, Economic Research Service.

Reeder, Richard J., and Anicca A. Jansen. 1995. "Rural Government—Poor Counties 1962–1987." Washington DC: US Department of Agriculture.

Rigby, E., and G. C. Wright. 2011. "Whose Statehouse Democracy: Policy Responsiveness to Poor versus Rich Constituents in Poor versus Rich States." In *Who Gets Represented?* ed. P. Enns and C. Wlezien, 223–46. New York: Russell Sage.

Saez, Emmanuel. 2013. "Income Inequality: Evidence and Policy Implications" Arrow Lecture, Stanford University. http://elsa.berkeley.edu/~saez/lecture_saez_arrow.pdf.

Schatz, Edward, ed. 2009. *Political Ethnography: What Immersion Contributes to the Study of Power.* Chicago: University of Chicago Press.

Schneider, Anne, and Helen Ingram. 1993. "Social Construction of Target Populations: Implications for Politics and Policy." *American Political Science Review* 87 (2): 334–47.

Schudson, Michael. 2002. "The News Media as Political Institutions." *Annual Review of Political Science* 5:249–69.

——— 2003 *The Sociology of News.* New York: W. W. Norton.

Schwartz-Shea, Peregrine, and Dvora Yanow. 2012. *Interpretive Research Design: Concepts and Processes.* New York: Routledge.

Sears, David O., and Jack Citrin. 1982. *Tax Revolt: Something for Nothing in California.* Cambridge, MA: Harvard University Press.

Sears, David O., and P. J. Henry. 2005. "Over Thirty Years Later: A Contemporary Look at Symbolic Racism." *Advances in Experimental Social Psychology* 37:95–150.

Sears, David O., and Donald R. Kinder. 1985. "Whites' Opposition to Busing: On Conceptualizing and Operationalizing Group Conflict." *Journal of Personality and Social Psychology* 48:1141–47.

Seely, Ron. 2011. "Mining in Wisconsin: Promise or Peril?" *Wisconsin State Journal,* October 9.

Shor, Boris. 2014. "How U.S. State Legislators are Polarized and Getting More Polarized (in 2 Graphs)." *Monkey Cage* (blog), *Washington Post,* January 14. www.washingtonpost.com/blogs/monkey-cage,

Siewert, Shereen. 2014. "Wis. Tribe Languishes as it Awaits Casino Decision." *USA Today,* August 23. *http://www.usatoday.com/story/news/nation/
2014/08/23/tribe-languishes-as-it-awaits-casino-decision/14511223/.*

Sigal, Leon V. 1973. *Reporters and Officials.* Lexington, MA: D. C. Health.

Skocpol, Theda. 1997. *Boomerang: Health Care Reform and the Turn against
Government.* New York: W. W. Norton.

Skocpol, Theda, and Vanessa Williamson. 2012. *The Tea Party and the Remaking of Republican Conservatism.* Oxford: Oxford University Press.

Smith, Tom. 1987. "That Which We Call Welfare by Any Other Name Would
Smell Sweeter: An Analysis of the Impact of Question Wording on Response
Patterns." *Public Opinion Quarterly* 51:75–83.

Soroka, Stuart N., and Christopher Wlezien. 2008. "On the Limits of Inequality
in Representation." *PS: Political Science and Politics 41* (2): 319–27.

Soss, Joe. 2006. "Talking Our Way to Meaningful Explanations: A Practice-
Centered Approach to In-Depth Interviews for Interpretive Research." In
Interpretation and Method, ed. Dvora Yanow and Peregrine Schwartz-Shea,
127–49. New York: M. E. Sharpe.

Soss, Joe, Richard C. Fording, and Sanford F. Schram. 2011. *Disciplining the
Poor: Neoliberal Paternalism and the Persistent Power of Race.* Chicago:
University of Chicago Press.

Soss, Joe, and Sanford F. Schram. 2007. "A Public Transformed? Welfare Reform as Policy Feedback." *American Political Science Review* 101 (1): 111–27.

Stonecash, Jeff. 2014. "The Two Key Factors Behind Our Polarized Politics." *Monkey Cage* (blog), *Washington Post,* January 24. http://www
.washingtonpost.com/blogs/monkey-cage/wp/2014/01/24/the-two-key-factors
-behind-our-polarized-politics/.

Tajfel, Henri. 1981. *Human Groups and Social Categories: Studies in Social Psychology.* Cambridge: Cambridge University Press.

Tajfel, Henri, M. G. Billig, R. P. Bundy, and Claude Flament, 1971. "Social Categorization and Intergroup Behavior." *European Journal of Social Psychology* 1:149–78.

Tajfel, Henri, and John Turner. 1986. "The Social Identity Theory of Intergroup
Behavior." In *Psychology of Intergroup Relations,* ed. Stephen Worchel and
William G. Austin, 7–24. Chicago: Nelson-Hall.

Taylor, Charles. 1971. "Interpretation and the Sciences of Man." *Review of Meta-
physics* 25 (1): 3–51.

Tenenbaum, David. 2014. "Town Meets Gown to Explore Wisconsin's Trempealeau Mounds." *University of Wisconsin–Madison News,* July 23. http://www
.news.wisc.edu/23014.

Tesler, Michael. 2012. "The Spillover of Racialization into Health Care: How
President Obama Polarized Public Opinion by Racial Attitudes and Race."
American Journal of Political Science 56 (3): 690–704.

Tuchman, Gaye. 1978. *Making News*. New York: Free Press.

Turner, John C., Michael A. Hogg, Penelope J. Oakes, S. D. Reicher, and Margaret S. Wetherell. 1987. *Rediscovering the Social Group: A Self-Categorization Theory*. Oxford: Blackwell.

Turner, John C., Penelope J. Oakes, S. Alexander Haslam, and Craig McGarty. 1994. "Self and Collective: Cognition and Social Context." *Personality and Social Psychology Bulletin* 20:454–63.

Ura, Joseph Daniel, and Christopher R. Ellis. 2008. "Income, Preferences, and the Dynamics of Policy Responsiveness." *PS: Political Science and Politics* 41 (4): 785–94.

USDA Economic Research Service. 2015. "Geography of Poverty." Last updated, April 9. http://www.ers.usda.gov/topics/rural-economy-population/rural-poverty-well-being/geography-of-poverty.aspx#.UbYa1IWGFJh.

Valentino, Nicholas. 1999. "Crime News and the Priming of Racial Attitudes during Evaluations of the President." *Public Opinion Quarterly* 63 (3): 293–320.

Valentino, Nicholas, Vincent Hutchings, and Ismail White. 2002. "Cues That Matter: How Political Ads Prime Racial Attitudes during Campaigns." *American Political Science Review* 96 (1): 75–90.

Varenne, Hervé. 1977. *Americans Together: Structured Diversity in a Midwestern Town*. New York: Teachers College Press.

Vargas-Cooper, Natasha. 2011. "We Work Hard, but Who's Complaining?" *New York Times,* April 2.

Varghese, Jeji, Naomi T. Krogman, Thomas M. Beckley, and Solange Nadeau. 2006. "Critical Analysis of the Relationship between Local Ownership and Community Resiliency." *Rural Sociology* 71 (3): 505–27.

Veenstra, Gerry. 2007. "Social Space, Social Class and Bourdieu: Health Inequalities in British Columbia, Canada." *Health and Place* 13 (1): 14–31.

Vincent, Stephen A. 1999. *Southern Seed, Northern Soil: African-American Farm Communities in the Midwest, 1765–1900*. Bloomington: Indiana University Press.

Weaver, David Hugh, and G. Cleveland Wilhoit. 1996. *The American Journalist in the 1990s: U.S. News People at the End of an Era*. Mahwah, NJ: Lawrence Erlbaum.

Weber, Bruce, Leif Jensen, Kathleen Miller, Jane Mosley, and Monica Fisher. 2005. "A Critical Review of Rural Poverty Literature: Is There Truly a Rural Effect?" *International Regional Science Review* 28 (4): 381–414.

Wendt, Alexander. 1998. "On Constitution and Causation in International Relations." *Review of International Studies* 24 (5): 101–18.

White, Ismail K. 2007. "When Race Matters and When It Doesn't: Racial Group Differences in Response to Racial Cues." *American Political Science Review* 101 (2): 339–54.

Williams, Allison, Peter Kitchen, Lily Demiglio, John Eyles, Bruce Newbold, and David Streiner. 2010. "Sense of Place in Hamilton, Ontario: Empirical Results of a Neighborhood-Based Survey." *Urban Geography* 31 (7): 905–31.

Williamson, Vanessa, Theda Skocpol, and John Coggin. 2011. "The Tea Party and the Remaking of Republican Conservatism." *Perspectives on Politics* 9:25–43.

Winter, Nicholas. 2006. "Beyond Welfare: Framing and the Racialization of White Opinion on Social Security." *American Journal of Political Science* 50 (2): 400–20.

———. 2008. *Dangerous Frames: How Ideas about Race and Gender Shape Public Opinion*. Chicago: University of Chicago Press.

Winters, Jeffrey A., and Benjamin I. Page. 2009. "Oligarchy in the United States?" *Perspectives on Politics* 7 (4): 731–51.

Wong, Cara. 2010. *Boundaries of Obligation: Geographic, National, and Racial Communities*. Cambridge: Cambridge University Press.

Wong, Cara, Jake Bowers, Tarah William, and Katherine Drake Simmons. 2012. "Bringing the Person Back In: Boundaries, Perceptions, and the Measurement of Racial Context." *Journal of Politics* 74 (4): 1153–70.

Wright, Erik Olin. 1997. *Class Counts: Comparative Studies in Class Analysis*. Cambridge: Cambridge University Press.

Wuthnow, Robert. 2013. *Small-Town America: Finding Community, Shaping the Future*. Princeton, NJ: Princeton University Press.

Zaller, John R. 1992. *The Nature and Origins of Mass Opinion*. New York: Cambridge University Press.

Zernike, Kate. 2011. "Wisconsin's Legacy of Labor Battles." *New York Times*, March 5. http://www.nytimes.com/2011/03/06/weekinreview/06midwest.html.

Zimmerman, Julie N., Sunny (Seonok) Ham, and Sarah Michelle Frank. 2008. "Does It or Doesn't It? Geographic Differences and the Cost of Living." *Rural Sociology* 73 (3): 463–86.

Index

The letter *f* following a page number denotes a figure.

Chicago Studies in American Politics

A SERIES EDITED BY BENJAMIN I. PAGE, SUSAN HERBST,
LAWRENCE R. JACOBS, AND ADAM J. BERINSKY

different to be able to perform on an instrument with this same degree of subtlety.[19]

Perhaps after many years of basic experimentation in all areas of music, adequate performance tests can be constructed. Someday, sophisticated instrumentation may make it possible for a student to perform before a machine that will quickly assess many variables of performances simultaneously (for example, intonation, timbre, rhythmic stability, subtle nuances) and provide a print-out sheet with exact data expressed in easily-understood terminology. This is certainly within the grasp of our highly specialized technology, but it necessitates an exact classification system followed by research. Statements such as "Blow through the notes," "Support the upper notes," and "Taper the end of the phrase" will have to be modified into more precise terminology that can be experimentally tested. Of course, some musicians will object to such a mechanical device, but the question still remains: What are the alternatives? Such an instrument could serve as a teaching aid as well as a prognostic tool. Over the years, "norms" could be established for different levels of development, and perhaps then the profession could incorporate many of the benefits initially predicted for tests concerning music abilities.

MUSIC IN THERAPY

Stereotypes are extremely common and perhaps no one knows this better than the music therapist. It is difficult, if not impossible, to explain to the layman "What is a music therapist?" and "What is his work?" Most people have several misconceptions of music therapy, and often it is as difficult to explain music therapy as it is to convince a layman that all psychotherapists do not have beards and practice some deep dark ritual over a patient lying on a couch. Surprisingly some music therapists evidence stereotyped thinking concerning the value of research and portray the attitude that while experimental research is respectable, it often has little "practical" value.

The music therapist should be eager to seek scientifically-based procedures and should constantly strive toward greater objectivity. The very nature of the music therapist's work demands a particular objectivity which is essential. If the therapist is not objective in interpersonal relationships, he cannot survive in the therapeutic situation and will

---

19 Frederick W. Vorce, Jr., "The Effect of Simultaneous Stimulus on Vocal Pitch Accuracy" (Doctoral dissertation, Florida State University, 1964).

cease to function.[20] However, concerning research as a mode of action, evaluation, and prognostication, the music therapist needs much more knowledge. There are many questions concerning the scientific practice of music therapy that should be investigated: Are accurate records kept of music activities prescribed for patients? Precisely how much time does a patient spend in music activities? How is it decided that a patient should engage in a music activity? Which is better, group participation or individual participation? How is improvement evaluated for each patient? What types of music activities should be available? What are the relative benefits of differing music activities? On what basis does the therapist change a patient's therapy program? Is fine musical performance better than activity therapy? and so on.[21]

Many of these questions could presently be answered by the music therapist. However, answers such as, "Well, it depends," or "I believe the patient should have a chance to express himself," or "We try to help those individuals who show they can benefit most from the music experiences" do not constitute scientific justification. If answers are to contribute to the establishment of rapport, the promotion of socialization, and so on, then these terms should be defined in regard to specific overt behaviors and positive amelioration for each patient. For example, if music is indeed "a socializing agent," then operational definition seems prerequisite to subsequent testing. To state that patients singing side by side are "socializing" is somewhat misleading; to equate this "socializing" with a public community choir and a professional orchestra might be irrelevant; and to assume that this "socializing" is monolithically good appears extremely questionable. To place a patient in the hospital chorus for specific reasons pertaining to his particular malady appears wise. If the reason the patient was institutionalized was in part that he could not sing songs side by side with other people, then the speculative positive benefits from this experience seem advisable. Perhaps a patient cannot even approximate any societal interaction except through group music activities. In this case, benefits that might accrue, especially pertaining to stimulus generalization, are obvious.[22] To consider just the

---

[20] Ardo M. Wrobel, "Roles of the Music Therapist in the Open Institution," in *Music Therapy*, ed. Erwin H. Schneider, National Association for Music Therapy (Lawrence, Kansas: The Allen Press, 1963), p. 48.

[21] Some of these questions were raised by Donald E. Michel in a descriptive study reported in NAMT *Music Therapy* (Lawrence, Kansas: The Allen Press, 1959), pp. 137–52.

[22] Sally H. Baird, "Some Clinical Uses of Music with Geriatric Patients: A Case Report," in *Music Therapy*, ed. E. Thayer Gaston (New York: The Macmillan Company, 1968), pp. 289–90.

wonderful experience of being in a musical group for all the socializing benefits seems naive.

The field of music therapy has moved a long way toward greater scientific respectability since its inception. Many problems will continue to present challenges to the research therapist. It would appear advisable for the aspiring therapist to gain as much research skill as possible.

MUSIC IN INDUSTRY

There are two areas for research that should be mentioned in a discussion of music in industry: (1) the use of music in industry including the various means by which production or some aspect of a particular skill are involved; and (2) music as an industry. The latter includes the many elements by which music activities can be identified as commercial activities.

Music in industry has been used in connection with a multitude of commodities, skills, and attitude enhancements.[23] Muzak[24] has enjoyed a growing clientele for a number of years, and many diverse institutions, professional offices, and commercial retail stores evidence the use of music. Research needs to be done in this entire area by competent investigators. It is difficult to believe that music would be as prevalent in commercial use as it is without the careful industrial research that definitely demonstrates "business is better," "production is greater," or "workers' attitudes are improved" because of music. However, basic projects need to be carried out that delve deeper into the problems and future possibilities concerning music in industry. Many questions should be asked regarding just what specific effects music has upon shoppers, factory workers, and production rates. What relationships exist between these aspects and music education, music therapy, and music performance? Does the constant bombardment of sound to which most people are continuously subjected increase musical discrimination? Does it help negate cortical responsiveness? Does it contribute to decreased activity, increased activity? Specific questions in this area might lead to research that would not only benefit industry but perhaps have far greater implications for education, therapy, and music performance.

Music as an industry raises questions regarding the "business of music." Academic researchers are sometimes noted for concern about

---

23 Lundin, *An Objective Psychology of Music,* pp. 291–304.
24 *Ibid.,* pp. 294–95.

traditional "Master Works," [25] but the actual or partial *control* of most of the nation's music activities may be substantially apart from anything that is currently being investigated. Records, music instrument sales, participant activities, radio, TV, movie scores, and all other commercial aspects of music need more intensive investigation, and results made available.

Unfortunately, "popular music" or "commercial pursuits" often appear to lie outside the proper province of serious academic researchers. While studies are conducted to determine the need for musicians to teach and engage in music as a financially remunerative *profession*,[26] there appears to be a dearth of investigation concerning "music and money." It may be a rather tainted subject, but it may provide key answers directly relating to other areas of more immediate concern to the profession. It appears unwise not to recognize the many financial aspects of music as a business and the popular music that is being employed by the vast majority of people in the nation.

CONCLUSION

There are many psychological bases for music experimentation. While music has been called "a universal language" as well as a means of "non-verbal communication," the specific nature of this communication needs to be assessed. Music effects people differently, and therefore separate areas of mood affects, musical taste, and musical abilities need extensive experimental investigation toward greater specificity. Research in these areas would be of special interest to music therapists, who need much more specific information concerning the use of music for physiological and psychological amelioration. Research in this area might use current "behavioral methods" to test the effectiveness of music in shaping appropriate adaptive behaviors. The use of music in industry, and allied "professional" considerations, might also be investigated. Implications from these areas should be of concern to music educators and to applied musicians.

Issues should not be confounded for the therapist, performer, or educator. The "either-or" of many diverse music aspects should be initially understood before the investigator proceeds with an experi-

---

[25] Paul R. Farnsworth, "Elite Attitudes in Music as Measured by the Cattell Space Method," *Journal of Research in Music Education*, X, No. 1 (Spring, 1962), 65.

[26] Fred K. Grumley, "A Study of the Supply and Demand for College Level Music Teachers with Doctoral Degrees, 1964–1970" (Doctoral dissertation, Florida State University, 1964).

ment; the researcher should not combine several areas and variables that need to be assessed separately. While implications can be assessed for interpretation in all areas of music, the researcher must isolate specific variables to be tested in reference to any primary area. Language should not be confused with mood; musical abilities should be separated from taste; status quo studies should be separated from the process of music education; and aspects of the affective domain need to be tested by assessing specific music effects.

STUDY QUESTIONS

1. What is the nature of "music communication"?
2. What are factors that contribute to a person's musical taste? How may taste be studied objectively?
3. What are some of the differences in behavior elicited by music and how might they be of interest to the music therapist?
4. What is meant by the phrase "music as a business"?
5. List and discuss several topics concerning the psychological bases of music that seem appropriate for experimental research.

CHAPTER FIVE

pedagogical bases for music experimentation

One of the most consequential aspects of experimental research concerns music education. Although most research in music comes from the theses and dissertations written in partial fulfillment for degrees in graduate schools, a most unfortunate aspect of this research is that it usually stops upon completion of the degree. Just when the student has attained the sophistication to conduct independent research (*after* the completion of a dissertation), he usually stops this particular pursuit, never to continue. Even at the professorial levels there are many who just vaguely remember the design and statistical concepts that they so ardently pursued as graduate students. While some continue to supervise research throughout their professional lives, it would appear that a greater number only remember research as the last hurdle toward the completion of the graduate degree.

Experimental research does not begin to enjoy the respect and popularity it should have in the teaching profession, particularly in relationship to basic research in teaching and learning. As one reviews existing experimental literature, one is often left with the thought that many experimental studies were designed to prove a particular point of view or teaching technique. It has been said that "all educational experiments are doomed to success." Seldom can much real knowledge arise from an investigation determined to prove that which one already "knows." There is a lack of investigation in the most basic issues relating to the teaching-learning situation and the most elementary aspects of music. It is probable that significant progress in these areas will be made in the future.

ATTRIBUTES OF MUSIC

Since many of the most fundamental aspects of music seem to be the most elusive, this chapter deals with the most obvious considerations of music for the teacher, and presents them with foremost simplicity. This is not intended to represent the totality of issues or problems concerning music education.

The first question concerning the music teacher would seem to be, What is music? The next question would concern the attributes of music, that is, What can one do with music? The third question, Can these attributes of music be learned? The fourth, Can they be taught? And lastly, How does one go about teaching them?

Music is organized sound and silence in time. Music can be (1) composed, (2) performed, (3) listened to, (4) verbalized, (5) conceptualized, and (6) used for extra-musical purposes.

COMPOSITION

Music is composed. The process of composition is generally thought of as synonymous with "creativity," although the general category of composition may also include arranging and orchestration. Is creativity simply a reorganization of past experiences, or is it mystical or supernatural, unexplainable in the empirical world? That Mozart wrote occidental music instead or oriental music would seem to support the first point regarding reorganization of past experiences. That Mozart wrote the quality of music he did at such a tender age seems extremely difficult to explain at all.[1]

Questions for teachers concerned with composition and creativity would seem to be, Can creativity be learned and can it be taught? If it can be *taught* but not learned, the pursuit seems irrelevant. If it can be *learned* but not taught, then perhaps the teacher should be concerned

---

[1] W. J. Turner, *Mozart: The Man and His Work* (New York: Doubleday Company, Inc., 1956).

with the *situation* where this learning can take place. Other questions arise at this point. Can the student create from nothing? If not, what implements and information does he need? If instruction in the use of these tools is given, does progressive instruction inhibit future creativity? These are questions that need to be answered not only by thoughtful teachers concerned with music composition, but also by those concerned with other creative music activities.

Possible answers might lie in the precise point at which instruction in manipulation of specific tools of the art should end and in whether evaluation of a creative work should come from the teacher and/or the student. Experimentation with very young children would seem invaluable in answering some of these questions.[2]

PERFORMANCE

The area of performance appears to be the major concern for many within the teaching profession. Most of what constiutes music education is the teaching and learning of performance skills. The necessary prerequisite for performance is listening, which will be discussed later. *Music performance is an active endeavor, which for the most part consists of perfecting neuro-muscular responses in relationship to judgmental aural discriminations.*

One significant problem encountered in discussing music performance skills is the chasm that has developed regarding neuro-muscular responses and other similar activities. Tightrope artists, football artists, juggling artists, and singing artists have a great deal in common: they develop neuro-muscular skills to an extremely high level. Learning to type and learning to play the piano are somewhat similar pursuits. The analogy is quite obvious in the initial states of developing skill on the two "instruments" and can be carried quite far. Of course, there are differences and these differences are extremely important. Nevertheless, the development of patterns of responses is quite similar for many activities. Many musicians abhor these comparisons. It is an insult to refer to a physician as "a butcher," regardless of how skillfully the physician uses a knife. The distinction, however, concerns societal status, consequences of the act, and many other related issues, not necessarily how adroitly one performs a neuro-muscular skill. For example, it is evident that the human organism must maintain a certain bodily temperature to function

---

2 *See* Gene Simons, "Comparisons of Incipient Music Responses Among Very Young Twins and Singletons," *Journal of Research in Music Education*, XII, No. 3 (Fall, 1964), 212–26.

at peak neuro-muscular effectiveness.[3] Athletes have known this for hundreds of years. They usually "warm up" before engaging in demanding physical pursuits. This warm-up consists of some simple activity to increase bodily functions and generate heat in preparation for performance. The common charley horse is partially caused by the contraction of a cold muscle, and usually a little skin-to-skin rubbing, which generates heat, will relieve the contraction. The entire idea of "warming up" is placed in perspective by most athletes. Contrast this concept with that evident in some music study. The initial concept of physiological preparation is almost completely lost in hundreds of lip slurs, long tones, vocalises, articles, and testimonials, which may have little if any relationship to "warming up." Thus, neuro-muscular preparation is confused with making music. The major point here is not the example. *Music is an aesthetic art, and because it is capable of eliciting intense emotive responsiveness, many teachers confuse the art object* (that is, the finished performance) *with the pedagogical process.* When discrimination between the process and the object is lacking, cultism flourishes.

Performance also necessitates imitation for the development of skills. Most imitative behaviors can be studied scientifically. Experiments can be designed that assess visual, neuro-muscular, and aural elements of performance as well as direct and vicarious modeling effects.[4] For example, conducting necessitates all of the aforementioned imitative behaviors. Again it should be stated that the scientific study of music performance demands analysis and experimental verification in order to know which specific behaviors should be shaped and the best methods by which this can be accomplished. Music as an art has nothing to lose from the application of scientific method. Objectification should not be confused with insensitivity.

LISTENING

Listening to music seems prerequisite to all other musical pursuits. *Discrimination* is the basis for listening. The first level of discriminatory perception is whether music is being heard or not being heard. The point is not so obvious when one considers the many situations where it is difficult to ascertain whether music is really "on" or "off." Background

---

3 M. Gladys Scott, *Analysis of Human Motion* (New York: Appleton-Century-Crofts, 1963), p. 180.
4 For information on modeling, *see* Albert Bandura, "Behavioral Modification Through Modeling Procedures," *Research in Behavior Modification*, eds. Leonard Krasner and Leonard P. Ullmann (New York: Holt, Rinehart & Winston, Inc., 1966).

music exists in our culture in large proportions, and most people are conditioned to being "bathed in sound." Listening to music, as far as the educator is concerned, should transcend this "on-off" level and include additional discriminations. An old cliché states that "all of life is like a bath, once one gets used to it, it's not so hot." Perhaps this is especially applicable to music. There seem to be many people who "enjoy" listening to music, but their attention to the music wanes appreciably after the initial stimulus, and they prefer to daydream and "drift with a mood." Hence, there appears to be little concentration on the music. Mood affects are often extremely desirable and especially vital to the music therapist. Mood affects are also very important in music education, but these experiences should not be confused with developing listening skills.

Partial answers to questions concerned with enhancing the listening experience might lie in investigations that attempt to test the effects of different types of successive programs aimed at teaching effective discrimination. One such program might experiment with two pitches contrasting the respective differences of the two sounds. As successive pitches are presented, the elementary concept of introducing form might be investigated. For example, one might start with one pitch and from one pitch go to two, to three, to a group, to a phrase, to a melody, to an embellishment of the same melody (variation form), then to a different melody (binary form), and back to the original melody (ternary form). The melody could be presented to "chase itself" (canon) and to chase itself with the same melody at a different interval (fugue). The simple song forms could be extended to encompass larger forms (sonata, rondo, etc.). This process could provide many experiments concerning the development of discrimination skills.

Another approach could experimentally test effective discrimination programs involving the differentiation of the *composite* sounds of an ensemble. The student could be given *something specific to listen for,* (high-low, loud-soft, fast-slow, short-long) and progress to greater discriminations (for example, tutti-concertino, strings-winds, strings-brass, trumpets-trombones, trumpets-horns, trumpets-trumpets) with the experimenter testing effective discrimination presentations. This approach might gradually encompass subtleties of orchestration with experimental verification. Another program might concentrate on the awareness of specific motifs, both rhythmic and harmonic, testing the subtle discriminations in harmony and style (theoretical analysis).

Listening is one of the most significant aspects of music; therefore, it is important enough to investigate thoroughly. Myriad experiments are awaiting the skillful investigator. The above processes in the programs being tested are conjectural. All variables concerning aural discrimination need to be tested and retested. New approaches await the verification of controlled research. The novice researcher should not be "looking for a topic," he should be delimiting from his vast musical experiences those specific topics that are vital and exciting for experimental research.

VERBALIZATION

Verbalization is of two kinds, oral and written. *Oral* aspects of music have to do with talking about music, and talking represents a very large part of the total time devoted to the study of music. Man's greatest differentiation from other species is this ability of communication—it warrants precise investigation. Most music instruction falls into this category. It would seem that since most teaching involves talking, the various ways teachers talk about music should make a great difference in teaching effectiveness.[5] Many experiments should be conducted that only test the effect of verbal instruction on music performance. To a large degree, talking is the major activity of the music teacher.

Written aspects of music verbalization concern history and terminology (notation, dynamic markings, etc.) Historical aspects of music might seem outside the province of experimental research, but this is not the case. Many experiments can be conducted concerning historical implications for music education. Many of the old concepts of the relatedness of historical perspectives, music performance, composition, and "appreciation" need to be examined. Does the assimilation of historical knowledge really improve performance? How much historical information should accompany basic appreciation courses, elementary school music series, and applied methodology? These are answerable questions once the goals of study are defined and operational definitions are established. (See the section on Historical Research in Chapter Two.)

Written aspects of music include notation as well as all written symbols used for music. These symbols are of extreme importance in the study of music and should be investigated. The thoughtful investigator might pick up a favorite score and ask himself, "If I were forced to eliminate written symbols from this page, what would constitute the finished hierarchy? Should the title go first or perhaps the composer's name? Are the measure lines important, the metronomic markings, the meter signature, the dynamic markings? Where would one stop? Where would one stop and still have something that could be performed? What on the page is helpful? What is necessary?" These questions should pro-

---

[5] *See* Frank A. Edmonson III, "The Effect of Interval Direction on Pitch Acuity in Solo Vocal Performance" (Doctoral dissertation, Florida State University, 1967).

vide many ideas for experimentation. The effects of specific rhythmic notations on performance might provide a lifetime of research; the way rhythms *should* be notated could perhaps fill another.[6]

CONCEPTUALIZING

To *think* about music requires information and is defined as the process one uses to analyze, criticize, and choose alternatives. Music students can be taught to think about music, and obviously all other aspects of music learning are concomitant with these thought processes. Thinking does seem quite difficult. It is much easier to "believe" than to think. Believing is not only easier, it often provides a good way to absolve individual responsibility and, therefore, blame someone else when things go wrong. ("That teacher wrecked my voice." "I'd play horn better now if it were not for my previous teacher." "That is what the tempo mark said! How was I supposed to know he wanted a decrescendo?") Clear thinking and individual responsibility are imperative for the researcher since the research product must stand on its own merit.

The term *conceptualization* is also used to refer to that aspect of intellectualization that concerns aesthetic appreciation. This is an area which needs much careful objective inquiry. Webster lists the Greek *"aisthētikos*—sense perception—to perceive," [7] in definition of the word aesthetic. This is understandable. Webster continues with "1 a: relating to or dealing with aesthetics or the beautiful; b: artistic. 2: appreciative of, responsive to, or zealous about the beautiful." [8] This too, is understandable, but the "aesthetic experience," which some say represents a somewhat mystical entity, continues to be elusive. Perhaps this "mystical aesthetic experience" represents *the composite emotional and intellectual responsiveness to music which is modified and reinforced through time and always defined as good.* It should be emphasized that the experimental researcher must deal with overt behavioral responses. If aspects of aesthetic appreciation are to be investigated, terminology must be specific and responses demonstrable and measurable.

---

[6] *See* Bernard Linger, "An Experimental Study of Durational Notation" (Doctoral dissertation, Florida State University, 1966).

[7] *Webster's Seventh New Collegiate Dictionary* (Springfield, Mass.: G. & C. Merriam Company, Publishers, 1963), p. 15.

[8] *Ibid.*, p. 15.

EXTRA-MUSICAL ASPECTS OF MUSIC

Extra-musical considerations are defined as all aspects of music encompassing areas outside the art for its own sake. These include music therapy, music in industry, music for dancing, and music used for recreation as well as other less specific areas such as music for socialization, cooperation, citizenship, understanding, and the many other positive qualities often attributed to the study of music.[9] How wonderful the world might be if music were capable of so much.

It would appear that transfer of learning is extremely unlikely, unless the teacher specifically teaches for transfer effects.[10] Yet many music teachers continue to justify music activities by alluding to many types of extra-musical benefits that transfer from the music program (for example, cooperation, socialization, moral enhancements). Experimentation would corroborate or reject some of this speculation. While there appears to be some justification for an indirect route to a particular goal, it would seem that if one wishes to learn music, one should study music, not mathematics, dancing, or citizenship. Conversely, if one wishes to study mathematics, dancing, or world understanding, the study of music may prove to be a poor substitute.

While many auxiliary benefits might accrue from music activities, these benefits need to be demonstrated. Even if verified, extra-musical elements may not constitute the raison d'être for music education. This is a question for philosophical inquiry. It would be wiser for the researcher to direct his time toward investigating instruction through carefully-controlled experimentation than to defend the status quo with claims about extra-musical attributes that may inhibit increased acceptability and that, perhaps, do not exist.

CONCLUSION

There appears to be a dearth of expertise in and acceptance of experimental research, perhaps because many professional educators fail to continue formal research after completion of a degree. Investigation needs to be continued in all aspects of the learning and teaching of music.

---

9 For an evaluation of extra-musical justifications, *see* Charles Leonhard and Robert N. House, *Foundations and Principles of Music* (New York: McGraw-Hill Book Company, 1959), pp. 96–102.

10 See B. F. Skinner's *Cumulative Record,* rev. ed. (New York: Appleton-Century-Crofts), 1961.

It is unfortunate when teaching and research represent an "either-or."

Music is defined as organized sound and silence in time, and six attributes are evident. Music can be: (1) composed, (2) performed, (3) listened to, (4) verbalized, (5) conceptualized, and (6) used for extra-musical purposes. The major questions for the educator are: (1) Can these attributes be learned? (2) Can they be taught? (3) What are the best ways to go about teaching them? Experimental research concerning all of the above seems limitless.

Aesthetic appreciation should continue to reign supreme in the domain of introspective subjectivity, although it is apparent that the researcher can only measure the attributes of the empirical world. If the aesthetic experience is indeed above scientific scrutiny and defies operational definition and subsequent testing, then it would appear wise to leave it with other transcendental experiences and not attempt the impossible task of "proving" the supernatural world by contriving "evidence" from measured reality. It should be remembered that the poet and philosopher have most often foreshadowed the achievements of the inventor and scientist. Theoretical abstraction is certainly a worthy pursuit, but the scientific investigator must always remember in what mode of inquiry he is engaged.

STUDY QUESTIONS

1. What is creativity? Can it be learned? Can it be taught?
2. Discuss the statement, "Music performance is an active endeavor, which for the most part consists of perfecting neuromuscular responses in relationship to judgmental aural discriminations."
3. What experimentation could be designed to test various levels of listening discrimination?
4. List aspects of music study that concern verbalization. Relate them to the conductor, applied teacher, and elementary music teacher.
5. Define the "aesthetic experience." Can any aspect of your definition be tested?

PART TWO

CHAPTER SIX

quantification in research

For thousands of years man has had difficulty with his environment. Some problems concerned the procurement of food, the threat of a thief, a place to live, and to what extent he could manipulate his surroundings. Some situations were different from others, some seemed the same, but the more he observed, the more things he saw. After some time and with apparent difficulty, he devised a method for general classification—he learned to count.

CLOSED SYSTEMS

Over the years, man has developed many closed systems—arithmetic, geometry, English, German, Arabic, music notation, the overtone series, and statistics to name but a few. The term "closed system" is used to advance the concept that these various systems are often intrinsically consistent; that is, internal relationships are always constant, but extrinsically invalid (closed). The systems are defined as "closed" because they lose intrinsic consistency when applied to each other or to different phenomena. For example, the relationships between the arithmetic numbers 1 to 2 to 3 is always invariate. These three numbers represent the same relationship as do the numbers 2 to 4 to 6. Also, 1 + 2 always equals 3. A problem arises, however, when this simple arithmetic system is used to quantify other areas, activities, or products. To state that "one apple plus one apple equals two apples" presents only slight difficulty. To state that "one apple plus one kumquat equals two pieces of fruit" is perhaps justified, but to state that "one apple plus one atom plus one universe equals three things" seems rather tenuous. The same difficulty applies to other closed systems. How much Arabic could one learn with an Arabic dictionary if one knew nothing about the symbols or their "meaning." Since every word in a dictionary is nothing more than a "definition" of every other word, one could not even get started without transferable relationships. Music notation has no meaning for a plumber except in relationship to other factors that have been learned through the *transfer* of perceived phenomena; for example, it may be that the plumber sings in church.

Some systems are related, and transfer is easier, for example, English and French with 46 percent cognates, arithmetic and algebra with digits and some symbols in common, the overtone series and some chord structures. Pitch is quantified in terms of frequency and loudness in terms of decibels. However, even with common elements, transfer can still be a problem when moving from one system into another. One of the basic rationales of the now old "New Math" was to avoid the pitfalls of learning one closed system after another. Because of the difficulties encountered when transferring from arithmetic, to algebra, to geometry, to trigonometry, and so on, modern mathematics now teaches most of these various systems *simultaneously,* using the concept of "sets." Quantification (counting, classifying) is considered less tenuous when any well-defined collection of objects (for example, oranges, limes, lemons, tangerines) is thought of as a set.

Questionable as is the process of transferring closed systems and subsequently inferring meaning, it represents a major resourcefulness of man and distinguishes him from other animals. Man's accomplishments in quantification have provided tremendous progress. It is the quantification of specific responses and subsequent logical methods of analysis that provide the background for experimental research.

SCIENCE AS A DEDUCTIVE METHOD

The rules of logical *deduction* are rules for arriving at true consequences from true premises. *Induction* is the process of reasoning from a part to a whole, from particulars to generals. Once a theory or principle has been established, it can be tested deductively and repeated observations can ascertain its validity. A problem arises for the empirical scientist: how does one go about arriving at the "truth" of the *initial* proposition? Since it is impossible for the scientist to observe all possible situations, he must generalize from what he thinks true of some observations to what is true for all possible observations. This represents a problem of induction, and any empirical science begins with particular observation and subsequent generalization. Mathematical systems such as probability theory are by their very nature *deductive*. Once the experimenter can make assumptions about what is true, then statistical theory based upon probability indicates how likely he is to observe particular results considering the laws of chance. Thus, experimental research combines these two processes; deduction is used to test observed data as a ground for induction.

METHODS FOR EXPERIMENTAL RESEARCH

Specific rationales for experimentation (observation under controlled conditions) were advocated by John Stuart Mill, who analyzed the search for causes in experimental research in order to identify the means by which experimentation may be achieved. These constitute the five Mill's Canons, or rules for experimental research.[1]

1. Mill's *Method of Agreement* proposes that if the circumstances leading up to a given event have in every case only one common factor, that factor probably is the cause. Thus, if through controlled experimentation it could be found that in the vast possibilities of musical experience only one factor could be found in common to some specific attribute (that is, perfect pitch, tone deafness, and so on), that factor would be the cause of the attribute. Many experimental designs using the One-Sample Method approximate this principle when attempting to assess the effect of manipulation of one variable at a time. The limitations of this method are appreciable because of the assumption concerning the *dis*similarities of *all* other factors. It is an extremely tenuous assumption to assess causality on the basis of single rather than multiple variables unless a functional analysis is performed.

2. Mill's *Method of Differences* proposes that if two or more sets of circumstances are alike in every respect except for one factor and if a given result occurs only when that factor is present, the factor in question probably is the cause of that result. It is difficult, if not impossible,

---

[1] John Stuart Mill, *A System of Logic*, Book III, Chapter 8 (New York: Harper and Brothers, 1873).

to create experimental conditions where all sets of circumstances are alike in every respect. Yet, this principle constitutes the major rationale for much experimentation (Equivalent-Sample Method) where individuals are matched, divided into control and experimental groups, and subjected to scientific manipulations, after which differences are assessed.

3. The *Joint Method* combines the above two methods. First, the one factor common to the occurrence is found (Method of Agreement), and second, the factor is withdrawn to determine if the phenomenon occurs *only* when the factor is present. When conditions of both the Method of Agreement and the Method of Differences are satisfactorily met, identification of causes should be reasonably conclusive. Sophisticated experimental designs (techniques alternating individual, group, or variable measures) use the rationale of the Joint Method. Specific factors are isolated and assessed, after which these factors are omitted and/or replaced with subsequent assessment. Often, the process is continued over extended periods with many rotations. The major difficulty in a rotation design is the factor of "learning" (or order effects), which tremendously complicates the assessment of the individual factor (variable) *after the initial rotation*.

4. The *Method of Residues* assesses causes by the process of elimination. This method proposes that when the specific factors causing certain parts of a given phenomenon are known, the remaining parts of the phenomenon must be caused by the remaining factor or factors. This is an uncertain procedure for specific conclusions; yet, it most aptly describes the entire process of *continued experimentation,* where unknown factors are constantly being found and evaluated to explain the additional aspects of a phenomenon.

5. The *Method of Concomitant Variations* proposes, in effect, that when two things consistently change or vary together, either the variations in one are caused by the variations in the other, or both are being affected by some common cause. Often, it is impossible or undesirable to isolate only one factor for study, that is, to conduct an experiment. When this is the case, inferences must be drawn from assessing the relationship among factors (correlation) and taking into account extrinsic variables (growth analysis, trend studies, causal comparative studies).

These five methods of investigation apply to individuals and groups as well as to inanimate objects, which are much more easily controlled. They represent methods by which the experimenter can begin to structure a design appropriate to the investigation of the proposed topic, see chart pp. 84–85.

While experimental design texts do not generally discuss Mill's Canons and apply them to research, the importance of a verbal rationale for those who have had little background in the scientific disciplines is apparent.

DESCRIPTIONS IN MUSIC QUANTIFICATION

Prior to proceeding to elementary principles of experimental design and statistics (Chapters Seven and Eight), a few brief descriptions of separate and related areas of experimental quantification are advisable.

Statistics is the collection and classification of facts on the basis of relative frequency of occurrences as a ground for induction.

Data processing involves the use of computers for any number of diverse computations including classifying and amassing separate data and statistical analysis.

A *computer programmer* is a person who writes a "program" or instructions by which data are analyzed by the computer.

There are many *computer programs* for statistical analysis. Prewritten programs for common statistical tests are available in any university computer center. Thus, a music student may use a pre-written program rather than going through the long process of working out by hand complex statistical formulas.[2]

Experimental design is the process by which scientific experiments are structured to measure a defined variable. This process requires knowledge of the subject area and some knowledge of elementary principles underlying statistics. Experimental design does not require any knowledge of computer usage. However, this knowledge can be extremely helpful in saving time when a pre-written statistical "program" can be used or a new program developed. This is of particular interest in many music experiments where thousands of separate observations regarding individual pitches and rhythms need to be analyzed.

Programmed instruction is a separate area and should not be confused with a "computer program." Programmed instruction usually refers to a process of self-instruction with instantaneous "feedback" (for example, a programmed textbook). Complex programmed instruction (for example, Computer Assisted Instruction) uses a computer for immediate evaluation and appropriate reinforcement of specific responses. This programmed instruction necessitates not only the hardware (computer), but also the software (that is, programs from subject matter specialists)

---

2 W. J. Dixon, ed, *BMD Biomedical Computer Programs* (Los Angeles: University of California Press, 1967).

for its actualization. Writing a programmed text requires knowledge of the subject matter area and principles of programming. If any instructional program is to be tested in comparison to other instructional media, then knowledge of experimental design and statistics is necessary for valid comparisons and interpretation.

Specifically different from any of the above is *computer music.* Music that is actually written (programmed) for, and/or performed by, a computer.

Competency in any of the above areas demands strenuous preparation; it is rare indeed to find a person well qualified in all.

LIMITATIONS OF QUANTIFICATION

It is purported that Disraeli once said, "There are three kinds of lies: lies, damn lies, and statistics." When the student views a television commercial and is told that four dentists out of five recommend a certain mouthwash, that might actually be the case—the total number of dentists equals five. Or perhaps after interviewing 800 dentists in groups of five, the company found 4 and only 4, out of one group of 5 that would recommend the product. A student can be the "highest in the class" and not be able to find either side of his desk with both hands. Alternately, a student may be in the "lowest part of the class" and demonstrate a firm command of the subject matter. If only partial information is given, "numerical tricks" can be deceptive.

It also appears that some people who work with numbers over an extended period of time come to "believe them." Most students have had the experience of questioning the basis on which their grade was given. The student may find himself looking over numbers in a roll book as though the roll book numbers were responsible for his grade. Each instructor usually chooses the text, determines the content of the course, constructs the tests, decides what responses are "right or wrong" and their relative weighting, and decides how much individual tests and assignments will count toward determining the final grade. For the teacher to then view *his* amassed numbers as though they had some extrinsic absolute worth may represent a case where "numbers are believed." It should be stated that most teachers use many statistical concepts to assess a student's work and arrive at individual grades with as much objectivity and genuine fairness as possible.

It must be remembered that application of numbers or mathematical systems per se do not necessarily establish "truth." Even if four dentists out of every five recommend a mouthwash, this does not tell much about the mouthwash or firmly establish that it is "good." The value and meaning of products, circumstances, situations, and all aspects of phenomena are always open to interpretation. While it would be unwise to jump off a building hoping to discount the laws of gravity, to assume dental expertise without professional training, or to believe that regardless of one's grades, graduation is still imminent, other activities of life seem more questionable. This is particularly evident in the quantification of some aspects of an *art* such as music.

CONCLUSION

Quantification and the many systems that man has developed over the years have provided the major basis for his environmental sophistication. Various systems of quantification combined with logical methods of analysis provide the base for experimental research. These systems are intended as vehicles toward greater understanding and should not be viewed as ends in themselves.

The student is cautioned to maintain and develop a tolerance for ambiguity. The necessity of not assuming an "either-or" attitude is again advised in relationship to quantification. The fact that man strives imperfectly toward knowledge and the development of methods to attain knowledge does not indicate that everything but the most gross subjectivity and personal biases should prevail. Many aspects of the art of music can be studied quantitatively. Perhaps, the best indication of a "closed mind" is the statement, "Well, if all that isn't *really true,* then why not forget about it." A conscientious student is capable of much more.

STUDY QUESTIONS

1. Define a "closed system." Name several in music.
2. What is meant by the statement, "Deduction is used to test observed data as a ground for induction"?
3. Devise simple experiments that illustrate each of the five Mill's Canons.
4. Give some examples of the use of numbers to give erroneous information.
5. Why should one continuously strive toward greater objectivity when quantification and mathematical systems per se do not necessarily establish truth?

CHAPTER
SEVEN

the experimental process

Experimentation is just one area of research. Research in its largest definition is a process of inquiry necessitating careful and diligent investigation and studious examination. It is aimed at the discovery of interpretation of facts or practical applications of such facts. The research process is a way man has learned to *control* his inquiry. The controls one uses in the process of answering questions increase the likelihood of the answers being acceptable and functional. Scientific experimentation does not establish absolute truth, but it does move man forward in his knowledge and understanding. It is this *process* of inquiry that occupies the researcher, and the actualities that result from this controlled inquiry that provide the greatest information.

STATEMENT OF THE PROBLEM

The initial concern for the researcher is the problem to be investigated. The experimenter speculates, analyzes, and criticizes a topic deemed appropriate for research. Thus, a basic idea is advanced and analyzed to ascertain its worth and feasibility. It is criticized from known information and various points of view. Finally, it is formulated into a specific statement (hypothesis) that is testable with appropriate statistical tests.

The necessary questions pertaining to the problem are:

1. Is the logic of the problem analysis sound?
2. Is the statement of the problem in agreement with all known facts?
3. Is the problem consistent with well-known theories, and if not, how does if differ?
4. Is the problem testable and are answers attainable?

During this initial process it usually helps to talk about the project with both musicians and researchers. See if it can be explained and try to state exactly what is to be attempted. Reciprocal communication helps clarify the problem, and when it can be verbalized clearly and succinctly, it can usually be developed into a sound research design.

When the researcher begins to construct an experimental design, the basic topic is almost always altered (restricted in scope) in ways that permit it to be experimentally tested. However, a clear concept of the initial problem is still prerequisite. Even when the problem seems minutely restricted, it usually necessitates much finer delimitation before it generates specific hypotheses that can be tested. The construction of specific hypotheses represents the first refinement in the experimental process.

THE HYPOTHESIS

The word hypothesis is used in research to refer to many things. It may be the initial guess or hunch of the experimenter, it may be the tentative conclusion that is assessed after the experimental study, or it may constitute the formal statement that is to be tested. The term hypothesis (*hypo,* less than or to put under; *thesis,* position or proposition) is generally used to indicate initial supposition on a continuum from hypothesis through theory to law. A *hypothesis* is a tentative explanation; *theory* implies a greater range of evidence; *law* implies a statement of order and relation in nature that has been found to be invariable under the same conditions.

Not infrequently, the young researcher confuses a hypothesis with a law and appears determined to prove a certain position for all time. The hypothesis is the first consideration toward "truth." It is not as important for the researcher to speculate correctly as it is to investigate with extreme care. Experimentation is one method for attaining greater knowledge—it is not a game to determine "who wins." It is unlikely that the music profession will drastically change because one study "proves" a certain position. Truth is often extremely elusive. It is important that the researcher ask meaningful questions and pursue each topic carefully and *honestly*. If a tentative explanation seems unfounded, then it is important that the unfounded idea or supposition have adequate appraisal. Often, "negative results" are extremely meaningful in the structure of new experiments.

The final hypothesis should constitute the best formulation of the problem of which the experimenter is capable. While one hypothesis is often adequate, sometimes several hypotheses are necessary. The number of hypotheses depends upon the nature of the problem to be studied and upon the experimental design. It should be remembered that the rejection or substantiation of particular suppositional statements does not constitute the entire benefits of experimentation. Many times, incidental aspects of research provide the most information. Mistakes, chance factors, and research obstacles often provide new directions for the investigator. Scientific literature is replete with examples of meaningful diversions that arise from "negative aspects" of experimentation.[1]

There is a growing number of researchers who choose *not* to use formal statements to be tested (hypotheses). Instead, these experimenters prefer to investigate certain areas and let the results stand alone. They think it inadvisable to accept or reject certain sentences as being "true" or "false" and prefer to: (1) describe the area of investigation, (2) present detailed information concerning experimental procedures, and (3) present the analyzed results. For example, a researcher studying perfect pitch might initially present research literature concerning "perfect pitch." He might then state that one hundred musicians purported to have "perfect pitch" were tested on their ability to recognize fifty intervals aurally. Detailed accounts of the selection of subjects, equivalent groups, intervals, trials, evaluation of performance, and so on would be given in the design description, after which results would be presented. While statistical tests would be used to evaluate subjects' ability to recognize intervals and the differences between subjects, intervals, and so on, no attempt would be made to confirm a stated hypothesis. There would *not* be the traditional statement: "The hypothesis that subjects purported to have 'perfect pitch' recognize more selected intervals than do subjects without 'perfect pitch' is confirmed at the .05 level of significance."

Experimentation without stated hypotheses is perhaps more sophisticated and less cumbersome than traditional reporting. For the begin-

---

[1] W. I. B. Beveridge, *The Art of Scientific Investigation* (New York: Vintage Books, 1957), p. 43.

ning researcher, however, the major benefit of formulating hypotheses is the process of stating exactly what is to be investigated and tested. This process helps clarify the entire study. Of course, the *problem* of a study is always implied in the experimental design, but the initial efforts of beginning researchers are often vague at best. Therefore, all processes that help clarify the study are recommended. The hypothesis can be an initial guess, or it may represent a more general theory that is based on careful and thorough study of other research results. Regardless, the stated hypothesis needs to be specific and testable.

Hypotheses may be presented in null form (hypothesis of no difference) or, on the basis of prior research, in directional form (hypothesis of predictable difference). The researcher should realize that only well-formulated hypotheses can be tested statistically. However, the entire rationale for statistical inference makes it impossible to prove a hypothesis (Chapter Eight). When a hypothesis is said to be confirmed at the .05 level, this indicates that results could be expected to occur on the basis of *chance alone* only five times in a hundred. Truth is not established, it is approximated.

REVIEW OF LITERATURE

A necessary process in experimentation is to search the literature for specifically and generally related studies. The researcher may wish to change some aspects of the original statement of the problem after reviewing related literature. It is also strongly recommended that the researcher first review many diverse experimental studies before attempting to structure an experimental design. While it is advantageous to spend as much time in the library as possible, there are many unique topics that arise from an individual's music experiences and not from other research. These topics present a challenge because it seems that they do not have a backlog of related literature. In this case, the beginning researcher may think that an intensive review of literature would be unnecessary. However, it is most likely that: (1) a vast amount of previous research has been done in the area (although perhaps difficult for the young researcher to find), and (2) the student should demonstrate that he is aware of research in the general area even though it is not directly relevant to his topic.

Reviewing experimental literature is an exciting pursuit once the library is found. Many institutions offer courses in how to find desired information (library science, for example), but usually each student has to go through a rather difficult process in order to find exactly what he wants. Since libraries are staffed with professional personnel, it usually helps to *ask*. It is suggested that the student begin this venture when he has ample time and is relatively free from anxiety. The literature should be reviewed carefully and diligently. All possible sources should be sought (periodicals as well as books). Titles not locally available may generally be procured through inter-library loan. If the researcher is unable to locate a specific source, he should ask the librarian about other possibilities. A list of pertinent periodicals in experimental research in music and related disciplines is presented in Appendix A.

When examining the literature, it is extremely important to keep detailed accurate records of all materials for future reference and possible inclusion in the formal report. (A 4×6 card file is adequate.) Very often the researcher finds it necessary to go back to sources he has previously reviewed. It is much less difficult if these sources are immediately available. (It is somewhat like practicing your instrument—how much more practice would you get in if, when the spirit moved you, you found yourself instantaneously in the practice room with all necessary materials?) If the time it takes to keep accurate records seems exorbitant, it does not compare with the time involved in trying to find the material again— ask any advanced graduate student.

Reviewing experimental literature not only provides source material for the proposed topic, it should also help the student begin to evaluate other experiments. The student should search particularly for those experiments that appear extremely simple, for he shall soon learn that this apparent simplicity was usually earned at a tremendous price of time and effort. Design clarity often demonstrates that the researcher knew his business and was able to structure the study without undue verbiage and confusion. The student should not be deceived by thinking the process is simple. It has been said that "there are only two types of people, muddle heads and simple minds—simplicity must be earned."

THE ELEMENT OF CONTROL

The proposed hierarchy of experimental design is to: choose a topic, state the problem, construct the hypothesis, select the sample, gather the data, and analyze the results in accordance with the stated hypothesis. This sounds simple, but in fact all of these elements need to be considered simultaneously. For beginners, not only is it imperative that statistical tools (Chapter Nine) be chosen before the *collection* of the data, but also it must be remembered that when one minute aspect of the design is altered, the entire design may collapse, necessitating total revision. The student will not appreciate the many different avenues an initial topic may take until he goes through this process.

The foremost element of design is *control*. The experiment is useless unless the finished design demonstrates that all aspects of the experimental process were controlled and could not bias the experimental variable(s) other than as intended by the experimental design. The supreme concern is to know *what is influencing what*. There are countless complexities, including everything from the most obvious (precise measuring equipment) to the apparent ridiculous (color of the room in which the experiment takes place). However, many aspects previously thought ridiculous are later found to be highly significant. The researcher cannot be too careful.

The greatest single difficulty in experimental research is that the experimenter almost always has to go through many revisions before the design achieves proper scientific control. Therefore, it is preferable that the beginning researcher choose an appropriate "model experiment" for his first venture and either replicate it exactly or change just one small aspect. This is perhaps the best starting point in order for the student to *gradually* become aware of the many necessary requirements of scientific investigation. If a student chooses to go through the entire process for his initial experiment, he should be content to accept the knowledge he learns from his *mistakes* and not believe that any subsequent results should be taken seriosuly.

A FIRST EXPERIMENT

Experimentation is an exciting and rewarding experience, but like any other endeavor it has various levels of sophistication, and true competence must be earned. It is much like composition in that most musicians can write a simple tune, but a *fine* symphony takes time, artistry, and highly developed skill. Consider the case of Joe:

> Joe is a first-year graduate student and must complete a research project for a one semester course in Research Methods. Being a clarinetist, he has always wanted to know if small differences in mouthpiece sizes can be detected. This seems like an easy little experiment until someone asks how he is going to control different reed strengths, models of clarinets, and so on. He thinks about this for awhile and decides this particular experiment would be too difficult. He then decides to check trumpet mouthpieces, because it seems easier. But what brand and sizes should he test? He finally decides to test the Bach brand, because he remembers reading somewhere that they were used more often. He finally manages to obtain a "selection of Bach mouthpieces" from the local music store

(value $150.00). The mouthpiece kit contains ten different sizes.

He approaches a trumpet graduate student to talk about his project. Not only is the trumpet major seemingly unco-operative, but he lets Joe know that *he* can *always* tell the differences between mouthpieces anytime, anywhere. Right then, Joe decides he is going to run the experiment with *high school* trumpeters. He contacts the local high school and finds that they do have nine trumpet students, but they cannot be excused from school to participate. He decides to contact them individually and after fifteen telephone calls has six that will meet him in the band room two weeks from Saturday. Things are looking up, thinks Joe.

"Now, how should I test them?" he ponders. "If everyone played on each of the ten mouthpieces for three minutes, that would be one-half hour each. Oh! What happens if they get tired? (and I must remember to take a good stopwatch). I guess I will use five mouthpieces—$3 \times 5 = 15$. I wonder if three minutes will be enough, or perhaps too much?" The next day Joe checks with another college trumpet student (not the graduate), and is told that probably one minute would be enough *if* all the trumpeters have a good warm-up. Warm-up. Joe had not thought about that. "What if they play any that morning before I can test them? I must remember to tell them not to play any before the experiment. Okay, how about the warm-up? I could give them, say, five minutes to warm up. Now, how many mouthpieces should I test?" After much deliberation, Joe decides to test just two mouthpieces, but which ones? He finally decides on the 7c and the 12c, because his trumpet friend (again not the graduate student) told him that these sizes were most often used. "Let's see now, two mouthpieces, five students—all set. Wait, how are they going to report the differences?" Joe decides to make up an answer sheet. "It could be same-different, same-different. Yeh! I will give every student the 7c, then the 12c, then the 7c, then the?? But, how much time will that take? . . . if everyone gets five trials on each mouthpiece?" Joe decides to have everyone play six times on each mouthpiece. Everything seems settled. "Now back to 'Form and Analysis' and what a tough course— it takes *so* much time. . . ."

Saturday arrives and Joe sets out with mouthpieces in hand. He arrives at the school. The heat is off and only four boys show up, one with a cornet into which the trumpet mouth-pieces will not fit. The first boy looks at the number on the side of the new mouthpiece before he starts to play. "Hey, this mouthpiece is just like the one I already use." "Oh no!" Joe places a postage stamp over the number. It is all he can find. "Why didn't I think of that? Besides, I already told him *not* to look at the number." "Boy, kids are dumb these days," thinks Joe. As the boy proceeds through the test, Joe becomes even more upset because the student cannot follow Joe's directions. After two more subjects and a very harrowing morning, Joe is tremendously upset. He decides to spend the afternoon in the library.

"How do all those other people run experiments?" Joe had previously read 25 abstracts for the Research Methods class and he had also completed a critical analysis of ten original research reports. Joe decides to read one of the ten he had already reviewed and handed in. Joe thinks about that particular review assignment and what a drag it was—busy work, busy work, and besides, wasn't that the same week he had taken a mid-term in Music History? "Doesn't matter— what a morning." The first study Joe looked for was not in the library; someone had it on inter-library loan. "Fifteen minutes to find out something is not there!" Joe finally settles down with another study, and after the girl across the table left, began to concentrate. "Introduction, same old jazz —review of literature." Joe was bored. He begins to count all the sentences that start, "It would appear that . . . or, it would seem . . ." "Wow, what dull junk—third person, no personal pronouns, I wonder if Brahms could get through something like this?"

He goes to the Experimental Design section. In earnest he begins to read and suddenly he begins to see things he had overlooked before. "Subjects were randomly selected from the student rolls of ten elementary schools." "A pilot test was conducted to determine the advisability of the project." "Subjects were used as their own controls to insure construct validity." "An analysis of co-variance was used to assess performance and assign subjects to equivalent control and experimental groups." "All possible combinations of trials were randomly presented to insure control for possible order effects." "Instructions were tape-recorded and consequently, identical for all subjects." "Consistent with previous experimentation in this area, each subject was tested for only twenty minutes to control for possible fatigue." "Interims between trials were filled with recorded music to help destroy past tonal associations, which might conceivably affect results on subsequent performances." "Recordings were made in an acoustically designed studio and performances analyzed after completion of the collected data." "A detailed description of all apparatus used in the experiment is found in Appendix A." "Raw data are presented in Table IV, however, the data are quite misleading unless the statistical Table V is viewed." "While the raw data concerning subjects in Group II indicate improvement after experimental manipulation, the statistical analysis shows this to be non-significant." "The statistical analysis demonstrated individual differences to be the greatest source of variation and this could possibly account for the higher total score, but non-significance of Group II. . . ."

Joe continues to read through the report, now with greater enthusiasm. When the report refers the reader to a table, Joe actually studies the table. When he is referred to an Appendix to read instructions given to subjects, he looks in the Appendix. Joe decides to reread the entire study. He starts at the beginning and then something stops him in the middle of a page. He remembers how cold the school building was when he had tested that morning; how cold the instruments were, and how the pitch changed as the sun finally came through the windows and the room got warmer. The study he is reading concerns intonation. Joe thinks, "What about temperature? Yeh, what about temperature?" Joe hurriedly goes through the study. "Recordings were made in an acoustically designed studio," but nothing about temperature. "How about that! So this guy was a Ph.D. now and nothing about temperature." Joe looks at the beginning of the study. Sure enough, "In partial fulfillment of the degree of Doctor of Philosophy." He skips a page, "So he loves his wife and acknowledges his professors, but no temperature control and even if he did keep the temperature constant, he should have stated it."

Joe has regained his equilibrium and decides to leave. He even thinks kindly of the matronly old lady who asks to check his books. As he leaves the library, he notices how dark it has become and is only now aware of how long he has stayed, and how much he still has to do. He walks quickly toward the music building. "Yes sir, control. Control is extremely important—control all those variables that are not of experimental manipulation. No temperature, *no temperature*—if that guy can get a doctor's degree, I can, too."

CONCLUSION

The following questions are imperative in evaluating the experimental design.[2]

1. Are the experimental variables singular and not confounded with other factors or each other?
2. Are all non-manipulative variables randomized?

---

[2] Expanded coverage of these questions may be found in D. B. Van Dalen, *Understanding Education Research* (New York: McGraw-Hill Book Company, 1966).

3. Is consideration given to the possibility of the experimenter or experimental procedures signaling or otherwise biasing the results?
4. Are all precautions taken to obtain equivalence of subjects, groups, or other necessary aspects of the experiment?
5. Is the sample adequate in kind and number?
6. Are the techniques of pairing or matching valid?
7. Are there items or factors in the tests, measures or instruments, which might bias the results?
8. Was there an adequate pretesting of all aspects concerning the experiment (materials, instruments, facilities, etc.)?
9. Do the proposed samples, analysis of data, and assumptions satisfy the use of the proposed statistical procedures?
10. Can you be sure that experimental findings are the result of intended manipulations?

The "either-or" concept is never more crucial than in relationship to the experimental design. Every aspect of the design has to be considered *independently and collectively*. The experimenter is cautioned to start with an extremely simple topic and to begin to revise and limit until all of the above considerations are adequately met. Experimental design with necessary *controls* is the most important and consequently the most difficult aspect of experimental research. After the design has been structured, it represents a "recipe" that can be carried out with little difficulty. The written report should contain a specific detailed account of what actually took place in order that future researchers will be able to duplicate the study exactly without additional information. The music professions will benefit greatly from results derived from such careful experimentation.

STUDY QUESTIONS

1. What questions should be asked about the statement of the problem?
2. Select a well-known fact and trace its evolution from hypothesis through theory to law.
3. Discuss the benefits of reviewing experimental literature. What should the experimenter do if he is just completing a study and finds that it has already been done?
4. Why is *control* the most important aspect of experimental design?
5. In what ways and to what extent can you identify with Joe? Could this identification confuse, upset, or anger a person? Why?

CHAPTER EIGHT

statistical theory and musicians

Most musicians do not possess detailed knowledge of advanced statistics; in fact, many might have difficulty with simple arithmetic. These same musicians may know little about the internal combustion engine, yet they drive cars; they may not understand electronics, yet they operate phonographs; they may become confused if asked to repair a lock, yet their keys open doors. Life is far too complex to know even a small part of the world and its many attributes or man's myriad activities. However, one can usually take advantage of many products and processes if one can differentiate between them and understand *how they work*.

USES OF STATISTICS

Statistics may also be used by musicians who know very little about statistics compared to professional statisticians. This is not to advocate that the serious researcher should not learn as much as possible about statistics—and all tools of research—nor is this text intended as a substitute for formal courses in statistics. However, in any activity one must begin. Many experiments can be conducted without advanced statistical knowledge. More important, there are usually competent statisticians in institutions where research is conducted who will help the musician interested in experimental research. The musician needs to know enough to be able to effectively communicate with statisticians. It is then possible to arrive at an appropriate design with adequate evaluation of results. Computer analyses can be very useful to the experimenter because there is a large number of pre-written statistical programs that will analyze data on the basis of common statistical tests.[1] The primary concerns for the musician are: (1) to understand the general theories and vocabulary of statistics; (2) to know which statistical tools are appropriate for particular problems (design), and (3) what the results mean, that is, how to interpret the statistical findings.

Statistics are used in experimentation to: (1) describe the data, and (2) calculate relative frequency of occurrences as a ground for induction (predicting). Descriptive statistics do not present a great problem. Students are familiar with many descriptive statistics: average salary, 94th percentile, price reduction 50%, and grade point average = 3.0. Statistics used to calculate the accuracy of observations however, present a more difficult problem and necessitate some understanding of probability theory.

THEORY OF PROBABILITY

Pascal was one of the first mathematicians to explore the theory of probability in detail. Reportedly, his interest was aroused in connection with a discussion about gambling odds. He pursued the question for some time and reported many of his conclusions, published posthumously in the *Treatise on the Arithmetic Triangle* (1665).[2]

For some time afterward, the theory of probability was developed to serve as a model for games of chance. As probability theory developed, it found many uses in addition to calculating the odds for rolling dice, spinning a roulette wheel, or playing card games. It became apparent that it could also be used to serve as a model for calculation of data in science

---

[1] Assistance in the choice and application of prewritten statistical programs is generally available to students at any university that maintains a computer center.

[2] Blaise Pascal, *Treatise on the Arithmetic Triangle* (1665). See Albert Maire, Bibliographie Générale des Oeuvres de Blaise Pascal, Paris: L. Giraud Badin, 1925.

and empirical experimentation.[3] A common characteristic of the gambler and scientist is that neither knows precisely what each individual outcome will be. Each must calculate in relation to the long run. *Given that certain things are true,* deductions may be made concerning what should be true *in the long run.* Every student who is faced with a decision goes through a similar process, although perhaps not as stringently. Underlying all statistical calculations is one basic tautology. *Events may be expected to move in the direction in which it is most probable they will move.* Thus, if the initial premise is true, or assumed to be true, it can be tested using the theory of probability for verification and possible prediction.

For example, most of us assume that the probability for tossing a coin either heads or tails is .50. Suppose that one was given a coin and asked to devise an experiment to see if the coin was fair, that is, if the probability of tossing heads is indeed .50. (The student is asked to take a coin and conduct this experiment.) Suppose that we decide to toss the coin ten times, keeping an accurate account of the occurrences of heads. Do it. If the student did this, he should not be surprised if the number of heads was less or more than five. Now suppose the coin is tossed ten more times and the total number of heads from the first ten tosses combined with that from the second ten tosses. Still the student should not be surprised if the total number of heads was more or less than ten. This process could be continued indefinitely. At what point (number of samplings) could one be reasonably sure that the coin was indeed fair? Put another way, if your life depended upon your correct assessment of the fairness of *your* coin, how many trials would you prefer to make before declaring that your coin is fair or biased? Think about it. If the student actually conducted this simple experiment and contemplated correct assessment in terms of his own life, he should begin to realize some of the attributes of the theory of probability and the number of trials required for accurate judgment. In addition, the uncertainty of absolute assessment, regardless of how many tosses, should be apparent. If the coin is indeed fair (proportion of heads = .50), then one can expect the observed proportion to approach .50 in the long run. A statement of probability tells us what to *expect* about the relative frequency of an event, given that enough sample observations are made at random. Since similar observations have previously been made many times regarding coins, we know (or at least strongly suspect) that the probability that our coin will turn up heads = .50. Thus, we can make the statement

---

[3] For an excellent historical overview of the beginnings of probability theory, see the classical work by I. Todhunter, *A History of the Mathematical Theory of Probability* (Cambridge: MacMillian, 1865).

of probability "that for any given toss of the coin, the probability of heads is .50." The thoughtful student may realize that if this is the case *for each trial*, then the possibility exists that the coin may come up heads every time. While this is possible, it is tremendously unlikely. One need only engage in a little gambling to fully realize this concept.[4] There would be no need for probability theory if *all* observations could be assessed. It is the necessity for ipso facto decisions which requires some basis for calculation. Without probability theory, generalization would be without method, and scientific experimentation would have little meaning.

Statistical theory and the laws of probability have become very important in modern life. Constantly, one hears the phrases, "in all probability," "the law of averages," or "relatively constant." These are statistical concepts concerning the laws of chance. Insurance companies represent an excellent example. If it were not for calculations based on the laws of probability, these companies could not exist. While it is not possible to predict the exact time any one person, age twenty, will die, an actuary is able to predict quite accurately how many twenty-year-olds will die this year, next year, and so on. Another example is the beginning of banking, when the old safe owner found that he could loan out another's money because not all of his depositors came to take their money out at the same time. Provisions have subsequently been made to insure depositors' money because of early speculation that sometimes proved excessive. Rates for this insurance (FDIC) are again based on the number of faulty speculations and thus the laws of probability. It is difficult to imagine many aspects of modern life that do not use and benefit from the application of this theory.

REQUIREMENTS FOR STATISTICAL DESCRIPTIONS

It should be apparent from foregoing discussions (Chapter Six) that the first requirement for statistical analysis is a means whereby data can be quantitatively assessed. *Measurement* involves assignment of numbers to observable phenomena. The process, as previously indicated, represents a tenuous transfer; however, it is the best means available, and careful procedures will assure greater "meaning" of the results. It is important not to ascribe numbers to aspects of data that are indeed

---

4 Gambling houses capitalize on the independence of trials (if the houses are fair). For example, if one were to bet on red continuously on a roulette wheel, he would "in the long run" lose some of his money. Remember that there are "green" spaces. These are certainly not included for reasons of aesthetic interior decor.

different and then treat them as if they were similar. Each particular event of observation within an experiment should represent a point in a well-defined area of·investigation. Thus, if one is measuring intonation, some objective numerical terminology is necessary that *does not include many different aspects simultaneously.* A negative example would be a rating scale that included only one numerical classification combining flatness, sharpness, type of instrument, grade level, I.Q., years of study, and so on. Discrimination and separate differentiation of categories with appropriate numerical description are imperative.

There are four general types of measurement scales used in experimentation: (1) nominal, (2) ordinal, (3) interval, and (4) ratio. The *nominal,* or "naming," scale is used solely for classification, for example, flat–sharp, good–bad, large, improvement. The only relation involved in the nominal scale is of equality or differences, and members must be identifiable by the property being scaled. For example, a large chorus is easily classified nominally into soprano, alto, tenor, or bass. The nominal scale represents the weakest basis for assessment, and only non-parametric statistics (discussed later) are appropriate for these kinds of data.

The *ordinal* scale not only allows comparisons of equality and differences but also permits the rank ordering of members of a group or events. Statements such as less than ($<$) or greater than ($>$) can also be designated, but the *number of times* one member is greater than or less than another or the *relative differences* between observations cannot be assessed. The assignment of orchestral parts within a section on the basis of assessed proficiency (auditions) is an excellent example of ordinal scaling by the conductor. Again, only non-parametric statistics are appropriate.

An *interval* scale permits measurement of equality and differences of *intervals* and also greater-than and less-than measurements. This scale permits the assessment of intervalic comparisons. The chromatic scale on the equal-tempered piano represents interval scaling at its best, that is, C$\sharp$ is to D as D is to D$\sharp$, and so on. An interval scale does not need an absolute zero point; however, the distances between points on the scale are of known size (common examples are the metronome, thermometer, and calendar). An interval scale is perhaps the strongest scale that can be used for most experimental research in music. More powerful methods of statistical analysis, that is, parametric statistics, are possible when interval scaling can be achieved.

The *ratio* scale has all of the above characteristics but also has an absolute zero point. This allows values to be doubled, tripled, etc. Some apparatus for measuring pitch and duration (for example, Stroboconn, electric clock) represent possibilities for ratio scaling, for example, stroboscopic analysis of pitch in plus or minus cent deviations and timings of durational rhythmic patterns. The ratio scale meets all the requirements for parametric statistical analysis and is to be preferred whenever possible.

After any of the above measurements have been made, often there needs to be some orderly arrangement of the observations so that pertinent facts may be *described.* Some assessment needs to be made concerning the extent to which these observations differ in magnitude and how they are distributed in value. One process for accomplishing this is called a *frequency distribution.* This consists of recording all the possible scores and then counting the number (frequency) of scores having each particular score value. When this is accomplished, the experimenter can then describe in what interval class (classes) most of the scores are concentrated and, also, where there is a sparsity of scores.

CENTRAL TENDENCY

A frequency distribution is a summary of data, but for many purposes it is necessary to summarize still further. Two characteristics of an observed distribution are its measures of *central tendency* and *variability.* If a student were instructed to choose one score from a group of many scores to best describe an entire distribution, an "average" score would probably be chosen. However, there are at least three different "averages" that could be specified: (1) the most frequent or commonly attained score—*mode,* (2) the point exactly midway between the top and bottom scores of the distribution—*median,* or (3) the familiar arithmetic average of the distribution—*mean.* If the mean, mode, and median are the same, then the distribution of scores is symmetrical. A common representation is the familar bell-shaped curve.

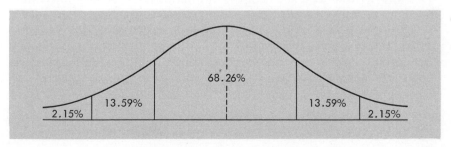

2.15%   13.59%   68.26%   13.59%   2.15%

"NORMAL" DISTRIBUTION

In any kind of measurement regardless of how careful observers try to be, small differences will occur. Thus, if 1000 musicians were given stopwatches and instructed to measure the precise time it takes for an individual to perform a certain rhythmic pattern, there would be many slightly different timings. If these timings (observations) were charted, it is extremely likely that the graph constructed from the distribution of these measurements would constitute a *normal curve*. This amazing characteristic of observations falling into a normal distribution can be demonstrated in such natural phenomena as sizes of feet, colors of hair, and heights of trees, and in the chance distribution of factors upon which the theories of probability rest.[5] For example, consider the probability of tossing different numbers of heads for ten coins, much like your earlier experiment. However, instead of tossing one coin ten times, think of tossing ten coins one time each. What would be the probability of obtaining 0, 1, 2, 3, . . . , 10 heads?

No. of Heads	Probability
10	1/1,024
9	10/1,024
8	45/1,024
7	120/1,024
6	210/1,024
5	252/1,024
4	210/1,024
3	120/1,024
2	45/1,024
1	10/1,024
0	1/1,024

It is easily observed that the above probabilities (binomial distribution) are approximated by the normal curve. The normal curve is regarded as a mathematical ideal and comparisons between samples of observation and this mathematical ideal provide the basis for important inferences.

Any index of central tendency, whether it be the mean, mode, or median, summarizes only one aspect of a distribution. Most experimental distributions have at least one other attribute called *spread* or *dispersion*. This is the tendency for observations to depart or deviate from central tendency. Descriptive statistics of this type are called measures of *variability*.

---

[5] A discussion of the principles upon which these ideas rest can be obtained through study of any good elementary textbook. Selected references for students of music are included in Appendix B.

Two measures of variability generally used in research are the *standard deviation* and the *variance*. The standard deviation is simply the square root of the variance. To compute the variance, we: (1) subtract each score from the mean (the result is called a deviation), (2) square each deviation, (3) add the squared deviations, and (4) divide by the number of scores minus 1. To compute the standard deviation, we simply extract the square root of the variance. Also, by subtracting the mean from an individual score and dividing by the standard deviation, the individual score is transformed to a *standard score* (z score). The use of standard scores allows a description of a subject's position in a given distribution with respect to both mean and variability, and makes direct comparisons with other distributions possible. Through the use of tables, the $\acute{z}$ scores can be converted to *percentile ranks*.[6]

The mean, standard deviation, and standardized scores are useful devices for summarizing data. However, the essence of these simple devices is that they provide fundamental cornerstones for inferential statistics.

SAMPLING AND RANDOMNESS

Since one of the foremost requirements for all statistical inference is the necessity of proper sampling techniques, the concepts of sampling and randomness need to be understood. The process of gathering data is called *sampling*. The results themselves are called observations, and a collection of observations is called a *sample* (a collection of observed sample events).

The term *random* is another extremely important term, denoting several important statistical procedures. The basic concept of randomness is simple. It signifies that each element of the sample has an equal and independent probability of being the sample selected; that is, *there is a lack of fixed pattern or order.* Before a die is thrown, the six possibilities are random because there is not a fixed order or pattern for each throw (that is, each throw represents a single miniature experiment). Each of the six numbers has an equal probability of coming up. (The student is reminded that it was the problem of calculating the odds for certain gambling possibilities that initiated the study of statistical inference.) The importance of this "randomness" permeates experimental research. If various possibilities of events are to remain free from systematic bias, then randomness must be assured. No one would desire to

---

6 Problems of this type, in addition to many others, can be solved with elementay knowledge and a source including various conversion tables. See Appendix B.

walk into a gambling situation where someone held "loaded dice." In a dice game, the possibilities (twelve numbers) need to be known and the participant must be assured that each possible number has an equal opportunity of coming up, that is, of being selected. Such is the case with statistics. After the experiment is completed, the researcher wants to be certain that the results were free from any systematic bias; that differences resulting from experimental manipulation (treatments) were caused by the manipulation, and did not result from uncontrolled factors. The essence of *experimental control* is that (1) aspects of the experiment that should be random are indeed randomly determined (sampling techniques), and (2) aspects not free to vary are controlled so they do not bias the results (experimental methodology). When researchers speak of rejecting experiments "that are not controlled," they are referring to inadequacies concerning sampling or methodology.

Randomness is usually thought of in reference to selecting samples, but it can also refer to selecting trials, mixing up orders of trials and presentations, assigning subjects to various treatment groups, and any other procedure of experimentation that necessitates controlling for undesired bias. For example, a researcher may take great care in selecting subjects at random but then proceed to give trials (for example, pitches) that have a fixed order that could bias the experiment (order effect). In this case, how does one know that the *order of presentation* (sequential pitches) is not influencing the results; that any differences in one trial are not caused by another trial or by the accumulation of successive presentations? This particular aspect of testing order effects could represent a separate experiment in itself, where the researcher presents certain trials in a fixed order to test if the *order* makes any difference.

The primary consideration in the process of randomness is to insure that all possibilities have an equal chance of being selected. If the experimenter selects every third student from a chosen population, or presents every second rhythmic variation from a group of selected rhythms, this would not represent randomness, because a fixed pattern would be evident. Random selection or random arrangement can be made by using tables of random numbers, by drawing numbers from a hat, by mixing up all possibilities and selecting by chance, or upon any other basis that insures equal possibility of selection or arrangement.

Sampling and randomness are extremely important. It should also be noted that there is no way to "cheat" the laws of probability regarding sampling and methodology. If the manipulation of experimental variables produces a statistically-significant variation different from what would be expected by chance alone, this variation will be evident. If the effect of experimental manipulation is not greater than that expected by chance only, then there will be no statistically-significant differences. It should be remembered that statistical tools constitute a "double-edged sword." If "expected results" are forthcoming in an experiment where the design is suspect because of uncontrolled variables, then "results" are discounted. If the structure of the design is inadequate to test desired information because principles of random selection are ignored and *cancel a real variation,* the experiment still fails because it does not demonstrate results that *actually may exist.* Even predictions of professional statisticians have been subsequently proven wrong many times. This happens not because the statistical tools are inadequate, but because methods of sampling were biased and not truly representative of what later proved to be the actual case; that is, the real population or uncontrolled variables were left free to vary. The experimenter is advised to design carefully. The more subtle the variables being investigated, the more precise the design needs to be.

Concerning sampling, the question has been asked many times—*how large does the sample need to be?* The answer is that the sample should be as large as necessary to accord with the importance of the question under investigation. Remember your coin-tossing experiment. How large would you want the sample (number of tosses) to be if your life depended on it? In this instance, the larger the sample the better. Obviously, the larger the sample, the greater is the possibility of ascertaining the actual case. However, sample size alone should not be confused with the importance of the study. Many results that are statistically significant because they are based on a large sample are neither musically nor actually important. The question "if your life depended on it" is far-fetched for many instances, yet daily life evidences certain risks. While many do not choose to play "Russian Roulette," we still drive automobiles, hunt, smoke, and engage in many activities if we feel the odds are in our favor. Perhaps we do not even think about it. Almost all man's activities have been calculated statistically, because *adequate sampling techniques* have made it possible. The beginning researcher should examine many studies in various disciplines to see what others consider an adequate sample, and determine whether the area warrants further investigation. If a significant result is obtained with a sample of 30, it can be generally assumed that the area is worthy of more extensive investigation. The student will find that time and physical circumstances usually help to determine the size of the sample. He should try to make the sample as large as is feasible, depending on his value judgments to determine the importance of the area. A large sample might produce significant results with very small differences that would not be worthwhile for anyone to know. Statistical significance is a tool for making judgments and is not the ultimate court of psychological, musical, or practical importance. If slight deviations in muscle tension are studied in 2000 violin players by means of an EMG, and we find significantly more tension in those who play poorly, but no teacher is able to detect the difference, then we have a statistically-significant result of no practical application. However, any study may lead to cumulative knowledge that might eventually produce practical application. The larger the sample, the greater is the probability that it represents the actual or theoretical population—*if random selection is insured.*[7]

CONCLUSION

Statistical methods and measurements cannot be separated. They do *not* constitute an "either-or"; both need to be considered simultaneously. Statistics are useless without measurements, and without statistics experimental investigation would not provide much useful information. Statistical evaluations provide the researcher with many advantages.

1. They permit a more exact description.
2. They necessitate clear thinking and exactness in experimental design.
3. They enable summarization of results in more interpretable forms.
4. They provide a method whereby inferences can be made to predict other eventualities.[8]

STUDY QUESTIONS

1. How are statistics used in experimental research?
2. Explain the theory of probability. What common uses does this theory have?
3. Name the four general types of measurement scales and give examples of each.
4. What is meant by central tendency? To what does it apply?
5. Define sampling and randomness. How do they interrelate? How are they different? What is meant by "systematic bias?"

---

[7] This section represents an extremely condensed overview for the neophyte music researcher. Entire volumes have been written pertaining to only a few of the many concepts advanced in these few pages (e.g., fixed-random variables, areas of rejection under Ho, Type I & II errors, etc.). The instructor may wish to pursue some of these concepts in greater detail; the student is referred to Appendix B.

[8] Adapted from J. P. Guilford, *Fundamental Statistics in Psychology and Education* (New York: McGraw-Hill, 1965), pp. 3–4.

CHAPTER NINE

elementary statistical tests

This chapter deals with some common statistical tests deemed appropriate for research designs in music. The statistical test should be chosen before the experiment is conducted. Again, it should be stated that this is imperative for the beginning researcher. However, the musician should not become distressed. Statistics should not represent a mystical or frightening void for the beginner. The process of choosing the appropriate statistical test is not a problem of "working out an experiment and then worrying about finding something to evaluate it." Statistical tests are structured to *coincide* with the experimental design. These tests have been developd with the express purpose of evaluating data, and most experimental designs are very similar in all fields of scientific investigation. Areas of experimental interest, populations, and observations under investigation may be quite different, but the basic experimental designs are really quite simple and similar.

PARAMETRIC AND NON-PARAMETRIC STATISTICS

Statistical tests are separated into two distinct groups, *parametric* and *non-parametric*. A parameter is a quantity that describes a population. A population is defined as that particular set of observations, however measured, from which samples of observations may be drawn. A population of observations is determined by the experimenter. He may be interested in observations of a group of people, a colony of mice, a selection of instruments, brands of mouthpieces, a range of pitches, differential rhythmic patterns, or any other conceivable population of defined experimental interest. If a mean were computed for the different sizes of mouthpieces representing a defined population (all trumpet mouthpieces), this mean could be a parameter. Parametric tests do not require the experimenter to know all of the actual population values. If all values were known, there would be no reason for the tests. Statistical manipulations make it possible to make inferences about the parameters of the population from which the samples were drawn, hence the term, parametric tests.

There are three assumptions upon which parametric tests are based:

1. That samples are drawn from a population with a known distribution. (Normal distributions are generally assumed.)
2. That variances of all samples are homogeneous.
3. That variables to be measured achieve *interval* measurement (cf., p. 70).

All of the above, especially the third assumption, are necessary for parametric tests. Parametric statistical tests require interval scale measurement, whereas non-parametric tests do not specify all of these conditions. A ratio scale is preferred to an interval scale if the data qualify. For example, intonation investigations where performances are measured on the chromatic stroboscope (Stroboconn) represent ratio measurement. Parametric tests are more *powerful;* that is, they generally yield the same results with smaller samples, and should be used when interval measurements are achieved. Among the most common parametric tests for testing differences in means are the various *t* tests, and analyses of variance.

The primary characteristic of *non-parametric* tests is that they do not require interval measurement and can deal with nominal and ordinal (ranking) measurements. The only assumption necessitated by these tests is that observations are independent. Non-parametric tests are used when interval measurement cannot be achieved or when ordinal measurement is preferred (for example, the use of chi square in questionnaire analysis).

The qualifications and specific requirements of the data to be analyzed are much more important than the choice concerning parametric or non-parametric tests. Statistical analysis is not a "game" where one chooses any test which might demonstrate the greatest "results." Extreme care should be taken to seek professional advice *before* the data are collected to assure the experimenter that adequate precautions have been taken in the structure of the design in the collection of data and in the employment of appropriate statistical tests that best assess the significance of the variables being investigated. The usual procedure is to state the null hypothesis and (1) select a significance level that minimizes the likelihood of rejecting this null hypothesis if it is indeed true (Type I error), and (2) select a sample size (N) that minimizes the likelihood of accepting this null hypothesis when it is indeed false (Type II error). There is a direct relationship between these two errors. However, intervalic measurement, as opposed to ranking, generally decreases the probability of making the Type I error. Also, as N increases, the probability of making the Type II error generally decreases.

CORRELATIONS

In a controlled experiment, samples are generally manipulated in some manner, and the effect of the manipulation is assessed (for example, effects of programmed instruction in sight singing). Often, the researcher does not or cannot use certain techniques because of ethical considerations (for example, will a tone stimulus of 200 db cause deafness?). A researcher may choose to study the relationship between two different sets of observations. In this case, correlations are made between two sets of scores or variables (for example, deafness and factory noise). The degree of correspondence between two sets of scores is expressed as a *correlation coefficient* (r) whose obtained value is expressed from +1.00 to −1.00. A value of +1.00 indicates a *perfect positive* correlation, a value of zero indicates no correlation and a value of −1.00 indicates a *perfect inverse* relationship. A high coefficient or, in fact, any relationship *does not imply causality*. Although, if it is known that a high r exists between two variables, it is possible to predict one of these variables by knowing the other. At what level a correlation should be taken seriously poses a difficult question. It is generally accepted that anything over .70 represents a high correlation; however, interpretation depends upon the variables and the sample size, and is also based upon the purpose for which the r was calculated. (A correlation of .70 should never be confused with 70 percent or the 70th percentile. These statistics represent three separate descriptions.)

The *Spearman correlation coefficient* and *Kendall's Tau* are nonparametric techniques that can be used to calculate correlations when measurements are ordered according to rank. *Pearson's product-moment* correlation is another technique generally computed on the basis of actual scores.

ONE-SAMPLE METHOD

The one-sample study consists of determining whether the selected observations came from a specified population, either theoretical or known. After the observations have been quantified, the data are compared to a theoretical distribution to see how "good it fits" (*goodness-of-fit tests: χ^2, binomial test, Kolmogorov-Smirnov one-sample test*). If interval measurement has been achieved, a *t* test (parametric) can be used to determine whether the mean of the sample is the same or different from the mean of the theoretical population distribution. If nominal measurements are achieved, then the chi square (χ^2) one-sample test or binomial test should be used. The *Kolmogorov-Smirnov one-sample test* is used for ranked data. If interval measurements are achieved, the *t* test is preferred.

The rationale for the goodness-of-fit tests as *tests of significance* is based on the assumption that after samples have been drawn at random from a specified population, the error in sampling can be assessed in relationship to the theoretical distribution so that inferences can be made about the sample. The process of goodness-of-fit testing represents: (1) assuming a known or theoretical distribution for a particular population, (2) extracting samples from the larger population, and (3) checking these observations against a theoretical distribution on the basis of sampling error. The experimenter may be concerned with whether or not observations are the *same* as the theoretical distribution, whether or not observations are *significantly different* from results obtained on the basis of chance alone, or other questions that will determine the statement of the hypothesis.

The chi square enjoys great popularity in analyzing questionnaire results where the investigator wishes to know if results deviate significantly from an expected frequency. He might hypothesize that all responses will fall evenly over the possible answers, and this becomes the *expected frequency*. The *observed frequency* for each answer is compared to each expected frequency, and significance determined. The χ^2 may also be used to assess the significance of before and after treatment designs when responses obtained prior to treatment are considered to be the expected frequencies, responses after treatment, the observed frequencies.

TWO-SAMPLE METHOD

When samples from a defined population are assigned to two independent groups or to two equivalent (matched) groups, the experimenter has a control sample for comparison with the experimental sample. This two-sample design is generally superior to the one-sample method because of extra control and should be used if possible. The one-sample method usually makes comparisons based on a non-existent "theoretical control group." In the two-sample method, a control group actually exists; therefore, the question is asked, is there a difference between the two samples *after* treatment? That is, do they now come from the same or different populations? Appropriate statistical tests for the two-sample independent method include the *t* test for independent samples (parametric), the *Mann-Whitney U test* (ordinal) and the chi square (χ^2) for independent samples (nominal).

When the two samples can be matched according to some appropriate criterion, the design is called an *Equivalent Sample Method.* Matching may be achieved on the basis of prior information or current tests (for example, I.Q., G. P. A., music tests, sex, socio-economic scales, age, music experience), or a pre-test may be constructed. *Unless the matching procedure is specifically appropriate to the experiment, it is better to assign subjects randomly to the control and experimental treatments.* A frequent mistake in educational research is to match subjects on commonly-used tests that may have nothing to do with the experiment except to interfere with equality of groups. For example, using I.Q. scores to assign sixty musicians to either a sight singing manipulation or to a control group might bias the experimental results without serving as a matching device. A relevant pre-test that indeed serves to match subjects and thereby insures equality of groups may be specially-constructed. Important benefits can be derived from the pre-test–post-test designs: (1) subjects can be used as their own controls; that is, performance of each subject can be compared for before and after treatment effects; (2) subjects can be randomly assigned to control and experimental groups on the basis of pre-test scores; and (3) "matched" subjects more narrowly define the population and represent a more monolithic group.

Appropriate statistical tests for two equivalent matched samples are the *t test* (interval), the *sign test* (nominal), *The McNemar test for the significance of changes* (nominal), and the *Wilcoxon matched pairs signed-rank test* (ordinal).

MULTIPLE-SAMPLE METHOD

The *multiple-sample method* designs are considered to represent sophisticated methods of experimental research. As with the two-sample methods, samples are either equivalent or independent.

If the experienced investigator is able to obtain the use of a pre-written statistical computer program or the services of a professional statistician, he should strongly consider one of the more sophisticated designs (that is, a design with a control group[s]). Unless the nature of the topic of experimental interest is prohibitive, the researcher should try to achieve all of the aforementioned qualifications of parametric statistics and advanced design. It is often more difficult to design an experiment that is vague, inadequate, and lacking in control than to strive for quality research. If evaluation equipment is available to achieve interval measurement, it should be used (stroboscope, oscilloscope, standard time, and so on). If interval or ratio measurement can be attained, the experimenter should not settle for anything less. If it is appropriate to the study that subjects be matched, if pre-test and post-test measures are constructed, and/or if possible rotation of groups is accomplished, the researcher should not be content to do inadequate research. If the researcher plans to spend a great amount of time on the research project, it would appear wise to construct the best design possible.

Rotation of experimental variables (subjects, groups, trials, stimuli, and so on) is a process of changing or alternating situations. The experimenter may also choose to alternate samples in a multiple sample study to assess observed results when different samples are exposed to treatment, or he may desire to assess the relative effect(s) of a variable change (for example, intensity, rate, duration, or order). Various *factorial* designs abound to (1) provide the researcher with methods that evaluate the presentation of several variables and their interactions simultaneously, and to (2) statistically *evaluate* the singular and interactive effects of these many variables (*analyses of variance tests*).

A word of caution should be given the beginning researcher. When variables are presented in different combinations or when the researcher desires to control or randomize many variables, he must consider the magnitude of vast possibilities. For example, the possible combinations of two events are expressed $2 \times 1 = 2$. The possibilities of three are expressed $3 \times 2 \times 1 = 6$, of four $4 \times 3 \times 2 \times 1 = 24$, of five $5 \times 4 \times 3 \times 2 \times 1 = 120$, and so on. Not only does this magnitude apply to structuring the experimental events (trials, rotations, and so on), it also necessitates appropriate statistical tests (for example, *factorial analysis of variance*) and increased complexity of interpretation. It is the problem of evaluating designs of this magnitude that generally *requires* the use of a computer. It should be remembered that the pre-written computer programs ("canned programs") may be used for almost all of the common statistical tests, regardless of the magnitude of the data.

Statistical tests for two or more *independent samples* include the parametric *analysis of variance*, the non-parametric *Kroskal-Wallis one-way analysis of variance by ranks*, and the *chi square* (x^2) *test for more than two independent groups.* Appropriate statistical tests for more than two equivalent samples include the various parametric *analyses of variance and co-variance.* The non-parametrics include the *Cochran Q test* and the *Friedman two-way analysis of variance by ranks.*

The parametric *analyses of variance* are perhaps the most widely used in all of experimental research in the behavioral sciences. These tests are sometimes referred to as *F* tests and provide information to evaluate significance levels from an *F* table. The analysis of variance is a technique for dividing the variation observed in experimental data into different parts, each assignable to a known source, cause, factor, or interaction. The relative magnitude of variation resulting from different sources can be assessed and the hypotheses of experimental interest either accepted or rejected. (See Edwards for discussion of one- and two-tail tests.) In its simplest form, the analysis is used to test the significance of the differences between sample means. If data qualify, the one-way or two-way analysis is recommended. The three-way, four-way, or more complex analyses of variance are extremely useful when many separate observations of different pitches or rhythms need to be analyzed, thus necessitating the calculation of many interactions. Expanded coverage of principles, tests, and design problems is available to the more sophisticated researcher but necessitates advanced work in statistics and experimental design. Following is a chart of selected research designs and statistical tests.[1]

CONCLUSION

Experiments may generally be classified in one of three groups: (1) the One-Sample Method, where a sample is drawn from a population and compared, assessing the chance factors of sampling (null hypothesis) to the larger sample from which it was drawn or by the preferred pre-test–post-test design; (2) the Two-Sample Method, where samples are drawn, treated differently, and the differences between samples compared (independent samples), or matched and compared to each other (equivalent samples); and (3) the Multiple-Sample Method (independent or equivalent), which may represent three-way, four-way, or other factorial comparisions. Rotation of samples may be used in any of the above categories. Rotation designs sometimes provide greater control and greater informa-

---

[1] A more comprehensive discussion of experimental design and statistical tests will be found in two excellent sources: *Experimental and Quasi-Experimental Designs for Research,* Donald T. Campbell and Julian C. Stanley (Chicago: Rand McNally & Co., 1963) and *Nonparametric Statistics, Sidney Siegel* (New York: McGraw-Hill Book Company, 1956).

SELECTED RESEARCH DESIGNS AND STATISTICAL TESTS

Hypothesis of No Difference (two-tail) **Hypothesis of Predictable Difference (one-tail)**

Area of rejection when $p = .05$

	One-Sample	Two-Sample				Multiple-Sample			
		Equivalent		Independent		Equivalent		Independent	
	Post-test only / Post-test / Pre-test-Post-test	Post-test only	Pre-test-Post-test	Post-test only	Pre-test-Post-test	Post-test only	Pre-test-Post-test	Pre-test-Post-test (Counterbalance)	Pre-test-Post-test (Temporal)
	$XO \quad X_1X_2O \quad O_1XO_2$	$M\ \dfrac{XO}{O}$	$M\ \dfrac{O_1XO_2}{O_1\ O_2}$	$\dfrac{XO}{O}$	$\dfrac{O_1XO_2}{O_1\ O_2}$	$M\ \dfrac{XO}{XO}\ O$	$\dfrac{MO_1XO_2}{MO_1\ O_2}\ \dfrac{M\ XO_1}{M\ O_1}$	$\dfrac{O_1X_1O_2}{O_1X_2O_2}\ O_1\ O_2$	$\dfrac{O_1XO_2}{O_1\ O_2}\ \dfrac{XO_1}{O_1}$
	Classification or ranking		*Pre-test-Post-test*		*Pre-test-Post-test*	*Matching by Counterbalance*	*Temporal.*	*Counterbalance*	*Temporal*
	Subjects as own control								
	$O_1O_2O_3O_6$ etc. $\quad O_1XO_2XO_3$	$M\ \dfrac{X_1O}{X_2O}$	$O_1M\ \dfrac{XO_2}{O_2}$	$\dfrac{X_1O}{X_2O}$	$O_1\ \dfrac{XO_2}{O_2}$	$\begin{matrix}X_1OX_2OX_3OX_4O\\X_2OX_4OX_1OX_3O\\X_3OX_1OX_4OX_2O\\X_4OX_3OX_2OX_1O\end{matrix}$	$\begin{matrix}MO_1X_1O_2X_2O_3X_3O_4\\MO_1\ O_2X_2O_3X_3O_4\\MO_1\ O_2\ O_3X_3O_4\\MO_1\ O_2\ O_3\ O_4\end{matrix}$	$\begin{matrix}X_1OX_2OX_3OX_4O\\X_2OX_4OX_1OX_3O\\X_3OX_1OX_4OX_2O\\X_4OX_3OX_2OX_1O\end{matrix}$	$\begin{matrix}O_1X\ O_2O_3O_4O_5\\O_1O_2X\ O_3O_4O_5\\O_1O_2O_3X\ O_4O_5\\O_1O_2O_3O_4X\ O_5\\O_1O_2O_3O_4\ O_5\end{matrix}$

NOMINAL MEASUREMENT — χ^2

χ^2 *One-Sample Test.* Goodness of fit for testing expected vs. observed frequencies (e.g., preferences among defined categories on questionnaire, performance rating scale, etc.). *Binomial Test.* Goodness of fit for testing two discrete categories (e.g., flat-rank order judgments).

McNemar Test for Significance of Changes. Used when the two categories are not related in measurement levels i.e., when one or both categories achieve only nominal level (e.g., comparing musical judgments good-bad with correct-incorrect, sharp, loud-soft, correct-incorrect). Excellent when subject acts as own control.

Fisher Exact Probability Test. Used with small N to test differences between samples on basis of central tendency in a 2×2 table. χ^2 *Test for Independent Samples.* Used to test differences between samples on basis of *any* discrete differences between the two populations.

Cochran Q Test. Used to test whether three or more matched sets differ significantly among themselves on the basis of dichotomous data (e.g., yes-no, flat-sharp, correct-incorrect). Matching may be between different subjects or on different observations for each subject.

χ^2 *Test for Multiple Independent Samples.* Used to test significant differences among samples.

ORDINAL MEASUREMENT	*Kolmogorov-Smirnov One-Sample Test.* Goodness of fit for testing ranked data (e.g., pre- vs. post-test measures, questionnaire, performance rating scale). Preferred to χ^2 if sample is small. *Wilcoxon Matched Pairs.* Used when measurements achieve ordinal level both *between* and *within* pairs. *Sign test.* Used when ordinal measurements achieved only within pairs.	*Mann-Whitney U.* Used to test differences in samples on basis of central tendency. Most powerful alternate to the parametric t test. *Kolmogorov-Smirnov Two-Sample Test.* Used to test significance between samples on basis of *any* differences between populations (two-tail) or central tendency (one-tail).	*Friedman Two-Way Analysis of Variance.* Used to test whether three or more matched sets differ significantly among themselves on basis of mean ranks for each set.	*Kruskal-Wallis One-Way Analysis of Variance.* Used to test significant differences among samples on basis of ranks. This test is always preferred to χ^2 if data qualify.
INTERVAL OR RATIO MEASUREMENT	t Test. Used to test significance between the sample mean and theoretical distribution or of different scores. *Walsh Test.* Used to test significance between samples of pre- and post-test differences.	t Test. Used to test significance between related sample means or means of different scores. *Randomization Test for Two Independent Samples.* Used to test significance between independent sample means. Should be used with small N.	*Analysis of Variance.* Used to test whether three or more matched samples differ significantly among themselves on basis of variance between sample means.	*Analysis of Variance.* Used to test whether three or more independent samples differ significantly on basis of variance between sample means.

X = Experimental Variable (treatments)
O = Observation (measurements)
M = Matching on basis of known attributes or pre-test by pairs of subjects, groups, or by using each subject as own control

tion, although it should be stated that these designs are often more difficult to structure and evaluate.

Comparisons are based on the laws of probability, as are, in fact, all statistical tests. The student may imagine that in the simplest experiment (like the one conducted in Chapter Eight concerning the fairness of your coin) only one theoretical distribution is being employed (binomial). As each new dimension is added in an experiment, interpretation becomes more complex. The entire rationale for statistical comparisons concerns the laws of probability based upon various distributions (normal, χ^2, t, and so on). Statistical tests should be chosen with primary regard to the qualification requirements of the data in relationship to the entire experimental design.

STUDY QUESTIONS

1. List the differences between the requirements and uses of parametric and nonparametric tests.
2. Discuss the advisability of using a two-sample method as opposed to using a one-sample method.
3. In what types of investigations would correlation techniques be advisable? What is meant by a perfect positive correlation; perfect inverse relationship?
4. What is the null hypothesis? What is the rationale for rejecting it? What is meant by a one-tail test as opposed to a two-tailed test?
5. Discuss the three groups of experimental classifications. How do these differ? How do they compare to the Mill's Canons?

CHAPTER
TEN

completion of an experiment

The student has been introduced to experimental control, decisions involving the choices of common statistical tests, and the fact that all aspects of experimental procedures need to be considered before structuring the design. The student should now consider instrumentation of the experiment. As instrumentation is developed, the design will gradually be formulated, and statistical tests can be chosen with regard to numerical classifications.

INSTRUMENTATION

Instrumentation involves tests, appraisal instruments, evaluating apparatus, or any implements necessary to measure observed data. The basic question of instrumentation is how responses are to be measured. For example, a study of intonational performance accuracy may be measured by the chromatic stroboscope and data recorded in plus and minus cent deviations from equal temperament. A rhythmic study may be assessed in time deviations from an established standard as measured by an electric metronome or standard timer. A study of the influence of music on behavior (affective responses to music) may be measured by written responses on a numerical scale constructed by the investigator, and so on. Some problems arise concerning elaborate measuring devices, but many simple experiments can be conducted with the use of a tape recorder, metronome, Stroboconn, record player, or other available apparatus (Descriptions of common measuring devices and uses are presented in Appendix D).

After the student decides how responses are to be measured (that is, after he structures the dependent variable), he should construct a graph that charts separate observations according to the independent variables of experimental interest. Thus, the total picture can be seen, and choices concerning the number of observations and treatments (manipulations) will be developed concurrently. The experimenter's time is almost always the determining factor; most experimental designs start out as good ten-year studies and become restricted to the time available. When the graph is constructed, simultaneous consideration of statistical tests will help structure the statistical evaluation.

STRUCTURING THE DESIGN

It is apparent that there is not a fixed hierarchy for designing an experiment. It is almost impossible even to get started without knowledge of all related aspects concerning experimentation. However, since the novice researcher has been introduced to many necessary concepts, procedures are now presented for structuring the composite design.

It is suggested that the investigator:

1. Review a great deal of experimental literature and evaluate published experiments on the basis of the criteria presented at the conclusion of Chapter Seven, pages 64–65.
2. Choose an area of investigation and delimit this area to a small topic while formulating appropriate hypotheses.
3. Go again to the literature and review all experiments that are related to the chosen topic.
4. Choose appropriate instrumentation for measuring observations (quantification). If appraisal instruments are not available, construct an objective measuring device that fits the topic (e.g., numerical rating scale).
5. If the topic does not generate its own experimental design, either (a) borrow a design that has previously been used in a similar experiment, or (b) study the Methods of Research Chart in Chapter Two; study Mill's canons in Chapter Six; study the Selected Research Designs and Statistical Tests chart, pp. 84–85; review statistical tests Chapter Nine, and then choose a composite design that fits the topic (e.g., two-sample independent—one-way analysis of variance).
6. Construct a graph that charts the number of separate observations on the

basis of the variables of experimental interest. For example, consider an experiment concerned with intonation: Title: "The Effect of Verbal Conditioning on Intonational Performance of College Vocalists." Hypothesis: Verbal conditioning will significantly improve performance as measured by the Stroboconn in plus and minus cent deviations from equal temperament. Total $N = 100$ subjects (randomly-selected sophomores) divided into an experimental group and a control group. Each subject performs on a pre-test (20 pitches) and a post-test (same 20 pitches). Therefore, total separate observations [pre-test $= (20 \times 50) + (20 \times 50)$] [post-test $= (20 \times 50) + (20 \times 50)$] $= 4,000$ pitches. If the total of separate observations gets too large, go back and limit some aspect(s) of the design to the point where the entire study can be accomplished in the time available.

7. Make sure that the methods of instrumentation and quantification, the methods of sampling and randomness, and the statistical test all are in harmony

8. In a word, *control*. Be certain that the design is "tight" so that results can be interpreted on the basis of the intended design. Remember that *orders* of presentation need to be randomized unless you are specifically checking order effects. Often, there are many different randomizations in each simple experiment, for example, selection of subjects, assignment to pre-test, assignment to treatments, assignment to post-test, selection of pitches, presentation of pitches, etc. Initial rigor will insure greater scientific control. Start with an extremely simple topic and work for even greater refinement.

THE PROSPECTUS

If the experiment is conducted for a thesis or dissertation, a prospectus (proposal) is generally written prior to the investigation. It is advisable to write a prospectus regardless of whether or not it is required. The prospectus provides many benefits: (1) It necessitates a complete structural design before the collection of data; (2) it provides a sound basis for conducting the experiment without irrevocable mistakes; (3) if it is well written, it is substantially identical to the entire first part of the finished report and therefore the student has only to write the Results, Discussion, and Conclusion sections; and (4) it provides a contract that protects the student from inadequate research. If the student's prospectus is approved, the topic and methods of research are deemed appropriate. The prospectus can then be used as a basis for formal approval of the project in every respect. Undue stress on the student is greatly reduced by the writing and subsequent approval of a prospectus.

SCHOLARLY STYLE

Research is most often presented in what constitutes scholarly writing. Scholarly writing is unique, and most students have not had previous experience with this particular manner of expression. Scholarly research reporting is contrasted with essay style. The essay may analyze a problem, provide thoughtful inquiry and even possible solutions or points of view. The research report, on the other hand, constitutes an addition to knowledge and as such should present only the facts. The discussion section of the research report provides the scholar with a section intended to move beyond the limitations of the problem. However, it should also be written in scholarly style and not include personal conjecture that is not related to the general area of the experimental topic or the results.

Most papers written in scholarly style read as though they all could have been written by the same person. There is justification for this. The scholarly report should constitute the most objective presentation possible. Therefore, all attempts are made to discount the individual writing style of the researcher. When a scientist reads a research report, it is read for the scientific information it contains. While the reviewer is indeed concerned with *scientific opinions* of the researcher, he mainly desires concrete information based on the facts of the study, the researcher's experience in obtaining the results, and implications for further research. The scientist does not want to be entertained.

In scholarly writing, there should also be an "open-mindedness" that demonstrates a lack of absolutism or dogmatism. Hence, the researcher writes in the third person and refrains from the use of personal pronouns. The researcher most often "believes" in the results of his experiment, but does not make statements that might portray an opinionated disrespect for divergent points of view and additional research. Some research reports are immediately considered suspect because the writing style seems to betray a lack of objectivity, which indicates the researcher may have had such a preconceived bias that the experiment could not have demonstrated results contrary to these expectations. Research reporting should be free from ambiguity and be as concise as possible.

The student may practice scholarly writing by taking a paragraph of an essay or novel and rephrasing it to conform to scholarly style. For example, the phrase, "I want to know if practicing makes a difference in performance," might be phrased, "Differences concerning performance in relationship to practice will be assessed." The phrase, "I think practice helps performance," might be stated, "It would appear that practice improves performance." Scholarly style might seem both affected and cumbersome, yet the student needs to develop this technique. If the student begins writing without the use of I, he, she, you, and so on, most other conventions of scholarly writing will be forthcoming. Often, scholarly writing is not suitable in conveying or eliciting desired communication. Much of this text is written in essay style. However, research reports should conform to scholarly style, especially if a researcher wishes to have the formal report published.

THE FORMAL REPORT

Writing the formal research report is the final aspect of experimentation. After data have been gathered, classified, analyzed, and statistically evaluated, they constitute the raw material for the formal research report. There are many "models" for the research report, and the investigator is usually required by the institution in which he is studying to conform to the details of a prescribed style. Institutional and/or professional requirements must be checked for details of format. However, every report should include: (1) the problem, (2) the method, (3) the results, (4) a discussion of the results, and (5) a summary or abstract either at the beginning or the end, depending upon the style of the scientific area or prospective journal for publication.

The *title* of the report should be as succinct and informative as possible. Any investigator who has reviewed experimental literature knows how distressing it is to be misguided by an inappropriate title. Some research reports also include a brief summary of the entire study at the beginning. This is extremely beneficial to the reader and is recommended if it does not conflict with the specified format of the parent institution. The *introduction* section should provide an initiation into the topic, after which the *problem* should be presented with as much clarity as possible. Usually, *literature* is reviewed, *hypotheses* are stated, and *limitations and terminology* of the study are presented. Sometimes a *need for the study* section is also included. Clarity and good organization are imperative. It is sometimes suggested that the student outline each subject and paragraph before attempting to write the formal report.

The *method* section of the formal report constitutes the experimental design section. The student should have little difficulty with this section if the design has been well-constructed. The method section should be easily written using the step-by-step experimental procedures employed in the collection of data. All aspects of the design should be included.

The *results* section is the most informative section in the experimental report. Appropriate graphs and tables should be used to represent the results visually. Statistical tests need to be described and the original hypotheses either confirmed or rejected. The *discussion* section is the appropriate place for the experimenter to discuss the possible meaning and interpretation of the findings. Often, resultant information that was initially unexpected is provided by the study. Sometimes, the design does not prove adequate to test certain hypotheses of the topic. The investigator can then discuss these negative aspects with suggestions to further researchers. Implications of the study for other areas, and scientific opinions gained by the investigator, are presented in the discussion section. It is sometimes wise to inform the reader that this section does not constitute experimentally-tested hypotheses and therefore represents conjecture. The *conclusion* or *summary* section is usually extremely short and merely states the problem and lists the results of the *tested* hypotheses. Sometimes a *recommendations for further research* section is included.

CONCLUSION

This text is intended as an introduction to experimental research. Many musicians recognize the need for experimentation within the disciplines of music, but do not know how to get started. This text presumes to get the student started. Therefore, it is written specifically for the student. The sophisticated musician might find reasons for argument in Part One, the sophisticated researcher in Part Two.

The student is reminded that conjecture is conjecture regardless of intent or consequences. Some of the material included in the first five chapters is conjecture and should not be construed as representing experimental justification. It is presented to stimulate needed testing of various research topics.

This text has as an underlying theme the relation of an "either-or" attitude to many aspects of music and research. "Either-or" aspects of life need constant examination, leading toward greater discrimination. Some situations are definitely mutually exclusive, as with the control of an experiment where issues must be firmly differentiated. Conversely, many problems seem to arise because of an "either-or" attitude toward the many aspects of life that may be mutually reinforcing. Such is the case with music as an art and a science. Scientists are not necessarily insensitive; musicians are not necessarily non-thinking.

Another underlying aspect of "either-or" concerns the gradual process of inquiry toward greater knowledge and understanding. Man is often prone to extremes in this process and has a tendency both to magnify tentative results and to reject that which appears inconsequential. It is sometimes difficult to see the value of getting started, of adding a little to knowledge, of maintaining a quest for truth in the totality of ambiguity. Indeed, a tolerance for ambiguity seems essential in experimentation where one constantly strives to establish as much "truth" as possible, yet must be content with fragments of information and imperfect knowledge. Experimental research in music is at least one important event in life's greater sample space. If well done, it may prove extremely beneficial to the art of music. The researcher is challenged to deal with the acquisition of knowledge as a continuous process and seek to integrate the best from the past and present in order to develop capacity for that systematic and imaginative inquiry that extracts knowledge from information and wisdom from knowledge.

STUDY QUESTIONS

1. Summarize the steps to be taken in structuring an experimental design. What is the basic question regarding the relation of instrumentation to the design? Relate instrumentation with quantification.
2. What are some values derived from writing a prospectus?
3. Why are research reports written in scholarly style?
4. List and explain each of the parts of a formal report.
5. How is the "either-or" concept related to the gradual acquisition of knowledge in experimentation?

APPENDIX
A

selected periodicals

Acta Psychologia
Acta Psychotherapeutica et Psychosomatica
American Annals of the Deaf
American Archives of Rehabilitation Therapy
American Journal of Mental Deficiency
American Journal of Occupational Therapy
American Journal of Orthopsychiatry
American Journal of Physical Medicine
American Journal of Psychiatry
American Journal of Psychology
American Journal of Psychotherapy
American Journal of Sociology
American Music Teacher
American Psychologist
American Rehabilitation Committee, Bulletin
American Sociological Review
American String Teacher
Annales Medico-Psychologiques
Année Psychologique
Archives of Diseases of Children
Archives of General Psychiatry

Archives of Neurology
Archives of Otolaryngology
Archivio de Psicologia, Neurologia e Psichiatria
Arquivos Brasileiros de Psycotecnica

Behavioral Science
Behavior Research and Therapy
Brain
British Journal of Educational Psychology
British Journal of Psychology
British Medical Journal

California Journal of Educational Research
Cerebral Palsy Review
Child Development
Child Psychiatric Techniques
Child Welfare
Community Mental Health Journal
Comparative Psychiatry
Contemporary Psychology
Council for Research in Music Education
Crippled Child

Diseases of the Nervous System
Dissertation Abstracts

Education
Educational and Psychological Measurement
Elementary School Journal
Exceptional Children

Franklin Institute, Journal

Genetic Psychology Monographs
Gesundheit und Wohlfahrt
Gravesano Review

Hahinukh
Hinrichsen's Musical Yearbook

Instrumentalist
International Journal for the Education of the Blind
International Journal of Social Psychiatry

Journal de Psychologie Normale et Pathologique
Journal of Abnormal Psychology
Journal of Aesthetics and Art Criticism

Journal of American Medical Association
Journal of Applied Behavior Analysis
Journal of Applied Psychology
Journal of Clinical Psychology
Journal of Comparative Physiological Psychology
Journal of Consulting Psychology
Journal of Education
Journal of Educational Psychology
Journal of Educational Research
Journal of Experimental Child Psychology
Journal of Experimental Education
Journal of Experimental Psychology
Journal of General Psychology
Journal of Genetic Psychology
Journal of Heredity
Journal of Musicology
Journal of Music Therapy
Journal of Nervous and Mental Disease
Journal of Neurology and Psychiatry
Journal of Pediatrics
Journal of Personality
Journal of Personality and Social Psychology
Journal of Psychology
Journal of Rehabilitation
Journal of Research in Music Education
Journal of School Psychology
Journal of Social Issues
Journal of Social Psychology
Journal of Special Education
Journal of Speech and Hearing Disorders
Journal of the Acoustical Society of America
Journal of the American Musicological Society
Journal of the American Psychoanalytic Association

Lancet

Menninger Clinic Bulletin
Mental Health
Mental Hygiene
Mental Retardation
Merrill Palmer Quarterly
Music
Musical Courier
Music and Letters
Music Educators Journal (see also state publications, for example, *Florida Music Educator*)
Music Journal

Music News
Music Teachers National Association, Proceedings
Music Therapy, Yearbooks of the NAMT

National Association for Music Therapy, Bulletin
Nature
Neurology
New Biology

Occupational Therapy and Rehabilitation
Overture

Perceptual and Motor Skills
Personnel Psychology
Philips Technical Review
Plastic and Reconstructive Surgery
Psyche
Psychiatric Quarterly
Psychiatric Quarterly Supplement
Psychoanalytic Quarterly
Psychoanalytic Review
Psychologi
Psychological Abstracts
Psychological Bulletin
Psychological Monographs
Psychological Reports
Psychological Review
Psychology in the Schools
Psychology Today
Psychometrika

Quarterly Journal of Experimental Psychology

Recreation
Revista de Psicologia General y Aplicada
Revue Belge de Psychologie et de Pédagogie

School Musician
Schweitzer Archiv für Neurologie, Neurochirurgie und Psychiatrie
Science
Scientific Monthly
See and Hear
Social Forces
Sound
Spastics Quarterly
State medical journals (Pennsylvania, New York, West Virginia, etc.)

Teachers College Record: Columbia University
Today's Health
Tohoku Psychologica Folia

Volta Review
Voprosy Psikhologii

Yearbook of Psychoanalysis
Young Children

Zeitschrift für Experimentelle und Angewandte Psychologie
Zeitschrift für Psychotherapie und Medizinische Psychologie

APPENDIX
B

selected statistical references

Self-instruction in statistics is not preferred and, in fact, should be discouraged. Nevertheless, the following texts will provide a complete background in statistics *if* the texts are studied and used in the order indicated.

1. Huff, Darrell. *How to Lie with Statistics.* New York: W.W. Norton & Company, Inc., 1954. Excellent first book to be read before any elementary texts. Contains humorous examples of deceptive statistical tricks. Read seriously, it prevents later errors of similar kind.
2. McCullough, H., and Celeste and Loche Van Atta. *Statistical Concepts: A Program for Self Instruction.* New York: McGraw-Hill Book Company, 1963.
3. Siegel, Sidney. *Nonparametric Statistics for the Behavioral Sciences.* New York: McGraw-Hill Book Company, 1956. Easily-understood text. Best available source for the use of nonparametric statistics (twenty-seven nonparametrics techniques with examples). Includes step-by-step calculation procedures and can be read without prior experience in statistics.
4. Edwards, Allen, L. *Statistical Analysis.* New York: Holt, Rinehart & Winston, 1958. Excellent text for beginners. Covers *t* tests, analysis of variance, and correlation coefficients.
5. Hays, William L. *Statistics for Psychologists.* New York: Holt, Rinehart &

Winston, 1963. Text builds from a basis of set theory and covers all common parametric statistics, gives some experimental design as well as some nonparametrics. Considered by many the best available text for elementary and advanced statistics.

6. Winer, B.F. *Statistical Principles in Experimental Design.* New York: McGraw-Hill Book Company, 1962. Most comprehensive advanced source for experimental design. Includes many model designs and all appropriate tables, but should not be consulted without a statistician's aid or prior experience.

7. Lindgren, B.W. *Statistical Theory.* New York: The Macmillan Company, 1962. Highly advanced text in statistical theory. Should not be read without advanced mathematical background.

APPENDIX
C

glossary of statistical terms and tests

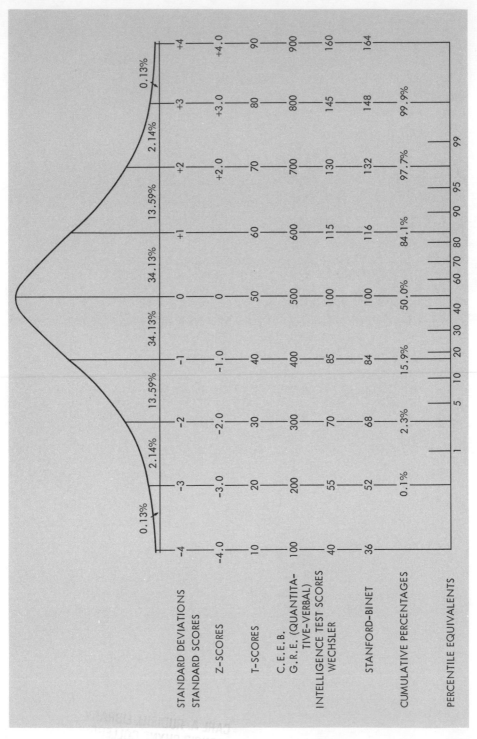

NORMAL CURVE WITH APPROXIMATIONS AMONG DERIVED SCORES

Analysis of Covariance — Original data on a variable of experimental interest are adjusted on the basis of known pre-experimental differences as measured on some other variable. This analysis permits elimination of that part of the variability accounted for by pre-experimental differences. Any bias in apparent experimental manipulation can thereby be reduced to a greater extent than when randomization is used. (*See:* Winer, *Statistical Principles in Experimental Design,* pp. 578–618.)

Analysis of Variance (one-way) — One of two basic designs for comparing groups of subjects after experimental manipulation. Analysis of variance involves three or more *independent* random samples, not necessarily of the same size. The test compares experimental group means. (*See:* Edwards, *Statistical Analysis,* pp. 141–47.)

Analysis of Variance (two-way) — Another basic design (see above) for comparing three or more groups on two separate variables simultaneously. The same individuals, cases, or groups are compared under both conditions. The tests compares differences in means. (*See:* Edwards, pp. 141–47.)

Arithmetic Mean—Mean—Generally called the "average," except in statistics. The mean is equal to the sum of the scores divided by the total number of scores. Computational symbols: $\frac{\Sigma X}{N} = \overline{X}$ ($\overline{X}$ = arithmetic mean). Σ = Greek capital letter sigma used to indicate the "sum of a series of measures." X = a raw score (your data) in a series of measures. ΣX = the sum of all the measures adding the measures with a cumulative total. N = the number of measures (total number of observations taken in a particular series).

Chi Square (χ^2) Used when measurements are classified in frequencies, i.e., when the number of subjects who fall into two or more categories is the basic data. The question to be answered is whether or not the frequencies observed in the categories are significantly different from some expected frequencies. The expected frequencies are normally derived from the null hypothesis. Formula: $\chi^2 = \Sigma \frac{(O - E)^2}{E}$. O = observed frequency. E = corresponding expected frequencies. After computation, degrees of freedom are used in consultation with χ^2 Table. (*See:* One-sample χ^2, Siegel, *Non-parametric Statistics for the Behavioral Sciences,* pp. 42–47; Two-sample χ^2, Siegel, pp. 104–11; χ^2 for independent samples, Siegel, pp. 175–79).

Cochran Q Test — A method for testing whether three or more matched sets of frequencies or proportions differ significantly among themselves. (*See:* Siegel, pp. 161–66.)

Confounding — Concurrent changing of two or more variables. Thus, results cannot be said to be attributed to a single variable.

Control Group — Ideally, this is a group which is like the experimental group in every way that would affect the outcome of the experiment, except for one manipulated variable.

Correlation — The interrelation between two or more conditions or events. Correlations are generally used when variables under study cannot be experimentally controlled. Correlations never indicate causality and rarely even indicate whether either variable is influencing the other. Correlations are measures of relationships and are expressed as positive, negative, or zero correlations. A positive correlation exists when scores tend to be the same on both variables. A negative correlation exists when low scores on one variable are associated with high scores on another variable. A zero correlation exists when there is little or no relationship between the scores on two variables.

Dependent Variable — The phenomenon that appears, disappears, or changes when the independent variable is applied, removed, or varied. The dependent measure is usually the test score.

Descriptive Statistics — Characteristics of a set of scores given in statistical terms. Descriptive statistics are used to describe rather than to predict.

Element of a Sample — Each entity or thing within a collection of things, grouped together on any basis, is termed an element of that collection. The assumption exists that states that each individual element of a sample can be distinguished from every other element.

Empirical — Methods based entirely upon experimentation and observations.

Equivalent-Sample Technique — A method of "matching" to overcome the difficulty that results because extraneous differences exist between groups of experimental subjects. Thus, the samples studied are related before the fact. Matching may best be achieved by using each subject as his own control, but many experiments pair subjects and then assign the two members of each pair to two different experimental conditions.

Experimental Group — The experimental group for which the experimenter attempts to hold constant all but one of the factors that might affect the outcome of the experiment, or the group or groups to which particular treatments are applied.

Experimental Variables — Any variables that can be manipulated or varied in accordance with the demands of the experimenter.

Fisher Exact Probability Test — An exact probability test used with small sample size to test differences between samples on the basis of central tendency. (*See:* Siegel, pp. 96–104.)

Friedman Two-Way Analysis of Variance by Rank—Can be used to test the hypothesis that two or more samples have been drawn from the same population. Data from the matched samples must be in at least an ordinal scale. (*See:* Siegel, pp. 166–72.)

Homogeneous — Composed of similar or identical elements or parts; uniform.

Independence of Observation — Independence indicates that each observation is not influenced by other observations. Some statistical tests are used to test for independence of observations.

Independent Groups — Different groups of subjects selected separately. An experiment that uses different groups of subjects for each condition of the experiment is based on independent groups.

Independent Variable — The factor purposively manipulated to ascertain its relationship with the dependent variable. Sometimes thought of as the "cause" of the dependent measure of "effect."

Inferential Statistics — The procedure whereby descriptive statistics are used to make predictions in either of two general ways: (1) The concept of reliability can be viewed as a prediction that what once was is still the same; (2) more sophisticated types of prediction are those in which descriptions at a given time and under certain conditions are used to guess (predict) what the descriptions will be at a later time and under slightly different conditions.

Interactions in Analysis of Variance — The use of two variables in the same experiment permits the assessment of any effects of either variable on a measured outcome. In addition, it is possible to gain information about the *combined* effects of both variables. When interactions between variables are discovered, the resulting outcome is better predicted by using such information than by using information about each variable separately.

Kendall's Tau — A measure of relationship between two sets of ranked numbers. This correlation is based on a probability analysis of all possible rank orders and the probability of the ranks reversing relative positions on two different rank-order scales. (*See:* Siegel, pp. 213–29; Hays, pp. 647–55.)

Kolmogorov-Smirnov One-Sample Test — A "goodness of fit" test for ranked data. (*See:* Siegel, pp. 47–52.)

Kolmogorov-Smirnov Two-Sample Test — A test of significance for two independent samples. (*See:* Siegel, pp. 127–36.)

Kruskal-Wallis One-Way Analysis of Variance by Ranks — A useful test for deciding whether two or more independent samples are from different populations. (*See:* Siegel, pp. 184–93.)

Mann-Whitney U — With ordinal measurement the Mann-Whitney U is used to determine whether two independent groups have been drawn from the same population. This test is an alternative to the parametric t test. (*See:* Siegel, pp. 116–27.)

McNemar Test for the Significance of Changes — This test is applicable to designs where persons are used as their own controls. Measurement should be of either a nominal or an ordinal scale. (*See:* Siegel, pp. 63–67.)

Median — Another label for the fiftieth percentile. The point above which 50% of the cases fall and below which 50% of the cases fall.

Mode — The score that occurs most frequently in a series of scores.

Null Hypothesis — The assumption that there is no difference between the population measured and the value under test. The null hypothesis is usually formulated for the express purpose of being rejected, in which case the alternative hypothesis may be accepted.

One-Sample Technique — One-sample techniques usually involve drawing on a random sample and testing whether or not the sample was drawn from a parent population with any hypothesized distribution. A common technique is to assess the difference between an observed (sample) mean and the expected (population) mean through the use of a t test. (*See:* Edwards, pp. 126–33). Non-parametric tests are also available. (*See:* Siegel, pp. 36–38.)

Pearson's Product-Moment Correlation — A method to determine whether or not some observed association in a sample of scores indicates that the variables under study are most probably associated in the population from which the sample was drawn. The Pearson r requires scores that represent measurement in at least an equal-interval scale. The value of the Pearson *r* is actually equal to the average of the *z*-score products for the two pairs. (*See:* Hays, *Statistics for Psychologists,* pp. 493–538.)

Percentile — The percentile rank of any specific score is a value indicating the percent of cases in a distribution falling at or below this score.

Pre-Written Statistical Programs — Maɪty universities have computer programs which can be used by persons who have no knowledge of computer programming (often called "canned programs"). The particular programs are pre-written and it is only necessary to know how to "plug-in" to the program. Consult your nearest computer center for this service.

Probability — The probability that any event will occur is generally expressed as a number from 0 to 1.00. Two methods are used: (1) The *relative frequency* method compares the occurrence of an event over some number of occasions on which the event could have occurred. This proportion is said to be equal to the probability of the event; (2) the *mathematical limits* method requires that one make certain mathematical assumptions that allow one to describe the relative frequency of the event in question, by means of an equation. If it can be shown that this relative frequency value approaches some stable value (limit) as the number of trials approaches infinity, then this limiting value of the relative frequency of an event is defined as the probability of the event.

Proposition — A fundamental assumption not meant to be tested, such as a statement concerning empirical observations. A set of propositions is often used within a given logical framework to yield further propositions implied by the original set. The further propositions (theorems) derived will depend upon the rules for deduction as well as upon original statements. Propositions may be tested indirectly by observing the concurrence or lack of it between theorems and observations.

Reliability — The degree to which one obtains the same result with a measuring device when the same variable is measured twice (or more).

Sample Size — Dependent upon the experimental design and the purposes of the experiment. Formulas can also be used to determine the sample size. (*See:* Hays, p. 204–6.)

Sets — Any collection of things grouped together for any reason may be called a set. Each entity or thing within such a collection will be termed an element or member of that set. It is assumed that each element or member of a set can be distinguished from every other element.

Sign Test — This test uses plus and minus signs rather than any other kind of measurement. The test emphasizes direction of difference between two scores or series of matched scores. The idea is to find if the conditions are different (for example, before and after experimental treatment). (*See:* Siegel, pp. 68–75.)

Spearman Rank Correlation Coefficient — A measurement of association requiring that both variables be measured in at least an ordinal scale. Objects or individuals under study may be ranked in two ordered series. This statistic is called rho. (*See:* Siegel, pp. 202–13).

Standard Deviation — An average of deviation scores or the root mean square deviation. A particular type of average wherein all scores are taken into consideration. Standard Deviation is a statistic that describes variability of measures. Generally, it is a figure that represents overall about one-sixth of the total range of a group of scores.

Calculation:

1. Find the mean (X) by summing all the raw scores and dividing by the total number of scores (N).
2. Subtract the mean from each raw score and square each result = $(X - X)^2$.
3. Sum the squares (Σx^2).
4. Divide the sum by the total observations minus one (N-1).
5. Take the square root of this figure.

Therefore, standard deviation $= \dfrac{\Sigma x^2}{N}$.

Standard Score (z score) — A value that indicates the amount by which a raw score deviates from the mean ($\overline{X}$) in standard deviation units. z scores from different distributions of scores are directly comparable. If the raw score is below the mean ($\overline{X}$) the z score is given a minus value. z scores normally range from -3.00 to $+3.00$ (6 standard deviation units). When a raw score equals the mean, $z = 0$.

A T score is another form of standard score. T scores avoid the use of negative numbers by placing the mean raw scores equal to a T score of 50 and equating the raw score standard deviation to 10 T-score points. Thus, a score 1 standard deviation above the mean (z score of 1) would have a T score of 60, that is, $50 + 10$. A score 1 standard deviation below the mean (a z score of -1) would have a T score of 40.

t Test — Used to statistically compare differences between means. The *t*-test is essentially a z score and actually shows the number of deviation units from a mean. (*See:* Edwards, pp. 126–33.)

Trend Studies — A study designed to assess the difference between groups over time when subjected to a series of experiences or manipulations.

Validity — The degree to which a test actually measures what it purports to measure. The determination of validity requires independent external *criteria* of whatever the test is designed to measure.

Variability — The extent of individual differences around the central tendency of a group of scores, the central tendency being a measure that provides a single, most typical, or representative score to characterize the performance of the entire group. Variability may be reported in terms of the *range* between the highest and lowest scores, the deviation of each individual score from the mean of the group, the *standard deviation,* or the *variance* or *mean square deviation.*

Variance (Equal to the Standard Deviation Squared) — This is generally called the mean square rather than the variance especially when dealing with analysis of variance routines. An excellent measure of variability both within a single series and for comparing one distribution with another.

Wilcoxen Matched Pairs Signed Rank Test — A test that utilizes information concerning both the direction of the differences within pairs and the magnitude of that difference. (*See:* Siegel, pp. 75–83.)

APPENDIX
D

equipment descriptions

The following equipment has been found useful for many experiments in music. The beginning researcher should be aware of the importance of precise instrumentation. However, he should realize that many experiments can be conducted with resourceful use of equipment at his disposal.

CATHODE-RAY OSCILLOSCOPE

The oscilloscope is used to obtain a picture of the wave form of a circuit. Controls on the oscilloscope enable the experimenter to view a constantly changing signal as if it were drawn on graph paper. From the display, the wave form can be evaluated in terms of time and amplitude characteristics. Resultant wave forms can be compared (matched) when used in conjunction with an overlay pattern; when the overlay is affixed to the screen of the oscilloscope comparative analyses can be drawn.

When used in conjunction with a microphone and an amplifier, the oscilloscope can be used to display various vocal patterns, i.e., differentiation of vowel sounds and the individual wave patterns produced on various musical instruments. Connect the microphone to the input of the amplifier and the output of the amplifier to the vertical input of the oscilloscope. This instru-

mentation suggests investigation into the areas of speech and instrumental techniques of tone production.

The oscilloscope not only is a valuable tool in the measurement of signal
voltages; but as a read-out and visual monitoring device it provides versatile
application in the field of research. Additional utilization of the instrument will
become apparent to the experimenter as he proceeds into the area of testing and
measurements.

Electronic Switch

The Electronic Switch serves as an accessory to be used in combination
with the oscilloscope. It enables the experimenter to view two signals at the
same time on the screen of the scope. Separate positioning controls are provided
to superimpose or separate the signals for comparative analysis or individual observation. Additional controls include: separate gain controls for each channel,
variable switching rate control, and a synchronous output control, which locks
the scope sweep to the signal output of the switch. A typical example of its use
is to simultaneously observe a signal before and after any additional modulation
or modification takes place, i.e., viewing the wave form of a signal as it appears at
both the input and output stages of an amplifier.

Audio Generator

The audio generator can provide signal sources of known frequency, form,
and amplitude. Some generators produce both sine and square waves, which
may be viewed separately or simultaneously on an oscilloscope without affecting
either wave form. Typical laboratory application of the instrument would include using the generator as an audiometer, i.e., testing the frequency and
threshold responses of subjects. In testing for pitch discrimination, it would be
advisable to obtain an instrument that provides a continuous (sweep) coverage
from 10 cps — 20 kc. A metered output, calibrated in volts and decibels, is available on some instruments, from which frequency response curves can be established.

D.C. Power Supply

The D.C. power supply has numerous applications in the laboratory,
especially where a source of variable, low-power, filtered, D.C. voltage is required. Specifications should include: a rated fused output of at least 1 ampere
and a variable voltage output from 0 — 48 volts. Most instruments provide a continuously metered output of voltage and current.

Multimeter — Vacuum Tube Voltmeter

The multimeter or volt-ohmmeter provides wide voltage, current, and
resistance measurements. The vom is self-powered, providing portable use in
the design and repair of electronic equipment. Occasionally, it becomes necessary to perform voltage checks on equipment without disturbing the electrical
characteristics of a particular circuit. Under these conditions, use a vacuum tube

voltmeter. The vtvm draws so little current from the circuit that the resultant voltage drop becomes negligible.

Capacitance—Resistance Decades

Capacitance and resistance decades provide convenient switch-selection of desired capacitance or resistance values in a circuit. The decades can be used to show effects of different capacitance or resistance values on circuit operation, and in servicing to estimate proper values for component replacement in "burned-out" circuitry.

Electric Chronoscope

The chronoscope is essentially a motor-driven electric clock with a sweep-1/100-second hand. It provides a convenient measurement of "on-task" time intervals during a "trial" period. The clock may be started and stopped mechanically or electrically. It records in seconds and hundredths of a second.

Pulse-Activated Switch

The pulse-activated switch, when used in conjunction with a microphone or tape recorder, can provide reliable and instantaneous "on" and "off" switching of an electrical circuit. A typical use of the switch is to activate the electric clutch (on time-recording devices) upon commencement of a sound or electronic impulse. The switch may also be touch-activated. A variable sensitivity control is usually provided on the instrument.

Stroboscope (Stroboconn-Strobotuner)

The stroboscope is designed to detect variances in pitch. It is tuned to A-440 cps. A strobe-light is modulated by the pitch of the sound produced and is focused on rotating discs, markings on which seemingly move forward or backward depending on sharpness or flatness of the note produced. A control knob is provided to stop the motion of the markings, at which time a direct reading is available in "cents" sharp or flat from exact pitch; a cent is 1/100 of a semi-tone (C.G. Conn, Ltd., Elkhart, Indiana).

Tempo/Tuner

The tempo/tuner is a small battery operated instrument designed as a combination metronome/audio generator. Because of its small size and portability, it is an ideal instrument for many simple experiments. (Model W2-1000, Electronic Research Products, Los Altos, California, distributed by Selmer, Elkhart, Indiana.)

Johnson Intonation Trainer

The Johnson Intonation Trainer is a portable electronic keyboard instrument with *adjustable* tuning for the twelve tones of the chromatic scale. It has a three octave keyboard and four possible timbres. The adjustable tuning (each of the 37 tones has a tunable range of about six semitones) makes this an excellent instrument for many possible experiments in perception as well as in educational research (E.F. Johnson Company, Waseca, Minnesota).

ADDITIONAL EQUIPMENT

4-Track Stereo Tape Recorder w/microphones, separate record/playback heads
Stereo phonograph w/integrated stereo amplifier system
Tuning forks, A = 440, B = 466.16, C = 261.63
Variac Transformer (variable A.C. power supply)

Soldering gun (medium duty)
Roll resin flux core solder—60/40 alloy
Multi-purpose screwdriver set—slotted and Phillips
Hollow-shaft nutdriver set (1/16"–1/8")
Combination pliers
Diagonal cutters—4½"
Long nose pliers—6"
Wire stripper
Lock pliers
Hammer—16 oz. head
Hacksaw
Hand-reamer—1/8" point
Center punch
Adjustable wrench—6"
Hand drill
Drill set—1/16"–1/4"
Tool box
High-intensity lamp
Magnifying glass
Vise—medium size
Rubber floor strip—3' wide, length to suit (minimizes shock hazard when using
    electrical equipment)

Resistor assortment, 1 watt
Resistor assortment, 5–15 watts
Capacitor assortment—600 volt rating
Electrolytic capacitor assortment—450 volt rating
Hook-up wire assortment
Tube socket assortment (octals—7- and 9-pin types)
Assorted hardware—nuts, screws, washers, etc.
Digital counter, 110 VAC, pulse-activated
Digital counter, 12-24 VDC, pulse-activated
Toggle switch assortment, SPST, SPDT, DPST, DPDT, etc.
Binding post assortment, red and black
Pushbutton switch assortment, SPST
Indicator lamp, socket, and jewel assortment
Time-delay relay, adjustable 1-10 sec., DPDT, 10 amp. rated

For additional information about electrical instrumentation see: Cornswett, Tom N., *The Design of Electric Circuits in the Behavioral Sciences* (New York: Wiley and Sons, Inc., 1963).

Electronic Equipment and Parts Catalogues:

Allied Electronics
100 N. Western Avenue, Chicago, Illinois 60680

Lafayette Radio Electronics
111 Jericho Turnpike, Syosset, L. I. New York 11791

Radio Shack Corporation
730 Commonwealth Avenue, Boston, Massachusetts 02215

KITS

Heathkit Electronics
3462–66 W. Devon Avenue, Chicago, Illinois 60680

Eico Electronic Instrument Company, Inc.
131–01 39th Avenue, Flushing, New York 11352

index